Baillière's
CLINICAL
HAEMATOLOGY
INTERNATIONAL PRACTICE AND RESEARCH

Baillière's

CLINICAL HAEMATOLOGY

INTERNATIONAL PRACTICE AND RESEARCH

Volume 1/Number 2
June 1987

Haematological Problems in the Elderly

T. J. HAMBLIN DM, FRCP, FRCPATH.
Guest Editor

Baillière Tindall

London Philadelphia Toronto Sydney Tokyo

Baillière Tindall 24–28 Oval Road
W.B. Saunders   London NW1 7DX, UK

West Washington Square
Philadelphia, PA 19105, USA

1 Goldthorne Avenue
Toronto, Ontario M8Z 5T9, Canada

Harcourt Brace Jovanovich Group (Australia) Pty Ltd
Post Office Box 300, North Ryde, NSW 2113, Australia

Exclusive Agent in Japan:
Maruzen Co. Ltd. (Journals Division)
3–10 Nihonbashi 2-chome, Chuo-ku, Tokyo 103, Japan

ISSN 0950-3536

ISBN 0–7020–1214–9 (single copy)

Baillière's Clinical Haematology is published four times each year by
Baillière Tindall. Annual subscription prices are:

TERRITORY	ANNUAL SUBSCRIPTION	SINGLE ISSUE
1. UK & Republic of Ireland	£35.00 post free	£15.00 post free
2. USA & Canada	US$60.00 post free	US$25.00 post free
3. All other countries	£45.00 post free	£18.50 post free

The editor of this publication is David Dickens, Baillière Tindall,
24–28 Oval Road, London NW1 7DX, England.

Baillière's Clinical Haematology was published from 1972 to 1986 as *Clinics in
Haematology*.

Printed in Great Britain at the Alden Press, Oxford

Contributors to this issue

MICHAEL A. BAKER MD, FRCPC, FACP, Director, Division of Haematology, Department of Medicine, and Professor of Medicine, University of Toronto. Head, Department of Haematology and the Oncology Program, Toronto General Hospital, 657 University Avenue, Toronto, Ontario, M5G 1L7, Canada.

J. ADRIAN COPPLESTONE MRCP, MRCPath, Senior Registrar, Department of Haematology, Southampton General Hospital, Southampton SO9 4XY, UK.

MICHAEL FREEDMAN MD, Professor of Medicine, Director, Division of Geriatrics, New York University School of Medicine, 550 First Avenue, New York, NY 10016, USA.

TERRY HAMBLIN DM, FRCP, FRCPath, Consultant Haematologist, Royal Victoria Hospital, Bournemouth. Visiting Professor, Southampton University, Southampton, UK.

ANTON KRUGER MB ChB, MRCP, Senior Registrar, Royal Victoria Hospital, Shelley Road, Boscombe, Bournemouth, BH1 4JG, UK.

ROBERT A. KYLE MD, Chairman, Division of Haematology, Mayo Clinic, William H. Donner Professor of Medicine and Laboratory Medicine, Mayo Medical School, Rochester, MN 55905, USA.

MARIA MESSINEZY MA (Oxon), MRCP, MRCPath, Clinical Assistant, Department of Haematology, St Thomas's Hospital, Lambeth Palace Road, London SE1 7EH, UK.

D. G. OSCIER MA, MB, B.CHIR, MRCP, MRCPath, Consultant Haematologist, Royal Victoria Hospital, Bournemouth, UK.

T. E. PARRY, MB, FRCPath, FRCP, Honorary Consultant Haematologist South Glamorgan Health Authority; Formerly Consultant Haematologist Llandough Hospital, Penarth, South Wales and Clinical Teacher in Haematology, University of Wales, College of Medicine, UK.

T. C. PEARSON MD, MRCPath, Reader, Division of Haematology, United Medical and Dental Schools of Guy's and St Thomas's Hospitals, Lambeth Palace Road, London SE1 7EH, UK.

FIONA RANDALL MRCP, Consultant in Continuing Care at Macmillan Unit, Christchurch Hospital, Christchurch, Dorset, BH23 2JX, UK.

BARRY M. SCHULTZ MD, Clinical Instructor in Medicine, New York University School of Medicine, New York. Geriatric Consultant, Goldwater Memorial Hospital, Franklin D. Roosevelt Island, New York, NY 10044, USA.

JOHN W. SWEETENHAM BSc, MB, BS, MRCP, Senior Registrar in Medical Oncology, CRC Wessex Medical Oncology Unit, University of Southampton, CF99, Southampton General Hospital, Southampton SO9 4XY, UK.

CHRISTOPHER J. WILLIAMS DM, FRCP, Senior Lecturer in Medical Oncology and Honorary Consultant Physician, CRC Wessex Medical Oncology Unit, University of Southampton, CF99, Southampton General Hospital, Southampton SO9 4XY, UK.

KENNETH W. WOODHOUSE MD, MRCP, Senior Lecturer in Medicine (Geriatrics) and Clinical Pharmacology, Wolfson Unit of Clinical Pharmacology, The University, Newcastle-upon-Tyne, NE1 7RU, UK.

HILARY WYNNE MB, BS, MA, MRCP, Lecturer in Geriatric Pharmacology, Wolfson Unit of Clinical Pharmacology, University of Newcastle-upon-Tyne NE1 7RU, UK.

Table of contents

RECENT ISSUES

August 1986
Acute Leukaemia
R. P. GALE
A. V. HOFFBRAND

November 1986
Myelodysplastic Syndromes
J. D. GRIFFEN

March 1987
The lymphomas
T. J. McELWAIN
T. A. LISTER

Foreword

After fifteen years on the Costa Geriatrica I am well aware that blood diseases are very common in the elderly. In fact, I sometimes think that they only occur in the elderly. As we progress towards the twenty-first century amid predictions that one third of the population will be old-age pensioners, this issue of Bailliere's Clinical Haematology is timely in reminding us of the special problems of the old. Just as children cannot be regarded simply as small adults, so the elderly have more than mere age to contend with.

There is, first of all, considerable controversy over what is normal in old age. Is it reasonable to accept changes in normal ranges with age, or is this an indicator of remediable disease? As part of the wearing out of organs and tissues there are readily observable changes in metabolism – especially of drugs – which have major implications. Even relatively trivial conditions such as mild haemophilia assume much greater significance when added to 'the thousand natural shocks that flesh is heir to'. The immune system in particular appears to degenerate in old age and resultant autoimmune processes may have profound effects on the blood. When does normal ageing become disease?

Clonal disorders become more common with age. I suspect that those that we detect in the blood are no more common than those we miss in the skin or bowel. However, benign proliferations of red cells or platelets may have disastrous effects while expansions of lymphocytes or plasma cells may set us diagnostic puzzles.

The impression that the general public has of leukaemia as a disease of children is good for fund raisers but thankfully inaccurate. Leukaemias are most common in old age. Two of them, the myelodysplastic syndrome and chronic lymphocytic leukaemia are almost confined to old age. Both have been misunderstood in the past because of natural reluctance of physicians to perform investigations in the elderly. In both conditions new information has become available recently which has allowed a clearer perspective. Acute leukaemia in the elderly certainly differs from that seen in younger adults and demands new strategies of management. In both leukaemia and lymphoma the nearness of natural termination of life imposes constraints on therapy in that the quality of every day's life is paramount. Those concerned with the care of the dying have special problems with haematology patients. In many, hope awakened has to be quelled; in others there is a tension between striving for cure and relief of symptoms. This issue addresses all of these themes. I thank the contributors for their diligence and perspicacity, and the publishers for their vision and efficiency.

TERRY HAMBLIN

1

The limits of normality in elderly patients

ANTON KRUGER

The distinction between age related changes and pathological events in the elderly is central both to the correct diagnosis and treatment of disease in this group and to the understanding of the ageing process itself. The term 'elderly' is relative and encompasses a wide age range, the lower limit for which will depend on the viewpoint of the observer and on the age distribution of local populations. An elderly population might, therefore, consist of a group of individuals whose ages span four decades and should not necessarily be regarded as homogeneous.

As individual patients the needs of the elderly are no different from those of younger individuals. Their disorders need to be diagnosed and corrected where possible and appropriate, although there may be profound differences from younger patients in the best means for achieving this end. It is often tempting to attribute variations from reference ranges and clinical norms which have been established for younger healthy adults, to 'old age' although this is justifiable in the minority of situations only. On the other hand, over-zealous investigation and treatment of minor changes specifically related to ageing is also undesirable. Superficially, age dependent reference ranges should be helpful in achieving a balance between these two extremes, but in practice many of the observed variations are of little value. Statistically significant differences do not necessarily imply clinical significance and this chapter will examine haematological tests in the aged in relation to their clinical application as well as from the descriptive viewpoint.

THE AGEING PROCESS, HAEMATOLOGY AND REFERENCE RANGES

Senescence can be seen as beginning in infancy when tissues and organs such as neurones and muscles lose their ability to divide. In the haemopoietic and immune systems, however, haematologists are concerned with dynamic elements that continue to undergo active replication and production throughout life. Certain age related changes are nevertheless commonly noted. Haemopoietic marrow is observed to progressively involute in its distribution and cellularity with advancing years (Custer and Ahlfeldt, 1932; Hartsock et al, 1965) and clinical and laboratory observations have led to the conclusion that marrow reserve declines with age (Lipschitz et al, 1981). Early experimental cell culture data were thought to indicate a finite lifespan and number of divisions for human diploid cells (Hayflick, 1966) although this was not confirmed for the haemopoietic system in later work (Lajtha and Schofield, 1971). It is now apparent that specific stromal tissue is vital for long term in-vitro cell cultures (Wolf and Trenlin, 1968; Johnson and Dorshkind, 1986) and for normal in-vivo haemopoiesis (Wolf, 1979). Non-pathological age related deterioration in marrow function is therefore likely to have its origin in the haemopoietic microenvironment and in humoral changes rather than in the stem cell itself.

Senescent changes are also observed in the lymphoid and immune system and will be discussed in more detail later. Observations on these changes have led to the proposition of immunologic theories of ageing. Age related changes in other tissues and organs also have an influence on haematological tests and observations. For example, vitamin B_{12} levels are observed to be low in patients with atrophic gastritis without clinical evidence of deficiency (Chanarin, 1985). Should these patients be regarded as haematologically normal? The answer is not entirely clear; although careful evaluation may uncover biochemical and morphological evidence of deficiency (Blundel et al, 1985), clinical studies have demonstrated no benefit from B_{12} therapy in this situation (Hughes et al, 1970) and long term follow-up is usually uneventful (Waters et al, 1971).

Reference ranges

'The normal range' is a somewhat ambiguous term commonly used to describe what is actually a reference range. The term is open to misinterpretation since a reference range cannot by itself define normality or the presence or absence of illness. It merely represents a defined proportion of observations that reflects the population from which it is derived and the methods used in its derivation. The use of the word 'normal' can also be confused with the statistical term which implies a particular distribution of values. Measurements in nature often are not gaussian in their distribution and it is best avoided. The International Committee for Standardization in Haematology (ICSH) (1981) has proposed standardized nomenclature for the definition of reference populations and ranges as described in Table 1.

Discussion of the theory of selection of reference samples is beyond the scope of this chapter as is a detailed description of the methods of expressing the data obtained from tests done on these samples, although a few points are addressed. Uniformity of reporting of reference ranges in the literature is lacking, most surveys being expressed either as a mean plus or minus, a multiple of the standard deviation for normal or log normal samples, or as common percentiles. These may be improved by more complex mathematical manipulations less sensitive to variation in the distribution of biological data (Shultz et al, 1985) but these concepts are less likely to be understood by the average clinician.

Table 1. Definition of key terms used in relation to reference ranges*.

Term	Definition
Reference individual	An individual selected on the basis of defined criteria
Reference population	All possible reference individuals. A natural population consists of all individuals unselected for disease or other criteria and may still serve as a reference population
Reference sample group	A statistically adequate number of individuals selected to represent the reference population. Selection may be random or the reference sample may be a subset of the reference population
Reference value	The value obtained by observation or measurement of a particular quantity in the individuals of the reference sample group
Reference distribution	A distribution of reference values
Reference limit	Derived from the reference distribution
Reference interval	The interval between and including two reference limits

* From the International Committee for Standardization in Haematology (1981) *The theory of reference values.*

The major disadvantage of the use of mean and standard deviation is obvious: many biological data are not normally distributed. Common percentiles, on the other hand, require no assumptions about the distribution of test values and are therefore less sensitive to variations in the distribution form. They are also ideally suited to the establishment of percentile charts which are useful in the graphic representation of age related trends (Kelly and Munan, 1977). Common percentiles, however, are prone to large variance which becomes apparent as a lack of smoothness in data when small numbers are examined. This disadvantage can be limited by the use of weighted percentiles (Harrell and Davis, 1982) which will produce smoother and more predictive curves. This will, however, be at the expense of the simplicity of the common percentile. Ash et al (1983) have compared the differences between standard deviation and log normal gaussian methods and the common percentile in establishing confidence limits for a variety of chemistry tests without demonstrating clinically important variations.

The choice of a reference population lies between a natural population, unselected for disease, or a selected population of healthy individuals as defined by specific criteria. Either method is acceptable although a reference interval derived from a natural population is likely to include a greater number of truly 'abnormal' values representing unhealthy individuals, than a comparable interval derived from a selected sample. This apparent disadvantage can be counted by reducing the size of the reference interval to include fewer than the conventionally accepted 95% of the sample population.

Deciding whether or not to rigorously standardize collection procedures and the preparation of reference individuals depends on: (a) the test being performed and (b) the likely application of the reference interval. For example, strenuous exercise prior to coagulation testing will result in an accelerated activated partial thromboplastin time (Mandalaki et al, 1980). On the other hand, a reference interval for the haemoglobin level that might be used to detect the presence of anaemia in a community survey should be established on ambulatory reference individuals in a situation similar to that in which the sample will be obtained from the population screened. In general, reference intervals that are likely to be used for tests performed in a clinical setting and to guide clinical judgement require minimal preparation of the reference individuals. Venesection should, of course, be performed with as little trauma and venous stasis as possible. Reference intervals that are to be used for experimental work or laboratory standardization might require a much more rigorous approach to ensure comparability of test and reference groups.

Once established, reference intervals need to be tested in the clinical setting in order to establish their clinical utility. This is especially important for the elderly, a group afflicted with the highest incidence of physical disorders in the natural lifespan and in whom the definition of normality is particularly difficult.

THE FULL BLOOD COUNT

The full blood count (FBC) is the test most commonly requested of the haematology laboratory. Over the past three decades the information generated in response to this has been subject to changes of a qualitative and quantitative nature. The advent of automated cell counters has allowed the rapid and precise reporting of the traditional red cell measurements and the white cell and platelet counts. As a result the investigation has become a useful screening tool enabling a reduced dependence on labour intensive examination of blood films. In addition to the well known indices, more variables have been made available by the later generations of blood counters, including red cell and platelet size distribution indices. The red cell distribution width (RDW) has shown some promise in the aetiological classification of anaemias (Bessman, 1983; Bessman et al, 1985) and the platelet distribution width (PDW) is particularly useful in combination with a mean platelet volume (MPV) in distinguishing between reactive thrombocytosis and high platelet counts associated with myeloproliferative disease (Bessman et al, 1985; Van Der Lelie et al, 1986).

Automated white cell differential counts are becoming more reliable and are likely to make a substantial impact on haematology laboratory practice (Koepke and Ross, 1985; Rumke, 1985). However, until the latest generation of multipart differential counters have been adequately tested in the clinical setting, careful blood film examination will remain an important part of the full blood count providing information additional to machine generated values.

Some of the variables reported in the FBC show age dependent changes in the elderly but, in general, these have not proven to be of great clinical significance, for reasons that will be considered below.

Haemoglobin

The haemoglobin level has been shown in several surveys to vary with age (Htoo et al, 1979; Jernigan et al, 1980; Lipschitz et al, 1981; Munan et al, 1978; Zaino, 1981). In the elderly this is usually characterized by a gradual decline from the sixth decade with a more rapid fall in median and mean levels over the age of 70. This is best illustrated in tables produced by the Sherbrooke group (Munan et al, 1978). In common with other surveys of natural populations, the decline shown in these is more marked in men and accompanied by a widening of the reference interval at the lower range of haemoglobin levels. A possible explanation for the latter observation might be thought to lie in the small sample size of the very old and the high likelihood of including unwell individuals in this unselected group. However, it is interesting to note that when analysed separately, a subsample of the total population which was selected and excluded for illness showed a similar fall in the lower limit for the haemoglobin level.

Other investigators have demonstrated no significant age related decline in the haemoglobin level for the elderly (Caird et al, 1973; Purcell and Borzovic, 1974; Viteri et al, 1972). The weight of evidence, however, favours a gradual fall in the mean, median and lower reference limits for the haemoglobin level from the seventh decade onwards, the fall being more marked in males.

However, clinical observations do not entirely favour the use of unique reference limits for haemoglobin in the elderly. Several studies in older people have demonstrated a high incidence of anaemia (as defined by limits for healthy young adults), to be associated with reversible pathology (Evans, 1971; Htoo et al, 1979; Mclennan et al, 1973; Milne and Williamson, 1972; Thomas and Powell, 1971) although other investigators have demonstrated little clinical benefit from following up minor abnormalities in older people (Jernigan et al, 1980; Lipschitz et al, 1981). Between 1984 and 1985 we undertook a survey of all patients over the age of 54 years who were registered with a single community practice in our district. Of 2926 eligible subjects, 1388 (47%) volunteered to have a single blood sample taken for FBC analysis. Samples were tested between one and six hours from aspiration on an automated blood counter (Ortho ELT-800) and a standard blood film was examined by a single observer. The sample population was thought to be representative of most social classes in the district and the survey was conducted in order to establish the prevalence of haematological illness in the community. No data are available on reasons for patients not volunteering for the study and we do not consider the sample adequate for the purposes of establishing a reference range for our local population. This survey detected 69 females and 55 males with haemoglobin levels below 11.5 g dl^{-1} and 13 g dl^{-1} respectively (see Table 2). Of the females, two-thirds had immediately identifiable causes for their anaemia, approximately half of these being related to iron deficiency. Lowering the haemoglobin cut-off level to 11 g dl^{-1} in females would have resulted in a 40% reduction in those classified as being anaemic. Sixty per cent of these had either an untreatable cause for the low haemoglobin level, such as an active chronic illness or no abnormality was found. Nevertheless, the number of treatable disorders discovered in this

Table 2. Prevalence of anaemia by haemoglobin level and age.

Males

Age range	No. tested	Mean Hb. (g dl^{-1})	Number below minimum haemoglobin: No. (%)		
			Min. Hb. (g dl^{-1})	11	12	13
55+	541	14.5		9(1.7)	27(5)	55(10.2)
55–59	56	14.8		1(1.8)	2(3.6)	2(3.6)
60–64	90	14.8		0	0	2(2.2)
65–69	103	14.5		1(1)	6(5.8)	11(10.7)
70–74	115	14.4		3(2.6)	6(5.2)	12(10.4)
75–79	105	14.6		0	5(4.8)	11(10.5)
80+	72	13.9		4(6.3)	8(10)	17(23)

Females

Age range	No. tested	Mean Hb. (g dl^{-1})	Number below minimum haemoglobin: No. (%)		
			Min. Hb. (g dl^{-1})	10.5	11	11.5
55+	845	13.3		29(3.4)	42(5)	69(8.2)
55–59	35	13.8		1(2.9)	2(5.7)	2(5.7)
60–64	95	13.5		1(1.1)	3(3.2)	4(4.2)
65–69	147	13.6		6(4.1)	7(4.8)	12(8.2)
70–74	200	13.3		6(3.0)	8(4)	18(9)
75–79	195	13.3		8(4.1)	12(6.2)	14(7.2)
80+	173	13.8		7(4)	10(5.6)	19(10.9)

group would make a reduction in our current lower limits of normal unjustifiable for the elderly. There was no age differential in the incidence of definable or treatable abnormality in this age range.

It seems that little has changed since this topic was discussed over a decade ago (Lewis, 1976; Thomas and Powell, 1971) and that age dependent reference ranges for the haemoglobin level are still of limited value in the investigation of the individual patient. Whether this holds true for large scale screening remains an open question. Increased automation and the use of computerized record keeping will almost certainly open further avenues for investigation in this field. We intend to conduct a follow-up survey on our own cohort of subjects which should help to confirm whether an individual's haemoglobin level will follow a percentile with ageing in much the same way that an infant's height and weight can be measured serially, as suggested by Kelly and Munan (1977). If this assumption is correct, it would be wise not to conclude that a low haemoglobin level in an elderly person is age-related rather than due to pathology unless this could be demonstrated by comparison with previous values to be on the normal percentile level for the individual concerned. For the very old, Zaino (1981) has argued that in the ninth and subsequent decades a lower limit of 11g dl^{-1} would be appropriate for the haemoglobin level. Since his survey of nonagenarians was based on a relatively large reference sample group and the results correspond with other large studies (Munan et al, 1978) this seems a reasonable approach for isolated low values, especially if there is no supporting evidence for a pathological process, such as abnormal red cell indices or a suggestive clinical history.

Red cell indices

Useful age-dependent reference ranges for the red cell indices are even less well defined than for the haemoglobin level although comprehensive tables do exist (Munan et al, 1978). This survey and others (Croft et al, 1974; Giorno et al, 1980; Okuno, 1972) have generally shown a small rise in the mean cell volume (MCV) with increasing age. This is of little clinical significance and other causes of macrocytosis should always be considered in the elderly. It should be noted that the mean cell haemoglobin concentration (MCHC) as derived on many automated counters has limited clinical value since it is a calculated parameter dependent on the measured MCV, haemoglobin and red cell count, the first of these being prone to errors in its measurement that are dependent on the true MCHC. Machines that are able to measure the MCHC directly may increase its clinical value. Despite the potential utility of the red cell distribution indices there is little evidence for any age-dependency for these.

Platelet count

The platelet count varies little with age although in one study it showed an age related decline which was more marked in women, who had higher mean counts than men at younger ages (Stevens and Alexander, 1977). These findings have little significance for the investigation of the individual elderly patient and variations from reference ranges established in younger people are always assumed to represent an abnormal process in our own unit.

White cell count (WBC)

There is little significant change in the total leucocyte count in the aged (Nagel et al, 1983; Zacharski et al, 1971; Zaino, 1981) although some investigators have shown a small fall in women (Cruikshank and Alexander, 1970) and in both sexes (Caird, 1972).

The absolute neutrophil count does not fall in elderly people, and although most of the cases of mild neutropenia with counts in the range of $1-2 \times 10^9 \, l^{-1}$ that have been followed up in our unit have demonstrated no treatable disorder, persistently low counts in this range and those with severe neutropenia of less than $1 \times 10^9 \, l^{-1}$ need to be investigated as it may indicate serious underlying pathology. Transient neutropenia in the elderly is most often assumed to be associated with viral infections although this is usually difficult to prove. Cyclical neutropenia can be confirmed by two-weekly blood counts over a six week period and may be responsive to steroid therapy if symptomatic (Loughran et al, 1986). Bone marrow examination is essential in the diagnostic evaluation of severe or persistent neutropenia along with a full history and clinical examination. We have seen several haematological malignancies in the elderly including myeloma, non-Hodgkin's lymphoma and myelodysplasia present with an isolated neutropenia.

Most of the reported age related variations in the WBC involve a reduction in the lymphocyte count (Allan and Alexander, 1968; Cruickshank and Alexander, 1970; Ferguson et al, 1977; Nagel et al, 1983) although other surveys have shown little change (Davey and Huntington, 1977; Sparrow et al, 1980; Zacharski et al, 1971.

The monocyte count has been variably reported in older subjects. One survey showed no change in an unselected group but a gentle decline when any subject who gave a history of recent illness was excluded from the analysis (Ferguson et al, 1977). The Sherbrook group has shown a similar decline with age (Munan and Kelly, 1978). Our own population who were not selected according to health status demonstrated a rise in the monocyte count from 55 to 85 years of age with an increase in the range of values. There is little reported on the usefulness of this variable in detecting disease in the elderly. We have found moderately increased counts in the range of $1-2 \times 10^9 \ 1^{-1}$ helpful in directing investigations to the diagnosis of myelodysplasia, although none of the three cases identified in our community survey demonstrated a monocytosis. The utility of the monocyte count when performed manually suffers from a low degree of precision due to the small number of cells seen within the normal range. Reliable automated monocyte counts may be able to improve on this and increase the value of the monocyte count as a screening variable.

Few data are available on the effect of age on the two other granulocytes normally present in the blood for similar reasons. Eosinophil counts have been reported to increase over the age of 70 in men with little change in women (Munan et al, 1978).

Undirected routine manual differential counts have been demonstrated to be of little clinical value (Rich et al, 1983; Shapiro et al, 1984) and when performed without a careful further examination of the blood film will often miss the presence of abnormal cells (Rumke, 1985). The value of an extended microscope examination of selected blood films including a low power scan is not as easily quantified and will probably not be replaced by automated counters for some time although reliable machines that have been effectively standardized are anticipated (Koepke and Ross, 1985). The choice of technique for automated counting lies between digital image processing systems and flow through systems (Bentley and Lewis, 1977). Although the former are likely to produce results closest to those achieved by conventional morphology the technique does not appear to have been widely adopted, probably for reasons of expense and speed. Flow through systems are on the other hand less directly comparable but require only a single sample manipulation, are relatively quick and do not require a second machine separate from the blood counter. At present multipart differentials are most useful in screening for samples that require further examination. The true test of man versus machine will have to concentrate on comparing careful examination of the blood film including a low power scan and the data produced by an automated counter.

GRANULOCYTE FUNCTION

It has been stated that the neutrophil response to infection is retarded in older individuals (Thomas, 1971). Other observers of the same period failed to document a difference in the degree of neutrophilia between younger and older individuals with acute appendicitis (Sasso et al, 1970; Peltokallio and Juahiainen, 1970). Although the latter studies did find some correlation between the neutrophil count and severity and extent of inflammation, there was a large overlap of the range seen with that in normal uninfected individuals. It is likewise well recognized that the absence of neutrophilia in younger patients does not exclude the presence of severe infection nor does its presence confirm it. The same holds true for older individuals and as a discriminating variable in reactive states the neutrophil count needs to be treated with circumspection and interpreted in the light of clinical findings. There are few data available that correlate the presence of band forms, toxic granulation and other features of neutrophil response with age and it is our impression that these occur as commonly in the presence of inflammation in older patients as in younger. The differential count alone has little diagnostic power in this situation and film examination should be oriented to looking for abnormal cells which might indicate an underlying abnormality.

The granulocyte response to steroid administration has also been reported to be retarded in the elderly (Baldwin and Roath, 1983; Cream, 1968) whilst opsonic activity appears to be unrelated to age (Phair et al, 1978). Neutrophil function is affected by both age and malnutrition in mice (Lipshitz and Udupa, 1986) and it is likely that observed responses in humans will be affected by a host of factors some of which may be age dependent. Despite the fact that the concept of a true reduction in granulocyte reserve in the elderly remains unproven, in-vitro and in-vivo studies of granulocyte function in the elderly should be conducted and interpreted with controls of ages comparable to test groups.

LYMPHOCYTES AND IMMUNE FUNCTION

Certain infections, autoimmune diseases and malignancies occur more frequently in the elderly. Correspondingly, there are many studies reporting age related changes in the immune system and its function. Recent advances in the understanding of the interrelationships between the various components of the immune response hold much promise for further developments in this field and for the explanation of the ageing process itself. Clinical applications of lymphocyte marker studies are, however, limited and beset by pitfalls which have been eloquently described by Preud'homme (1984). In the clinical setting, age has little impact on the results of these studies aside from the age related incidence of disease. As a research tool, however, they remain valuable and do show several age related variations which need to be accounted for.

Morphology

Certain elements of the lymphoreticular system show definite morphological changes with ageing. Thymus involution is observed at a morphological and functional level with alterations in the relationship of thymic epithelial cells and lymphocytes and reduce production of thymic hormone (Baroni et al, 1983; Kay, 1979; Lewis et al, 1978). Peyer's patches undergo changes in their morphology and distribution (Cornes, 1965) and bone marrow lymphoid nodules increase in number with age (Navone et al, 1985) although most of the latter observations were made in subjects with haematological and other diseases.

Lymphocyte subsets: T cells

Comparison of the many reported studies of lymphocyte subsets in relation to age is hampered by a number of factors. These include:

(1) varying methodologies and reagents used in defining the subsets;
(2) variability in the age ranges and age and sex distributions of the subjects tested;
(3) lack of standardization in methods of expressing data and statistical methods used for analysis;
(4) inconsistent and unreported admission criteria for studies aiming to establish the effect of age on variables sensitive to nutrition and health status.

These deficiences are being addressed. Cell markers can now be classified according to their target antigens in the cluster determinant system (CD), an advance that owes much to the increased understanding of the immune system. Ligthart et al (1984) have proposed admission criteria for immuno-gerontological studies which provide useful guidelines for the selection of adequate controls. Statistical analysis of age related trends is probably best performed by regression methods rather than testing between arbitrarily chosen age groups, since this is less likely to be influenced by age dispersion within age ranges and more likely to detect changes at the extremes of life (Cobleigh et al, 1980). Data need to be expressed in absolute terms as well as in proportions.

Total lymphocyte numbers have shown a slight fall with ageing in many studies (Table 3). The major component of this decline appears to be in the absolute number of T lymphocytes (Jamil and Millard, 1981; Ligthart et al, 1985; Mascart-Lemone et al, 1982; Nagel et al, 1983; Teasdale et al, 1976). However, others have not confirmed a reduction in T-lymphocyte numbers (Cobleigh et al, 1980; Davey and Huntington, 1977) and perhaps the most consistent observation that can be made about T cells is that their numbers do not rise with age.

In addition to changes in T-cell numbers, several age related variations in T-cell subsets have been observed (Cobleigh et al, 1980; Mascart-Lemone et al, 1982; Nagel et al, 1983; Thompson et al, 1984). These have shown changes in helper–suppressor cell ratios or changes in absolute numbers in either group, but have not provided consistent data.

Analysis of numbers of circulating B cells in age has also produced conflicting results, showing increases (Del Pozo Perez et al, 1973), no change (Davey and Huntington, 1977; Jamil and Millard, 1981; Phair et al, 1978), and decreases (Cobleigh et al, 1980; Ligthart et al, 1985) and evidence for consistent trends remains unavailable. This absence of defined trends and the wide variation in ranges reported in various age groups necessitate the evaluation of lymphocyte subset studies with age matched controls and careful exclusion or consideration, by multivariant analysis, of possible confounding factors.

Assays of lymphocyte function are as important as subset analysis in the understanding of the immune response and its interactions with and influence on the ageing process. B cells can be assessed in terms of mitogen responsiveness and antibody production in vitro and in vivo. Functional assays for T cells include a variety of proliferative responses, cytotoxic assays, tests for T–B and T–T collaboration and mediator production (Janossy and Prentice, 1982). These have their in-vivo counterparts in the skin hypersensitivity tests.

Several investigators have demonstrated reduced mitogen responsiveness in lymphocytes from older subjects although some discrepancies are noted (Table 3). Speculation that reduction in PHA responsiveness may be due to alterations in T subset ratios were not confirmed when addressed in one study (Cobleigh, 1980) where no correlation was found between phytohaemagglutinin responsiveness and relative and absolute numbers of T-cell subsets as defined by immunoglobulin sensitized ox red blood cells. Humoral factors may also play a part in mitogen responsiveness as evidenced by the modification of lymphocyte proliferative activity in the elderly by cyclooxygenase inhibitors (Finkelstein et al, 1982) and the effect of protein calorie malnutrition (Bistrian et al, 1975) and zinc deficiency (Bistrian, 1975; Allen et al, 1982; Winchurch et al, 1984). However, it is interesting to note that lymphocyte PHA responses and skin test results have been shown to be similar in healthy and in ill subjects in one group of elderly people (Goodwin et al, 1982) implying a true relationship between the depressed response and age and not age related illness.

Natural killer activity has been shown to deteriorate in old mice but generally appears normal or enhanced in elderly humans (Krishnaraj and Blandford, 1984; Thompson et al, 1984) although zinc deficiency in elderly lung cancer patients appears to impair natural killer function (Allen, 1982). Interleukin-2 (IL-2) production was impaired in a small group of centenarians (Thompson et al, 1984) and mouse and other human studies have shown a fall off in production with age (Gillis et al, 1981; Inamizu et al, 1985). Delayed type hypersensitivity responses are generally depressed with advancing years which may correlate with the increased incidence of tuberculous activation in the elderly (Powell and Farar, 1980) and increased severity of infections by other

Table 3. Studies relating to lymphocyte function in the aged.

Reference	Con. A	PWM	PHA	Total count	T cells (Total)	B cells	T-cell subset changes	NK activity	Skin test response	Interleukin-2 production	IgA	IgM	IgG	IgE
Cobleigh et al, 1980			R	N	N*	R	P				I	N		
Davey et al, 1977				N	N	N						N	N	
Del Pozo Perez et al, 1973			R			I					N	N		
Dworsky et al, 1983	R	R	I	R					R					
Ferguson et al, 1977				R	R									
Fernandez et al, 1976			R†		N	R								
Krisnaraj & Blandford, 1984								I						
Mascart-Lemone et al, 1982					R		P‡				I	N	I	
Moulias et al, 1984			N	N	R				N					
Nagel et al, 1983				R	R		P§							
Radl et al, 1975											I¶	N¶	I¶	
Schwab et al, 1985			R											
Teasdale et al, 1975		R	R		R	N	P‡							
Thompson et al, 1984			R	N		I‖		N		R	N	N	N	N

N—Normal; P—Present; R—Reduced; I—Increased; Con. A—Concanavalin A; PWM—Pokeweed mitogen.

* Subset of T cells reduced.
† After four day culture. Increased after eight days.
‡ Reduced helper cells.
§ Reduced suppressor/cytotoxic cells, helper/suppressor ratio constant.
¶ Over 95 years.
‖ Increased early B cells.

intracellular organisms such as legionella. Lymphopenia induced by bacterial infections in the elderly has been shown to be a predictor of a fatal outcome (Proust et al, 1985) with no such discriminating power in younger patients.

Paradoxically, immunological changes responsible for reduced resistance to infection and tumour establishment in the elderly may be responsible for the observation that, once established, tumours grow more slowly than in younger individuals (Ershler, 1986).

IMMUNOGLOBULINS

Immunoglobulin levels are known to change with age (Table 3), most consistently reflected in the elderly in increased levels of IgA and IgG (Radl et al, 1975; Buckley et al, 1974; Moulias et al, 1984). IgM levels are generally reported to remain stable (Moulias et al, 1984). Others have shown no significant changes in all Ig classes including IgE (Thompson et al, 1984; Dworsky et al, 1983) and it is apparent that selection of study groups will be of some significance when measuring immunoglobulin levels. The magnitude of the age related variations reported are such that they are unlikely to be of much clinical significance.

Qualitative abnormalities in immunoglobulins are also seen in the aged. The presence of monoclonal immunoglobulin in the absence of overt illness, monoclonal gammopathy of unknown aetiology, has long been recognized to increase steadily in incidence from the third decade (Axelsson et al, 1966) and to be present in up to 20% of people over the age of 95 (Radl et al, 1975). Antibody production in response to vaccination is impaired in the elderly, an example being the poor response to pneumococcal vaccine (Amman et al, 1980). The accumulation of autoantibodies with age is well recognized, particularly anti-thyroglobulin and gastric parietal cell antibodies (Moulias et al, 1984; Reisen et al, 1976; Roberts-Thompson et al, 1974).

The significance of these in healthy subjects remains uncertain. They may represent defects in T-suppressor function or in the formation of anti-idiotypic antibodies. It is important, however, to recognize the phenomenon and interpret positive results in autoantibody screens in the elderly with caution when these have been performed for diagnostic reasons. On the other hand it is equally important not to attribute the presence of other autoanti-bodies solely to age. Intrinsic factor antibody, for example, is rarely found in the absence of pernicious anaemia.

ERYTHROCYTE SEDIMENTATION RATE (ESR)

The ESR is a non-specific test sensitive to technical variables in its performance such as tube inclination and ambient temperature. In crowded modern laboratories full of automated equipment, it is often seen as being out of place and is a rather labour intensive and time consuming test, a fact not appreciated by many clinicians. It is also sensitive, in an unpredictable manner, to the haemoglobin level and shows a diurnal variation (Mallya et al,

1982). An alternative does exist in the measurement of plasma viscosity. Although this is also sensitive to variation in technique it is not affected by the haemoglobin level (Dacie and Lewis, 1984b) and is the preferred test in many laboratories.

Nevertheless it seems unlikely that the ESR will be supplanted readily (Bottiger, 1982). It does have some value in diagnosis and in our experience will often guide the haematologically inexperienced clinician towards investigations directly relevant to the diagnosis of myeloma, when this might have been missed. It is also of use in monitoring of treatment and the course of illnesses, particularly polymyalgia rheumatica, when interpreted in the light of its shortcomings. The mean value for the ESR as well as the range of values increases with age (Sharland, 1980; Lewis, 1980; Ash et al, 1983) with high values of up to 69 mm h^{-1} in well elderly women with no detectable illness (Sparrow et al, 1981). This may be attributable to increased fibrinogen levels observed in the elderly. It is also interesting to note that in the longitudinal survey of Sparrow et al, the ESR was not significantly related to the risk of death in the over 45s whereas it was in the under 45s. This fact may reflect the reduced predictive capacity of the test due to its wider reference limits in the elderly. With these further limitations in mind, interpretation of an 'abnormal' ESR in an older patient should be made with even more caution than in the younger age group. Furthermore, although an upper limit of 30 mm h^{-1} has been suggested for the over 50s (Bottiger, 1982) definite limits are probably not practicable in older patients.

BONE MARROW ASPIRATION AND BIOPSY

Indications for and the methods of examining bone marrow smears and biopsies in the elderly are no different from younger patients. Slight technical difficulties may be experienced in obtaining intact biopsy cores from trephine needles owing to the often fragile nature of osteoporotic bone in older patients. Sharp needles and a careful technique are essential. Iliac crest marrow cellularity decreases with age to about 30% in the over 70s (Hartsock et al, 1965) but this rarely presents a problem in interpretation. Careful examination of sections and films is advisable in order to detect the often subtle changes found in myelodysplasia. There are no morphological changes in the haemopoietic cell lines that are specific to ageing although distinction between changes attributable to B_{12} or folate deficiency and myelodysplasia may be difficult. Lymphoid nodules in the absence of overt clinical disease are more common than in younger ages but are more often associated with a variety of disorders (Navone et al, 1985).

HAEMATINICS

Deficiencies and disorders relating to B_{12}, folate and iron will be discussed in detail elsewhere in this issue. From the viewpoint of screening we have found that low B_{12} levels are common in the elderly and that these do not necessarily predict the presence of B_{12} malabsorption, anaemia or even macrocytosis. This is similar to the experience of others. For this reason screening for deficiency of the vitamin should be directed towards clinical and laboratory features of a functional effect of the deficiency, such as anaemia, macrocytosis or typical neurological signs. Utilizing the B_{12} level as a screening investigation will uncover many abnormal levels in the elderly in the absence of other features of deficiency and may provoke unnecessary investigation and even treatment of these individuals.

Folate and iron deficiency are also common in the elderly (Batata et al, 1967; Girdwood et al, 1967) but screening for these is best directed towards the detection of anaemia and changes in the MCV. Consequently, observed changes in reference limits for the serum iron (Pririe, 1952) are unlikely to be of clinical significance.

CONCLUSIONS

Although much energy has been focused on studying the unique effects of the ageing process on clinical and laboratory measurements in haematology, there are few firm conclusions to be drawn. The high incidence of illness in the elderly and the apparent increase in biological variability ensure that 'normality' is a difficult entity to define in this group and although age related trends may be noted, this often has little relevance to the clinician faced with an individual patient. In general, functional diagnoses are more useful than descriptive tests in establishing whether a variation from the norm is part of a pathological process. For example, a reticulocyte response and rise in haemoglobin level following cobalamin administration are better indicators of vitamin B_{12} deficiency than the measurement of a lower serum level of the vitamin.

In addition, minor changes with no currently recognized cause should not necessarily be attributed to age alone. Simple observation has led to the recognition of myelodysplasia as a defined clinical disorder responsible for changes that might easily have been passed as 'age related' little more than a decade ago. Advances in the fields of immunology and cellular biology will almost certainly uncover explanations for other age related observations.

REFERENCES

Allan RN & Alexander MK (1968) A sex difference in the leukocyte count. *Journal of Clinical Pathology* **21:** 691.

Allen JR, Bell EM, Oken MM et al (1982) Zinc deficiency, hyperzincuria and immune dysfunction in lung cancer patients. *Clinical Research* **30:** 342A.

Amman AJ, Schiffman G & Austrian R (1980) The antibody responses to pneumococcal capsular polysaccharides in aged individuals. *Proceedings of the Society for Experimental Biology and Medicine* **164:** 312–316.

Ash KO, Clark SJ, Sandberg LB, Hunter E & Woodward SC (1983) The influences of sample distribution and age on reference intervals for adult males. *American Journal of Clinical Pathology* **79:** 574–581.

Axelsson U, Bachmann R & Hallen J (1966) Frequency of pathologic protein in 6995 sera from an adult population. *Acta Medica Scandinavica* **179:** 235–247.

Baldwin C & Roath S (1983) The evaluation of neutropenia: the use of the granulocyte mobilisation test. *Clinical Laboratory Haematology* **5:** 353–360.

Baroni CD, Valtieri M, Stoppacciaro A et al (1983) The human thymus in aging: histologic involution paralled by increased mitogen response and by enrichment of OKT3 lymphocytes. *Immunology* **50:** 519–528.

Batata M, Spray GJ, Bolton FG, Higgins G & Wollner L (1967) Blood and bone marrow changes in elderly patients with special reference to folic acid, vitamin B_{12}, iron and ascorbic acid. *British Medical Journal* **2:** 667–669.

Bentley SA & Lewis SM (1977) Automated differential leucocyte counting: the present state of the art. *British Journal of Haematology* **35:** 481–485.

Bessman JD (1985) Normal haematological values. In: Denheim MJ & Chanarin I (eds) *Blood Disorders in the Elderly*, pp 6–9. Edinburgh, New York: Churchill Livingstone.

Bessman JD, Williams LJ & Gardner FH (1983) Improved classification of anaemia with MCV and RDW. *American Journal of Clinical Pathology* **78:** 150–153.

Bessman JD, Gilmer PR & Gardner FH (1985) Use of mean platelet volume improves detection of platelet disorders. *Blood Cells* **11:** 127–135.

Bistrian BR, Blackburn GL, Scrimshaw NS et al, (1975) Cellular immunity in semistarved states in hospitalised patients. *American Journal of Clinical Nutrition* **28:** 1148–1155.

Blundell EL, Matthews JH, Allen SM, Middleton AM, Morris JE & Wickramasinghe SE (1985) Importance of low serum B_{12} and red cell folate concentrations in elderly hospital inpatients. *Journal of Clinical Pathology* **38:** 1179–1184.

Bottiger LE (1982) Is it time to abandon the ESR? *Acta Medica Scandinavica* **212:** 353–354.

Buckley III CE, Buckley EG & Dorsey FC (1974) Longitudinal changes in serum immunoglobulin levels in older humans. *Federation Proceedings* **33:** 2036–2039.

Caird FI (1973) Problems of interpretation of laboratory findings in old age. *British Medical Journal* **4:** 348–351.

Caird FI, Andrews GR & Gallie TB (1972) The leucocyte count in old age. *Age and Ageing* **1:** 239–244.

Chanarin I (1985) Megaloblastic anaemia. In: Denham MJ & Chanarin I (eds) *Blood disorders in the elderly*, pp 52–54. Edinburgh, New York: Churchill Livingstone.

Cobleigh MA, Baun DP & Harris JE (1980) Age-dependent changes in human peripheral blood B-cells and T-cell subsets: correlation with mitogen responsiveness. *Clinical Immunology and Immunopathology* **15:** 162–174.

Cornes JS (1965) Number size and distribution of Peyer's patches in the human small intestine. Part II. The effect of age on Peyer's patches *Gut* **6:** 230–233.

Cream JJ (1968) Prednisolone-induced granulocytosis. *British Journal of Haematology* **15:** 259.

Croft RF, Streeter AM & O'Niell BJ (1974) Red cell indices in megaloblastosis and iron deficiency. *Pathology* **6:** 107–117.

Cruickshank JM & Alexander MK (1970) The effect of age, sex, parity, haemoglobin level and oral contraceptive preparations on the normal leucocyte count. *British Journal of Haematology* **18:** 541–550.

Custer RP & Ahlfeldt FE (1932) Studies on the structure and function of bone marrow. Variations in cellularity in various bones with advancing years of life and their relative response to stimuli. *Journal of Laboratory and Clinical Medicine* **17:** 960–965.

Dacie JV & Lewis SM (1984a) Basic haematological techniques. In *Practical Haematology*, 6th edn. Edinburgh: Churchill Livingstone.

Dacie JV & Lewis SM (1984b) Plasma viscosity. In: *Practical Haematology*, 6th edn, pp. 422–423. Edinburgh: Churchill Livingstone.

Davey FR & Huntington S (1977) Age related variation in lymphocyte subpopulations. *Gerontology* **23:** 381–389.

Del Pozo Perez MA, Prieto Val Tuena J, Gonzalez Guilabert MI & Velasco Alonso R (1973) Effects of age and sex on T and B lymphocyte populations in man. *Biomedicine* **19:** 340–344.

Dworsky R, Paganini-Hill A & Pavker J (1983) Immune responses of healthy humans 83–104 years of age. *Journal of the National Cancer Institute* **71:** 265–168.

Ershler WB. (1986) Why tumours grow more slowly in old age. *Journal of the National Cancer Institute* **77:** 837–839.

Evans DM (1971) Haematological aspects of iron deficiency in the elderly. *Gerontology Clinics* **13:** 12–30.

Ferguson T, Crichlon DN & Price WH (1977) Lymphocyte counts in relation to age. (Letter) *Lancet* **ii:** 35.

Fernandez LA, MacSween JM & Langley GR (1976) Lymphocyte responses to phytohaemagglutinin: age related effects. *Immunology* **31:** 583–587.

Finkelstein MS, Freedman ML & Nadel H (1982) Modification of lymphocyte proliferative activities in the elderly by orally administered cyclooxygenase inhibitors. *Gerontologist* **22:** 234.

Gillis S, Kozak R, Duisuile M et al (1981) Immunological studies of aging: decreased production of and response to T cell growth factor by lymphocytes from aged humans. *Journal of Clinical Investigation* **67:** 937–942.

Giorno R, Clifford JH, Beverly S & Rossing G (1980) Haematology reference values. *American Journal of Clinical Pathology* **74:** 765–770.

Girdwood RH, Thomson AD & Williamson J (1967) Folate status in the elderly. *British Medical Journal* **2:** 667–669.

Goodwin JS, Searles RP & Tung SNK (1982) Immunological responses of a healthy elderly population. *Clinical & Experimental Immunology* **48:** 403–410.

Harrell FE & Davis CE (1982) A new distribution free quantile estimator. *Biometrika* **69:** 635–640.

Hartstock RJ, Smith EB & Pelly CS (1965) Normal variations with ageing on the amount of haemopoietic tissue in bone marrow from the anterior iliac crest. *American Journal of Clinical Pathology* **43:** 326–331.

Hayflick L (1966) In: Shock NW (ed), *Perspectives in Experimental Gerontology*. p. 195. Springfield, Illinois: CC Thomas.

Hersey P, Haran G, Hasic E & Edwards A (1983) Alteration of T cell subsets and induction of suppressor T cell activity in normal subjects after exposure to sunlight. *Journal of Immunology* **131:** 171–174.

Htoo MS, Kofkoff RL & Freedman ML (1979) Erythrocyte parameters in the elderly: an argument against new geriatric normal ranges. *Journal of the American Geriatrics Society* **27:** 547–551.

Hughes D, Elwood PC, Shinton NK & Wrighton RJ (1970) Clinical trial of the effect of vitamin B_{12} in elderly subjects with low serum B_{12} levels. *British Medical Journal* **2:** 480–486.

Jamil NAK & Millard RE (1981) Studies of T, B and 'null' blood lymphocytes in normal persons of different age groups. *Gerontology* **27:** 79–84.

Janossy G & Prentice HG (1982) T cell subpopulations, monoclonal antibodies and their therapeutic applications. *Clinical Haematology* **11:** 631–660.

Jernigan JA, Gudat JC, Blake JL, Bowen L & Lezotte DC (1980) Reference values for blood findings in relatively fit elderly persons. *Journal of the American Geriatrics Society* **28:** 308–314.

Johnson A & Dorshkind K (1986) Stromal cells in myeloid and lymphoid long-term bone marrow cultures can support multiple hemopoietic lineages and modulate their production of hemopoietic growth factors. *Blood* **68:** 1348–1354.

Kay MMB (1979) The thymus: clock for immunological aging. *Journal of Investigative Dermatology* **73:** 29–33.

Kelly A & Munan L (1977) Haematological profile of natural populations: red cell parameters. *British Journal of Haematology* **35:** 153–160.

Koepke JA & Ross DW (1985) White blood cell differential: a call for standards. *Blood Cells* **11:** 1–9.

Krishnaraj R & Blandford G (1984) Quantitative and qualitative difference in natural killer cell activity in aging. *Gerontology* **24:** 162.

Lajtha LB & Schofield R (1971) Regulation of stem cell renewal and differentiation of possible significance in aging. *Advances in Gerontology Research* **3:** 131.

Lewis R (1976) Anaemia – a common but never normal concomitant of aging. *Geriatrics* Dec., 53–60.

Lewis SM (1980) Erythrocyte sedimentation rate and plasma viscosity. *ACP Broadsheet No. 94.* London: British Medical Association.

Lewis VM, Twomey JJ, Bealmear P et al (1978) Age, thymic involution and circulating thymic hormone activity. *Journal of Clinical Endocrinology* **18:** 145.

Ligthart GJ, Gorberand JX, Fournier C et al (1984) Admission criteria for immunogerontological studies in man: the SENIEUR protocol. *Mechanisms of Ageing and Development* **28**; 47–55.

Ligthart GJ, Schmit HRE & Hijmans W (1985) Subpopulations of mononuclear cells in aging: expansion of the null cell compartment and decrease in the number of T and B cells in human blood. *Immunology* **55**: 15–21.

Lipschitz DA & Udupa KB (1986) Influence of aging and protein deficiency on neutrophil function. *Journal of Gerontology* **41**: 690–694.

Lipschitz DA, Mitchell CO & Thompson C (1981) The anaemia of senescence. *American Journal of Hematology* **11**: 47–54.

Loughran TP, Clark EA, Price TJ & Hammond WP (1986) Adult onset cyclic neutropenia is associated with increased large granular lymphocytes. *Blood* **68**: 1082–1087.

Mallya RB, Berry H, Mace BEW, De Beer FC & Pepys MB (1982) Diurnal variation of erythrocyte sedimentation rate related to feeding. *Lancet* **i**: 389–391.

Mandalaki T, Dessypris A, Panayotopoulou C & Dimitriado C (1980) Marathon run III. Effects on coagulation, fibrinolysis, platelet aggregation and serum cortisol levels. *Thrombosis and Haemostasis* **43**: 49–52.

Mascart-Lemone F, Delespesse G, Servais G & Kunstler M (1982) Characterization of immunoregulatory T lymphocytes during aging by monoclonal antibodies. *Clinical and Experimental Immunology* **48**: 148–154.

Mclennan WJ, Andrews GR, Macleod L & Caird FI (1973) Anaemia in the elderly. *Quarterly Journal of Medicine* **42**: 1–13.

Milne JS & Williamson J (1972) Haemoglobin, haematocrit leucocyte count and blood grouping in older people. *Geriatrics* **27**: 118–122.

Moulias R, Proust J, Wang A et al (1984) Age related increase in autoantibodies (Letter). Lancet **i**: 1128–1129.

Munan L, Kelly A, Petitclerc C & Billon B (1978) *Atlas of blood data*. Prepared by the: Epidemiology Laboratory and Laboratory of Clinical Biochemistry, University of Sherbrooke, Quebec.

Nagel JE, Chrest FJ, Pyle RS & Adler WH (1983) Monoclonal antibody analysis of T lymphocyte subsets in young and aged patients. *Immunology Communications* **12**: 223–237.

Navone R, Valpreda M & Pich A (1985) Lymphoid nodules and nodular lymphoid hyperplasia in bone marrow. *Acta Haematologica* **74**: 19–22.

Okuno T (1972) Red cell size as measured by the Coulter model S. *Journal of Clinical Pathology* **25**: 599–602.

Peltokallio P & Jauhiairien K (1970) Acute appendicitis in the aged patient: study of 300 cases after the age of 60. *Archives of Surgery* **100**: 140–143.

Phair JP, Kauffman CA, Bjornson A et al (1978) Host defences in the aged: evaluation of components of the inflammatory and immune responses. *Journal of Infectious Diseases* **138**: 67–73.

Powell KE & Farar LS (1980) The rising age of the tuberculous patient: a sign of success and failure. *Journal of Infectious Diseases* **142**: 946–948.

Preud-homme J-L (1984) Lymphocyte markers: diagnostic help or costly vogue. *Diagnostic Immunology* **2**: 242–248.

Pririe R (1952) The effect of age upon serum iron in normal subjects. *Journal of Clinical Pathology* **5**: 10–15.

Proust J, Rozenzweig C & Debouzy RM (1985) Lymphopenia induced by acute bacterial infections in the elderly: a sign of age-related immune dysfunction of major prognostic significance. *Gerontology* **31**: 178–185.

Purcell Y & Borzovic B (1974) Red cell 2,3 diphosphoglycerate concentration in man decreases with age. *Nature* **251**: 511–512.

Radl J, Sepers JM, Skvaril F, Morell A & Hijmans W (1975) Immunoglobulin patterns in humans over 95 years of age. *Clinical and Experimental Immunology* **22**: 84–90.

Reisen W, Keller H, Skvaril F, Morell A & Barandun S (1976) Restriction of immunoglobulin heterogeneity, autoimmunity and serum protein levels in aged people. *Clinical and Experimental Immunology* **26**: 280–285.

Rich EC, Crowson TW & Connolly DP (1983) Effectiveness of differential leucocyte count in case finding in the ambulatory care setting. *Journal of the American Medical Association* **249**: 633–638.

Roberts-Thompson IC, Whittingham S, Youngchaiyua U & MacKay IR (1974) Aging, immune response and mortality. *Lancet* **ii:** 368–370.

Rumke Chr L (1985) Statistical reflections on finding atypical cells. *Blood Cells* **11:** 141–144.

Sasso RD, Hanna EA & Moore DL (1970) Leukocytic and neutrophilic counts in acute appendicitis. *American Journal of Surgery* **120:** 563–566.

Shapiro MF, Hatch RL & Greenfield S (1984) Cost containment and labour intensive tests. The case of the leucocyte differential count. *Journal of the American Medical Association* **252:** 231–234.

Sharland DE (1980) Erythrocyte sedimentation rate. The normal range in the elderly. *Journal of the American Geriatric Society* **28:** 346–348.

Shultz EK, Willard KE, Rich SS, Gonnely DP & Critchfield GC (1985) Improved reference-interval estimation. *Clinical Chemistry* **31/12:** 1974–1978.

Sparrow D, Silberg JE & Rowe JW (1980) The influence of age on peripheral lymphocyte count in men: a cross sectional and longitudinal study. *Journal of Gerontology* **35:** 163–166.

Sparrow D, Rowe JW & Silbert JE (1981) Cross-sectional and longitudinal changes in the erythrocyte sedimentation rate in men. *Journal of Gerontology* **36:** 180–184.

Stevens RF & Alexander MK (1977) A sex difference in the platelet count. *British Journal of Haematology* **37:** 295–300.

Teasdale C, Thatcher S, Whitehead RJ & Hughes LE (1976) Age dependence of T lymphocytes (Letter) *Lancet* **i:** 1410–1411.

Thomas JH & Powell DEB (1971) *Blood disorders in the elderly.* Bristol: John Wright.

Thompson JS, Wekstein DR, Rhoades JL et al (1984) The immune status of healthy centenarians. *Journal of the American Geriatric Society* **32:** 274–281.

Van der Lelie J & Van Dem Borne AEG (1986) Platelet volume analysis for differential diagnosis of thrombocytosis. *Journal of Clinical Pathology* **39:** 129–133.

Viteri FE, De Tuba V & Guzman MA (1972) Normal haematological values in the Central American population. *British Journal of Haematology* **23:** 189–204.

Waters WE, Withey JC, Kilpatrick GS & Wood PHN (1971) Serum vitamin B_{12} concentrations in the general population – a ten year follow-up. *British Journal of Haematology* **20:** 521–526.

Winchurch RA, Thomas DJ, Alder WH & Lindsay TJ (1984) Supplemental zinc restores antibody formation in cultures of aged spleen cells. *Journal of Immunology* **133:** 569–571.

Wolf NS (1979) The haemopoietic microenvironment. *Clinics in Haematology* **8:** 469–484.

Wolf NS & Trenlin JJ (1968) Haemopoietic colony studies. V. Effect of haemopoietic organ stroma on differentiation of pluripotent stem cells. *Journal of Experimental Medicine* **127:** 205–214.

Zacharski LR, Elveback LR & Linman JW (1971) Leucocyte counts in healthy adults. *American Journal of Clinical Pathology* **56:** 148–150.

Zaino EC (1981) Blood counts in the nonagenarian. *New York State Journal of Medicine* **81:** 1199–1200.

2

Iron deficiency in the elderly

BARRY M. SCHULTZ
MICHAEL L. FREEDMAN

Iron deficiency is usually discovered during the evaluation of a newly diagnosed microcytic anaemia. In the elderly, the degree of iron loss needed to produce an iron-deficient state nearly always results from bleeding. This is because while we lose less than 1 mg of iron per day, the average diet in the industrialized world contains 15–16 mg per day. Consequently, iron deficiency due to inadequate dietary intake would be very rare. In fact, in the absence of blood loss, there appears to be a gradual accumulation of iron in the body with ageing as long as the diet contains iron. Even in populations where the majority of younger people are iron deficient, the elderly are not (Marcus and Freedman, 1985).

STAGES OF IRON DEFICIENCY

There are four well-described stages of iron deficiency (Table 1), only the last two of which are reflected in the red blood cell indices (Marcus and Freedman, 1985). Before the overt haematological effects of iron deficiency manifest themselves, only bone marrow stains for iron or serum ferritin can be used to detect the earlier stages of iron depletion. In the first stage, known as iron depletion, serum ferritin is the most useful indicator because it is not practical to use bone marrow aspiration as a screening test. As iron deficiency progresses, bone marrow iron remains reduced or absent and serum ferritin remains low while other biochemical and haematological changes occur. In the second stage, iron deficiency without anaemia, there is a fall in the serum iron with a corresponding rise in the transferrin. In early iron-deficiency anaemia, the third stage, bone marrow iron is absent but the red blood cells are usually still normocytic normochromic. Additionally, the supply of transport iron becomes limited for haemoglobin synthesis, and the erythrocyte protoporphyrin is elevated. In the fourth and final stage of iron deficiency the classic haematological findings of microcytic, hypochromic anaemia are seen.

Table 1. Progression of iron deficiency.

	Bone marrow iron	Serum Fe/TIBC	Serum ferritin	Erythrocyte protoporphyrin	RBC morphology
Iron depletion	Decreased	Normal	Low	Normal	Normal
Iron deficiency without anaemia	Decreased or absent	Low	Low	Normal	Normal
Early iron-deficiency anaemia	Absent	Low	Low	High	Normal or slightly microcytic
Late iron-deficiency anaemia	Absent	Low	Low	High	Microcytic hypochromic

Reprinted with permission from Marcus and Freedman 1986).

Table 2. Limitations of tests used to diagnose iron deficiency.

Test	Limitation
Haemoglobin/Haematocrit	Anaemia is a late finding. Does not distinguish it from other causes.
Microcytosis	Late finding. Other anaemias cause microcytosis.
Serum ferritin	Normal level not accurate with chronic disease or liver disease.
Transferrin saturation	Low transferrin also found in the elderly and those with chronic disease.
Serum iron	Levels may fluctuate.
Free erythrocyte protoporphyrin	Late finding. Does not distinguish it from lead poisoning
Red-cell distribution width (RDW)	Not sensitive enough for screening.

DIAGNOSIS OF IRON DEFICIENCY

Tests used to detect iron deficiency have various levels of diagnostic accuracy (Table 2). The limitation of each measurement must be kept in mind. Using anaemia as a screening test for iron deficiency is limited because it is a late finding, and does not distinguish iron deficiency from the other causes of anaemia (Freedman, 1983 a & b). Decreased mean corpuscular volume (MCV) is also a relatively late finding. Additionally, other anaemias which may be microcytic and difficult to distinguish from iron deficiency based on MCV are thalassemia minor, anaemia of chronic disease, and sideroblastic anaemia (Marcus and Freedman, 1985).

Other tests, often useful in detecting iron deficiency before an overt anaemia develops, can present several problems from the standpoint of diagnostic accuracy. Whereas a low serum ferritin always indicates iron deficiency, a normal level does not assure adequate iron stores, as serum ferritin is often elevated into the normal range in the presence of chronic inflammation and liver disease (Freedman, 1983). Low transferrin saturation is unreliable because iron and serum transferrin levels are often decreased in the elderly as well as in those with chronic disease (Freedman and Marcus, 1980). The serum iron may be inaccurate because it may fluctuate depending on the time of the day (Speck, 1968). Free erythrocyte protoporphyrin levels increase around the same time that microcytosis develops and are therefore a relatively late finding. Additionally, high levels of erythrocyte protoporphyrin may not distinguish iron deficiency from lead poisoning (Marcus and Freedman, 1985).

Thompson et al (1987) have evaluated the accuracy of the red cell distribution width (RDW), MCV, and transferrin saturation in the diagnosis of iron deficiency in hospitalized patients. The RDW measures the variability in red cell size (anisocytosis). In contrast to previous reports, the authors found that none of these tests were sensitive or specific enough to be considered an accurate screening test for the diagnosis of iron deficiency anaemia in hospitalized patients and the elderly.

NONERYTHROID FUNCTIONS OF IRON

As well as playing a vital role in the production of haem, iron is responsible for many other metabolic processes, either directly through iron-containing enzymes or as a cofactor. These biochemical functions of iron have in most cases been described through the effect of iron deficiency on the various processes involved.

Iron is present at the subcellular level in the mitochondria, where it functions in several metabolic processes as a component of various iron-containing enzymes. The presence of iron is essential in mitochondria for the generation of energy in the form of ATP by oxidative phosphorylation. Several enzyme components of the respiratory electron transport chain contain iron, including cytochrome oxidase (containing two haem groups), succinate dehydrogenase (an iron flavoprotein), and other non-haem containing compounds (Jacobs, 1982). By itself and as a part of haem, iron exerts a controlling effect on protein synthesis in the mitochondrion, and may help maintain the integrity of the organelle (Marcus and Freedman, 1986).

The cellular concentration of haem exerts crucial control of protein synthesis chain initiation and polyribosome formation in reticulocytes (Rabinovitz et al, 1969). As haem concentration falls below a critical level, a translational repressor of initiation forms (the haem-controlled repressor or HCR) from a noninhibitory form of the same protein found in the postribosomal supernatant, and stops cytoplasmic protein synthesis (Freedman et al, 1974).

In sufficient amounts, haem can inhibit the formation of this repressor and reverse its activity (Freedman and Rosman, 1976). HCR in its inhibitory form has also been found in mature human and rabbit erythrocytes (Freedman et al, 1974), while in reticulocytes that are actively synthesizing protein it is found in its inactive or 'proinhibitor' form. This is considered to be evidence

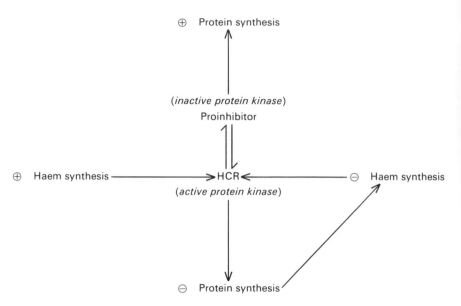

Figure 1. Working model for haem control of cytoplasmic protein synthesis. HCR = haem-controlled repressor. Reprinted with permission from Marcus and Freedman (1986).

that HCR plays a physiological role in the maturation and cessation of protein synthesis in erythroid cells.

Freedman et al (1977) have shown that HCR is a cyclic AMP-independent protein kinase that appears to act by phophorylating and thus inactivating initiation factor eIF-2 that mediates the binding of met-tRNA$_f$ to the 40S ribosomal subunit. Phosphorylated eIF-2 is as efficient as unphosphorylated eIF-2 in the formation of the 40S and 80S initiation complexes in a reconstituted system with highly purified components (Ranu and London, 1976). More recent evidence has shown that the formation of the ternary complex (eIF-2-GTP-met-tRNA$_f$) and its subsequent binding to the 40S subunit involves other factors in addition to eIF-2 (Trachsel and Staehelin, 1978) and the phosphorylation of eIF-2 may inhibit its interaction with these factors (de Haro et al, 1978). It has been further demonstrated that cAMP acts at the level of mitochondrial δ-aminolaevulinic acid synthetase (ALA-S) in reticulocytes (Ibrahim et al, 1979).

Freedman and Marcus (1986) have proposed a working model for haem control of cytoplasmic protein synthesis (Figure 1). A decrease in haem synthesis results in diminished protein synthesis. Haem synthesis is also partially regulated by endproduct inhibition (by haem) of the rate-limiting enzyme ALA-S (Ibrahim et al, 1978). Consequently, when haem accumulates, ALA-S is inhibited and further haem synthesis stops. This model helps explain the balanced haem and globin synthesis seen in erythroid cells.

This model of haem control of protein synthesis is consistent with other evidence showing that haem synthesis is essential in erythropoiesis. Erythropoietin has been shown to first stimulate ALA-S and haem synthesis before affecting globin synthesis (Beuzard et al, 1973). Using a system of bone marrow precursors in tissue culture, the authors have shown that haem synthesis is maximal in the earliest precursor cells and decreases with cell maturity. This is consistent with the theory of Lodish and Desalu (1973) that in erythrocytes there must be sufficient intracellular haem to convert HCR from its inhibitory to a noninhibitory state before protein synthesis may proceed.

Haem control of protein synthesis seems to be fairly universal. Various nonglobin proteins have been shown to require haem for protein synthesis, including those of the reticulocyte (Gross and Rabinovitz, 1972), Krebs ascites tumour cells (Rhoades et al, 1973), platelets (Freedman and Karpatkin, 1973), and cells from brain and liver (Hayashi et al, 1969), as well as mRNAs for nonmammalian proteins (Lodish, 1974).

Thus, the control of haem synthesis is essential to the translational control of cytoplasmic protein synthesis. Further investigation of haem synthesis would require that attention be directed to the mitochondrion. It contains four of the haem synthetic enzymes: δ-aminolaevulinic acid synthase, coproporphrinogen oxidase, ferrochetalase, and protoporphrinogen oxidase (Deybach et al, 1985). Additionally, although ALAS, the rate-limiting enzyme of haem synthesis, is synthesized in the cytoplasm, it is then transported into the mitochondrion, where it binds to a protein synthesized by the mitochondrial protein synthesizing system (DeLoskey and Beattie, 1984). The structural integrity of the mitochondrial inner membrane is necessary for the normal activity of all of the mitochondrial haem synthetic enzymes (Marcus et al, 1984).

The investigation of mitochondrial protein synthesis has involved examining the synthesis of inner membrane proteins (Marcus et al, 1982). Other products of mitochondrial protein synthesis include coproporphyrinogen oxidase as well as a subunit of the cytochrome c oxidase. Most mitochondrial proteins, however, are synthesized on cytoplasmic ribosomes (under nuclear genetic control) and subsequently transferred into the mitochondrion (Freedman and Marcus, 1980). Marcus et al (1980) have shown that ferrous iron is required for maximal mitochondrial protein synthesis. In the presence of the ferrous iron chelator a,a-dipyridyl, mitochondrial protein synthesis was inhibited by almost 50%. The inhibition was reversed by the addition of ferrous ammonium sulphate. Additionally, ferrous iron protected against a,a-dipyridyl inhibition whereas haem did not. Thus, ferrous iron appears to be required for mitochondrial protein synthesis through a mechanism independent of haem concentration.

For normal cell growth to occur, there must be an integration of the synthesis of mitochondrial proteins at both the cytoplasmic and mitochondrial sites. There is stimulation of mitochondrial protein synthesis when mitochondrial proteins synthesized in the cytoplasm accumulate (Tenhunen et al, 1970). As would be expected, it has also been shown that when

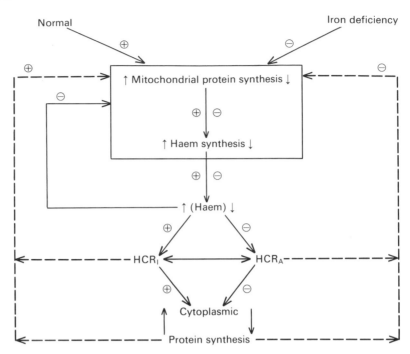

Figure 2. Proposed interrelationship between mitochondrial and cytoplasmic protein synthesis. Under normal conditions (+) there is maximal mitochondrial protein synthesis (↑), which allows maximal haem synthesis (↑) and sufficient cytoplasmic haem to maintain the haem-controlled repressor (HCR) in the noninhibitory form (HCR$_I$). Thus, under normal conditions (+) cytoplasmic protein synthesis is maximal (↑). In iron deficiency (−) mitochondrial protein synthesis falls (↓), haem synthesis and concentration drop (↓), and HCR is activated (HCR$_A$) to inhibit cytoplasmic protein synthesis. If haem levels are supranormal (i.e., where there is primary inhibition of cytoplasmic protein synthesis), mitochondrial protein synthesis would be inhibited by haem (−). As shown (− − − −) there appears to be a mechanism for cytoplasmic protein synthesis to signal mitochondrial protein synthesis. This could conceivably be via the cytoplasmic proteins themselves, HCR, or some other mechanism. Reprinted with permission from Marcus and Freedman (1986).

mitochondrial proteins synthesized in the cytoplasm decrease, the mitochondrial portion of protein synthesis is inhibited (Freedman and Marcus, 1980).

A working model has been proposed by Marcus et al (1980) on the basis of the above work to explain the interrelationship between mitochondrial and cytoplasmic protein synthesis (Figure 2). In the model, iron deficiency exerts a negative effect on mitochondrial protein synthesis and there is decreased synthesis of the inner mitochondrial membrane. This results in a decrease in haem synthesis, a fall in cellular haem concentrations and activation of the haem controlled repressor (HCR$_A$). Consequently, cytoplasmic protein synthesis is decreased which, in turn, results in a decrease in cytoplasmically synthesized mitochondrial proteins that may also involve the HCR$_A$. Therefore, in a situation where there is a primary inhibition of cytoplasmic protein synthesis, free haem levels will rise and could also contribute to a decrease in mitochondrial protein synthesis. Elevated levels of haem will immediately result in feedback inhibition of ALAS. Thus the effect of haem on mitochondrial protein synthesis would be a long-term and indirect way for the cell to control haem synthesis and integrate mitochondrial and cytoplasmic protein synthesis.

The relationship between iron metabolism and protein synthesis seems to be more than casual. Ferrous iron is inserted into protoporphyrin to form haem in the final step of the haem synthetic pathway. The reaction is catalysed by the mitochondrial enzyme ferrochetalase (Dallman, 1982). The haem is then transported out of the mitochondrion, and may serve to regulate cytoplasmic protein synthesis. For example, haemoglobin tetramer formation in the erythrocyte involves the release of globin chains from the ribosome, followed by the rapid formation of complete haemogobin molecules (De Matteis and Gibbs, 1972); the reaction requires only haem.

Cytochrome P-450 is an important component of the hepatic drug-metabolizing enzyme system. It contains haem, and depends upon the availability of haem for its biological activity. Haem production is regulated in hepatocytes by the balance between and haem synthesis, controlled by ALAS (Granick and Sassa, 1971), and haem degradation, controlled by microsomal haem oxygenase (Tenhunen et al, 1970). The regulation of ALAS and haem oxygenase is thought to be controlled by a 'regulatory haem pool'. This also seems to control the supply of haem to the apo form of the various haem proteins, including cytochrome P-450. Free haem itself probably does not regulate the synthesis of cytochrome P-450 haemoproteins (Griger and Meyer, 1981), but there seems to be an alternative haem pool available, such as tryptophan pyrolase (Badaway, 1982) or haemopexin (Davies et al, 1979). Cytochrome P-450 is a part of the microsomal mixed function oxidase system, which is responsible for the biotransformation of many drugs. A drug substrate binds with oxidized cytochrome P-450; the drug– cytochrome complex is then reduced by the redox component of the system, and the reduced complex then combines with molecular oxygen. A second electron and two hydrogen atoms are acquired from the NADPH component of the system to produce an oxidized metabolite (drug) and water, and regeneration of oxidized cytochrome P-450.

Iron is specifically required for DNA synthesis because of the iron dependence of the rate-limiting enzyme, ribonucleotide reductase. Other specific examples of iron dependence include the enzymes tyrosine hydroxylase (Moore and Dominic, 1971), phenylalanine hydroxylase (Fisher et al, 1972), monoamine oxidase (Youdim et al, 1975), aconitase (Gawron et al, 1974), proline hydroxylase (Prockop, 1971), xanthine oxidase, catalase, myeloperoxidase, and cytochrome c reductase.

Other nonenzyme iron-containing proteins include myoglobin and cytochrome c. Myoglobin is a nonerythroid haem protein accounting for 10% of total body iron and functions as a muscle store for oxygen which is utilized during contraction. Cytochrome c is another iron-containing protein which functions as a component of the mitochondrial electron transport chain involved in oxidative metabolism.

In summary, in addition to its contribution to red blood cell production, iron is an integral component of many cellular functions. Because of iron's ubiquitous presence in cell metabolism, it is feasible that many of the changes associated with ageing could be due to iron deficiency. It would therefore seem reasonable to screen all elderly patients for iron depletion.

TISSUE DEFECTS IN IRON DEFICIENCY

In addition to the biochemical effects of iron deficiency which result in decreased concentrations of various enzymes, defects in tissues (Table 3), primarily of the gastrointestinal tract, have been well described. The lack of tissue iron seems to have a profound effect on various mucosal surfaces, resulting in several clinical entities. The mouth has been found to be affected by iron deficiency in a number of ways, including glossitis and angular stomatitis (Beveridge et al, 1965). Additionally, several reports have described altered histology in the buccal mucosa of iron-deficient patients (Jacobs, 1959, 1960).

The effects of iron deficiency on the oesophagus have received much attention, beginning with the reports of Paterson (1919), Kelly (1919) and Vinson (1922). Sideropenic dysphagia, also known as Paterson–Kelly syndrome and Plummer–Vinson syndrome, is characteristically associated with a mucosal web found in the postcricoid region of the hypopharynx. Although in most cases the web is found to consist of normal epithelium, carcinoma in situ is occasionally demonstrated (Entwistle and Jacobs, 1965). Several investigators consider the postcricoid obstruction of Paterson–Kelly syndrome to be a premalignant lesion (Ahlbom, 1936; Wynder et al, 1957; Jacobs 1960). The Paterson–Kelly syndrome has also been found to be associated with a variety of autoimmune disorders, including Sjogren's syndrome, Hashimoto's thyroiditis and pernicious anaemia (Jacobs and Kilpatrick, 1964; Chisholm et al, 1971a,b), all of which are common in the elderly.

The integrity of the gastric mucosa is affected adversely by a lack of iron. Iron deficiency is associated with a high frequency of atrophic gastritis. The

Table 3. Tissue defects in iron deficiency.

Location	Defect
Mouth	Glossitis
	Angular stomatitis
	Altered histology
Oesophagus	Mucosal web (premalignant)
Stomach	Atrophic gastritis
Small intestine	Mucosal changes similar to sprue
Fingernails	Koilonychia (spoon nails)
Mitochondria	Enlarged and translucent
Lymphocytes	Swelling
	Vacuolation
	Cristae rupture
	Membrane rupture

loss of normal acid production in iron-deficient subjects may be secondary to the development of autoantibodies to gastric parietal cells (Markson and Moore, 1962; Dagg et al, 1964). Atrophic gastritis and achlorhydria seem to be reversible when iron is replaced before the age of 30, but the changes appear to be permanent if treated after that age (Jacobs et al, 1966; Stone, 1968). Iron deficiency may also affect the mucosa of the small intestine; mucosal changes similar to those seen in sprue have been seen in children with iron deficiency anaemia. The mucosa can revert to normal following iron replacement (Jacobs, 1982).

There is evidence that adequate tissue levels of iron are necessary for normal growth and skeletal development. Iron-deficient children have been shown to be significantly underweight, and when iron was replaced weight gain occurred (Judish et al, 1966).

As previously mentioned, iron appears to be necessary to maintain the normal integrity of mitochondria. When iron is deficient, gross abnormalities of mitochondrial structure are seen in the rat liver and heart (Dallman, 1974). The mitochondria are found to be enlarged and translucent; this enlargement may be responsible for the cardiac hypertrophy seen in iron-deficient hearts (Jacobs, 1982).

Inadequate tissue iron levels seem to be responsible for structural abnormalities of lymphocytes. These include swelling, vacuolation, rupture of cristae and rupture of the outer membrane (Dallman, 1974).

FUNCTIONAL EFFECTS OF IRON DEFICIENCY

Work capacity

Iron deficiency results in certain physiological effects which may be directly related to the metabolic changes. One of the most important functional consequences of iron deficiency anaemia is the significant limitation seen in certain types of physical activity. This association was evaluated in a study by Ekblom et al (1972), who found that exercise performance was reduced in those who were made mildly anaemic by venesection. Among the exercise tests evaluated was a brief, intense run on a treadmill. Both maximal running time and maximal oxygen uptake were found to be reduced after the removal of approximately 1 l of blood. The reduction in maximal oxygen uptake corresponded closely with the percentage of total haemoglobin removed. The results indicated that the loss of a small percentage of total body haemoglobin was associated with a corresponding reduction in the performance of a brief but intense exercise task.

Several studies have been conducted in developing countries to evaluate the relationship between anaemia and work performance. Changes in work performance have been shown to reflect the socioeconomic sequelae of the nutritionally related iron deficiencies seen in third world countries. A study by Viteri and Torun (1974) in the lowlands of Guatemala evaluated the exercise performance of a group of chronically anaemic agricultural labourers normally engaged in physically demanding tasks. In this study a close correlation was seen between mean haemoglobin concentration and a standardized aerobic activity in the form of the Harvard Step Test. The significant finding here is that small decreases in haemoglobin within the normal range resulted in lower exercise performance. When a group of these subjects were given iron and folate, resulting in an improvement of haemoglobin level, a progressive improvement in exercise performance was observed when compared to a control group. This was the first study to provide evidence that even mild degrees of iron deficiency can impair performance in occupations requiring a heavy energy expenditure.

A similar study was performed by Gardner et al (1977), who evaluated the physical work capacity of 75 female subjects employed on a tea plantation in Sri Lanka. Work performance was determined using a multistaged treadmill test in which the percentage of grade was progressively increased at 3 min intervals until a maximal possible work time of 18 min was attained. Performance was correlated with haemoglobin levels, which ranged from 6 to 13 g/dl. Higher haemoglobin concentrations resulted in improved performance both in total time on the treadmill and in the percentage of persons reaching the highest workload. There was also a close correlation between mean haemoglobin concentration and the percentage of increase in mean heart rate. An important finding also seen in previous studies showed that even mild degrees of anaemia (haemoglobin 11–12 g/dl) can result in a significant diminution (20%) in work tolerance. These findings resulted in recommendations by the authors for the correction and prevention of iron deficiency on the basis of economic as well as health considerations. These studies provide convincing evidence that iron deficiency anaemia impairs performance in a brief, intense type of exercise and that treatment with iron results in improvement. Other studies have attempted to evaluate the effect of iron deficiency on prolonged activity of the endurance type, which is more likely to reflect true work performance. Basta et al (1979) attempted to evaluate work performance in economic terms in a study of latex tappers employed at an Indonesian rubber plantation. Work output could be precisely determined because the daily pay of each worker was based on the weight of latex he collected. Of the 302 workers evaluated, 45% were anaemic based on a haemoglobin of < 13 g/dl. Haemoglobin levels of 10–16 g/dl were found to correlate closely with income. In those anaemic workers treated with iron, work output improved in proportion to the increase in the haemoglobin level.

Additional support for the theory that correction of iron deficiency anaemia improves work performance of the sustained endurance type is provided in a study by Edgerton et al (1979), who observed 199 women working on a tea plantation in Sri Lanka. Work output was again determined by recording the daily weight of tea collected before and after iron supplementation or treatment with a placebo. As in the previous study, women given iron supplementation picked significantly greater quantities of tea than the placebo group. The degree of improvement in work output was directly related to the severity of the original anaemia. An additional component of this study was determining the level of voluntary physical activity by means of a small movement-sensitive recording device strapped to the subject's body. Twenty-four hour recordings of physical activity revealed that women who received iron treatment were about 60% more active within 3 weeks than matched subjects who were given a placebo. The results were interpreted as direct evidence for the assertion that symptoms of tiredness and weakness could be attributed to iron deficiency.

Impaired work performance is usually attributed to the anaemia of iron deficiency rather than to the metabolic effects. A study by Finch et al (1976) in rats indicates that the deficit in tissue iron may also be important. Normal and iron-deficient rats were subjected to a brief, intense treadmill exercise to assess work performance. Just prior to testing, the haemoglobin levels of both groups were adjusted to identical levels by exchange transfusion to eliminate the effects of the anaemia. Iron-deficient rats demonstrated impaired performance as compared to normals with matched haemoglobin levels. Work output improved within 4 days of correcting the iron deficiency, indicating that the metabolic abnormalities imposed by iron deficiency are rapidly reversible. Following this a group of rats was subjected to prolonged endurance exercise on a treadmill. Two groups emerged. One was able to run over 70 min, with blood lactate levels reaching a plateau of moderate elevation. The second group became exhausted within less than 20 min, and developed a rapid and continuous rise in blood lactate. These results were taken as evidence that the capacity of oxidative phosphorylation may reflect work performance shown in an exercise of endurance.

Additional evidence pointing to the important consequences of a deficit in tissue iron comes from a study by Schoenc et al (1983). The authors evaluated the effect of 2 weeks of iron therapy on exercise performance and exercise-induced lactate in iron-deficient trained athletes. Whereas performance on a bicycle ergometer remained unchanged after iron therapy, blood lactate levels at maximum exercise decreased significantly. These results were interpreted as a reflection of the important role iron plays in oxidative metabolism. Based on the involvement of iron as an integral component of several enzymes contained within the electron transport chain of the mitochondria, it was postulated that iron-depleted muscles had to switch from aerobic to anaerobic metabolism, resulting in greater lactate production.

A study by Holloszy (1967) provides further evidence linking endurance exercise to the enzymes of oxidative phosphorylation. Endurance training resulted in improved maximum duration, increased mitochondrial content of skeletal muscle, and a doubling of the activity of oxidative enzymes.

This relationship was further defined by Davies et al (1981), who were able to measure the effects of different forms of exercise on V_{O_2} max and muscle oxidative capacity. Endurance training only increased the V_{O_2} max by 14% while doubling the muscle oxidative capacity. In contrast, sprint training of rats did not affect muscle oxidative capacity, although it did result in an increase in V_{O_2} max. The authors therefore hypothesized that impaired V_{O_2} max and aerobic work capacity would be associated primarily with anaemia, whereas decreased endurance would be more closely related to loss of muscle oxidative capacity.

This hypothesis was then tested by Dallman (1982) in a study in which young rats were made severely iron-deficient. Muscle cytochrome oxidase and pyruvate oxidase were 44 and 21% of control. Aerobic work capacity and V_{O_2}

max in the deficient rats were approximately 50% of control, while endurance capacity was 7% of control. Iron-deficient rats were then given a diet rich in iron, and various parameters were followed daily. Haemoglobin and haematocrit increased promptly within 3 days, while Vo_2 max and aerobic work capacity recovered after 5 days. Improvements in muscle cytochrome oxidase and pyruvate oxidase, mitochondrial content of muscle, and endurance capacity occurred only after the fifth day of initiation of iron treatment. Similar patterns in improvement occurred with mitochondrial concentrations of cytochromes and flavoproteins, and rates of oxidation with succinate and pyruvate–malate as substrates. Another group of rats underwent exchange transfusions where the haemoglobin concentrations were raised to an intermediate value of 9.5 g/dl in iron-deficient and control rats, respectively. In iron-deficient rats with corrected haemoglobin, Vo_2 max and aerobic work capacity were corrected to within 15% of control values. In contrast, exchange transfusion with correction of haemoglobin did not significantly improve the endurance capacity of iron-deficient animals.

In summary, human studies have described the effects of iron deficiency on work performance as measured in both cardiovascular and economic terms. Animal studies have demonstrated that cellular iron depletion and iron deficiency anaemia contribute to reduced work capacity in different ways. Anaemia seems to comprise cardiovascular function, resulting in an impaired capacity to perform brief, intense forms of exercise reflected by the Vo_2 max. In contrast the loss of iron at the cellular level results in a reduction in the levels of muscle oxidative enzymes, resulting in an impairment in the performance of endurance-type exercise. Physicians caring for the elderly should be aware of the adverse effects of iron deficiency when advising patients interested in starting an exercise routine.

Immunity and infection

The relationship between iron deficiency and the risk of infection is controversial as well as confusing. Some evidence points to iron depletion causing impaired cell-mediated immunity and phagocytosis with resulting predispositon to infection. Other evidence has suggested that rapid correction of iron deficiency can predispose to certain life-threatening infections.

Early clinical evidence by MacKay (1928) suggested that the administration of iron during infancy may reduce the frequency of common infections. Two other studies done in infants have yielded opposite results (Andelman and Sered, 1966; Burman, 1972). A study by Basta et al (1979) in adults on a rubber plantation in Indonesia found a significant reduction in the prevalence of enteritis and influenza-type illness when the workers were treated with iron. The impairment in epithelial structure and function which occurs with iron deficiency may be responsible for the predisposition to chronic mucocutaneous candidiasis reported by Higgs and Wells (1973). Similarly, the association between iron deficiency and recurrent Herpes simplex (Vayas and Chandra, 1984) may result from an effect on mucosal surfaces.

An impairment in cell-mediated immunity has been demonstrated repeatedly in patients with iron deficiency. One report describes an impairment of lymphocyte transformation and migration inhibition factor production on stimulation with *Candida* antigen and purified protein derivative in a small group of subjects with iron-deficiency anaemia (Joynson et al, 1972). Other evidence for impaired cell-mediated immunity includes reduced lymphocyte proliferation and response to mitogens in iron deficiency (Chandra and Saraya, 1975) as well as a correlation between the lymphocyte stimulation index and the transferrin saturation (Macdougal et al, 1975). Lastly, a significant improvement in the mean stimulation indices for *Candida* antigen occurred in iron-deficient infants when they were treated with iron. Thus there is ample evidence pointing to a defect in T lymphocyte function in iron deficiency.

A defect in neutrophil function attributed to an impairment in myeloperoxidase activity is another demonstrated defect in the immune system which may predispose iron-deficient individuals to repeated infections (Sagone and Balcerzak, 1970). Chandra (1973) found that deficient functions in iron-depleted neutrophils included intracellular bacterial killing and reduction of nitroblue tetrazolium, while the opsonic activity of the plasma and phagocytosis were normal.

In contrast to evidence linking iron deficiency with a predisposition to infection, there is information suggesting that rapid correction of iron deficiency may promote certain bacterial and parasitic infections (Cook and Lynch, 1986). Iron is known to be a necessary nutrient for the normal growth of micro-organisms. The presence of the iron-binding proteins transferrin and lactoferrin in human tissues results in reduced availability of iron and impaired multiplication of many pathogens. Normal human serum has impressive bacteriostatic and bacteriocidal properties which can be overcome by saturating the iron-binding sites with iron (Sussman, 1974). In fact, the virulence of certain bacteria has been shown to be due, in part, to their ability to acquire iron from their host (Payne and Finkelstein, 1978).

There are several reports of situations in which the administration of large amounts of iron preceded the onset of serious infection. The administration of parenteral iron dextran to newborn Polynesian infants in the early 1970s as a prophylaxis against iron-deficiency anaemia was associated with a tremendous increase in the incidence of Gram-negative neonatal sepsis. When the programme was discontinued after 5 years, the incidence of Gram-negative neonatal sepsis fell from 17 to 2.7 in 1000 births. Most of the cases of sepsis were due to *Escherichia coli*, and occurred between day 4 and day 10 following administration of iron (Barry and Reeve, 1977).

Cook and Lynch (1986) have suggested that the increased incidence of neonatal sepsis may have resulted from several factors, including the deep intramuscular injection or the reticuloendothelial cell blockade which may have been produced by the iron dextran complex. However, the sudden availability of iron dextran in the circulation and tissues of these infants must also be included as a possible cause for the increase in sepsis. Iron dextran remains in the circulation for several days following intramuscular injection, and iron released during that time would reduce the level of unsaturated circulating transferrin and could thereby impair the bacteriostatic properties of the plasma against *E. coli*. In contrast to the case with infants, there is no evidence that parenteral iron is hazardous to adults with a normal immune system. For example, there is no known evidence suggesting that women given parenteral iron during pregnancy have an increased incidence of bacterial sepsis (Cook and Lynch, 1986).

Weinberg (1984) has postulated that iron deficiency may act as a defence mechanism against infection by preventing access to bacteria, fungi and protozoa. One study in support of this theory examined the frequency of infection in 100 anaemic patients admitted to an adult medical ward in East Africa (Masawe et al, 1974). Those with iron-deficiency anaemias had a much lower prevalence of infection than those with other forms of anaemia. Explanations for this observation include a protective effect of iron deficiency resulting in a decreased availability of iron to pathogens. Additionally, the commonly observed increase in infections in anaemic patients with normal or increased levels of iron, as seen in those with sickle cell anaemia or bone marrow failure, is another possible explanation. The mechanism in this case is felt to be haemolysis resulting in an increase in the supply of iron to bacteria (Bullen et al, 1978).

The incidence of iron deficiency has been shown to be increased in those with malaria. Additionally, exacerbation of malaria was common in a group of iron-deficient patients given replacement iron therapy (Bullen et al, 1978). Murray et al (1978) showed that iron therapy may predispose to the development of malaria in a group of Somali nomads. The cause of this phenomenon may be related to the reticulocytosis following iron therapy resulting in an increase in malarial parasitaemia.

The potential implications of studies linking a risk of increased infection to iron therapy relate to policies to replace iron in severely malnourished populations. Further controlled studies must be done to define the risk of iron replacement in these groups. Fleming (1982) has suggested that because iron-deficiency anaemia in the tropics may lead to severe morbidity, frequently resulting in death, severely anaemic patients should be treated with iron while being protected against malaria, and should be treated for bacterial infections when they occur. In otherwise healthy populations there does not seem to be any reason to believe that treating iron deficiency would be dangerous from the standpoint of increasing the risk of infection. Because of pre-existing immune defects, it may be advisable to closely monitor elderly patients for infections when treating them for iron deficiency. In those with active infection it would seem prudent to treat the infection first and to limit the use of parenteral iron.

Cognitive function

There is much evidence relating deficiency of iron to central nervous system dysfunction in animals and humans. Common causes of cognitive dysfunction in the elderly, such as Alzheimer's disease or multi-infarct dementia, may interfere with any attempts to examine an association between iron deficiency and cognition. Consequently, there have been few reports attempting to link iron deficiency with dementia in the elderly. However, studies of an association between impaired cognitive function and iron deficiency in younger populations and animals may permit hypotheses of how similar mechanisms can occur in the elderly.

Iron-deficient rats displayed marked behavioural changes which reversed on treatment with iron, as reported by Youdim and Green (1977). The authors suggested that these changes may be related to an abnormality in monoamine neurotransmission. A marked reduction in spontaneous movements and a reversal in the normal diurnal pattern of iron-deficient rats was reported by Glover and Jacobs (1972). Oral iron supplementation caused reversal of these abnormalities in 2 days. Other investigators have reported similar findings in iron-deficient rats, mostly relating to decreased responsiveness (Weinberg et al, 1980; Williamson and Ng, 1980).

In addition to poor scholastic performance, chronic fatigue and other non-specific symptoms have been attributed to iron deficiency in studies done with children. Many of the earlier studies have been limited by their inability to distinguish the effects of iron deficiency from other factors such as nutritional and social deprivation (Pollitt and Leibel, 1976). However, enough evidence has been gathered in several more recent carefully controlled investigations to indicate a pattern of age-related neurological dysfunction that is associated with iron deficiency.

Studies attempting to relate changes in mental development and performance to iron deficiency in infants have been based on the Bayley Scales of Infant Development (BSID). The BSID has severe limitations, including difficulty of administration and poor correlation between different tests in the same subject. Despite these problems, consistent findings include impaired attention span and cognitive development studies that have included infants around the age of 2 years (Oski and Honig, 1978; Deinard et al, 1981; Lotzoff et al, 1982; Walter et al, 1983). Studies done in preschool and school children have pointed primarily to a deficit in directing attention rather than to true learning rate deficiency (Webb and Oski, 1973; Pollitt et al, 1983; Soemantri et al, 1985). Studies in adults have yielded results with somewhat confusing associations between iron deficiency and cognitive function. For example, Tucker et al (1984) found an association between impaired nonverbal auditory task performance and high serum ferritin levels.

A behavioural abnormality frequently associated with iron deficiency in adults is a perversion of taste leading to the consumption of nonfood items (pica). One of the more commonly encountered forms in the USA is pagophagia, the compulsive eating of ice (Elwood and Wood, 1966). Pagophagia resolves after treatment with doses of iron less than those required to correct anaemia or repair an iron-storage deficit (Coltman 1969). Other forms of pica occur in various parts of the world, and are most frequently observed in children and pregnant women. In some cases the pica serves to replace the lost iron, but in others the substance may consume iron and inhibit its absorption, contributing to the deficiency state (Bothwell et al, 1979). Additionally, it should be noted that iron deficiency is not the only cause for pica (Sayers et al, 1974).

There have been no studies directly linking biochemical changes in the brain with behavioural or cognitive abnormalities in iron-deficient states in humans. However, a deficit of brain nonhaem iron may alter the metabolism of substances in the brain that affect behaviour. Alterations in several central nervous system neurotransmitters that are thought to affect behaviour have been described in iron-deficient rats. A reduction in the activity of aldehyde oxidase, an iron-containing mitochondrial enzyme, has been shown to result in an increase in serotonin and other 5-hydroxyindole compounds in iron-deficient rat brains (Mackler and Finch, 1982). Another iron-containing enzyme, phenylalanine hydroxylase, is necessary for the conversion of phenylalanine to tyrosine. Iron deficiency results in a reduction in the activity of phenylalanine hydroxylase in the liver, leading to an accumulation of phenylalanine and its toxic byproducts. The resulting impairment in mental function may resemble that seen in phenylketonuria, which is caused by a hereditary deficiency in phenylalanine hydroxylase (Mackler and Finch, 1982). Youdim et al (1982) have described a reduction in the dopamine-D2 receptor of iron-deficient rats, with resulting behaviour abnormalities. Alterations in monoamine metabolism in the brains of iron-deficient rats have been described (Sourkes, 1982). Although the rate of synthesis of serotonin in the brain does not appear to be affected by iron deficiency (Youdim et al, 1980), ferrous iron seems to facilitate the in vitro binding of serotonin to a soluble brain protein located in the synaptosomes (Tamir et al, 1976). Several biochemical changes resulting in increased levels of catecholamines could affect various aspects of behaviour (Marcus and Freedman, 1985). Aldehyde dehydrogenase is an iron-containing enzyme which catalyses the conversion of aldehyde to the corresponding carboxylic acid in the monoamine oxidase reaction. Its reduction in the iron-deficient rat may lead to a decrease in the brain of acidic metabolites of monoamines, including 3,4-dihydroxyphenylacetic acid and homovanillic acid from dopamine, indoleacetic acid from tryptamine, and 5-hydroxyindolacetic acid from serotonin (Marcus and Freedman, 1985).

Catecholamines and thermogenesis

Various studies have demonstrated reduced monoamine oxidase activity in iron-deficient states. Symes et al (1971) reported decreased activity of monoamine oxidase in vivo in iron-deficient rats. The monoamine oxidase activity of human platelets was found to be reduced in iron-deficient patients (Woods et al, 1977). However, according to Youdim et al (1980), brain monoamine oxidase activity was not decreased in iron-deficient rats.

Monoamine oxidase is an important enzyme in the catabolism of noradrenaline. Because noradrenaline is felt to be one of the neurotransmitters which affects behaviour, Voorhess et al (1975) examined the urinary output of several catecholamines (including noradrenaline) in a group of iron-deficient children. Urinary noradrenaline levels were found to be more than two standard deviations above the mean for children in 9 of 11 subjects. Noradrenaline excretion returned to normal after treatment with iron. In contrast, urinary levels of dopamine, adrenaline, and metanephrine–normetanephrine did not change after treatment. Although reduced monoamine oxidase activity would logically explain the increased urinary noradrenaline levels seen in iron deficiency, the expected decrease in vanillylmandelic acid and increase in normetanephrine were not found. An alternative explanation may be that increased noradrenaline production is a compensatory response to the impaired control of body temperature seen with iron deficiency (Dillman et al, 1979).

Further investigation into the increased levels of catecholamines seen in iron-deficient rats led Dillman et al (1979) to conclude that this phenomenon is largely temperature-dependent. The investigators demonstrated that elevated levels of noradrenaline were associated with iron deficiency when the anaemia was corrected with exchange transfusions. During these investigations an unexpected impairment in the ability of cold-exposed rats to maintain normal body temperature became evident. Iron replacement resulted in the normalization of heat-generating ability in these animals. Normal heat production involves a combination of shivering, release of catecholamines, and the effects of triiodothyronine (T3). Catecholamine production increases within minutes of exposure to cold, whereas the response to thyroid hormone does not begin for several hours. An abnormality of thyroid function was considered because of the animals' impaired ability to maintain normal body temperature in the cold despite elevated levels of catecholamines.

The conversion of T4 (thyroxine) to T3 was subsequently shown to be impaired in iron-deficient rats (Dillman et al, 1979). This resulted in a reduction in the ratio of T3 to T4 to about half that in control animals. The plasma T3 response to hypothermia returned to normal with iron treatment over a 6 day period. To compare the heat-generating abilities of T4 and T3, the investigators gave thyroidectomized iron-deficient rats daily injections of one of these thyroid hormones. The ability of T3 to reverse energy-related abnormalities associated with iron deficiency was found to be better than that of T4. Subsequently, the effect of T3 on peripheral tissues was examined in biochemical studies carried out on brown fat, one of the major heat-producing tissues in rats. The activity of the mitochondrial electron transport system was found to be reduced in the brown fat of iron-deficient rats. Treatment with T3 improved the activity of the system by increasing the total amount of brown fat rather than by affecting the activity of specific enzymes. Therefore, T3 seems to affect the size of the heat production system and not its metabolic activity.

Similar abnormalities of catecholamine metabolism and thermogenesis have been reported in iron-deficient humans (Dillman et al, 1982). Elevated catecholamine levels have been reported in iron-deficient humans in the absence of anaemia. Additionally, impaired temperature maintenance has been demonstrated in iron-deficient subjects exposed to mild hypothermia.

CONCLUSION

Iron deficiency is common in the elderly. Although most of the research on the effects of iron deficiency has been done in non-geriatric populations, the information that has been generated can be extrapolated to the elderly. Reduced immunity to infection, decreased work capacity, diminished cognitive function (i.e. dementia), and impaired thermogenesis (i.e. hypothermia) are common problems in the elderly. It would therefore seem reasonable to screen elderly patients for iron deficiency. All patients evaluated in the New York University/Bellevue Hospital Center Geriatric Clinic have a serum ferritin level as part of the initial laboratory screen. Regarding iron treatment, it is important to point out that pharmacological doses of iron should not be used prophylactically in the elderly. The risks of iron overload include haemochromatosis and increased incidence of infection. In summary, it is hoped that this review will stimulate new investigations into the implications of iron deficiency in the elderly.

SUMMARY

Iron deficiency in the elderly almost always results from blood loss. The loss of iron can be viewed as occurring in four stages, which are reflected in the different tests used to diagnose iron deficiency. Tests used to diagnose iron deficiency have certain limitations regarding their ability to detect iron deficiency before the overt anaemia occurs. The tests which diagnose iron deficiency most accurately are low serum ferritin and reduced iron staining of a bone marrow aspirate.

Because iron is present in many metabolic processes besides the production of haemoglobin, iron deficiency results in a variety of defects which are manifested at biochemical, tissue, and functional levels. Iron is a component of several enzymes in the respiratory electron transport chain. Adequate haem and iron levels are necessary to control cytoplasmic and mitochondrial protein synthesis. Iron deficiency results in tissue defects, including those affecting the gastrointestinal tract, and defects of mitochondria and lymphocytes. Normal iron levels seem to be necessary for normal work capacity. A deficiency of iron, independent of the anaemia, results in reduced exercise capacity that can be measured in both physiological and economic terms. Elderly patients complaining of increased fatigue should therefore be screened for iron deficiency.

There is evidence to suggest that iron deficiency may predispose individuals to certain infections. Other information points to the promotion of certain bacterial and parasitic infections after rapid correction of iron deficiency. Thus elderly patients having iron replacement therapy should be followed closely. A deficiency of iron has been shown to result in certain behavioural and learning abnormalities. Iron deficiency has been shown to result in impaired control of body temperature, resulting in an increase in catecholamine levels. The impairment in heat-generating ability was shown to result from reduced conversion of T4 to T3 in the peripheral tissues.

REFERENCES

Ahlbom HE (1936) Simple achlorhydric anaemia, Plummer–Vinson syndrome and carcinoma of the mouth, pharynx, and esophagus in women. *British Medical Journal* **ii**: 331–336.
Andelman MF & Sered BR (1966) Utilization of dietary iron by term infants. *American Journal of Diseases of Childhood* **111**: 45–52.

Badaway AAB (1982) Evidence against involvement of cytochrome P-450 haem in the regulation of synthesis of mammalian liver 5-aminolevulinate synthase. *Biochemical Journal* **202:** 807–813.

Barry DMJ & Reeve AW (1977) Increased incidence of gram negative neonatal sepsis with intramuscular iron administration. *Pediatrics* **60:** 908–913.

Basta SS, Soerkirman MS, Karydi D et al (1979) Iron deficiency anemia and the productivity of adult males in Indonesia. *American Journal of Clinical Nutrition* **32:** 916–922.

Beuzard Y, Rodvien R & London IM (1973) Effect of hemin on the synthesis of hemoglobin and other proteins in mammalian cells. *Proceedings of the National Academy of Sciences USA* **70:** 1022–1031.

Beveridge BR, Bannerman RM, Evanson JM et al (1965) Hypochromic anaemia. A retrospective study and follow-up of 378 in-patients. *Quarterly Journal of Medicine* **34:** 145–153.

Bothwell TH, Carlton RW, Cook JD et al (1979) *Iron Metabolism in Man.* Oxford: Blackwell.

Bullen JJ, Rogers HJ & Griffiths (1978) Role of iron in bacterial infection. *Current Topics in Microbiology and Immunology* **80:** 1–12.

Burman D (1972) Hemoglobin levels in normal infants aged 3 to 24 months and the effect of iron. *Archives of Diseases in Childhood* **47:** 261–267.

Chandra RK (1973) Reduced bactericidal capacity of polymorphs in iron deficiency. *Archives of Diseases in Childhood* **48:** 864–870.

Chandra RK & Saraya AK (1975) Impaired immunocompetence associated with iron deficiency. *Journal of Pediatrics* **86:** 899–909.

Chisholm M, Ardran GM, Callender ST et al (1971a) A follow up study of patients with post-cricoid webs. *Quarterly Journal of Medicine* **40:** 409–414.

Chisholm M, Ardran GM, Callender ST et al (1971b) Iron deficiency and autoimmunity in post-cricoid webs. *Quarterly Journal of Medicine* **40:** 421–427.

Coltman CA Jr (1969) Pagophagia and iron lack. *Journal of the American Medical Association* **207:** 513–521.

Cook JD & Lynch SR (1986) The liabilities of iron deficiency. *Blood* **68:** 803–809.

Dagg JH, Goldberg A, Anderson JR et al (1964) Autoimmunity in iron deficiency anaemia. *British Medical Journal* **i:** 1349–1355.

Dallman PR (1974) Tissue effects of iron deficiency. In Jacobs A & Worwood M (eds) *Iron in Biochemistry and Medicine.* pp. 437–475. London: Academic Press.

Dallman PR (1982) Manifestations of iron deficiency. *Seminars in Hematology* **19:** 19–30.

Davies DM, Smith A, Muller-Eberhard U et al (1979) Hepatic-subcellular metabolism of heme from hemopexin: Incorporation of iron into ferritin. *Biochemistry and Biophysics Research Communication* **91:** 1504–1511.

Davies KJA, Packer L & Brooks GA (1981) Biochemical adaptation of mitochondria, muscle, and whole animal respiration to endurance training. *Archives of Biochemistry and Biophysics* **209:** 538–553.

de Haro C, Datta A & Ochoa S (1978) Mode of action of the hemin-controlled inhibitor of protein synthesis. *Proceedings of the National Academy of Sciences USA* **75:** 243–252.

Deinard A, Gilbert A, Dodds M et al (1981) Iron deficiency and behavioral deficits. *Pediatrics* **68:** 828–833.

DeLoskey RJ & Beattie DS (1984) The effects of insulin and glucose on the induction and intracellular translocation of delta-aminolevulinic acid synthase. *Archives of Biochemistry and Biophysics* **233:** 64–70.

De Matteis F & Gibbs A (1972) Stimulation of liver 5-amino-laevulinate synthetase by drugs and its relevance to drug-induced accumulation of cytochrome P-450. Studies with phenylbutazone and 3,5-diethoxycarbonyl-1,4-dihydrocollidine. *Biochemical Journal* **126:** 1149–1157.

Deybach JC, da Silva V, Grandchamp B et al (1985) The mitochondrial location of protoporphyrinogen oxidase. *European Journal of Biochemistry* **149:** 431–438.

Dillman E, Johnson DG, Martin J et al (1979) Catecholamine elevation in iron deficiency. *American Journal of Physiology* **237:** R237–R300.

Dillman E, Mackler B, Johnson D et al (1982) Effect of iron deficiency on catecholamine metabolism and body temperature regulation. In Pollitt E & Leibel RL (eds) *Iron Deficiency: Brain Biochemistry and Behavior,* pp 57–62. New York: Raven Press.

Edgerton VR, Gardner GW, Ohira Y et al (1979) Iron deficiency anaemia and its effect on worker productivity and activity patterns. *British Medical Journal* **2:** 1546–1549.

Ekblom B, Goldbarg AN & Gullbring B (1972) Response to exercise after blood loss and reinfusion. *Journal of Applied Physiology* **33:** 175–180.

Elwood PC & Wood MM (1966) Effect of oral iron therapy on the symptoms of anaemia. *British Journal of Preventive and Social Medicine* **20:** 172–180.

Entwistle CC & Jacobs A (1965) Histological findings in the Paterson–Kelly syndrome. *Journal of Clinical Pathology* **18:** 408–413.

Finch CA, Miller LR, Inamdar AR et al (1976) Iron deficiency in the rat: physiological and biochemical studies of muscle dysfunction. *Journal of Clinical Investigation* **58:** 447–453.

Fisher DB, Kirkwood R & Kaufman S (1972) Rat liver phenylalanine hydroxylase: an iron enzyme. *Journal of Biological Chemistry* **247:** 5161–5167.

Fleming AF (1982) Iron deficiency in the tropics. *Clinics in Haematology* **11:** 365–371.

Freedman ML (1983a) Anemias in the elderly. *Comprehensive Therapy* **9:** 45–53.

Freedman ML (1983b) Common hematologic problems: diagnosis and treatment. *Geriatrics* **38:** 119–131.

Freedman ML & Karpatkin S (1973) Requirement of iron for platelet protein synthesis. *Biochemistry and Biophysics Research Communications* **54:** 475–481.

Freedman ML & Marcus DL (1980) Anemia and the elderly: is it physiology or pathology? *American Journal of Medical Science* **280:** 81–85.

Freedman ML & Rosman J (1976) A rabbit reticulocyte model for the role of hemin-controlled repressor in hypochromic anemias. *Journal of Clinical Investigation* **57:** 594–603.

Freedman ML, Geraghty M & Rosman J (1974) Hemin control of globin synthesis: isolation of a hemin-reversible translational repressor from human mature erythrocytes. *Journal of Biological Chemistry* **249:** 7290–7302.

Freedman ML, Spieler PJ, Rosman J et al (1977) Cyclic AMP maintenance of rabbit reticulocyte haem and protein synthesis in the presence of ethanol and benzene. *British Journal of Haematology* **37:** 179–185.

Gardner GW, Edgarton VR, Senewiratne B et al (1977) Physical work capacity and metabolic stress in subjects with iron deficiency anemia. *American Journal of Clinical Nutrition* **30:** 910–917.

Gawron O, Waheed A, Glaid AJ & Jaklitsh A (1974) Iron and aconitase activity. *Biochemical Journal* **139:** 709–716.

Glover J & Jacobs A (1972) Activity pattern of iron deficient rats. *British Medical Journal* **2:** 627–633.

Granick S & Sassa S (1971) Control of heme synthesis. *Metabolic Regulation* **5:** 77–81.

Griger G & Meyer U (1981) Role of haem in the induction of cytochrome P-450 by phenobarbitone. *Biochemical Journal* **198:** 321–328.

Gross M & Rabinovitz M (1972) Control of globin synthesis by hemin: factors influencing formation of an inhibitor of global chain initiation in reticulocyte lysates. *Biochimica et Biophysica Acta* **287:** 340–352.

Hayashi N, Yoda B & Kikuchi G (1969) Mechanism of allylisopropylacetamide-induced increase of delta-aminolevulinate synthetase in liver mitochondria. IV. Accumulation of the enzyme in the soluble fraction of rat liver. *Archives of Biochemistry and Biophysics* **131:** 83–89.

Higgs JM & Wells RS (1973) Chronic mucocutaneous candidiasis: associated abnormalities of iron metabolism. *British Journal of Dermatology* **86**(supplement 8): 88–93.

Holloszy JO (1967) Biochemical adaptations in muscle. Effects of exercise on mitochondrial oxygen uptake and respiratory enzyme activity in skeletal muscle. *Journal of Biological Chemistry* **242:** 2278–2282.

Ibrahim NG, Gruenspecht NR & Freedman ML (1978) Hemin feedback inhibition at reticulocyte delta-aminolevulinic acid synthetase and delta-aminolevulinic acid dehydratase. *Biochemistry and Biophysics Research Communications* **80:** 722–730.

Ibrahim NG, Spieler PJ & Freedman ML (1979) Ethanol inhibition of rabbit reticulocyte haem synthesis at the level of delta-aminolevulinic acid synthetase. *British Journal of Haematology* **41:** 235–241.

Jacobs A (1959) Oral cornification in anaemic patients. *Journal of Clinical Pathology* **12:** 235–241.

Jacobs A (1960) The buccal mucosa in anaemia. *Journal of Clinical Pathology* **13:** 463–470.

Jacobs A (1982) Non-haematologic effects of iron deficiency. *Clinics in Haematology* **11:** 353–365.

Jacobs A & Kilpatrick GS (1964) The Paterson–Kelly syndrome. *British Medical Journal* **2:** 79–85.

Jacobs A, Lawrie JH, Entwistle CC et al (1966) Gastric acid secretion in chronic iron deficiency anaemia *Lancet* **ii:** 190–196.

Joynson DHM, Jacobs A, Walker DM et al (1972) Defect of cell mediated immunity in patients with iron deficiency anaemia. *Lancet* **ii:** 1058–1061.

Judish JM, Naiman JL & Oski FA (1965) The fallacy of the fat iron deficient child. *Pediatrics (New York)* **37:** 987–993.

Kelly AB (1919) Spasm at the entrance to the oesophagus. *Journal of Laryngology, Rhinology and Otology* **34:** 285–289.

Lodish HF (1974) Model for the regulation of mRNA translation applied to haemoglobin synthesis. *Nature* **251:** 385–392.

Lodish HF & Desalu O (1973) Regulation of synthesis of nonglobin proteins in cell free extracts of rabbit reticulocytes. *Journal of Biological Chemistry* **248:** 3420–3428.

Lotzoff B, Brittenham GM, Viteri FE et al (1982) Developmental deficits in iron-deficient infants: effects of age and severity of iron lack. *Journal of Pediatrics* **101:** 948–956.

Macdougal LG, Anderson R, McNab GM et al (1975) The immune response in iron deficient children: impaired cellular defence mechanisms with altered humoral components. *Journal of Pediatrics* **86:** 833–840.

MacKay HM (1928) Anaemia in infancy: its prevalence and prevention. *Archives of Diseases in Childhood* **3:** 117–122.

Mackler B & Finch C (1982) Iron in central nervous system oxidative metabolism. In Pollitt E & Leibel RL (eds) *Iron Deficiency: Brain Biochemistry and Behavior,* pp 31–38. New York: Raven Press.

Marcus DL & Freedman ML (1985) Clinical disorders of iron metabolism in the elderly. *Clinics in Geriatric Medicine* **1:** 729–745.

Marcus DL & Freedman ML (1986) Role of heme and iron metabolism in controlling protein synthesis. *Journal of the American Geriatric Society* **34:** 593–600.

Marcus DL, Ibrahim NG, Gruenspecht N et al (1980) Iron requirement for isolated rat liver mitochondrial protein synthesis. *Biochimica et Biophysica Acta* **607:** 136–143.

Marcus DL, Ibrahim NG & Freedman ML (1982) Age-related decline in the biosynthesis of mitochondrial inner membrane proteins. *Experimental Gerontology* **17:** 333–341.

Marcus DL, Halbrecht JL, Bourque AL et al (1984) Effect of cimetidine on delta-aminolevulinic acid synthase and microsomal heme oxygenase in rat liver. *Biochemical Pharmacology* **33:** 2005–2011.

Markson JL & Moore JM (1962) Autoimmunity in pernicious anaemia and iron deficiency anaemia. *Lancet* **ii:** 1240.

Masawe AEJ, Muindi JM & Swai GBR (1974) Infections in iron deficiency and other types of anaemia in the tropics. *Lancet* **ii:** 314–320.

Moore KE & Dominic JA (1971) Tryrosine hydroxylase inhibitors. *Federation Proceeding* **30:** 859–866.

Murray MJ, Murray AB, Murray MB et al (1978) The adverse effect of iron repletion on the course of certain infections. *British Medical Journal* **2:** 1113–1121.

Oski FA & Honig AS (1978) The effects of therapy on the developmental scores of iron-deficient humans. *Journal of Pediatrics* **92:** 21–28.

Paterson DR (1919) A clinical type of dysphagia. *Journal of Laryngology, Rhinology and Otology* **34:** 289–295.

Payne SM & Finkelstein RA (1978) The critical role of iron in host–bacterial interactions. *Journal of Clinical Investigation* **61:** 1428–1435.

Pollitt E & Leibel RL (1976) Iron deficiency and behavior. *Journal of Pediatrics* **88:** 372–381.

Pollitt E, Leibel RL & Greenfield DB (1983) Iron deficiency and cognitive test performance in preschool children. *Nutrition and Behavior* **1:** 137–142.

Prockop DJ (1971) Role of iron in the synthesis of collagen in connective tissue. *Federation Proceedings* **30:** 984–990.

Rabinovitz M, Freedman ML, Fisher JM et al (1969) Translational control in hemoglobin synthesis. *Symposia in Quantitative Biology* **34:** 567–574.

Ranu RS & London IM (1976) Regulation of protein synthesis in rabbit reticulocyte lysates: purification and initial characterization of the cyclic 3′:5′-AMP independent protein kinase of the heme-regulated translational inhibitor. *Proceedings of the National Academy of Sciences USA* **73:** 4349–4355.

Rhoads RE, McNight GS & Schimke RT (1973) Quantitative measurement of ovalbumin messenger ribonucleic activity. Localization in polysomes, induction by estrogen, and effect of actinomycin D. *Journal of Biological Chemistry* **248:** 2031–2037.

Sagone AL & Balcerzak SP (1970) Activity of iron containing enzymes in erythrocytes and granulocytes in thallassemia and iron deficiency. *American Journal of Medical Sciences* **259:** 350–355.

Sayers G, Lipschitz DA, Sayers M et al (1974) The relationship between pica and iron nutrition in Johannesburg Bantu adults. *South Africa Journal of Nutrition* **48:** 53–60.

Schoene RB, Escourrou P, Robertson HT et al (1983) Iron repletion decreases maximal concentrations in female athletes with minimal iron deficiency anemia. *Journal of Laboratory and Clinical Medicine* **102:** 306–311.

Soemantri AG, Pollitt E & Kim I (1985) Iron deficiency anemia and education achievement. *American Journal of Clinical Nutrition* **42:** 1221–1227.

Sourkes TL (1982) Transition elements and the nervous system. In Pollitt E & Leibel RL (eds) *Iron Deficiency: Brain Biochemistry and Behavior*, pp 1–29. New York: Raven Press.

Speck B (1968) Diurnal variation of serum iron and the latent iron binding capacity in normal adults. *Helvetica Medica Acta* **34:** 231–238.

Stone WD (1968) Gastric secretory response to iron therapy. *Gut* **9:** 99–104.

Sussman M (1974) Iron and infection. In Jacobs A & Woorwood M (eds) *Iron in Biochemistry and Medicine*. pp. 644–679. London: Academic Press.

Symes AL, Missala K & Sourkes TL (1971) Iron- and riboflavin-dependent metabolism of a monoamine in the rat in vivo. *Science* **74:** 153–155.

Tamir H, Klein A & Rapport MM (1976) Serotonin-binding protein: enhancement of binding by Fe^{2+} and inhibition of binding by drugs. *Journal of Neurochemistry* **26:** 871–878.

Tenhunen R, Marver HS & Schmid R (1970) The enzymatic catabolism of hemoglobin: stimulation of microsomal heme oxygenase by hemin. *Journal of Laboratory and Clinical Medicine* **75:** 410–417.

Thompson W, Meola T, Lipkin M et al (1987) The utility of the RDW, MCV and transferrin saturation in the diagnosis of iron deficiency (submitted for publication).

Trachsel H & Staehelin T (1978) Binding and release of eukaryotic initiation factor eIF-2 and GTP during protein synthesis initiation. *Proceedings of the National Academy of Sciences USA* **75:** 204–211.

Tucker DH, Sandstead HH, Penland JG et al (1984) Iron status and brain function: serum ferritin level associated with asymmetries of cortical electrophysiology and cognitive performance. *American Journal of Clinical Nutrition* **39:** 105–112.

Vinson PP (1922) Hysterical dysphagia. *Minnesota Medicine* **5:** 107–111.

Viteri FE & Torun B (1974) Anaemia and physical work capacity. *Clinics in Haematology* **3:** 609–617.

Voorhess ML, Stuart MJ, Stockman JA et al (1975) Iron deficiency anemia and increased urinary epinephrine excretion. *Journal of Pediatrics* **86:** 542–547.

Vyas D & Chandra RK (1984) Functional implications of iron deficiency. In Stekel A (ed.) *Iron Nutrition in Infancy and Childhood*, pp 45–59. New York: Raven Press.

Walter T, Kovalskys J & Stekel A (1983) Effect of mild iron deficiency on infant mental development. *Journal of Pediatrics* **10:** 519–525.

Webb TE & Oski FA (1973) Iron deficiency anemia and scholastic achievement in young adolescents. *Journal of Pediatrics* **82:** 827–833.

Webb TE & Oski FA (1974) Behavioral status of young adolescents with iron deficiency anemia. *Journal of Special Education* **8:** 153–160.

Weinberg ED (1984) Iron withholding: a defence against infection and neoplasia. *Physiological Review* **64:** 65–72.

Weinberg J, Dallman PR & Levine S (1980) Iron deficiency during early development in the rat: behavioral and physiological consequences. *Pharmacology and Biochemistry in Behavior* **12:** 493–502.

Williamson AM & Ng KT (1980) Activity and T-maze performance in iron deficient rats. *Physiology and Behaviour* **24:** 1157–1162.

Woods HF, Youdim MBH, Boudin D et al (1977) Monoamine metabolism and platelet function in iron-deficiency anaemia. In *Ciba Foundation Symposium 51, Amsterdam*, pp 227–248. Amsterdam: Elsevier.

Wynder EL, Hultberg S, Jacobsson F et al (1957) Environmental factors in cancer of the upper alimentary tract. *Cancer* **10**: 470–475.

Youdim MBH & Green AR (1977) Biogenic monoamine metabolism and functional activity in iron deficient rats: behavioral correlates. In Porter R & Fitzsimons DW (ed.) *Iron Metabolism*, pp. 201–221 Amsterdam: Elsevier/North–Holland.

Youdim MBH, Woods HF, Mitchell B et al (1975) Human platelet monoamine oxidase activity in iron-deficiency anaemia. *Clinical Science and Molecular Medicine* **48**: 289–295.

Youdim MBH, Green AR, Bloomfield MR et al (1980) The effects of iron deficiency on brain biogenic monoamine biochemistry and function in rats. *Neuropharmacology* **19**: 259–267.

Youdim MBH, Yehuda S, Ben-Shachar D et al (1982) Behavioral and brain biochemical changes in iron-deficient rats: the involvement of iron in dopamine receptor function. In Pollitt E & Leibel RL (eds) *Iron Deficiency: Brain Biochemistry and Behavior*, pp 39–56. New York: Raven Press.

3

Megaloblastic anaemia in the elderly

T. E. PARRY

The commonest cause of megaloblastic anaemia at any age is lack of vitamin B_{12} or of folic acid. A brief review of the functions of these two vitamins will therefore be given.

VITAMIN B_{12}

The two commercial preparations of vitamin B_{12} are cyanocobalamin and hydroxycobalamin. The former is now regarded as an artefact of isolation. It does not occur naturally although very small quantities have been detected in the sera of smokers (Wilson et al, 1971). Neither cyanocobalamin nor hydroxycobalamin are active biologically. They must be converted enzymatically to the two active coenzymes adenosylcobalamin and methylcobalamin. This involves reduction of the trivalent cobalt in the corin ring into the monovalent form. Nitrous oxide has the opposite effect. In humans, it oxidizes the cobalt (Banks et al, 1968) and inactivates the vitamin. Adenosylcobalamin, and to a lesser extent hydroxycobalamin, is the form of the vitamin that occurs in the tissues; methylcobalamin predominates in blood.

THE FUNCTIONS OF ADENOSYLCOBALAMIN

Adenosylcobalamin is a coenzyme in the methylmalonyl-CoA mutase reaction which brings about the molecular rearrangement of L-methylmalonyl-CoA to form succinyl-CoA (Figure 1.) Excessive amounts of the former, over 4 mg/24 h, are excreted in the urine in vitamin B_{12} deficiency which is corrected by vitamin B_{12} but not by folic acid. This suggests a causative role for adenosylcobalamin in subacute combined degeneration of the spinal cord, which likewise responds to vitamin B_{12} but not to folic acid (Cox and White, 1962). In most reported series the urinary excretion of methylmalonic acid in pernicious anaemia has been under 300 mg/24 h (Cox and White, 1962; Kahn et al, 1965; Bashir et al, 1966; Brozovic et al, 1967). Quantities greatly in excess of this, however, i.e. 6.0 g (Levine et al, 1966) and 1340 mg (Lindblad et al, 1968) have been reported, sometimes for very long

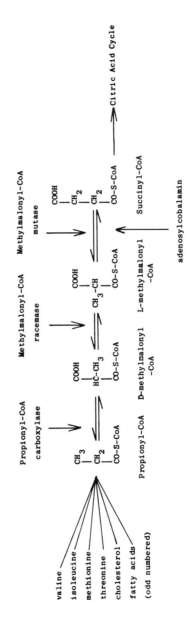

Figure 1. The propionyl-CoA succinyl-CoA pathway.

periods (Giorgio et al, 1976), in patients with congenital methylmalonic aciduria who were normal haematologically and neurologically, as well as in healthy siblings of affected infants (Ledley et al, 1984). This amply confirms the conclusion of Levin et al (1966) that the methylmalonyl-CoA mutase block, and therefore adenosylcobalamin, has no aetiological role either in the anaemia or in the neurological complications of vitamin B_{12} deficiency.

The methylmalonyl-CoA mutase reaction is the final stage in the conversion of propionic acid to succinic acid (Flavin et al, 1955) (Figure 1). This is a life-supporting pathway in ruminants, but not in humans, because propionate largely forms the end-product of bacterial fermentation of carbohydrate in the rumen. This does not enter the citric acid cycle directly. It has first to be metabolized along this pathway. Both succinate and acetate, the end-product of carbohydrate digestion in humans, do enter the cycle. Nevertheless, a number of other important metabolites are catabolized to propionate in humans. These include the four amino acids valine, isoleucine, methionine and threonine, the side chain of cholesterol, and fatty acids containing odd numbers of carbon atoms. These are all potentially glucogenic. Their rapid and early passage along this pathway into the citric acid cycle when the mutase block is relieved by adenosylcobalamin has been suggested as the metabolic basis for the striking early subjective improvement often experienced by patients with pernicious anaemia (Parry et al, 1981, 1985).

THE FUNCTION OF METHYLCOBALAMIN

Methylcobalamin is a coenzyme in the methionine synthetase reaction in which the methyl group is transferred from 5-methyltetrahydrofolate to homocysteine to form methionine (Weissbach and Taylor, 1966).

5-methyltetrahydrofolate + $HS\,CH_2\,CH_2\,CHNH_2\,COOH$ $\xrightarrow{\text{methylcobalamin}}$
(homocysteine)

tetrahydrofolate + $CH_3S\,CH_2\,CH_2\,CHNH_2\,COOH$
(methionine)

This reaction is regarded as a means of liberating tetrahydrofolate from the otherwise inactive methyl derivative apart from the synthesis of methionine itself. This is the only undisputed reaction in which both vitamin B_{12} and folate participate. Its significance will be further considered below.

FOLATE METABOLISM

Seventy-five per cent of food folate is in polyglutamate form containing between three and seven glutamic acid residues. These are broken down by conjugases and absorbed as monoglutamates in the upper jejunum The monoglutamate (folic acid, a conjugate of the base pteridine, p-aminobenzoic acid and glutamic acid; Figure 2) is reduced, probably in the cells of the jejunal mucosa, first to 7,8-di- and then to 5,6,7,8-tetrahydrofolate, which is methylated in the 5 position to form 5-methyltetrahydrofolate (5-CH₃-

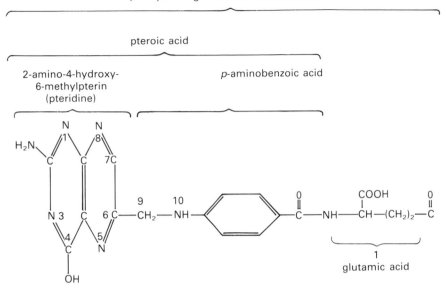

Figure 2. Pteroylmonoglutamic acid (folic acid).

H₄folate). This is the form in which folate is transported in the blood and enters the cells. In the latter it is demethylated by the methionine synthetase reaction (above) and the liberated tetrahydrofolate is converted enzymatically into the coenzyme forms (Figure 3). These are 10-formyltetrahydrofolate (10-CHO-H₄folate) and its sequentially reduced 5–10 bridge compounds, 5,10-methenyl-(5,10-5CH=H₄folate) and 5,10-methylene (5,10-CH₂—H₄folate), and finally 5-methylfolate (5CH₃—H₄folate). These four coenzymes are involved in the introduction of carbon atoms 2 and 8 into the purine ring, the methylation of deoxyuridine monophosphate to form deoxythymidine monophosphate, and the synthesis of methionine respectively. A fifth coenzyme, 5-formimino H₄folate (5-CH=NH-H₄folate), is involved in the transfer of the formimino group CH=NH from formiminoglutamic acid to H₄folate in the final stage of the conversion of histidine into glutamic acid. Finally, the coenzymes are polyglutamated into the original form in which they are found in food (Figure 3). The polyglutamate chain of 5–7 glutamic acid residues form a link between the coenzyme and the apoenzyme (Chanarin et al, 1980).

The formylation of folate and its reduction as far as 5,10-CH₂-H₄folate are reversible reactions. Its further reduction to 5-methyl-H₄folate is irreversible. Folate in this form can only re-enter the above circulation after first being demethylated. This is done in the methylcobalamin-dependent methionine synthetase reaction. In vitamin B₁₂ deficiency this reaction fails and folate accumulates in the otherwise inactive methyltetrahydrofolate form. This is the methyl folate trap hypothesis of vitamin B₁₂ action (Herbert and Zalusky,

1962). This has gained wide support (Metz et al, 1968; Waxman et al, 1969; Lavoie et al, 1974) but it has also been criticized (Chanarin, 1973; Parry, 1978; Lumb et al, 1980).

VITAMIN B₁₂ NUTRITION

Vitamin B_{12} can only be synthesized by micro-organisms which are present in soil, water and in the colons of humans and animals. That it is not absorbed from the latter is clear, because nutritional B_{12} deficiency occurs in humans. These organisms are present also in the rumen. Between 600 and 1000 μg of vitamin B_{12} is synthesized per day in the rumen of sheep on normal pastures (Marston et al, 1961). Sheep, cattle, pigs and other ruminants therefore form the main source of the vitamin for humans. Liver and kidney are particularly rich sources but it is present also in muscle. Fish, milk and milk products, and eggs, also contain the vitamin. Cow's but not goat milk is a particularly important source for vegetarians. Unlike folic acid, vitamin B_{12} is only slightly destroyed by cooking.

The daily requirement is in the order of 1–3 μg/day. Vitamin B_{12} deficiency of dietary origin, although well-documented (Stewart et al, 1970; Britt et al, 1971), is therefore rare. The common cause of vitamin B_{12} deficiency is failure to absorb the vitamin. For this the intrinsic factor of Castle, a glycoprotein secreted by the parietal cells of the stomach, is essential, and the vitamin B_{12} intrinsic factor complex is absorbed in the terminal ileum (Booth and Mollin, 1959). Once absorbed, the vitamin combines with the rapidly turning over transcobalamin II, a β-globulin present in fairly low concentrations in the plasma, and the main transport protein for the vitamin immediately after absorption and distribution to the organs. Circulating vitamin B_{12}, on the other hand, is attached to transcobalamins I and III, mainly the former. These are glycoproteins of the R binder type, present in the stomach. They have a much slower turnover rate, but their concentration in the serum is 10 times that of transcobalamin II. Severe vitamin B_{12} deficiency with normal serum vitamin B_{12} concentrations can occur when the biologically active transcobalamin II is deficient. Conversely, low serum vitamin B_{12} without vitamin B_{12} deficiency can result when the more abundant but inactive transcobalamin I is lacking (England and Linnell, 1979; Mathews and Linnell, 1979). The vitamin is stored mainly in the liver, which contains about 2–3 mg, approximately 1000 day's supply.

VITAMIN B₁₂ ASSAY

Vitamin B_{12} can be assayed microbiologically with *Euglena gracilis* or *Lactobacillus leishmanii*, or by radiodilution assay. *L. leishmanii* in particular is inhibited by antibiotics, and this can result in fallaciously low values. Normal values are 160–925 ng/l, and borderline values are 160–100 ng/l. They are invariably below 100, usually below 50, and not infrequently below 20 ng/l in pernicious anaemia. Radiodilution assays tend to give higher values and

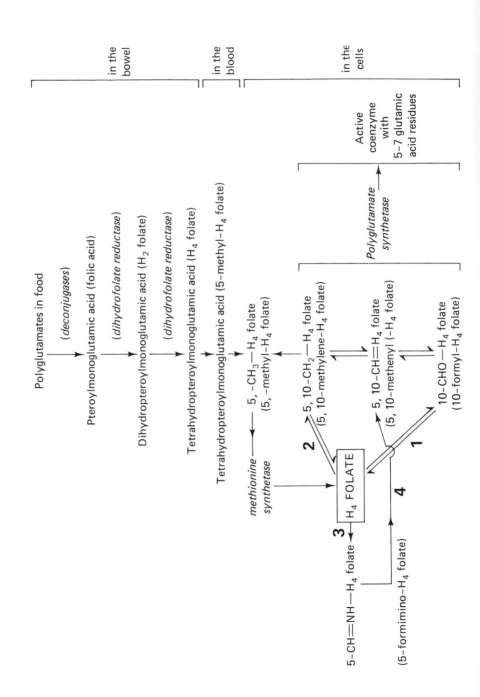

1 *Formyltetrahydrofolate synthetase*

$$HCOOH + ATP + H_4 \text{ folate} \rightleftharpoons 10\text{-}CHO\text{---}H_4 \text{ folate} + ADP$$
$$(10\text{-formyl-}H_4 \text{ folate})$$

2 *Serine hydroxymethyltransferase*

$$H_4 \text{ folate} + CH_2OHCHNH_2COOH \rightleftharpoons 5,10\text{-}CH_2\text{---}H_4 \text{ folate} + CH_2NH_2COOH$$
$$\text{(serine)} \qquad (5,10\text{-methylene-}H_4 \text{ folate)} \quad \text{(glycine)}$$

3 *Forminimoglutamate forminimotransferase* reaction

$$HOOC\text{---}CH_2\text{---}CH_2\text{---}CH\text{---}COOH + H_4 \text{ folate} \longrightarrow 5\text{-}CH{=}NH\text{---}H_4 \text{ folate} + HOOC\text{---}CH_2\text{---}CH_2\text{---}CH\cdot NH_2\text{---}COOH$$

$$\begin{array}{c} NH \\ \| \\ CH \\ | \\ NH \\ | \end{array}$$

$$\text{(forminimoglutamic acid)} \qquad (5\text{-formimino-}H_4 \text{ folate)} \qquad \text{(glutamic acid)}$$

4 5-Formimino-H_4 folate can be further converted into
5, 10-methenyl-H_4 folate in the 5-*forminimotetrahydrofolate*
cyclodeaminase reaction

$$5\text{-}CH{=}NH\text{---}H_4 \text{ folate} + H^+ \rightleftharpoons 5,10\text{-}CH{=}H_4 \text{ folate} + NH_3$$
$$(5\text{-formimino-}H_4 \text{ folate)} \qquad (5,10\text{-methenyl-}H_4 \text{ folate)}$$

Figure 3. Folic acid absorption and conversion to active coenzyme.

have given normal values in cases which were vitamin B_{12} deficient by all other criteria, including microbiological assay (Cooper and Whitehead, 1978; Kolhouse et al, 1978). The latter authors attributed this to the presence of biologically inactive cobalamin analogues in serum; these are bound by R protein binders, which constituted the main protein binder in 10 commercial kits which they examined. Intrinsic factor binds only biologically active vitamin B_{12}, and only when this is used as a protein binder will radiodilution assays yield reliable results.

SERUM VITAMIN B_{12} LEVELS IN THE ELDERLY

There have been numerous reports indicating that the mean serum vitamin B_{12} level falls with age (Mollin and Ross, 1952; Cape and Shinton, 1961; Grantz et al, 1983) and an almost equal number maintaining that they do not, reviewed by Hitzhusen et al (1986). Of greater concern, however, is that low values in the pernicious anaemia range have been encountered in nonanaemic geriatric patients (Thomas and Powell, 1971; Blundell et al, 1985) as well as in close relatives of patients with pernicious anaemia (Callender and Spray, 1962). They have also been encountered in normal population surveys (Kilpatrick and Withey, 1965; Elwood et al, 1971), where values below 100 ng/l were found in 8% and 3.4% respectively of subjects over the age of 65. Eight subjects with these low values in the former survey had similar values when re-examined after an interval of 10 years, but their haemoglobin levels had remained normal (Waters et al, 1971). A clinical trial involving 39 nonanaemic elderly subjects with values below 150 ng/l failed to demonstrate any psychiatric or subjective improvement following six injections of vitamin B_{12} over a period of 5 weeks (Hughes et al, 1970).

Vitamin B_{12} therapy is not therefore indicated when the serum vitamin B_{12} is low in the absence of anaemia, but the patients should be carefully followed. Attention must be paid to the MCV as well as to the haemoglobin, and when the former is above 90 fl the marrow should be examined. The finding of a normal red cell folate in these cases would argue against true vitamin B_{12} deficiency (Grinblat et al, 1986) (see below).

Nearly 30% of normal subjects over the age of 70 have histamine fast achlorhydria, and some of these have impairment of vitamin B_{12} absorption (Chanarin, 1969a). This could contribute significantly to the above findings. Other possible contributory causes are chronic pancreatic disease (see below), nutritional deficiency in certain groups, and possible loss of transcobalamin II binding sites in the elderly (Grantz et al, 1983).

THE CAUSES AND SYMPTOMS OF VITAMIN B_{12} DEFICIENCY

The causes of vitamin B_{12} deficiency are summarized in Table 1.

Pernicious anaemia

The overall incidence of pernicious anaemia is about 120/100 000, but it is considerably higher in the elderly population group considered here. The peak

Table 1. Causes of vitamin B_{12} deficiency in the elderly.

- Gastric causes:
  - Pernicious anaemia
  - Gastrectomy
    - Total
    - Partial

- Intestinal causes:
  - Malabsorption syndromes
    - Gluten-induced enteropathy
    - Tropical sprue
  - Diverticulae of duodenum and jejunum
  - Organic disease of the terminal ileum
    - Crohn's disease
    - Tuberculosis
    - Lymphoma
    - Scleroderma
  - Ileocaecal fistula
  - Blind loop syndrome
  - Resection/radiation damage to terminal ileum

- Parasites:
  - Fish tapeworm (*Diphyllobothrium latum*)

- Pancreatic disease

- Increased demand:
  - Hyperthyroidism
  - Malignant disease

- Inactivation:
  - Prolonged nitrous oxide administration

age incident is 60, with 11% of cases occurring before the age of 40. The male/female ratio is 7:10 (Chanarin, 1979). Symptoms may be due to the anaemia, to involvement of the gastrointestinal tract, or to neurological complications.

Symptoms due to anaemia

The onset is extremely insidious. The disease may be suspected from a routine blood count, but tiredness, listlessness, weakness, shortness of breath and palpitations on exertion are present on direct questioning in nearly every case. An anaemia of considerable severity, with the haemoglobin as low as 80 g/l, can develop without the patient being aware that there is anything seriously amiss. The haemoglobin may fall to 40 g/l or lower before the patient seeks medical advice, and not infrequently congestive cardiac or left ventricular failure may supervene. Infertility is common in women of child-bearing age and therefore more common in nutritional vitamin B_{12} deficiency. There is usually a leucopenia which may predispose to respiratory or urinary infections. Haemorrhagic manifestations are rare but occur when the platelets are very low, particularly in very anaemic patients.

Symptoms due to involvement of the gastrointestinal tract

Glossitis, sometimes painful, is present in half the patients. Anorexia, nausea and vomiting, together with some loss of weight, may suggest carcinoma of the stomach—a diagnosis which should always be excluded. Abdominal pain, sometimes colicky and not related to food, and diarrhoea are fairly common.

Symptoms due to neurological complications

Paraesthesias associated with sensory loss of 'glove and stocking' distribution, muscular weakness, muscular tenderness, and diminished reflexes are attributed to peripheral nerve involvement. Posterior column involvement is shown by loss of the senses of vibration and of position. Lateral column involvement is shown by spasmodic ataxia, increased reflexes, ankle clonus and an extensor plantar response. Often the ankle reflexes are absent because of the peripheral neuritis, and the knee jerk is exaggerated. Sphincter involvement is late. The occurrence of neurological changes bears no relationship to the anaemia and may precede the haematological changes.

Visual disturbances

In addition to being caused very rarely by macular haemorrhages, these can be due to retrobulbar neuritis, which may progress to bilateral optic atrophy. Although rare, it can occur in the absence of both anaemia and neurological complications. It occurs almost entirely in men who are heavy smokers. It has been claimed that tobacco amblyopia and retrobulbar neuritis in pernicious anaemia are identical conditions, and both have been attributed to chronic cyanide intoxication. Cyanocobalamin, which is usually absent or which constitutes less than 8% total plasma cobalamin, may be as high as 35% in these conditions, but it can also be raised in uncomplicated pernicious anaemia (Mathews and Linnell, 1979). These authors stress that cyanocobalamin may be harmful in the treatment of this condition. They advocate hydroxycobalamin as the preparation of choice to treat all vitamin B_{12} deficiency states.

Mental confusion, memory failure and depression may occur in pernicious anaemia and may respond to vitamin B_{12} therapy.

Physical examination

The patient is well-nourished although a history of some loss of weight is common. Premature greying of the hair, pallor, and mild icterus resulting in the 'lemon yellow tinge' are common but by no means invariable. Skin pigmentation, usually of the hands, as well as viteligo, are fairly common. The tongue is atrophic and smooth in half the cases. When the anaemia is fairly severe, signs of congestive cardiac failure or of left ventricular failure may supervene. In the absence of cardiac failure the myocardium is extremely vulnerable in severely anaemic patients.

The liver is enlarged in the absence of cardiac failure when the anaemia is severe. The spleen is palpable in less than 10% of cases.

The signs in the central nervous system have been described above.

LABORATORY INVESTIGATIONS

Blood

In an early case the haemoglobin may be over 120 g/l, but the red cell count will be in the region of $3.5 \times 10^{12}/l$. The red cell count rather than the haemoglobin gives the true indication of the severity of the disease. Similarly, the MCV, which is dependent on the red cell count, is the most sensitive indicator of the nature of the anaemia. The upper normal limit of the MCV is therefore important. This has been regarded as 94 fl (Raper and Choudhury, 1978) or 95 fl (Griner and Oranburg, 1978) but when trapped plasma is excluded by means of automatic blood counters, England et al (1972) give a normal range of 80–90 fl. It it usually between 110 and 130 fl in pernicious anaemia and may be as high as 140 fl. Much lower MCV values have, however, been occasionally reported in megaloblastic anaemia due mainly to folate deficiency, but in the abscence of iron deficiency, 72 fl (Zuelzer and Ogden, 1946), 90 fl (Royston and Parry, 1962) and 83 fl (Oscier and Hamblin, 1979).

The mean corpuscular haemoglobin. This is raised but the mean corpuscular haemoglobin concentration is normal unless complicated by iron deficiency.

The white cells. There is usually a leucopenia with counts much below $4.0 \times 10^9/l$, with depression of both polymorphs and lymphocytes. Occasionally there is a relative lymphocytosis.

Platelets. Thrombocytopenia with platelet counts under $140 \times 10^9/l$ is common, and counts as low as $20 \times 10^9/l$ have been reported (Smith et al, 1962).

Film appearance. Oval macrocytosis, anisocytosis, poikylocytosis and small fragments of red cells are striking features. Hypersegmented polymorphs with more than five nuclear lobes are present. Although these may be encountered in other conditions such as renal failure and iron deficiency, their presence, together with macrocytosis, is highly suggestive of vitamin B_{12} or folate deficiency. Platelets are reduced in numbers, sometimes strikingly so.

The marrow appearances. The marrow is usually highly cellular. The myeloid–erythroid ratio is diminished and often reversed, such is the degree of erythroid hyperplasia. Large nucleolated proerythroblasts with intensely basophilic cytoplasm and a perinuclear pale halo are greatly increased in number and may even predominate. These cells are present in small numbers in normal marrows and are increased in iron deficiency and in any marrow showing normoblastic hyperplasia. Although large they should not be referred to as megaloblasts. Nor are the terms pronormoblasts and pro-megaloblasts (coined in an endeavour to separate these cells, mainly on grounds of size, in normoblastic and megaloblastic marrows) helpful. Many of these early red cell precursors fail to mature, and die in the marrow (ineffective erythropoiesis).

Maturation normally proceeds along normoblastic lines, but in vitamin B_{12} or folate deficiency it proceeds along megaloblastic lines. Israels (1939) recognized early (basophilic), intermediate (polychromatic), and late (ortho-chromatic), normoblasts and megaloblasts respectively. The megaloblast is larger than the normoblast, and haemoglobinization is more advanced, but condensation of nuclear chromatin is delayed. Poor, belated attempts at chromatin condensation result in a finely stippled but open nuclear pattern, aptly described as the 'strawberry nucleus', of the well-haemoglobinized intermediate megaloblast. In the late megaloblast the nucleus is often trefoil, and although a considerable degree of nuclear condensation is now evident, open spaces are still apparent in a well-stained preparation. A good nuclear stain such as Jenner–Geimsa is essential. Leishman stain is not satisfactory.

It is not always easy to distinguish between the proerythroblast, the early normoblast and the early (basophilic) megaloblast, nor between the late normoblast and late megaloblast, as the latter may appear pyknotic in an overstained film. Attention should be concentrated on the haemoglobinized intermediate megaloblast, which is easily distinguished from the correspond-ing normoblast.

Under certain circumstances, such as acute haemorrhage or haemolysis, erythropoiesis is accelerated and cells mature earlier and are therefore larger in size. Erythropoiesis under these circumstances is described as macro-normoblastic. The macronormoblast nucleus, however, shows the same nuclear chromatin condensation as does the normoblast under normal conditions. The term transitional has been employed to describe erythroblasts intermediate in appearance between normoblasts and megaloblasts. In difficult cases an injection of vitamin B_{12}, or of folic acid if this deficiency is suspected, can be given and the marrow examined 4 days later. If either of these two vitamins are deficient there will be clear differences between erythropoiesis in the two samples. The term megaloblastoid should be avoided.

Myelopoiesis is usually less active than normal. Giant bizarre metamyelocytes with large horse-shoe nuclei and hypersegmented polymorphs are the two outstanding features.

Megakaryocytes likewise show nuclear hypersegmentation as well as morpho-logical changes in their nuclei similar to those seen in the megaloblast. Ineffective granulopoiesis as well as ineffective thrombopoiesis have been described in megaloblastic marrows (Epstein, 1949).

Stainable iron is usually abundant.

Table 2. Other causes of macrocytosis.

Haematological conditions:
  Rapid blood regeneration
    Acute haemorrhage, haemolysis, response to iron therapy
  Leucoerythroblastic anaemia
  Myelosclerosis, myeloma, secondary malignant deposits
  Myelodysplastic syndromes
  Myeloproliferative diseases
  Acute leukaemia
  Aplastic anaemia

Nonhaematological conditions:
  Alcohol
  Liver disease
  Hypothyroidism
  Chronic respiratory failure

Other causes of macrocytosis (Table 2). These are discussed in the text. In liver disease unaccompanied by dietary folate deficiency or by alcoholism, erythropoiesis is macronormoblastic in type, as it is in most of these conditions (see text).

BIOCHEMICAL CHANGES IN PERNICIOUS ANAEMIA

Evidence of haemolysis

The raised unconjugated bilirubin, the urobilinogenuria and the increased stercobilinogen excretion reflect intracellular (reticuloendothelial) haemolysis. Diminished or absent serum haptoglobin, the positive Schumm's test for methaemalbumin, and the haemosiderinuria, point to intravascular (extracellular) haemolysis. Diminished red cell lifespan, fragmentation of red cells in the peripheral blood and ineffective erythropoiesis all contribute to the haemolysis.

Enzymes

Serum lactate dehydrogenase (LDH) and 2-hydroxybutyrate dehydrogenase are greatly elevated in both vitamin B_{12} and folate deficiency (Emerson and Wilkinson, 1966). Normally the isoenzyme LDH_2 activity is higher than that of LDH_1 in red cells. This is reversed in megaloblastic anaemia (Winston et al, 1970).

Serum and red cell folate

Serum folate is normal or raised in pernicious anaemia but may be low in about 10% of cases. Red cell folate is lower than normal (see below).

Iron metabolism

Both serum iron and serum ferritin are raised in pernicious anaemia and both fall sharply within 48 h after vitamin B_{12} administration. Iron deficiency may subsequently supervene. Serum transferrin is normal or slightly reduced, resulting in high saturation levels. Values over 50% are often encountered and in the presence of severe anaemia are themselves highly suggestive of megaloblastic anaemia in the elderly (Thomas and Powell, 1971). Plasma iron turnover is considerably increased but iron incorporation into the red cells is reduced, reflecting ineffective erythropoiesis.

Urea and electrolytes

In the absence of renal failure the blood urea is normal. Serum and red cell potassium is usually low and both fall further following treatment (Lawson et al, 1972).

Methylmalonic, propionic and succinic acids (Figure 1)

The first has been considered above. Between 1.4 and 54.3 mg of propionic acid was excreted daily in the urine of eight cases of pernicious anaemia (normal 0.1–1.2 mg/24 h). This returned to normal within 10 days of commencing vitamin B_{12} therapy. It was normal in four cases of vitamin B_{12} deficiency complicated by iron deficiency and in three cases of folate deficiency (Cox et al, 1968). Succinic acid excretion was subnormal, below 2.0 mg/24 h in six of 15 patients with pernicious anaemia (Brozovic et al, 1967).

Acetate metabolism

An unexplained raised urinary excretion of acetate in pernicious anaemia which was slowly reduced by vitamin B_{12} but further raised by folate therapy was reported by Cox et al (1968). Acetate is metabolized in the acetyl-CoA ester form. The urinary excretion of free acetate would have a major metabolic advantage. It would conserve coenzyme A. This important metabolite is severely compromised proximal to the methylmalonyl-CoA mutase block in pernicious anaemia (Figure 1).

Serum amino acids

Serum methionine is subnormal but serum valine is normal in untreated pernicious anaemia. Methionine returns to normal within 48 h of commencing vitamin B_{12} therapy. Valine, on the other hand, falls sharply but transiently during the same period. The former reflects the action of methylcobalamin in the methionine synthetase reaction. The latter reflects the flux of valine and other glucogenic metabolites into the citric acid cycle consequent on the relief of the methylmalonyl-CoA mutase block by adenosylcobalamin (Parry, 1969; Parry et al, 1981, 1985). Interestingly, therefore, the behaviours of these two amino acids reflect the individual actions of the two vitamin B_{12} coenzymes.

INVESTIGATIONS SPECIALLY INDICATED IN PATIENTS SUSPECTED OF HAVING PERNICIOUS ANAEMIA

Serum vitamin B_{12}

Serum vitamin B_{12} levels of 160–100 ng/l are borderline. The values in pernicious anaemia are invariably below 100 ng/l, usually below 50 ng/l, and not infrequently below 20 ng/l.

Serum and red cell folate

This is discussed later under 'Folate'.

Antibodies

These can be directed against either intrinsic factor or parietal cells.

Intrinsic factor antibodies are of two types. Type I or blocking antibody prevents the attachment of intrinsic factor to vitamin B_{12} and is present in 55% of patients with pernicious anaemia. Type II or binding antibody prevents the attachment of intrinsic factor, whether free or in combination with vitamin B_{12}, to the ileal mucosa, and is present in 35% of cases. Very rarely, type I antibody has been reported in conditions other than pernicious anaemia, particularly thyroid diseases and diabetes, as well as in relatives of patients with pernicious anaemia. It is present also in the gastric juice of about 80% of patients with pernicious anaemia. Its presence together with a macrocytic anaemia, however, is strong evidence for pernicious anaemia.

Parietal cell antibodies are present in 85% of patients with pernicious anaemia but are present also in many other conditions, such as chronic gastritis, chronic active hepatitis and thyroid disease.

Gastric function

Gastric analysis. The volume of gastric juice is greatly diminished in pernicious anaemia. Acid pepsin and intrinsic factor are lost from the stomach in that order. The presence of free acid excludes the diagnosis of pernicious anaemia but mistaken diagnosis of folate deficiency, congenital absence of intrinsic factor (McIntyre et al, 1965) or congenital failure to absorb vitamin B_{12}– intrinsic factor complex with persistent albuminuria (Grasbeck et al, 1960) all of which have free acid in the stomach, have in the past led to the erroneous diagnosis of pernicious anaemia with acid in the stomach. Adequate gastric stimulation is essential and is provided by histamine 40 μg/kg body weight or preferably pentagastrin 6 μg/kg/h IM. Achlorhydria is present if the pH is above 3.5 and falls by less than one unit following maximal stimulation.

Intrinsic factor. One unit binds 1 ng of vitamin B_{12}. Approximately 2000 units are normally secreted per h. It is not demonstrable in the stomach in two-thirds of patients with pernicious anaemia. The remainder secrete less than 250 units/h.

Barium meal. This is indicated in all cases of pernicious anaemia. It confirms the gastric atrophy in 75% of cases, but its main use is to exclude gastric cancer, which is present in 6% of cases. This association is commoner in men. Two-thirds of the tumours are polypoid and are found in the body and fundus of the stomach.

VITAMIN B_{12} ABSORPTION STUDIES

The more reliable whole body counting and the more commonly employed Schilling's test will be described.

Whole body counting

This requires specialized equipment. One μg of labelled vitamin B_{12} is given by mouth, and an initial count representing the 100% value is taken after 1 h and repeated 7 days later to establish how much has been retained. Either [57]Co- or [58]Co-labelled vitamin B_{12}, or both, one bound to intrinsic factor, may be used. Between 25 and 40% is normally absorbed and the ratio of bound to unbound B_{12} is approximately 1:0. The ratio is usually above 1.5:0 in pernicious anaemia.

The Schilling test

One μg of [57]Co]cyanocobalamin is given by mouth followed immediately by a 'flushing dose' of 1000 μg nonradioactive vitamin B_{12} IM. *All* the urine is collected over the following 24 h, or 48 h after a second flushing dose at 24 h in renal disease. Between 12 and 15% of the isotope is normally excreted in 24 h. In pernicious anaemia less than 5% is excreted. It is increased to nearly normal levels if the test is repeated with labelled vitamin B_{12} bound to intrinsic factor.

The 'Dicopac' test

Two capsules, one containing [57]Co]cyanocobalamin bound to intrinsic factor and the other containing free [58]Co]cyanocobalamin (from the radiochemical centre, Amersham) are given by mouth and are followed immediately by a 'flushing' dose of 1000 μg nonradioactive vitamin B_{12} IM. The 24 h urine is collected and the isotopes counted differentially. The [57]Co/[58]Co urinary B_{12} ratio is above 2.0 in pernicious anaemia. Because the isotope ratio is used, urinary collection is not critical, a major advantage in the elderly. The test is, however, not as accurate as when the two labelled vitamins are given independently. Pathy et al (1979) found the test of limited diagnostic significance in one-third of 71 patients with pernicious anaemia between the ages of 60 and 95.

The dU suppression test (Killman, 1964)

When normal marrow is incubated for 1 h with labelled deoxythymidine the latter is readily incorporated into DNA. This is regarded as 100% incorporation. When the marrow is incubated with unlabelled deoxyuridine for 1 h and then for a second hour with labelled deoxythymidine the incorporation of the latter is suppressed to less than 5%. This is interpreted to demonstrate the ability of normal marrow to methylate deoxyuridine to deoxythymidine. This methylation is impaired both in vitamin B_{12} and in folate deficiency. Megaloblastic marrow will not therefore incorporate deoxyuridine to the same extent, and more deoxythymidine—about 15–20%—will be incorporated during the second hour.

Both vitamin B_{12} and folic acid, as well as folinic acid, will correct the test in vitamin B_{12} deficiency. Folic and folinic acid but not vitamin B_{12} will correct it in folate deficiency. Its correction by folinic acid alone—a tetrahydrofolate—implies a failure to reduce folate to H_4folate, e.g. by folic acid antagonists.

Formiminoglutamic acid (Figlu) excretion

This is considered later under 'Folate'.

Not one of the above tests in isolation is diagnostic of pernicious anaemia, although a single finding, the presence of acid in the stomach, will exclude the diagnosis. A combination of tests is therefore necessary. The author considers the following satisfactory: a full blood count, a marrow biopsy, serum B_{12} and serum and red cell folate assay, a histamine test meal, a vitamin B_{12} absorption test and a barium meal examination. For management, plasma electrolytes and red cell potassium levels are also necessary. Very often they can all be done on an outpatient basis. Reluctance to do marrow biopsies and gastric analysis on the very frail elderly is understandable, but they should be included whenever possible because of their high diagnostic content.

MANAGEMENT AND TREATMENT

Therapeutic trial

Vitamin B_{12} in physiological doses of 2 μg/day either orally in the case of presumed dietary deficiency or parenterally will produce a reticulocyte response in patients with vitamin B_{12} but not folate deficiency. The oral trial, if continued for a few weeks, will result in a full haematological remission. It can conveniently and advantageously be carried out with the patient at home taking his or, usually, her own ordinary unmodified diet. This is the only way in which nutritional vitamin B_{12} deficiency can be proved.

Treatment of pernicious anaemia

Time maybe an important factor in the management of these patients, even when the anaemia is only of moderate severity. Following a full clinical examination, blood is taken for serum B_{12}, serum and red cell folate, and urea and electrolytes, and a marrow biopsy is performed, the latter as an emergency out of hours procedure if necessary. The aim should be to institute treatment within hours of the patient's admission to hospital.

Hydroxycobalamin

One thousand micrograms IM should be given daily for 4 days. If the platelet count is under 40 000, all parenteral medication should be given IV to avoid troublesome haematomata. If the anaemia is severe or the cause unknown, folic acid 10 mg t.d.s. should be given as well. If the anaemia is very severe this also could be given parenterally. This may advance the reticulocyte response by some 24 h.

Potassium supplements

Slow K^+, 1 or 2 tablets t.d.s. should be given, as dictated by the plasma and red cell potassium.

Blood transfusion

This should be avoided if at all possible. It is not indicated in the majority of cases and is positively dangerous when the anaemia is severe. Because of its insidious nature, the anaemia has persisted over a longer period of time in pernicious anaemia than in any other anaemia, including that of folate deficiency. During this time profound fatty changes have taken place in the viscera. Nowhere are these more important than in the myocardium: the more severe the anaemia, the more dangerous is blood transfusion. It is in these cases that parenteral folic acid may be particularly helpful and prompt treatment rewarding. The heart should be supported by all means possible: rest, diuretics etc. If it becomes clear that the patient is not going to survive the 48–72 h until the reticulocyte response occurs, then blood transfusion becomes inevitable. Not more than 250–300 ml of concentrated red cells should be given, preferably with a diuretic and an equal volume of blood removed from the opposite arm. This was successfully carried out on an unconscious elderly female patient with a haemoglobin of 29 g/l. She recovered.

Subsequent management

Hydroxycobalamin 1000 μg should be continued once a week for 4–6 weeks and then once every 1, 2 or 3 months, depending on the response of the patient, and continued throughout the patient's life. It is most important that the need for this is clearly explained to the patient. The patient should be seen and the blood examined at least every 12 months.

Management of neurological complications

Hydroxycobalamin 1000 μg should be given once a week for at least 6 months. This should be continued, but at longer intervals, throughout the patient's life.

Pernicious anaemia and polycythaemia

Very rarely this combination occurs in the same patient. The pernicious anaemia should be fully treated as above and the polycythaemia managed independently. On no account should vitamin B_{12} be reduced in an attempt to control the polycythaemia. This could precipitate acute neurological complications.

Prognosis

Females with pernicious anaemia have a normal life expectancy. In males, however, this is slightly shortened by the increased tendency to develop carcinoma of the stomach.

OTHER CAUSES OF VITAMIN B_{12} DEFICIENCY IN THE ELDERLY

Total gastrectomy

Megaloblastic anaemia invariably follows total gastrectomy after an interval of about 2 years, but the peak incidence is about 5–6 years after the operation. Intrinsic factor and parietal cell antibodies are not seen. Parenteral vitamin B_{12} 1000 μg at monthly intervals should be given from the time of the operation.

Partial gastrectomy

Iron deficiency is common after this operation but megaloblastic anaemia occurs in approximately 6% of cases after an interval of 5–6 years. In the vast majority this is due to vitamin B_{12} deficiency, but in a small minority, about 10%, it is due to folate deficiency.

Disease resection or radiation damage to the terminal ileum

Vitamin B_{12} malabsorption occurs in Crohn's disease and in ileocaecal tuberculosis, and may follow resection of as little as 0.6 m of the terminal ileum. It can also follow radiation damage to the bowel following deep x-ray therapy for carcinoma of the bladder. If resection has been extensive, vitamin B_{12} by injection should be given from the time of the operation. Otherwise the patient should be monitored haematologically.

Surgical blind loop syndrome

Surgical blind loops, duodenal and jejunal diverticulae and the bowel lumen itself when stasis results from organic infiltration of the bowel wall, e.g. in scleroderma, lymphoma, Crohn's disease or tuberculosis, are colonized by bacteria, some of which avidly devour vitamin B_{12}. Intrinsic factor is without effect; but vitamin B_{12} absorption is improved by a course of a wide-spectrum antibiotic. In some cases the abnormal flora breaks down bile salts, and this interferes with fat absorption, leading to steatorrhoea with impaired absorption of vitamin B_{12}.

Fish tapeworm (*Diphyllobothrium latum* infestation)

Although this parasite has a wide prevalence, infestation of humans is virtually confined to Finland, and the diagnosis need therefore only be considered in those who have resided in that country. Megaloblastic anaemia occurs in approximately 2% of those infested, and the age incidence is similar to that of pernicious anaemia. Megaloblastic changes in the marrow, however, are more frequent, and vitamin B_{12} neuropathy and visual disturbances are not uncommon (Chanarin, 1969b). Diagnosis is readily established by finding the ova in the stools, and treatment consists of expelling the worm.

Gluten-induced enteropathy and tropical sprue

These are considered later under 'Folate'.

LOW SERUM VITAMIN B_{12} NOT ASSOCIATED OR VERY RARELY ASSOCIATED WITH MEGALOBLASTIC ANAEMIA

Nutritional vitamin B_{12} deficiency

This is well documented as a cause of megaloblastic anaemia in young Hindu women who are strict vegetarians. It has also been suggested, but not proved, as a possible cause of anaemia in the elderly (Elsborg et al, 1976; Blundell et al, 1985). The former authors excluded pernicious anaemia, folate deficiency and intestinal malabsorption in 40 of 273 geriatric patients with low serum vitamin B_{12} levels. A therapeutic trial was not, however, performed, but the serum vitamin B_{12} level was elevated by a hospital diet alone in 17 – an observation made also by Blundell et al (1985). The elderly on a mixed diet will not suffer from nutritional vitamin B_{12} deficiency, but this must be borne in mind in strict vegetarians, in those with dietary fads, and in those who for physical or mental reasons are not able to feed themselves adequately.

Pancreatic disease

Vitamin B_{12} malabsorption corrected by pancreatin but not by intrinsic factor has been reported in chronic pancreatitis (Veeger et al, 1962) and in fibrocystic disease of the pancreas. Vitamin B_{12} combines with R protein binders in the stomach as well as with intrinsic factor, but is not absorbed in the terminal ileum from the former complexes. Trypsin possibly acts by releasing the vitamin from the R protein binders, thereby allowing it to recombine with intrinsic factor.

Continuous sedation with nitrous oxide

This, for periods up to 18 days in the management of tetanus, resulted in megaloblastic anaemia, with two deaths from septicaemia consequent upon the severe granulocytopenia after recovery from the tetanus (Lassen et al, 1956). Megaloblastic changes in the marrow and an abnormal dU suppression test (Amess et al, 1978), as well as increased urinary excretion of methylmalonic acid (Rask et al, 1983) have been reported following continuous nitrous oxide administration for 24 h for open heart surgery, and elevated serum valine, and to a lesser extent isoleucine, attributed to adenosylcobalamin inactivation, have occurred after exposure for periods as short as 3 h (Parry et al, 1985). The effects of these fairly short exposures, however, are quickly reversed by discontinuing the anaesthetic.

FOLATE

Folate, mainly in the form of polyglutamate containing 4–7 glutamic acid residues, is present in nearly all foods. The richest sources are yeast (Marmite), liver, kidney, spinach, asparagus and nuts. It is present in all leafy vegetables (Latin folium = leaf) as well as in root vegetables, fruit, fish and beer. It is present also in cow's, but not goat's, milk and milk products. Folate is extensively destroyed by cooking, especially by boiling. The loss can be reduced by minimizing the water and reducing the cooking time.

The daily requirement has been variably estimated as 50 (Herbert, 1962), 100 (Hoffbrand, 1981) and 200 (WHO) $\mu g/day$. An intake of 200 ± 68 $\mu g/day$ was adequate to maintain folate status in adult males living in a metabolic unit (Milne et al, 1983). The body contains about 10 mg of folate, enough to last for only 4 months. Folate deficiency can therefore develop very rapidly.

Clinical features

In addition to anaemia, signs of other vitamin deficiencies or of disease causing folate malabsorption may be present. Folate-deficient megaloblastic anaemia was present in 7 of 100 consecutive elderly anaemic patients (Thomas and Powell, 1971), but only one of 90 cases of megaloblastic anaemia was due to uncomplicated folate deficiency in the series reported by Evans et al (1968); 35 had combined iron and folate deficiency. Apart from anaemia, sleeplessness, forgetfulness and irritability were among symptoms noticed by Herbert (1962) when on a low-folate diet of 5 μg/day, and more profound neurological disturbances have been encountered in folate-deficient patients.

Neurological complications

Normal serum vitamin B_{12} and low serum folate have been reported in patients with neurological disease who have responded to folic acid, sometimes after failing to respond to vitamin B_{12}. Out of 30 cases, 14 men and 16 women, 22 aged over 60 and 14 over 70 years, dementia was present in ten (Strachan and Henderson, 1967; Melamed et al, 1975; Manzoor and Runcie, 1976; Monaco et al, 1983), subacute combined degeneration of the cord or a 'neurological disease indistinguishable from it' (Manzoor and Runcie, 1976) in 19 [Hawkins and Meynell, 1958 (case 4); Ungar and Gowling, 1960; Anand, 1964; Ahmed, 1972; Pincus et al, 1972; Melamed et al, 1975; Manzoor and Runcie, 1976; Botez et al, 1978 (cases 2 and 3)] and peripheral neuropathy in 10 (Long et al, 1963; Hansen et al, 1964; Grant et al, 1965 (cases 4, 5 and 6); Fehling et al, 1974; Botez et al, 1978 (cases 1, 4 and 5); Monaco et al, 1983). Six were on anticoagulants and six had upper jejunal disease or resection resulting in folate malabsorption. Severe dementia responded completely or almost completely to folic acid alone in five cases. In subacute combined degeneration, folic acid produced 'remarkable improvement' (Ahmed, 1972), 'total neurological remission' (Pincus et al, 1972) (in both cases after vitamin B_{12} alone for 8–10 days had failed to produce a haematological response and was then discontinued), a resolution in 3 weeks (Melamed et al, 1975), and 'complete or almost complete reversal of the neuropathy' in five and a significant improvement in three of their 10 cases (Manzoor and Runcie, 1976). Extensor plantar responses were reversed bilaterally in seven cases and unilaterally in one case (Pincus et al, 1972; Melamed et al, 1975; Manzoor and Runcie, 1976). The peripheral neuropathy likewise improved on folic acid. Serum vitamin B_{12} level was 230–689 ng/l in all but two, who had levels of 150 and 130 ng/l (case 4 of Grant et al (1965) and case 9 of Manzoor and Runcie (1976)). Both responded neurologically to folate alone. Serum folate was between 3.0 and 4.8 μg/l in three, under 3 μg/l in 19, under 2 μg/l in 17, and 1 μg/l or under in nine. Three cases were reported as 'no growth' on microbiological assay. The haemoglobin ranged between 34 and 149 g/l, being 100 g/l or under in 14, and the MCV ranged between 80 and 122 fl. It was over 95 fl in 13 and over 100 fl in 12. Seven were treated with both vitamin B_{12} and folate but responded haematologically and neurologically only when folate was added. Vitamin B_{12} was discontinued in three. Twenty-three were treated with folate alone. The administration of vitamin B_{12} precipitated acute quadriparesis within 48 h in a 70 year old man who suffered from megaloblastic anaemia due to combined vitamin B_{12} and folate deficiency. It responded to folic acid thus proving the exact opposite to the usual aggravation by folate of vitamin B_{12} deficient neuropathy (Steiner and Melamed, 1983).

Although there are pitfalls in the interpretation of these results (reviewed by Reynolds (1976)), notably the possible presence of other vitamin deficiencies that could damage the nervous system (Grant et al, 1965), the neurotoxicity of anticonvulsants (often the cause of folate deficiency) and spontaneous change of mood in the elderly, these cases provide convincing evidence that an encephalomyeloneuropathy exists which is pharmacologically distinct from that caused by vitamin B_{12} deficiency. Folic acid cures the former and can precipitate the latter (Wilkinson, 1949). They can only be differentiated by the serum vitamin B_{12} and serum and red cell folate levels. They have been found mainly in patients on anticonvulsants or those with disease or resection of the upper jejunum and in the elderly. Vitamin B_{12} and folate assays are clearly indicated when any of the above neurological syndromes remain unexplained in the elderly.

Haematological changes

The blood and bone marrow appearances may be indistinguishable from those already described in vitamin B_{12} deficiency. Not infrequently, however, these are modified by the presence of iron deficiency, which tends to mask the megaloblastic changes in the marrow but enhances the nuclear hypersegmentation of the polymorphs. Under these circumstances it may be advisable to defer the marrow biopsy until iron therapy has been given.

Free acid may or may not be present in the stomach in folate deficiency.

Tests for folate function

These are as follows:

1. Folate assay in serum and red cells.
2. Folic acid absorption test.
3. Formiminoglutamic acid (Figlu) excretion test.
4. dU suppression test.

Folate assay

Folate can be assayed microbiologically with *Lactobacillus casei* both in serum (Herbert et al, 1960) and in red cells (Hoffbrand et al, 1966). Normal serum folate, mainly 5-methyltetrahydrofolate monoglutamate, ranges between 6 and 20 $\mu g/l$. In megaloblastic anaemia due to folate deficiency it is usually below 3 and in severe cases below 1 $\mu g/l$. Levels between 3 and 6 $\mu g/l$ are therefore borderline. High levels are encountered in vitamin B_{12} deficiency, in acute liver disease, and in the intestinal stagnant loop syndrome where the vitamin may be synthesized by abnormal bacterial flora. Serum folate is influenced by recent folate intake and may be low following temporary anorexia or a short period of coma. Conversely, abnormally high values may be encountered if the patient takes several days' medication all at once.

Red cell folate ranges from 160 to 640 μg/l with a mean of 316 μg/l. It represents the folate intake over a longer period represented by the age of the circulating red cells. It may therefore be normal in megaloblastic anaemia due to folate deficiency of rapid onset. Intracellular folate is in polyglutamate form with 4–7 glutamic acid residues. Polyglutamation is vitamin B_{12}-dependent, either by direct action of the vitamin on the formylation of H_4folate (Chanarin et al, 1980) (these authors consider formyl folate to be 'natural' substrata for polyglutamate synthesis) or by indirect action because tetrahydrofolate liberated in the methylcobalamin-dependent methionine synthetase reaction is a better substrate than 5-methyltetrahydrofolate and the 'preferred' substrate for polyglutamate synthetase (Shane and Stokstad, 1985). Red cell folate is therefore low in vitamin B_{12} deficiency. It has been suggested that a normal red cell folate in the presence of low serum vitamin B_{12} is evidence against tissue depletion of the latter (Grinblat et al, 1986). In the absence of vitamin B_{12} deficiency, red cell folate correlates well with the severity of folate deficiency as assessed both by polymorph nuclear lobe counts and by marrow morphology (Hoffbrand et al, 1966). Reticulocyte folate is higher than mature red cell folate, and misleadingly normal 'red cell' folate values can be obtained in haemolytic anaemia when the mature red cell folate is actually low. Microbiological assay can yield falaciously low results in patients on antibiotics or on folic acid antagonists.

Folate can be determined also by radioassay both in serum and in red cells. The results tend to be lower than those obtained by microbiological assay. Numerous commercial kits are available and have been compared with, and evaluated against, microbiological assay. This has been previously reviewed (Parry, 1980). Different kits vary considerably in their sensitivity and it can not be too strongly emphasized that each should be rigorously tested in each laboratory before being adopted for use.

Folic acid absorption tests

Folic acid absorption can be assayed by measuring folate in serum, following a standard dose of oral folate, or by measuring radioactivity in faeces, plasma or urine, following an oral dose of ^{3}H-labelled folate. Peak levels between 51 and 142 μg/l are obtained 1–2 h after an oral dose of 40 μg/l folic acid per kg body weight. The patient is given 15 mg of folic acid daily for 3 days prior to the test to saturate the tissues, and *Streptococcus faecalis*—which does not measure methyltetrahydrofolate normally present in the serum—is employed for the assay (Chanarin and Bennett, 1962).

Formiminoglutamic acid (Figlu)

Fifteen grams of histidine in distilled water is drunk by the patient after an overnight fast, and the urine is collected in 1M HCl between 3 and 8 h after the test dose (to avoid the high concentration of histidine excreted during the first 3 h). Figlu is converted enzymatically (reactions 3+4, Figure 3) into 5,10-methenyl-H$_4$folate, which is measured spectrophotometrically (Chanarin and Bennett, 1962). Between 1 and 18 mg are excreted by normal subjects. It is considerably elevated in most but not all cases of folate deficiency to between 20 and 1500 mg. Notable exceptions are the pregnant, epileptics on anticonvulsants, and those suffering from kwashiorkor. There is a moderate excretion in liver disease thyrotoxicosis and malignant disease. It is increased also in pernicious anaemia when the anaemia is severe, i.e. haemoglobin below 80 g/l.

dU Suppression test

This has been considered under 'Vitamin B$_{12}$'.

Serum and red cell folate in the elderly

Low serum and red cell folate attributed to inadequate folate intake has been reported in patients admitted to acute geriatric wards and to homes for the elderly (Read et al, 1965; Hurdle and Picton Williams, 1966; Varadi and Elwis, 1966; Batata et al, 1967; Raper and Choudhury, 1978; Blundell et al, 1985). Many of these, however, suffered from serious debilitating disease, and Raper and Choudhury studied a special group selected because the MCV was raised. Positive Figlu tests (Read et al, 1965; Hurdle and Picton Williams, 1966) as well as abnormal dU suppression tests (Blundell et al, 1985) and low serum folate have been reported in patients with normal haemoglobin and MCV. Girdwood et al (1967), however, did not find any difference between the serum folate levels of 72 elderly subjects, composed of 40 women (mean age 75.1) and 32 men (mean age 77.4) living at home (mean 6.4+3.5 μg/l), and 62 younger control groups, mainly medical students (mean 6.1±2.5 μg/l), but the mean serum folate of 39 geriatric patients, composed of 19 women (mean age 79.1) and 20 men (mean age 75.8), who had been in hospital for at least 3 months (mean 4.8±2.0 μg/l), was significantly lower. Elwood et al (1971) in a community survey in South Wales found 3% and 8% respectively of 533 subjects over the age of 65 with serum folate levels below 3 μg/l and red cell folate under 200 μg/l. The mean serum and red cell folate were 7.0 and 341 μg/l in men and 6.7 and 317 μg/l in women. There was no evidence of impairment to health which could be attributed to their findings. In another community survey in Albuquerque, New Mexico, Garry et al (1984) found the serum and red cell folate of 188 healthy elderly subjects living at home, and who were not taking any folate supplements, to be 5.4±2.36 μg/l and 259±126 μg/l respectively. They also concluded that folate and vitamin B$_{12}$ status was not a major problem among the 'free living healthy elderly'.

Somewhat lower levels were encountered in an older population in Manchester (Webster and Leeming, 1979). The red cell folate was not significantly different in 29 elderly subjects, all over the age of 75, in good health living at home (179 μg/l), 62 patients aged 66–94, mean 78 years, admitted to an acute geriatric ward (198 μg/l), and 32 patients mainly in the 8th and 9th decades who had been resident in a long-stay chronic geriatric ward for more than 2 years (234 $\mu g/l$), but they were significantly lower than in 29 young healthy controls, average age 27 (296 $\mu g/l$). The incidence of low red cell folate, under 100 $\mu g/l$, of 24%, 16% and 18% respectively, was not significantly different in the three elderly groups. Interestingly, the difference between the young and the old increased and that between the elderly groups diminished with increasing age. The daily food folate of patients on the long-stay ward was 140 $\mu g/day$, and the patients were selected for the survey partly because they were all 'good eaters', yet the red cell folate was under 100 $\mu g/l$ in six of the 32 patients (18%) in this group. The authors concluded that diet and hospitalization alone could not explain their findings and suggested that other factors such as malabsorption of folate could be implicated.

The conflicting results of these surveys can possibly be explained by the age of the populations surveyed. Significantly lower results for serum (Girdwood et al, 1967) and for red cell folate (Webster and Leeming, 1979) were obtained in the two surveys that involved the older age groups where the mean age groups varied between 75.1 and 79.1 years. Although these subjects were not anaemic, the finding of an abnormal Figlu test (Read et al, 1965) and abnormal dU suppression tests (Blundell et al, 1985) with low serum folate levels in the presence of normal haemoglobin and normal MCV shows that folate metabolism is impaired in some of these patients even in the absence of anaemia. Particular attention should be paid to the MCV, and if this is over 90 fl the marrow should be examined. This was abnormal in seven and the dU suppression test abnormal in 11 of 31 cases with low serum vitamin B_{12} and/or low serum and red cell folate (Blundell et al, 1985). Bearing in mind that the MCV can be normal when the marrow is megaloblastic in anaemic patients (see above), a case could be made for examining the marrow of all patients with a low serum vitamin B_{12} and/or serum and red cell folate, irrespective of the haemoglobin and MCV.

Most of the reports of low folate levels have come from Britain. Similar findings have not been reported from the USA (Rosenberg et al, 1982). It is interesting, therefore, that the two community surveys referred to above, that of Elwood et al (1971) in South Wales and that of Garry et al (1984) in New Mexico, produced very similar results after allowing for the different methods of assay employed—microbiological in the British, and radioassay in the American—and led to the same conclusions. Both surveys involved younger age groups than those referred to above. Sixty-two per cent of the patients studied by Elwood et al were between 65 and 75, and the mean age of the 270 subjects, including those on folate supplements, was 72 in the New Mexico survey.

THE CAUSES OF FOLATE DEFICIENCY IN THE ELDERLY

The causes of folate deficiency in the elderly are shown in Table 3.

Inadequate intake

This is the most important cause of folate deficiency at any age and is a contributory factor in the majority of patients with folate deficiency, whatever the primary cause. The elderly are particularly at risk. Poverty, immobility, physical and mental disability, medication, alcohol and in particular apathy, with a loss of interest in food leading to a 'tea and toast' diet, all contribute to the inadequacy.

Partial gastrectomy

Although iron deficiency is the common anaemia following partial gastrectomy, and megaloblastic anaemia when it occurs is usually due to vitamin B_{12} deficiency, about one-tenth of these cases are due to folate deficiency and respond only to the latter.

Impaired absorption

Gluten-induced enteropathy

Folate is absorbed in the upper jejunum. Folate absorption was normal but vitamin B_{12} absorption was zero after resection of all but the proximal 0.9–

Table 3. Causes of folate deficiency in the elderly.

Inadequate intake:
    Dietary deficiency
    Postgastrectomy

Impaired absorption:
    Gluten-induced enteropathy
    (i) Idiopathic steatorrhoea
    (ii) Dermatitis herpetiformis
    Other malabsorption syndromes
      Tropical sprue
      Jejunal resection

Increased utilization:
    (i) Haematological causes
      (a) Chronic haemolytic anaemia
      (b) Myelosclerosis
    (ii) Malignant disease: carcinoma, leukaemia, lymphoma, myeloma
    (iii) Chronic inflammatory disease:
      Crohn's disease, tuberculosis, psoriasis, exfoliative dermatitis

Excessive loss:
    (i) From intestinal epithelium congestive cardiac failure
    (ii) Liver disease
    (iii) Dialysis

Drugs:
    (i) folic acid antagonists
      (a) In humans—methotrexate aminopterin, dichlormethotrexate
      (b) In bacteria—trimethoprim
      (c) In protozoa—pyrimethamine
      (d) Diuretics—triampterine
    (ii) Sulphasalazine
    (iii) Those where the mode of action is not completely known
      (a) Anticonvulsants
      (b) Alcohol

1.2 m of small intestine for volvulus (Booth et al, 1964). In the gluten-induced malabsorption syndrome (idiopathic steatorrhoea) there is impaired absorption of fat, glucose, xylose and folate, leading to steatorrhoea, a flat glucose tolerance curve, abnormal xylose tolerance and megaloblastic anaemia respectively. A jejunal biopsy shows villous atrophy. This is more pronounced in the duodenum and upper jejunum and diminishes progressively towards the ileocaecal valve. Folate-deficient megaloblastic anaemia occurs in virtually all, and vitamin B_{12} deficiency in 40%, of cases. A gluten-free diet induces a slow haematological remission. In practice, vitamin B_{12} and folate are given as well. Iron may be necessary later.

Dermatitis herpetiformis. Upper jejunal lesions which appear to be identical with those of idiopathic steatorrhoea, including a response to a gluten-free diet, have been reported in dermatitis herpetiformis (Fry et al, 1967). Haematological and biochemical evidence of folate deficiency was present in nine of 12 cases investigated. Fat absorption was also impaired but xylose and vitamin B_{12} absorption was normal.

Tropical sprue. This usually has a lower age incidence. The whole of the small intestine is involved with malabsorption of fat, glucose, xylose, vitamin A, folic acid and vitamin B_{12}. Megaloblastic anaemia is present in 90% of cases and responds to folate in the acute form and to vitamin B_{12} in the chronic form.

Jejunal resection. Extensive resection of the upper jejunum results in impaired folate absorption and can result in megaloblastic anaemia. Vitamin B_{12} absorption is not affected.

Increased utilization

Haematological causes

Chronic haemolytic anaemia, particularly thalassaemia major, sickle cell disease, congenital spherocytosis and autoimmune haemolytic anaemia. Folate requirement may be increased up to 10-fold. Red cell folate may not reflect the true folate status, because of the high folate content of reticulocytes (see above). These patients can benefit from folate supplements but these should be given only when the vitamin B_{12} concentration is normal in serum, and then only for a short period. If long-term supplementation is contemplated, normal vitamin B_{12} absorption should first be ascertained.

Myelosclerosis. The MCV was over 90 fl in 26 and over 100 fl in 20 of 49 cases of myelosclerosis reported by Hoffbrand et al (1968a). Megaloblastic erythropoiesis was present in 33 of these and folate deficiency was established in 32. The authors drew attention to the life-saving action of folate in the severe cytopenias of this condition. Megaloblasts may be easier to find in the buffy coat of the peripheral blood, as adequate marrow samples are difficult to obtain. Folate deficiency should be suspected if there is a sudden increase in transfusion requirement or a sudden fall in white cells or platelets.

Malignant disease

Carcinoma, leukaemia, lymphoma and myeloma. These conditions increase demand for folic acid but megaloblastic anaemia is rarely seen. Megaloblastic changes are occasionally seen in the marrow in acute leukaemia.

Inflammatory conditions

Crohn's disease. Folate deficiency was established and vitamin B_{12} deficiency excluded in seven of 21 cases with active Crohn's disease out of 64 patients studied (Hoffbrand et al, 1968b). Marked subjective and haematological improvement followed folate therapy. There is also a high incidence of vitamin B_{12} deficiency in this condition, and this should be excluded before continuing folate therapy.

Excessive loss

This may occur in acute liver disease and to a lesser extent in congestive cardiac failure from folate loss in necrotic liver cells in the former as well as from intestinal epithelial cells in the latter.

Drugs

Folic acid antagonists

These are methotrexate, aminopterin and dichloromethotrexate. These act by inhibiting dihydrofolate reductase. This is the basis of their antitumour action. Their administration in acute lymphoblastic leukaemia is followed by profound megaloblastic changes in the marrow. The antibiotic trimethoprim and the antiplasmodial agent pyrimethamine likewise inhibit dihydrofolate reductase. The inhibitory action of methotrexate on the human enzyme is 100 000-fold that of trimethoprim (Sive et al, 1972). The antifolate action of trimethoprim is therefore weak, and although megaloblastic anaemia has been reported following its use in combination with sulphamethoxazole as co-trimaxazole (Septrin, Bactrim), its antifolate action in humans is virtually negligible (Jenkins et al, 1970; Salter, 1973; El Tamtany, 1974). Pyrimethamine (Hamilton et al, 1954; Waxman and Herbert, 1969), and the thiazide diuretic, triampterine (Dytol) (Corcino et al, 1970), have both caused megaloblastic anaemia by the same mechanism.

The action of folic acid antagonists acting in this manner is immediately counteracted by the administration of 5-formyltetrahydropteroylglutamic acid (folinic acid), which is available commercially as calcium folinate (calcium leucovorin).

Sulphasalazine

A megaloblastic anaemia was encountered in four of 75 (McConkey et al, 1980) and in seven of 50 (Prouse et al, 1986) patients treated with sulphasalazine for rheumatoid arthritis. This is a considerably higher incidence than that occurring following its use in ulcerative colitis. The MCV was dose-related, and the red cell, but not the serum, folate correlated inversely with the total amount of drug given (Longstreth et al, 1983). The drug interferes both with intestinal absorption and with intracellular folate metabolism (Selhub et al, 1978). The anaemia can be treated with folate without discontinuing sulphasalazine. Serum vitamin B_{12} levels, however, should be monitored.

Anticonvulsants

The most important drugs are diphenylhydantoin sodium (Dilantin, Epanutin) and primidone (mysoline) administered either alone, together, or in combination with phenobarbitone. Megaloblastic anaemia is rare after phenobarbitone alone. Serum, red cell and CSF folate (normally three times higher than serum folate) are all reduced in patients on anticoagulants (Reynolds, 1976). Their mode of action is not clear but folate malabsorption was not demonstrated by Girdwood and Lenman (1956) or by Melamed et al (1975).

Alcohol

Three haematological changes can be attributed to alcohol.

1. Macrocytosis which may or may not be associated with megaloblastic erythropoiesis. This is one of the commonest abnormalities in alcoholics in Britain (Wu et al, 1974).
2. Cytoplasmic vacuoles both in early erythroid and early myeloid cells.
3. Marked sideroblastic changes with ringed sideroblasts in the marrow. This is accompanied by considerable elevation of serum iron. The sideroblastic changes disappear and the serum iron falls dramatically within 3 days of alcohol withdrawal (Sullivan and Herbert, 1964; Hourihane and Weir, 1970).

The spontaneous reticulocytosis normally seen on alcohol withdrawal did not occur in alcoholics maintained on a low (5 μg) folic acid diet daily, nor was a reticulocytosis produced by the daily administration of 75 μg folic acid until alcohol had first been withdrawn (Sullivan and Herbert, 1964). These authors concluded that both alcohol ingestion and an inadequate folate intake had a role in producing pancytopenia in alcoholics. Neither Lindenbaum and Leiber (1969) nor Williams and Girdwood (1970) found alcohol-induced megaloblastic anaemia in the absence of nutritional folate deficiency. When borderline folate deficiency was present, however, alcohol precipitated megaloblastosis within the short period of 7–14 days, and this was preceded by a sharp fall in serum folate (Sullivan and Herbert, 1964; Eichner and Hillman,

1971). Intravenous feeding with an amino acid–sorbitol–ethanol preparation also produced megaloblastosis in the same short interval (Wardrop et al, 1975). Although Wu et al (1974) reported macrocytosis and megaloblastic erythropoiesis in alcoholics who were not folate-deficient, 'alcohol probably represents the single most important risk factor in folate deficiency among the elderly as well as among the nonelderly population' (Rosenberg et al, 1982).

Two difficulties beset the recognition of the haemopoietic effects of alcohol: (1) these are usually masked by the effect of alcohol on general nutrition and on the liver, and the predisposition to infection that it causes, all of which affect the haematological status; (2) chronic alcoholism is often unrecognized (Jarman and Kellet, 1979). A constant awareness of alcohol as a potential haematological toxin is clearly necessary. Unexplained macrocytosis, particularly in the presence of a normal haemoglobin (Chanarin, 1979), and vacuolation of erythroid and early myeloid cells, should immediately arouse suspicion. These may or may not be accompanied by sideroblastic and megaloblastic changes in the marrow. The final proof is provided by the reversal of these changes by alcohol withdrawal. This in turn must be monitored by serial liver function tests, as the enzyme γ-glutamyl transpeptidase (γ-GT) is particularly alcohol-sensitive and yields objective evidence where the clinical history is often unreliable.

MEGALOBLASTIC ANAEMIA DUE TO CAUSES OTHER THAN VITAMIN B_{12} OR FOLATE DEFICIENCY

These are shown in Table 4.

Table 4. Megaloblastic anaemia due to causes other than vitamin B_{12} or folate deficiency.

(1) The myelodysplastic syndromes—preleukaemia
(2) Atypical leukaemia
(3) Drugs:
    Pyrimidine inhibitors:
        fluorodeoxyuridine (thymidylate synthetase inhibitor)
        6-azauridine (orotic decarboxylase inhibitor)
    Purine inhibitors:
        6-mercaptopurine
        thioguanine
        azathioprine (Imuran)
    Ribonucleotide reductase inhibitors:
        cytosine arabinoside
        hydroxyurea

The myelodysplastic syndromes or preleukaemia

These are considered elsewhere in this book and will be discussed here only in so far as their differentiation from megaloblastic anaemia is concerned.

Five conditions are considered under the heading.

1. Refractory anaemia with erthyroid hyperplasia (RA).
2. Refractory anaemia with ringed sideroblasts (RARS).
3. Refractory anaemia with excess blasts (RAEB).
4. Chronic myelomonocytic leukaemia (CMML).
5. Refractory anaemia with excess blasts in transformation (RAEBT).

All have in common a refractory anaemia and, with the exception of CMML, the absence of hepatosplenomegaly and lymphadenopathy. All show a varying tendency to develop into acute myeloid leukaemia.

The anaemia occurs with pancytopenia in 50%, thrombocytopenia in 20% and leukopenia in 5% of the cases. Less than 5% have isolated monocytosis, leukopenia, thrombocytopenia, or leukocytosis, and blast cells are present in the peripheral blood. Oval macrocytosis, basophilic stipling and hypochromia are evident in the film (Koeffler, 1986).

The marrow shows hyperplastic erythropoiesis with megaloblastic or dyserythropoietic features. The latter include abnormalities of nuclear shape, nuclear budding, karyorhexis ringed sideroblasts and cytoplasmic vacuolation. Rarely, multiple nuclei and nuclear bridging may be seen.

Myelopoiesis invariably shows excess blasts, varying from < 5% in RA and RARS to 20–30% in RAEBT. Hypogranularity or agranularity of the more mature forms, and nuclear hyposegmentation, lead to a pseudo-Pelger–Huet appearance, and some of the myeloid cells may resemble monocytes.

Megakaryocytes are increased in 50%, diminished in 25% and show morphological abnormalities in 85% of cases (Linman and Bagby, 1976). The latter authors, as well as Koeffler (1986), stress the importance of excluding vitamin B_{12} and folate deficiency in these cases and suggest that if the results of serum folate and vitamin B_{12} levels are not immediately available then the patients should have the benefit of a therapeutic trial with pharmacological doses of vitamin B_{12} and folate. The present author would prefer physiological doses of folate.

Although these conditions are all preleukaemic, erythroid and megakaryocytic changes are more prominent than myeloid changes in the early stages, and marrow failure leading to haemorrhage and infection rather than leukaemic transformation is responsible for 40% of all deaths (Mufti et al, 1985).

Atypical leukaemia

Rarely, acute leukaemia can present with striking megaloblastic changes in the marrow. In one case examined by the author – a young man of 27 – erythropoiesis presented a florid megaloblastic picture completely indistinguishable from the megaloblastic erythropoiesis of pernicious anaemia. Giant metamyelocytes and hypersegmented polymorphs could not, however, be found. Myeloid cells were few in number and consisted mainly of promyelocytes, several of which contained Auer rods. Clinical trials with physiological doses of both vitamin B_{12} and folic acid failed to produce a reticulocyte response. The diagnosis was an atypical acute myeloid leukaemia.

More often, but still rarely, erythropoiesis is dyserythropoietic rather than megaloblastic; although the latter may prevail, the differential diagnosis will be the myelodysplastic syndrome (above) and acute erythroleukaemia. In the latter, macrocytosis may be evident in the peripheral blood, which in addition may contain nucleated red cells that may show megaloblastic features.

Drugs

These provide an interesting insight into the basic biochemical defect in the megaloblast. They all interfere with the synthesis of nucleotides, the building blocks of which both RNA and DNA are made. Impairment of thymidylate synthesis and ribonucleotide reduction (Table 4), affect DNA but not RNA synthesis. It has been suggested that both these lesions can result in single-stranded breaks in the DNA molecule which affect DNA replication and therefore mitosis without affecting RNA and protein synthesis, thus correlating with the deficient numbers but full haemoglobinization of the red cells in uncomplicated megaloblastic anaemia (Parry, 1966).

6-Azauridine inhibits the enzyme orotic decarboxylase (Table 4), one of the enzymes deficient in congenital oroticaciduria. It is active in the conversion of orotic acid to uridine monophosphate, and affects both RNA – and therefore mRNA and protein synthesis – as well as DNA synthesis. Megaloblastic anaemia in congenital oroticaciduria is invariably accompanied by severe hypochromia due to defective protein synthesis inherent in the disease, which does not respond to iron but does to uridine. Similarly, impaired purine ring synthesis affects both RNA and DNA synthesis. That hypochromia is not a feature of uncomplicated megaloblastic anaemia shows that defective purine ring synthesis, which would affect mRNA and protein synthesis, is not a significant factor in the megaloblast, although purine metabolism is affected in the disease, as shown by excessive urinary excretion of the purine precursor amino-imidazolecarboxamide. It is excessive also in haemolytic anaemia and liver disease (Luhby and Cooperman, 1962; Herbert et al, 1964).

A third major metabolic step in the synthesis of both RNA and DNA, namely the amination of the hydroxy bases uracil and hypoxanthine to form cytosine and adenine respectively, has received scant attention in the literature. The reverse process, however, the deamination of cytosine and adenine to uracil and hypoxanthine, has been extensively studied. This can be brought about chemically by nitrous acid (Schuster, 1960) as well as by the corresponding deaminases. These two deaminations provide the chemical basis for the mutagenic action of nitrous acid (Kaudewitz, 1959), and the molecular mechanisms by which they can produce base transitions, i.e. point mutations, in the DNA molecule have been fully documented (Vielmetter and Schuster, 1960; Freeze, 1963). Two possibilities therefore arise (Parry, 1986): (1) excessive enzymatic deamination of cytosine or adenine could under certain circumstances produce the same results; (2) the same mutagenic mechanism could reside in the reverse process, namely in any possible failure to aminate uracil and hypoxanthine to cytosine and adenine respectively, thereby providing the unique possibility of a metabolic block incorporating a mutagenic mechanism. The amination of the hydroxy bases uracil and hypoxanthine and the deamination of the amino bases cytosine and adenine could provide a fruitful field for future research.

REFERENCES

Ahmed M (1972) Neurological disease and folate deficiency. *British Medical Journal* **1:** 181 (letter).

Amess JAL, Burman JF, Rees GM, Nancekievill DG & Mollin DL (1978) Megaloblastic haemopoiesis in patients receiving nitrous oxide. *Lancet* **ii:** 339–342.

Anand MP (1964) Iatrogenic megaloblastic anaemia with neurological complications. *Scottish Medical Journal* **9:** 388–390.

Bahemuka M, Denham MJ & Hodkinson HM (1973) Macrocytosis. *Geriatrics* **3:** 421–422.

Banks RGS, Henderson RJ & Pratt JM (1968) Reactions of gases in solution. Part iii: Some reactions of nitrous oxide with transitional metal complexes. *Journal of the Chemical Society* A 2886.

Bashir HV, Hinterberger H & Jones BP (1966) Methylmalonic acid excretion in vitamin B_{12} deficiency. *British Journal of Haematology* **12:** 704–711.

Batata M, Spray GH, Bolton FG, Higgins G & Willner L (1967) Blood and bone marrow changes in elderly patients with special reference to folic acid, vitamin B_{12}, iron and ascorbic acid. *British Medical Journal* **2:** 667–669.

Blundell EL, Matthews JH, Allen SM et al (1985) Importance of low serum vitamin B_{12} and red cell folate concentration in elderly hospital inpatients. *Journal of Clinical Pathology* **38:** 1179–1184.

Booth CC & Mollin DL (1959) The site of absorption of vitamin B_{12} in man. *Lancet* **1:** 18–21.

Booth CC, MacIntyre I & Mollin DL (1964) Nutritional problems with lesions of intestine. *Quarterly Journal of Medicine* **33:** 401–420.

Botez MI, Peyronnard JM, Bachevalier J & Charron L (1978) Polyneuropathy and folate deficiency. *Archives of Neurology* **35:** 581–584.

Britt RP, Harper C & Spray GH (1971) Megaloblastic anaemia among Indians in Britain. *Quarterly Journal of Medicine* **40:** 499–520.

Brozovic M, Hoffbrand AV, Dimitriadau A & Mollin DL (1967) The excretion of methylmaluric acid and succinic acid in vitamin B_{12} and folate deficiency. *British Journal of Haematology* **13:** 1021–1032.

Callender ST & Spray GH (1962) Latent pernicious anaemia. *British Journal of Haematology* **8:** 230–239.

Cape RDT & Shinton NK (1961) Serum vitamin B_{12} concentration in the elderly. *Gerontologica Clinica* **3:** 163–172.

Chanarin I (1969a) *The Megaloblastic Anaemias*, p 607. Oxford: Blackwell.

Chanarin I (1969b) *The Megaloblastic Anaemias*, p 716. Oxford: Blackwell.

Chanarin I (1973) New light on pernicious anaemia. *Lancet* **ii:** 538–539.

Chanarin I (1979) *The Megaloblastic Anaemia*, 2nd edn, p 318. Oxford: Blackwell.

Chanarin I & Bennett MC (1962) A spectrophotometric method for estimating formimino-glutamic acid and urocanic acid. *British Medical Journal* **1:** 27–29.

Chanarin I, Perry J & Lumb M (1974) The biochemical lesion in vitamin B_{12} deficiency in man. *Lancet* **i:** 1251–1252.

Chanarin I, Deacon R, Lumb M & Perry J (1980) Vitamin B_{12} regulates folate metabolism by the supply of formate. *Lancet* **ii:** 505–508.

Chanarin I, Deacon R, Lumb M, Muir M & Perry J (1985) Cobalamin-folate interrelations: a critical review. *Blood* **66:** 479–488.

Cooper BA & Whitehead VM (1978) Evidence that some patients with pernicious anaemia are not recognized by radio dilution assay for cobalamin in serum. *New England Journal of Medicine* **299:** 816–818.

Corcino J, Waxman S & Herbert V (1970) Mechanisms of triamterene induced megaloblastosis. *Annals of Internal Medicine* **73:** 419–424.

Cox EV & White AM (1962) Methylmalonic acid excretion: an index of vitamin B_{12} deficiency. *Lancet* **ii:** 853–856.

Cox EV, Robertson-Smith D, Small M & White AM (1968) The excretion of propionate and acetate in vitamin B_{12} deficiency. *Clinical Science* **35:** 123–134.

Eichner ER & Hillman RS (1971) The evolution of anaemia in the alcoholic patient. *American Journal of Medicine* **50:** 218–232.

Elsborg L, Lund V & Bastrup-Madsen P (1976) Serum vitamin B_{12} levels in the aged. *Acta Medica Scandinavica* **200:** 309–314.

El Tamtany S (1974) Co-trimoxazole and the blood. *Lancet* **i:** 929 (letter).

Elwood PC, Shinton NK, Wilson CID, Sweetnam P & Frazer AC (1971) Haemoglobin vitamin B_{12} and folate levels in the elderly. *British Journal of Haematology* **21:** 557–563.

Emerson PM & Wilkinson JN (1966) Lactate dehydrogenase in the diagnosis and assessment of response to treatment of megaloblastic anaemia. *British Journal of Haematology* **12:** 678–688.

England JM & Linnell JC (1979) Haematological aspects of cobalamin deficiency. In Zagalek B (ed.) *Proceedings of the Third European Symposium on Vitamin B_{12}.* Berlin: DeGruyter.

England JM, Walford DM & Waters DAW (1972) Reassessment of the reliability of the haematocrit. *British Journal of Haematology* **23:** 247–256.

Epstein RD (1949) Cells of the megakaryocytic series in pernicious anaemia, in particular the effect of specific therapy. *American Journal of Pathology* **25:** 239–251.

Evans DMD, Pathy MS, Sanerkin NG & Deeble TJ (1968) Anaemia in geriatric patients. *Gerontologica Clinica* **10:** 228–241.

Fehling C, Jagerstad M, Lindstrand K & Ehmqvist D (1974) Folate deficiency and neurological disease. *Archives of Neurology* **30:** 263–265.

Flavin M, Oritz PJ & Ochoa S (1955) Metabolism of propionic acid in animal tissues. *Nature* **176:** 823–826.

Freeze E (1963) Molecular mechanisms in mutation. In Taylor JH (ed.) *Molecular Genetics*, part 1, pp 207–261. New York: Academic Press.

Fry L, Kier P, McMinn RMH, Cowan J & Hoffbrand AV (1967) Small intestinal structure and function and haematological changes in dermatitis herpetiformis. *Lancet* **ii:** 729–733.

Garry PJ, Goodwin JS & Hunt WC (1984) Folate and vitamin B_{12} status in a healthy elderly population. *Journal of the American Geriatrics Society* **32:** 719–727.

Giorgio AJ, Trowbridge M, Boone AW & Patten RS (1976) Methylmalonic aciduria without vitamin B_{12} deficiency in a adult sibship. *New England Journal of Medicine* **295:** 310–313.

Girdwood RH & Lenman JAR (1956) Megaloblastic anaemia occurring during primidone therapy. *British Medical Journal* **i:** 146–147.

Girdwood RH, Thomson AD & Williamson J (1967) Folate status in the elderly. *British Medical Journal* **ii:** 670–672.

Grant HC, Hoffbrand AV & Wells DG (1965) Folate deficiency and neurological disease. *Lancet* **ii:** 763–767.

Grantz J, Marcus D, Hernandez F & Freedman M (1983) Low vitamin B_{12} in the elderly. *Gerontologist* **23:** 140–141 (abstract).

Grasbeck R, Gordin R, Kanterio I & Kuhlback B (1960) Selective vitamin B_{12} malabsorption and proteinuria in young people. *Acta Medica Scandinavica* **167:** 289–296.

Grinblat J, Marcus DL, Hernandez F & Freedman ML (1986) Folate and vitamin B_{12} levels in an urban elderly population with chronic diseases. Assessment of two laboratory folate assays: microbiological and radio assay. *Journal of the American Geriatrics Society* **34:** 627–632.

Griner PF & Oranburg PR (1978) Predictive values of erythrocyte indices for tests of iron folic acid and vitamin B_{12} deficiency. *American Journal of Clinical Pathology* **70:** 748–752.

Hamilton L, Phillips FS, Sternberg SS, Clarke EA & Hutchings GH (1954) Haematological effects of certain 3,4-diaminopyrimidines, antagonists of folic acid metabolism. *Blood* **9:** 1062–1081.

Hansen HA, Nordqvist P & Sourander P (1964) Megaloblastic anaemia and neurological disturbances combined with folic acid deficiency. *Acta Medica Scandinavica* **176:** 243–251.

Hawkins CF & Meynell MJ (1958) Macrocytosis and macrocytic anaemia caused by anticonvulsant drugs. *Quarterly Journal of Medicine* **37:** 45–63.

Helman N & Rubenstein LS (1975) The effects of age, sex and smoking on erythrocytes and leukocytes. *American Journal of Clinical Pathology* **63:** 35–44.

Herbert V (1962) Experimental nutritional folate deficiency in man. *Transactions of the Association of American Physicians* **75**: 303–320.

Herbert V & Zalusky R (1962) Inter-relations of vitamin B_{12} and folic acid metabolism: folic acid clearance studies. *Journal of Clinical Investigation* **41**: 1263–1276.

Herbert V, Baker H, Frank O et al (1960) The measurement of folic acid activity in serum. A diagnostic aid in the differentiation of folic acid activity in serum – a diagnostic aid in the differentiation of megaloblastic anaemia. *Blood* **15**: 228–235.

Herbert V, Larabee AR & Buchanan JM (1962) Studies on the identification of a folate compound in human serum. *Journal of Clinical Investigation* **41**: 1134–1138.

Herbert V, Streife RR, Sullivan LW & McGeer PL (1964) Deranged purine metabolism manifested by aminoimidazolicarboximide excretion in megaloblastic anaemias, haemolytic anaemia and liver disease. *Lancet* **ii**: 45–46 (letter).

Hitzhusen JC, Taplin ME, Stephenson WP & Ansell JE (1986) Vitamin B_{12} levels and age. *American Journal of Clinical Pathology* **85**: 32–36.

Hoffbrand AV (1981) Megaloblastic anaemias. In Hoffbrand AV & Lewis SM (eds) *Postgraduate Haematology* p 95. London: William Heinemann.

Hoffbrand AV, Newcombe BFA & Motlin DL (1966) Method of assay of red cell folate activity and the value of the assay as a test for folate deficiency. *Journal of Clinical Pathology* **19**: 17–28.

Hoffbrand AV, Chanarin I, Kremenchuzky S et al (1968a) Megaloblastic anaemia and myelosclerosis. *Quarterly Journal of Medicine* **37**: 493–516.

Hoffbrand AV, Stewart JS, Booth CC & Mollin DL (1968b) Folate deficiency and Crohn's disease. *British Medical Journal* **2**: 71–75.

Hourihane DOB & Weir DG (1970) Suppression of erythropoiesis by alcohol. *British Medical Journal* **1**: 86–89.

Hughes D, Elwood PC, Shinton NK & Wrighton RJ (1970) Clinical trial of the effect of vitamin B_{12} in elderly subjects with low serum B_{12} levels. *British Medical Journal* **2**: 458–460.

Hurdle ADF & Picton Williams TC (1966) Folic acid deficiency of elderly patients admitted to hospital. *British Medical Journal* **2**: 202–205.

Israels MCG (1939) Pathological significance of the megaloblast. *Journal of Pathology and Bacteriology* **49**: 231–240.

Jagerstad M & Westesson AK (1979) Folate. *Scandinavian Journal of Gastroenterology* **14** (supplement 52): 196–202.

Jarman CMB & Kellet JM (1979) Alcoholism in the general hospital. *British Medical Journal* **2**: 469–472.

Jenkins CG, Hughes DTD & Hall PC (1970) A haematological study of patients receiving long term treatment with trimethoprim and sulphonamide. *Journal of Clinical Pathology* **23**: 392–396.

Kahn SB, Williams WJ, Barness LA et al (1965) Methylmalonic acid excretion, a sensitive indicator of vitamin B_{12} deficiency in man. *Journal of Laboratory and Clinical Medicine* **66**: 75–83.

Kaudewitz F (1959) Production of bacterial mutants with nitrous acid. *Nature* **183**: 1829–1830.

Killman SA (1964) Effect of deoxyuridine on incorporation of tritated thymidine: difference between normoblasts and megaloblasts. *Acta Medica Scandinavica* **175**: 483–488.

Kilpatrick GS & Withey JL (1965) The serum vitamin B_{12} concentration in the general population. *Scandinavian Journal of Haematology* **2**: 220–229.

Koeffler HP (1986) Myelodysplastic syndromes (preleukaemia). *Seminars in Haematology* **23**: 284–299.

Kolhouse JF, Kondo H, Allen NC, Peddel E & Allen RH (1978) Cobalamin analogues are present in human plasma and can mask cobalamin deficiency because radioisotope dilution assays are not specific for true cobalamin. *New England Journal of Medicine* **299**: 785–792.

Lassen HCA, Henriksen E, Neakrich F & Kristensen HS (1956) Treatment of tetanus. Severe bone marrow depression after prolonged nitrous oxide anaesthesia. *Lancet* **i**: 527–530.

Lavoie A, Tripp E & Hoffbrand AV (1974) The effect of vitamin B_{12} deficiency on methylfolate metabolism and pteroylpolyglutamate synthesis in human cells. *Clinical Science and Molecular Medicine* **47**: 617–630.

Lawson DH, Murray RM & Parker JLW (1972) Early mortality in the megaloblastic anaemias. *Quarterly Journal of Medicine* **41**: 1–14.

Lazer RB (1978) Myelopathy after prolonged exposure to nitrous oxide. *Lancet* **ii:** 1227–1230.

Ledley FD, Levy HL, Shih VE, Benjamin R & Mahoney MJ (1984) Benign methylmalonic aciduria. *New England Journal of Medicine* **311:** 1015–1018.

Levin B, Oberholzer VG, Burgess EA & Young WF (1966) Methylmalonic aciduria and pernicious anaemia. *Lancet* **ii:** 1415–1516.

Lindblad B, Lindblad BS, Olin P et al (1968) Methylmalonyl aciduria. A disorder associated with acidosis hyperglycinaemia and hyperlactatemia. *Acta Paediatrica Scandinavica* **57:** 414–424.

Lindenbaum J & Lieber CS (1969) Haematological effects of alcohol in man in the absence of nutritional deficiency. *New England Journal of Medicine* **281:** 333–338.

Linman JW & Bagby GC (1976) The preleukaemic syndrome: clinical and laboratory features. Natural course and management. *Blood Cells* **2:** 11–31.

Long MT, Childress RH & Bond WM (1963) Megaloblastic anaemia associated with the use of anticonvulsant drugs. *Neurology* **148:** 697–701.

Longstreth GF & Green R (1983) Folate status in patients receiving maintenance dose of sulphasalazine. *Archives of Internal Medicine* **143:** 902–904.

Luhby AL & Cooperman JM (1962) Aminoimidazole carboxamide excretion in vitamin B_{12} and folic acid deficiencies. *Lancet* **ii:** 1381–1382.

Lumb M, Deacon R, Perry J et al (1980) The effect of nitrous oxide inactivation of vitamin B_{12} on rat hepatic folate. Implications for the methyl folate trap hypothesis. *Biochemical Journal* **186:** 933–936.

Manzoor M & Runcie J (1976) Folate-responsive neuropathy: report of 10 cases. *British Medical Journal* **1:** 1176–1178.

Marston RH, Allen SH & Smith RH (1961) Primary metabolic defect supervening on vitamin B_{12} deficiency in sheep. *Nature* **190:** 1085–1091.

Mathews DM & Linnell JC (1979) Vitamin B_{12}: an area of darkness. *British Medical Journal* **2:** 533–535.

McConkey B, Amos RS, Durham S et al (1980) Sulphasalazine in rheumatoid arthritis. *British Medical Journal* **280:** 442–444.

McIntyre OR, Sullivan LW, Jeffries GH & Silver RH (1965) Pernicious anaemia in childhood. *New England Journal of Medicine* **272:** 981–986.

McLennan J, Andrews GR, Macleod C & Caird FI (1973) Anaemia in the elderly. *Quarterly Journal of Medicine* **42:** 1–13.

Melamed E, Reches A & Herschko C (1975) Reversible central nervous system dysfunction in folate deficiency. *Journal of the Neurological Sciences* **25:** 93–98.

Metz J, Kelly A, Swett VC, Waxman S & Herbert V (1968) Deranged DNA synthesis by bone marrow from vitamin B_{12} deficient humans. *British Journal of Haematology* **14:** 575–592.

Milne DB, Johnson LK, Mahalko JR & Sanstead HH (1983) Folate status of adult males living in a metabolic unit: possible relationship with iron nutriture. *American Journal of Clinical Nutrition* **37:** 768–773.

Mollin DL & Ross GLM (1952) The vitamin B_{12} concentration of serum and urine of normals and of patients with megaloblastic anaemia and other diseases. *Journal of Clinical Pathology* **5:** 129–139.

Monaco F, Sechi GP, Piras MR et al (1983) Brain atrophy, peripheral neuropathy and folic acid deficiency. *Italian Journal of Neurological Science (Milan)* **1:** 113–115.

Mufti GJ, Stevens JR, Oscier DG, Hamblin TJ & Machin D (1985) Myelodysplastic syndromes – a scoring system with prognostic significance. *British Journal of Haematology* **59:** 425–433.

Oscier DG & Hamblin TJ (1979) Megaloblastic anaemia with normal mean cell volume. *British Medical Journal* **1:** 389–390 (letter).

Parry TE (1966) Nucleotide derangement in the megaloblast nucleus. *Nature* **212:** 148–149.

Parry TE (1969) Serum valine and methionine levels in pernicious anaemia under treatment. *British Journal of Haematology* **16:** 221–229.

Parry TE (1978) Evidence against defective thymidylate synthesis being the main biochemical lesion in vitamin B_{12} deficiency. *British Journal of Haematology* **41:** 451–452 (letter).

Parry TE (1980) The diagnosis of megaloblastic anaemia. *Clinical and Laboratory Haematology* **2:** 89–109 (review).

Parry TE (1986) Adenosine deaminase (ADA) in leukemia. Clinical value of plasma ADA activity and characterization of leukemic cell ADA. *American Journal of Haematology* **21:** 431–432 (letter).

Parry TE & Blackmore JA (1976) Serum 'uracil and uridine' levels before and after vitamin B_{12} therapy in pernicious anaemia. *British Journal of Haematology* **34:** 575–579.

Parry TE, Blackmore JA & Roberts B (1981) The differentiation between methylcobalamin and adenosylcobalamin action in pernicious anaemia and in patients under nitrous oxide anaesthesia. *Journal of Clinical Pathology* **34:** 818 (abstract).

Parry TE, Laurence AS, Blackmore JA & Roberts B (1985) Serum valine, methionine and isoleucine levels in patients anaesthetized with and without nitrous oxide. *Clinical and Laboratory Haematology* **7:** 317–326.

Pathy MS, Kirkman S & Molloy MJ (1979) An evaluation of simultaneously administered free and intrinsic factor bound radioactive cyanocobalamin in the diagnosis of pernicious anaemia in the elderly. *Journal of Clinical Pathology* **32:** 244–250.

Pincus JH, Reynolds EH & Glaser GH (1972) Subacute combined system degeneration with folate deficiency. *Journal of the American Medical Association* **221:** 496–497.

Prouse PJ, Shawe D & Gumpel JM (1986) Macrocytic anaemia in patients treated with sulphasalazine for rheumatoid arthritis. *British Medical Journal* **293:** 1407.

Raper CGL & Choudhury M (1978) Early detection of folic acid deficiency in elderly patients. *Journal of Clinical Pathology* **31:** 44–46.

Rask H, Olesen AS, Mortensenm, JZ & Freund LG (1983) N_2O and urine methylmalonic acid in man. *Scandanavian Journal of Haematology* **31:** 45–48.

Read AE, Gough, KR, Pardoe JL & Nicholas A (1965) Nutritional studies on the entrants to an old peoples' home with particular reference to folic acid deficiency. *British Medical Journal* **2:** 843–848.

Reynolds EH (1976) Neurological aspects of folate and vitamin B_{12} metabolism. *Clinics in Haematology* **5:** 661–696.

Rosenberg IH, Bowman BB, Cooper BA, Halstead CH & Lindenbaum J (1982) Folate nutrition in the elderly. *American Journal of Clinical Nutrition* **36:** 1060–1066.

Salter AJ (1973) The toxicity profile of trimethoprine/sulphamethoxazole after 4 years of widespread use. *Medical Journal of Australia (Supplement 1. Supplement 2)* 70–74.

Schuster H (1960) The reaction of nitrous acid with desoxyribonucleic acid. *Biochemical and Biophysical Research Communications* **2:** 320–323.

Selhub J, Dhar GJ & Rosenberg IH (1978) Inhibition of folate enzymes by sulfasalazine. *Journal of Clinical Investigation* **61:** 221–224.

Shane B & Stokstad ELR (1985) Vitamin B_{12}–folate interrelationships. *Annual Review of Nutrition* **5:** 115–141.

Sive G, Green R & Metz J (1972) Effect of trimethoprim on folate dependent DNA synthesis in human bone marrow. *Journal of Clinical Pathology* **25:** 194.

Smith MD, Smith DA & Fletcher M (1962) Haemorrhage associated with thrombocytopenia in megaloblastic anaemia. *British Medical Journal* **1:** 982–985.

Steiner I & Melamed E (1983) Folic acid and the nervous system. *Neurology* **33:** 1634 (letter).

Stewart JS, Roberts PD & Hoffbrand AV (1970) Response of dietary vitamin B_{12} deficiency to physiological oral doses of cyanocobalamin. *Lancet* **ii:** 542–545.

Strachan RW & Henderson JG (1967) Dementia and folate deficiency. *Quarterly Journal of Medicine* **36:** 189–204.

Sullivan LW & Herbert V (1964) Suppression of haemopoiesis by ethanol. *Journal of Clinical Investigation* **43:** 2048–2062.

Thomas JH & Powell DEB (1971) *Blood Disorders in the Elderly*, pp 86–122. Bristol: John Wright & Son.

Ungar B & Gowling DC (1960) Megaloblastic anaemia associated with anticonvulsant drug therapy. *Medical Journal of Australia* **2:** 461–462.

Varadi S & Elwis A (1966) Folic acid deficiency in the elderly. *British Medical Journal* **2:** 410 (letter).

Veeger W, Abels J, Hellemans N & Nieweg HO (1962) Effect of sodium bicarbonate and pancreatin on the absorption of vitamin B_{12} and fat in pancreatic deficiency. *New England Journal of Medicine* **267:** 1341–1344.

Vielmetter W & Schuster H (1960) The base specificity of mutation induced by nitrous oxide on phage T_2. *Biochemistry and Biophysics Research Communications* **2:** 324–328.

Wardrop CAJ, Heatley RV, Tennant GB & Hughes EE (1975) Acute folate deficiency in surgical patients on aminoacid/ethanol intravenous nutrition. *Lancet* **ii:** 640–642.

Waters WE, Withey JL, Kilpatrick GS & Wood PHN (1971) Serum vitamin B_{12} concentrations in the general population – a ten year follow up. *British Journal of Haematology* **20:** 521–526.

Waxman S & Herbert V (1969) Mechanism of pyrimethamine induced megaloblastosis in human marrow. *New England Journal of Medicine* **280:** 1316–1319.

Waxman S, Metz J & Herbert V (1969) Defective DNA synthesis in human megaloblastic bone marrow. Effects of homocysteine and methionine. *Journal of Clinical Investigation* **48:** 284–289.

Webster SGP & Leeming JT (1979) Erythrocyte folate levels in young and old. *Journal of the American Geriatrics Society* **27:** 451–454.

Weissbach H & Taylor R (1966) Role of vitamin B_{12} in methionine biosynthesis. *Federal Proceedings* **25:** 1649.

Wilkinson JF (1949) Megaloblastic anaemia. *Lancet* **i:** 336–340.

Williams IR & Girdwood RH (1970) The folate status of alcoholics. *Scottish Medical Journal* **15:** 285–288.

Wilson J, Linnell JC & Mathews DM (1971) Plasma-cobalamins in neuro-ophthalmological diseases. *Lancet* **i:** 259–261.

Winston RM, Warburton FG & Stoff A (1970) Enzymatic diagnosis of megaloblastic anaemia. *British Journal of Haematology* **19:** 587–592.

Wu A, Chanarin I & Levi AJ (1974) Macrocytosis of chronic alcoholism. *Lancet* **i:** 829–831.

Zuelzer WW & Ogden FN (1946) Megaloblastic anaemia in infancy: a common syndrome responding specifically to folic acid therapy. *American Journal of Diseases in Childhood* **71:** 211–243.

4

Polycythaemia and thrombocythaemia in the elderly

T. C. PEARSON
M. MESSINEZY

The presenting feature of polycythaemia or primary thrombocythaemia is often some kind of vascular occlusion, a condition which becomes increasingly more frequent with age. Therefore, in dealing with any elderly patient who presents in this way, it is important to establish whether either of these haematological conditions is present.

In the past, when patients have presented with vascular occlusive, ischaemic or other symptoms, the index of awareness of the possibility of an underlying haematological disorder has not been high (Calabresi and Meyer, 1959). In a study of polycythaemia (Pearson, 1977), approximately one-third of the patients had had vascular occlusive events or abnormal blood counts, which had been left uninvestigated, within the 2 years preceding the definitive diagnosis. As routine screening becomes a feature of the management of the geriatric population, so early diagnosis and prevention of vascular occlusive events from undiagnosed polycythaemia and thrombocythaemia will be possible. While this is often easier when the haematological changes are marked, it can be difficult with less obvious changes, particularly in the elderly, where there are often a number of different pathological processes present.

In this chapter the presentation, investigation and management of the elderly patient with a raised PCV and/or platelet count will be discussed.

POLYCYTHAEMIA

The definition of a raised PCV

The PCV should be taken as the indicator of polycythaemia. The reasons for this are that it directly relates to the volume occupied by red cells and that, in iron deficiency, which is relatively common in the elderly (Sheridan et al, 1974), the Hb value, which some suggest is the more valuable index of polycythaemia, is relatively lower than the PCV. It is essential to remember that blood samples for PCV measurement should be taken without venous occlusion.

When there are significant reductions in MCV and MCH with a normal Hb value, the diagnosis of iron deficiency and polycythaemia should be considered. In addition, in the presence of microcytic hypochromic red cell changes, PCV measurement should be made by the microhaematocrit method, since in the presence of these changes electronic counters underestimate the true PCV (Guthrie and Pearson, 1982). Just occasionally patients present with an iron-deficient anaemia. Folate or B_{12} deficiency may much less commonly complicate polycythaemia. In these situations, monitoring the recovery of the full blood count and red cell indices following specific therapy is essential in making sure that polycythaemia is not missed.

Although there is probably a small decrease in Hb and PCV over the age of 60 years (Hawkins et al, 1954; Elwood, 1971), it would be reasonable to take similar values for PCV as indicating the need for further investigation by red cell mass and plasma volume measurement, as in younger patients. Therefore those patients with confirmed PCV values above 0.48 (females) and 0.51 (males) should be selected.

Red cell mass and plasma volume

Standard methods for the measurement of red cell mass (RCM) and plasma volume (PV) have been established (International Committee for Standardization in Haematology, 1980); each of these should be measured separately and not estimated from one to the other. There are no adequate publications establishing normal values for different age groups, and therefore the values established for the normal adult population should be used for elderly patients.

Traditionally, expressions of normal and measured values of RCM and PV are given in terms of body weight alone. However, in normal adults there is a poor correlation between RCM and body weight (Hyde and Jones, 1962). The reason for this is that fat tissue is relatively avascular. Therefore, ml/kg expressions give low measured values and high predicted normal values for obese individuals. The problem can be overcome by measuring the lean body mass (LBM), since there is a close correlation between LBM and RCM in normal individuals (Hyde and Jones, 1962). However, measurement of LBM at every RCM/PV study would be tedious. Fortunately, formulae for estimating normal RCM which include both height and weight give similar values as formulae using LBM (Pearson et al, 1978) and avoid the inaccuracy of using weight alone. Various formulae using either height/weight (Nadler et al, 1962; Pearson et al, 1978) or surface area (Hurley, 1975) have been proposed. The formulae we use in our laboratory are based on the normal blood volume prediction of Nadler et al (1962) and Pearson et al (1978), but those proposed by Hurley (1975) give similar predicted normal values (Pearson and Guthrie, 1984). Examination of the standard error of these estimates reveals that the normal range for each height/weight combination is wide, but that if the measured RCM exceeds the predicted normal value for the individual by more than 25% then such a patient can be regarded as having a raised RCM – absolute polycythaemia.

Similar limitations can be put forward for expressing measured PV results or normal predicted values in terms of body weight alone. Thus the use of height/weight formulae as for RCM has been advocated. Unfortunately, the predicted normal values given by the various formulae are not precisely the same (Pearson and Guthrie, 1984). However, their use is far superior to the use of body weight alone.

Classification of the polycythaemias

A patient with a raised PCV has some form of polycythaemia. On the basis of the result of the RCM measurement, patients are divided into those with an absolute polycythaemia (increased measured RCM) and those with an apparent or relative polycythaemia (RCM within normal range). Those with an absolute polycythaemia are further subdivided on the basis of clinical and further laboratory features. Various algorithms, such as that of Berk et al (1986), have been suggested as being useful in the assessment of these patients. A series of investigations are performed to exclude causes of secondary polycythaemia. Where there is no such cause, the criteria for the diagnosis of primary proliferative polycythaemia (PPP) are invoked (Berlin, 1975). Patients with an absolute polycythaemia, without secondary polycythaemia and with splenomegaly may be regarded as having PPP. In the absence of splenomegaly, a combination of two of the following are required to meet a diagnosis of PPP: platelet count in excess of $400 \times 10^9/l$, WBC greater than $12 \times 10^9/l$ in the absence of infection, raised NAP score, raised serum B_{12} (greater than 900 ng/l, or unbound B_{12} binding capacity (greater than 2200 ng/l). Those patients who do not meet these criteria or those of secondary polycythaemia are put in a separate group, termed idiopathic erythrocytosis.

The central importance of establishing the presence of splenomegaly as a hallmark of PPP has led to the use of isotopic techniques to complement clinical assessment (Bateman et al, 1978). The measurement of serum erythropoietin levels may be helpful in the individual case (Cotes et al, 1986). In PPP, erythropoietin levels are usually lower than normal, although some fall in the normal range. In secondary polycythaemia not all values are raised as might be expected, but a raised value would be against PPP. Culture of erythroid colonies (BFU-E) from samples of marrow or peripheral blood may be helpful. Growth of BFU-E in the absence of erythropoietin, so-called spontaneous colonies, supports the diagnosis of PPP but is not found in all cases (Eridani et al, 1983a).

Thorough investigation of all patients is essential. It is perhaps not surprising that in elderly patients often more than one particular process conducive of polycythaemia is established, e.g. chronic obstructive airways disease with hypoxaemia in the presence of PPP.

Primary proliferative polycythaemia

Nature and terminology

It is now established that PPP is a clonal disorder (Adamson and Fialkow, 1978). For this reason we feel that PPP is a more precise title than polycythaemia rubra vera (PRV), which literally means a true increase in red cells, and would obviously apply to other forms of absolute polycythaemia as well as to PPP.

Clinical presentation

Age and sex. Since 1968, PPP has been subject to cancer registration. A recent review (Prochazka and Markowe, 1986) of registrations and mortality (Figure 1) showed increasing incidence up to the 7th decade of life, with a slight male dominance. Thus PPP is predominantly a disease of the elderly.

Vascular occlusive complications. Between one-third and a half of patients present with vascular complications (Barabas et al, 1973). Untreated PPP has a median survival of 18 months, with death being mainly due to vascular occlusion (Chievitz and Thiede, 1962). This establishes the absolute need for awareness of the possibility of the diagnosis, and the simple requirement for a full blood count in elderly patients presenting with vascular occlusive symptoms.

In the detailed study of vascular complications of PPP in 200 patients at presentation by Barabas et al (1973), 34% presented with arterial, and 28% with venous, occlusive events. Thirteen per cent of patients had both arterial and venous complications, and both sexes were equally affected. Cerebrovascular events were four times as frequent as coronary artery occlusion. Ischaemia of the digits tended to occur before proximal occlusion. This ischaemia of the peripheries, and in some cases cerebral ischaemia, is probably caused by the raised platelet count (thrombocythaemia) which may accompany the raised PCV in PPP. These symptoms are discussed more fully under 'Primary Thrombocythaemia'.

The high incidence of cerebrovascular occlusion has been noted in other series (Chievitz and Thiede, 1962; Pearson and Wetherley-Mein, 1978). Completed stroke may be the presenting manifestation, but in some patients ischaemic symptoms of a transient nature are the initial feature. Although some of these are due to platelet emboli or local platelet aggregation, the relationship to the PCV level per se can occasionally be demonstrated by the improvement in symptoms following PCV reduction (Millikan et al, 1960; Ashenhurst, 1972). Just occasionally patients develop progressive neurological deficits which lead to an erroneous diagnosis of intracerebral neoplasm (Kremer et al, 1972). In addition, apart from specific symptoms, many patients complain of headache, loss of concentration or mental impairment. These nonspecific symptoms often improve with PCV reduction, and improvement in cerebral function following treatment has been measured (Willison et al, 1980).

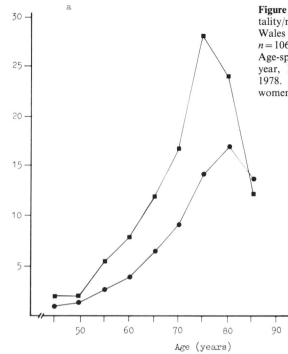

Figure 1. PPP (a) Age-specific mortality/million/year in England and Wales 1968–1982. (■) men, $n = 1068$; (●) women, $n = 886$. (b) Age-specific registration/million/year, England and Wales 1968–1978. (■) men, $n = 2712$; (●) women, $n = 1859$.

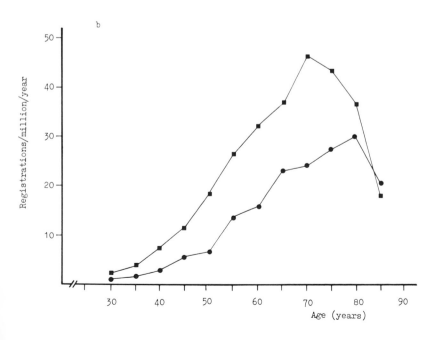

The reason that the cerebral circulation is at particular risk has not been totally established but is probably linked to two major factors. First, global cerebral blood flow (CBF) is low (Thomas et al, 1977), and second, whole blood viscosity is high, since the PCV is the major determinant of blood viscosity. The reason for the low CBF at presentation is almost certainly related to the rise in arterial oxygen content at high Hb and PCV values (Brown et al, 1985). Thus, despite the reduced flow, cerebral oxygen transport is maintained. If this were always so there would be no explanation of cerebral ischaemic symptoms, which improve on venesection. Wade (1983) demonstrated, however, that half the polycythaemia patients studied before and after PCV reduction showed no change in cerebral oxygen transport, while the other half showed improvement after lowering the PCV. These studies only examined global flow, but local arterial vessel disease may lead to impaired blood supply in a small area of cerebral tissue, and when vasomotor reserve is exhausted, the increased blood viscosity further limits flow and hence oxygen supply (Schmid-Schönbein, 1981). It is thus in the elderly, where vessel disease is maximal and therefore vasomotor reserve limited, that one would expect the highest incidence of cerebral ischaemia and infarction in PPP. This is supported by a postmortem study of a normal geriatric population with a mean age at death of 77 years (Tohgi et al, 1978). These authors found that the highest incidence of cerebral infarction was in patients with previous PCV values above 0.46 and with moderate to marked atheroma.

Other arterial vessels, such as coronary, lower limb, retinal and mesenteric, may be involved in occlusive disease in PPP, while improvement in intermittent claudication following PCV reduction has been documented (Edwards and Cooley, 1970).

Barbas et al (1973) found that the most common venous complication in PPP was superficial thrombophlebitis but that deep vein thrombosis, complicated in a few by pulmonary embolization, was almost as frequent. Other sites which may be involved include the splenic vein, the hepatic vein with a Budd–Chiari syndrome (Burris and Arrowsmith, 1953), and the portal veins within the hepatic substance, which may be obliterated, leading to nodular regenerative hyperplasia (Wanless et al, 1980). Since blood stasis is a factor in venous thrombosis (Clark and Cotton, 1968), the elderly are at particular risk because they are relatively immobile and more frequently develop heart failure than younger patients.

Haemorrhage. Excessive bruising or bleeding following trauma, but rarely spontaneously, may occur (Schafer, 1984) and is due mostly to abnormal platelet function, particularly in those with elevated platelet counts, although coagulation factor deficiencies have been described (Stathakis et al, 1974a).

Haemorrhage from peptic ulceration may lead to an iron-deficiency anaemia. Traditionally it has been considered that peptic ulceration is more common in PPP than in the normal population. However, although dyspepsia is occasionally a presenting symptom (Wasserman, 1954), proven ulceration has rarely been established, and this traditional view is probably mistaken (Pearson, 1977). Further, the suggested mechanism for the ulceration –

Table 1. Relation between the duration of haematological control and the incidence of complications after major surgery in primary proliferative polycythaemia. Data from Wasserman and Gilbert (1963).

	Duration of control			
	None ($n = 24$)	Immediate 0–7 days ($n = 9$)	Short 1–18 weeks ($n = 12$)	Long 18 weeks or more ($n = 16$)
Death	37%	0	16.5%	0
Complicated	46%	33%	16.5%	6%
Uncompli-cated	17%	67%	67%	94%

increased gastric acid due to increased histamine levels – has also been shown to be unlikely (Gray et al, 1982), and gastric acidity in PPP has been demonstrated to be reduced or normal (Delamore, 1961).

Surgery. In patients with PPP undergoing major surgery, the morbidity and mortality, mostly from thrombosis and haemorrhage, was significantly lower in those in whom the disease process was adequately controlled (Table 1; Wasserman and Gilbert, 1963). There is a tendency for less vigorous treatment of PPP in the elderly patient, but since as a group they are more likely to require surgery it is essential that their management should match that of younger patients.

Pruritus. Itching is relatively common, occurring in approximately 15% of patients at presentation. It is usually intermittent, and induced or enhanced by warmth, but may be precipitated by cold ambient temperatures (Steinman et al, 1987). The symptom is similar to aquagenic pruritus, which is found in some haematologically normal individuals in whom contact with water is the initiator (Kligman et al, 1986). The mechanism for pruritus in PPP is not totally established but increased histamine levels related to the basophil count (Gilbert et al, 1966), histamine release after water challenge (Steinman et al, 1987), platelet involvement (Fjellner and Hagermark, 1979) and iron deficiency (Salem et al, 1982) have been implicated. In the elderly without any underlying haematological disorder, aquagenic pruritus may occur. It differs in many features, such as dry skin and seasonal variation, from the condition in younger patients (Kligman et al, 1986). Obviously, however, in the elderly patient presenting with itching, PPP should be excluded.

Gout. During the course of PPP, gout occurs in approximately 10% of patients (Calabresi and Meyer, 1959). The serum urate level at which gouty arthritis develops is inversely proportional to age (Nuki, 1983). Thus gout is more likely in elderly patients with PPP. Diuretic therapy, frequently used in the elderly, also increases the risk, since it decreases uric acid excretion (Nuki, 1983).

PPP and other haematological disorders

Conditions that have been described in association with PPP, particularly in elderly patients, include chronic lymphatic leukaemia (Jacobsen et al, 1982) and myeloma (Franzen et al, 1966). Although the most likely explanation is the coexistence of two 'clonal' disorders, an alternative hypothesis has been proposed: that the two conditions arise as a result of expansion from a common abnormal pluripotent stem cell (Jacobsen et al, 1982). Usually, the acute leukaemic transformation of PPP, if it occurs, is myeloblastic. The finding that occasionally it is of a lymphoblastic type (Hoffman et al, 1978) adds some weight to the common aberrant stem cell proposal.

Occasionally, a fortuitous association between pernicious anaemia and PPP is found (England et al, 1968; Chanarin, 1969). Pernicious anaemia may develop in established PPP (Sage, 1969) but the megaloblastic anaemia is usually the first haematological manifestation. Often, polycythaemia becomes evident after B_{12} therapy. Serum B_{12} levels are either normal or increased in PPP (Rachmilewitz et al, 1977); a marginally low or obviously reduced B_{12} level in an elderly patient with PPP warrants further investigation.

The management of PPP in the elderly

During the initial assessment of the patient and subsequent investigation, the urgency and aggressiveness with which one needs to treat the condition should be ascertained. Presentation with a vascular occlusive lesion or ischaemic symptoms indicates the need for urgency.

Treatment can be divided between an early phase designed to lower the PCV, and definitive long-term treatment. In the initial phase, venesection is the simplest method of reducing the PCV. In the elderly it is unwise to exceed 150–250 ml (depending on the blood volume) on the first occasion, but if there is urgent need to reduce the PCV, and a larger volume is taken (or if there is evidence of myocardial or peripheral ischaemia), it is prudent to perform the procedure isovolaemically, since rare fatalities have been reported (Kiraly et al, 1976). Venesection may be carried out daily when relatively rapid lowering of the PCV is required. In patients with symptoms from thrombocythaemia, such as digital microvascular occlusion or transient ischaemic attacks, antiplatelet agents are indicated. Daily aspirin is effective, but the addition of another antiplatelet drug, e.g. dipyridamole, may confer additional benefit (Preston and Greaves, 1985). Since the elderly are particularly prone to gastrointestinal haemorrhage with the use of these agents (Tartaglia et al, 1986), this treatment should be discontinued as soon as the platelet count is reduced by myelosuppressive therapy.

In the maintenance phase of treatment there are a number of objectives and considerations. These include the patient's ability to attend hospital, drug-compliance and the availability of accessible peripheral veins. The PCV should be adequately controlled to minimize the vascular occlusive risk, and a value of less than 0.45 is ideal (Pearson and Wetherley-Mein, 1978; Messinezy et al, 1985). Any induced iron deficiency is rarely associated with symptoms (Messinezy et al, 1985), even in the elderly (Rector et al, 1982). If microcytic hypochromic red cell changes are present, then as long as the PCV is accurately measured – most easily by microhaematocrit—whole blood viscosity is no higher than in the presence of normochromic normocytic red cells (Van de Pette et al, 1986a). Compared with normal red cells, the relatively lower Hb and therefore reduced oxygen-carrying capacity when microcytic hypochromic changes are present (Van de Pette et al, 1986a) is rarely a problem in this form of polycythaemia. If iron therapy is ever given to these patients (and this is very rarely required) it should be in a low dosage and with close supervision of the haematological response, since a dramatic rise in PCV may occur.

The question of whether a high platelet count in PPP (thrombocythaemia) should be treated has been discussed (Berk et al, 1986). One study suggested that the higher the platelet count in the maintenance phase, the greater the incidence of vascular occlusive events (Dawson and Ogston, 1970). This observation has not been confirmed by other authors (Chievitz and Thiede, 1962; Pearson and Wetherley-Mein, 1978; Kessler et al, 1982). This may in part be due to the apparently dominant influence of the PCV level on larger vessel occlusive events in PPP (Pearson and Wetherley-Mein, 1978). High platelet counts may not be associated with any symptoms (Kessler et al, 1982), particularly in the younger patient (Hoagland and Silverstein, 1978). However, the incidence of microvascular lesions (Singh and Wetherley-Mein, 1977), neurological dysfunction (Preston et al, 1979) and haemorrhage in primary thrombocythaemia (Kessler et al, 1982; Van de Pette et al, 1986b), and the risks associated with untreated thrombocythaemia at surgery (Wasserman and Gilbert, 1963), suggest strongly that in the elderly patient the platelet count should be reduced, ideally to below $400 \times 10^9/l$. In a few, symptoms attributable to 'thrombocythaemia' occur at platelet counts at the upper end of the normal range. In these patients further cautious reduction of the platelet count is worthwhile.

The simplest treatment for elderly patients is radioactive phosphorus, ^{32}P (Wasserman, 1971; Berk et al, 1986). A single intravenous dose is effective in inducing long-term 'remission' in the majority of patients, so frequent hospital visits are unnecessary. Occasionally an additional lower dose of ^{32}P is required after 3 months to produce adequate control, although in some patients additional venesection is required. Acute leukaemic transformation and nonhaematological malignancies occur more commonly in patients treated with ^{32}P than in those managed with venesection alone (Berk et al, 1986). These transformations and malignancies begin to occur 4–5 years after the initiation of ^{32}P treatment (Berk et al, 1986). This time interval may be considered reassuring when treating patients already in the eighth decade.

When the haematological manifestations of PPP are limited to only modest elevations of the PCV and platelet count, peripheral veins are easily accessible, and hospital care is readily available, it is possible to treat PPP by venesection with the addition of low-dose intermittent busulphan to control any thrombocythaemia (Messinezy et al, 1985). This regime was not associated with an increased incidence of acute leukaemic transformation compared with venesection alone. However, if this regime is used, adequate treatment must be given to control the peripheral count (PCV < 0.45; platelets $< 400 \times 10^9/l$) to minimize the cardiovascular complications to which this age group is particularly prone (Wasserman et al, 1981).

Although originally advocated (Wasserman, 1971), there is no indication for the use of intermittent high-dose chemotherapy, such as chlorambucil, for the treatment of PPP. The frequent blood tests which are required, and the high incidence of acute leukaemia and other malignancies following its use, indicate its limitations (Berk et al, 1986).

Recently there has been renewed interest (Donovan et al, 1984) in the use of continuous hydroxyurea, which had previously been shown to be effective, in the long-term treatment of PPP. The advantage of hydroxyurea is that since it produces its effects by suppressing DNA synthesis by inhibiting ribonucleotide reductase, it is probably less mutagenic than the alkylating agents and ^{32}P. In 61% of 51 previously untreated patients a satisfactory long-term control was achieved with hydroxyurea supplemented as required by venesection (Kaplan et al, 1986). The complication rate (leukaemia and thromboembolic) was no greater than in patients in the venesection-only limb of the previous Polycythaemia Vera Study Group (PVSG) trial. However, since the two groups did not have similar haematological values at presentation, they are not strictly comparable. There may well be a place for the use of continuous hydroxyurea in the reliable elderly patient but this has not yet been totally evaluated.

Understandably, there are no figures for the median survival of elderly patients using the various regimes of treatment. Those available for all ages include the PVSG randomized trial of 8.9 years for chlorambucil, 11.8 years for ^{32}P, and 13.9 years for venesection alone (Berk et al, 1986) and the nonrandomized study of 11.1 years for venesection and intermittent low-dose busulphan (Messinezy et al, 1985).

Supportive measures in the management of PPP

Gout. Prophylactic allopurinol should be given to those with raised uric acid levels or who have had a previous attack of gout, which should be managed by standard methods with the use of a nonsteroidal analgesic anti-inflammatory drug (Nuki, 1983).

Pruritus. This can be difficult to control, although adequate myelosuppression is sometimes associated with improvement. Histamine antagonists, e.g. cyproheptadine (Gilbert et al, 1966), or H_2 antagonists, e.g. cimetidine (Scott and Horton, 1979) are occasionally effective. In addition, aspirin (Fjellner and Hagermark, 1979), cholestyramine (Chanarin and Szur, 1975), and (for those with marked iron-deficient changes) cautious low-dose iron therapy (Salem et al, 1982) may occasionally be helpful. Often these measures are of limited success and the patient has to resort to the avoidance of situations which precipitate pruritus.

Transitional myeloproliferative disorder

This term has been applied to a situation in patients with some features of PPP but before progression to myelofibrosis (Pettit et al, 1979). Some patients present at this stage; others, however, evolve to this phase after many years of having typical PPP (Pettit et al, 1979). Many of the patients involved are elderly. The features for defining this period are an elevated RCM, moderate to marked splenomegaly, leukoerythroblastic blood picture, hypercellular marrow with increased reticulin, and extramedullary erythropoiesis. Similar features were used by Najean et al (1984) to describe the 'spent' phase of PPP.

It is perhaps unnecessary to separate a distinct phase between PPP and myelofibrosis, except to recognize that the transition may be slow and it is usually impossible to define a precise starting point of myelofibrosis. The difficulty of definition of a separate transitional stage is confirmed by the considerable variation in the subsequent clinical course of the patients in the studies of Pettit et al (1979) and Najean et al (1984). The use of alkylating agents, splenic irradiation and, in some cases, splenectomy, may be of benefit in the management of the steady-state patient in this intermediate phase (Pettit et al, 1979). Radioactive phosphorus is inappropriate since extramedullary erythropoiesis is the dominant component.

Secondary polycythaemia

Causes of secondary polycythaemia are traditionally divided into two groups: those due to hypoxia with activation of the normal erythropoietin mechanism; and those due to inappropriate erythropoietin production from, for example, tumours and renal lesions. However, the measurement of serum erythropoietin levels is not always helpful in establishing the presence of a secondary polycythaemia (Cotes et al, 1986).

Not all of the various causes of secondary polycythaemia need to be considered in the elderly, since some forms, e.g. that associated with cyanotic congenital heart disease, are only seen in childhood and early adulthood.

The hypoxic polycythaemias

Lung disease. In general, values of arterial oxygen saturation (Sao_2) below 92% may be associated with the development of an absolute polycythaemia (Berlin, 1975). However, a single measurement should not be regarded as a reliable guide, since Sao_2 is variable and may fall, e.g. during sleep (Apps, 1983), and in the supine position (Ward et al, 1968). These intermittent reductions in Sao_2 may be sufficient to induce an absolute polycythaemia (Ward et al, 1968; Apps, 1983; Moore-Gillon et al, 1986).

In the elderly there are a number of age-related anatomical and physiological changes occurring in the lungs which tend to lower the arterial Po_2 and Sao_2 (Sorbini et al, 1968). These include a progressive fall in vital capacity and FEV_1 (Morris et al, 1971), and an increase in lung volume at which airway collapse occurs (Begin et al, 1975). In the individual patient other factors may also be involved, including obesity, postural effects, cerebral infarction due to either central or peripheral effects, Parkinson's disease and thoracospinal deformities (Freeman, 1978).

Chronic bronchitis increases in frequency with age. Some develop the clinical picture of chronic obstructive airway disease (COAD). Interestingly, arterial hypoxaemia is more likely in the younger patient than the older (Burrows et al, 1965). Some of the patients with COAD, who have significant arterial hypoxaemia, influenced additionally by sleep effects (Flenley, 1980) and smoking (Stradling and Lane, 1981), develop absolute polycythaemia. Occasionally, transitory increases in Hb, PCV and RCM are seen when an acute chest infection is superimposed on COAD, particularly when right heart failure occurs.

It is an incorrect view that the rise in Hb and PCV in secondary polycythaemia is an appropriate response to hypoxaemia and that no treatment need therefore be considered. The median survival of these patients is 18–30 months (Medical Research Council Working Party, 1981). Lowering of the PCV leads to a fall in blood viscosity, reduced right heart work and pulmonary artery pressure due to reduced total pulmonary resistance, improved exercise capacity and symptoms often attributable to hyperviscosity, including lethargy, headache and poor concentration (Harrison and Stokes, 1982). Probably the most effective way of lowering the Hb and PCV and targeting treatment at the 'underlying' problem is to give long-term domiciliary oxygen therapy for at least 15 h/day (Petty and Finigan, 1968). This therapy produces a significant improvement in prognosis (Medical Research Council Working Party, 1981). The clinical improvement in the elderly is similar to that seen in younger patients (Petty and Finigan, 1968).

In those patients for whom oxygen therapy is not practicable, reduction of PCV by venesection should be considered. The level of PCV which is optimal for these patients is not necessarily the same for all, but a general indication was given in the study of Weisse et al (1975). In this study, reduction of the elevated PCV (> 0.55) was in two stages: first, to 0.50–0.52, and second to 0.44. The first stage was associated with an improvement in cardiopulmonary function, but no further improvement occurred on greater PCV reduction. This study can be used to give a practical therapeutic approach to these patients. Reduction of PCV is unnecessary, in general, unless the PCV is 0.55 or above, and treatment is aimed at achieving a value of 0.50–0.52. The exception to this overall plan would be an individual with ischaemic symptoms at PCV values below 0.55, and those in whom specific symptoms are not relieved following reduction of the PCV to 0.50, after which cautious reduction to below 0.50 could be attempted. Although drugs such as pyrimethamine and dapsone have been suggested as useful in reducing the PCV in this situation (Pengelly, 1966), they require close supervision and are not generally advocated. Although venesection is not totally without risk (Constantinidis, 1979), it is safe if closely supervised. The procedure to be followed is that outlined under the management of PPP. Mild iron-deficiency red cell changes, unassociated with symptoms, may occur following repeated venesection. It is in these patients that the relatively lower Hb to PCV could be a theoretical disadvantage (Van de Pette et al, 1986a). If iron therapy is indicated there must be careful observation of the Hb and PCV, and more frequent venesection will probably be required to control the PCV.

Despite the subjective improvement that has been described following PCV reduction by venesection, there is no study establishing an improved prognosis by this treatment. It is highly unlikely that such a study of an adequate design will ever be performed.

Smoking. There appears to be a spontaneous reduction in tobacco consumption with advancing age (McKennell and Thomas, 1967). Thus, when investigating polycythaemia in the elderly, cigarette smoking emerges as a much less prominent consideration than at younger ages. Smokers have PCV values 0.02–0.03 higher than nonsmokers (Eisen and Hammond, 1956). Occasionally an absolute polycythaemia with a very high PCV value is found (Smith and Landaw, 1978). Smoking exerts its effect largely by stimulation of erythropoiesis, although a direct effect of lowering plasma volume may occur (Jackson and Spurr, 1978). The principal effect is to produce a significant level of carboxyhaemoglobin (COHb). Carbon monoxide has a much higher binding affinity for Hb than oxygen, hence reducing the amount of Hb available for oxygen carriage. In addition, the presence of COHb shifts the oxygen dissociation curve to the left (Collier, 1976), further reducing the tissue oxygen availability. Smoking also directly effects lung function (Ward et al, 1968) and undoubtedly exacerbates the effects of chronic lung disease, leading to a further reduction in oxygen saturation in these patients (Calverley et al, 1982).

Sleep hypoxaemia. In the young, SaO_2 at night does not change significantly from the daytime resting value, while with increasing age (particularly over 55 years) episodes of transient hypoxaemia, especially during rapid eye movement sleep, become more common (Flenley, 1985). Sleep apnoea and hypoxaemia are also more common in the obese, in hypertensives (Kales et al, 1984), and in patients with chronic lung disease (Apps, 1983). It is important to recognize sleep apnoea in the elderly, since the symptoms which may occur of enuresis, daytime sleepiness, intellectual deterioration and personality change (Flenley, 1985) may be put down as symptoms of 'old age'. Similarly, in patients with unexplained polycythaemia, nocturnal hypoxaemia should be considered, since an appropriate study is required for its identification (Moore-Gillon et al, 1986).

High oxygen affinity haemoglobin. There are a number of α and β globin chain variants which lead to a markedly left-shifted oxygen dissociation curve (Stephens, 1977). The condition is obviously genetically determined and is therefore usually discovered early in life. Just occasionally, however, it may go unrecognized until old age. The reasons for this are two-fold. First, the physiological adaptation to these Hb variants includes a variable increase in cardiac output and Hb level (Charache et al, 1978), and thus some patients may only have modest increases in Hb and PCV, the underlying mechanism for which may not be investigated. Second, these patients often do not present clinically, because they have a low incidence of vascular occlusion, the reason for which may be related to the observed increase in cardiac output and blood flow (Wade et al, 1980).

Renal lesions

Thorough renal investigation is essential in all patients presenting with unexplained polycythaemia. Various renal lesions have been associated with secondary polycythaemia. In the context of the elderly, these include hypernephroma, solitary renal cysts, polycystic disease, renal artery stenosis, hydronephrosis and diffuse parenchymal lesions of the kidney (Thorling, 1972; Hoppin et al, 1976).

There are a number of possible diagnostic difficulties. Up to 5% of patients with hypernephroma have polycythaemia, and up to 20% of these have an associated thrombocytosis and neutrophil leukocytosis (Thorling, 1972). Occasionally, therefore, the peripheral blood findings are similar to those in PPP. The development of simple renal cysts, both in incidence and size, is related to ageing, with an incidence of 40% in patients over 60 years (Laucks and McLachlan, 1981). The difficulty in the elderly is therefore knowing, having established the presence of polycythaemia and a renal cyst, whether these are causally related. If it is accessible, aspiration of the cyst fluid may be helpful; cytological examination might establish whether the cyst has arisen secondarily to a renal tumour. Measurement of the erythropoietin activity in the cyst fluid may be useful, but high levels may be found without associated polycythaemia and vice versa (Murphy et al, 1970). In addition, serum erythropoietin levels are not necessarily raised in patients with polycythaemia presumed to be due to an established renal lesion (Murphy et al, 1970; Cotes et al, 1986).

To establish that a particular renal lesion is causing the polycythaemia, the ultimate test is the surgical removal of the presumed causative lesion to establish the regression of the polycythaemia, but only rarely is this approach justified, except with a hypernephroma.

Hepatic lesions

There are a number of different hepatic lesions that may cause polycythaemia. It is found in up to 10% of patients with hepatocellular carcinoma, and is probably the result of tumour production of erythropoietin (McFadzean et al, 1967; Thorling, 1972). A hepatoma sometimes develops in patients with pre-existing cirrhosis which, even when uncomplicated by the tumour, may cause polycythaemia. This is either due to increased production of erythropoietin by the 'damaged' hepatic tissue (Kolk-Vegter et al, 1971), or to arterial hypoxaemia resulting from multiple abnormal pulmonary arteriovenous anastomoses (Wolfe et al, 1977). Splenomegaly is a common finding in the presence of primary hepatic pathology and this must be considered before making a mistaken diagnosis of PPP.

Other tumours and possible causative factors

An association between other tumours and polycythaemia has been documented, but this association is only occasionally found. Some of these tumours, such as fibroids (Wrigley et al, 1971) and cerebellar haemangioblas-tomas (Thorling, 1972) virtually never occur in the elderly. Others, e.g. phaeochromocytoma (Waldmann and Bradley, 1961), usually occur at a younger age, while bronchial carcinoma (Shah et al, 1979) and ovarian tumours (Ghio et al, 1981) are more commonly seen in the elderly.

Chronic ingestion of alcohol may produce polycythaemia by causing cirrhosis, and possibly by a direct depression of the respiratory centre, particularly in patients with arterial hypoxaemia from other causes (Moore-Gillon and Pearson, 1986). Finally, androgen therapy may cause an increase in Hb and PCV and an absolute polycythaemia, as demonstrated in a small number of elderly males (Gardner et al, 1968).

Idiopathic erythrocytosis

By definition, idiopathic erythrocytosis applies to a group of patients who have an absolute polycythaemia, but in whom, after adequate investigation, no underlying cause can be found, nor a diagnosis of PPP be supported.

Nature

These patients do not represent a single pathological entity. Up to 40% progress to PPP 6 months to 13 years after presentation, indicating that the RCM increase was just the first expression of the clonal disorder. If additional techniques are used, such as spleen scanning (Bateman et al, 1978), serum erythropoietin measurement (Cotes et al, 1986) and peripheral blood and marrow culture for 'spontaneous' erythroid colonies (Eridani et al, 1983a), it is occasionally possible to establish a diagnosis of PPP earlier.

A cause of secondary polycythaemia may emerge on further observation of the patient. The present authors have observed a delay of 1–2 years between initial presentation and the identification of a renal neoplasm. Further, it has been shown that some patients have significant nocturnal arterial oxygen desaturation to explain the RCM increase (Moore-Gillon et al, 1986). In addition, an occasional patient will have autonomous high erythropoietin production (Cotes et al, 1986). These findings demonstrate that very detailed investigation will establish an underlying cause in some additional patients, but a 'core' of patients with an unexplained absolute polycythaemia will remain.

Clinical features

The age distribution is similar to that of PPP, thus including the elderly. There is a predominance of males (Modan and Modan, 1968; Pearson and Wetherley-Mein, 1979; Najean et al, 1981). Larger vessel occlusive symptoms, e.g. intermittent claudication and deep vein thrombosis, are the commonest presenting features. Haemorrhagic manifestations are not found. Up to 20% of patients are asymptomatic (Pearson and Wetherley-Mein, 1979). There are no specific clinical signs. The presence of palpable splenomegaly would obviously change the diagnosis to PPP.

Haematological features

The abnormal findings are a raised Hb, PCV and RCM. Occasionally in the elderly patient, one additional haematological abnormality, e.g. a raised platelet count, is found. Alone this is insufficient for a diagnosis of PPP. It is in these patients that it is important to exclude an underlying malignancy, although the haematological changes may represent 'early' PPP.

Treatment

The current study of the Royal College of Physicians Research Group (Wetherley-Mein et al, 1987) includes patients with idiopathic erythrocytosis, and management is discussed later in this chapter under the treatment of relative and apparent polycythaemia. If the PCV is to be lowered, venesection is the treatment of choice (Pearson and Wetherley-Mein, 1979), since it is not associated with acute leukaemic transformation, which has been observed in a significant proportion of these patients when ^{32}P and chemotherapeutic agents have been used (Modan and Modan, 1968; Najean et al, 1981). In the occasional elderly patient, however, venesection might be impracticable or inadvisable because of cardiovascular disease. In such a patient the risks of using a myelosuppressive agent must be weighed against the risks of venesection.

Apparent and relative polycythaemia

There have been a number of different titles given to the group of patients who have a raised PCV but a measured RCM within their normal range. These titles include Geisbock's syndrome, stress, relative, pseudo-, spurious and apparent polycythaemia.

Previously, nearly all authors have interpreted measured RCM and PV data using ml/kg expressions. The limitations of using body weight alone rather than a combination of height and weight have been discussed earlier. The use of ml/kg give the impression that the only cause for a raised PCV associated with a normal RCM is a low PV. This is certainly not the case. There are, however, some patients who do have a reduced PV even with appropriate interpretation of results, and the term 'relative polycythaemia' should be reserved for them. For the remaining patients the term 'apparent polycythaemia' will be used in the remainder of this chapter.

Incidence

Relative and apparent polycythaemia are commoner in males than in females, and are said to be more common in middle age (Lawrence and Berlin, 1952), but the other published series include elderly patients (Burge et al, 1975; Weinreb and Shih, 1975). A study of the results of RCM/PV measurements in adult males with PCV values between 0.500 and 0.599 showed that 37% had absolute, 45% apparent, and 18% relative polycythaemia (Pearson et al,

1984). Half of the patients with apparent polycythaemia had a measured RCM that fell within the high normal range (12.5–25%) above their predicted normal value.

Causes

There are some authors who doubt whether these conditions are pathological entities and suggest that these individuals represent the end of the normal physiological distribution (Brown et al, 1971). This must apply to some but not to the majority.

There is a wide variety of causes which have been proposed for relative and apparent polycythaemia. Dehydration, e.g. from gastrointestinal loss, is more likely to reduce the PV in the elderly because of age-related impairment of renal concentration. The PV decrease may be sufficient to lead to a rise in the PCV above normal. Short-term high-dose diuretic therapy may cause quite marked PV reduction. Chronic low-dose diuretic therapy with thiazides has been shown to reduce the PV by about 5%, with a rise in PCV of 0.02–0.03 (Tarazi et al, 1970). In some hypertensive patients some reduction in PV can be demonstrated (Tarazi et al, 1970). However, in only a small number of patients has an increase in PV and a fall in PCV been demonstrated on the introduction of hypotensive therapy (Emery et al, 1974). Conversely, the introduction of diuretics for the control of hypertension has been shown to reduce the PV (Dustan et al, 1972).

The normal range of RCM is so wide that a patient's measured RCM may significantly increase without falling outside their normal range. All patients who eventually develop an absolute polycythaemia must have passed through this phase. Thus, in these patients any of the causes previously discussed under secondary polycythaemia may be present. These include arterial hypoxaemia from, for example, lung disease and sleep disturbance, renal lesions, various tumours and, less commonly in the elderly, smoking.

In many patients, despite adequate investigation, the cause of the raised PCV remains uncertain. All patients should be regularly followed up.

Clinical features

The rather nonspecific symptoms often associated with these forms of polycythaemia in younger patients (Burge et al, 1975; Weinreb and Shih, 1975), are uncommon in the elderly. There are no specific physical signs. It is debatable whether hypertension is more common in these patients than in the normal population, particularly in the elderly, where there is a very wide range of blood pressure in the normal population (Master et al, 1958).

Haematological and clinical course

The haematological course of these patients has not been precisely established. Some show a spontaneous fall in their PCV, while a few show a progressive increase in PCV and development of an absolute polycythaemia.

In the majority of patients, however, the PCV, RCM and PV remain unchanged over several years (Burge et al, 1975).

There are only two studies of the clinical course of these patients (Burge et al, 1975; Weinreb and Shih, 1975). Both are retrospective and neither examines the elderly patients separately. Burge et al (1975) found that the mortality rate, particularly from cardiovascular complications, was six times greater than that expected for age- and sex-matched individuals. These authors concluded that PCV reduction was a reasonable approach to management. Weinreb and Shih (1975) observed an increased incidence of cardiovascular complications in these patients, but particularly in those with hypertension. They suggested that the PCV level was not a risk factor on its own.

Treatment

Initially, attention should be directed to treating and modifying any possible underlying mechanism or risk factor. Dehydration clearly needs treatment if present. Hypertension, if discovered, should be treated as this is an established risk factor. However, the level of blood pressure indicating the necessity for treatment in the elderly is outside the scope of this chapter. Treatment should if possible avoid the use of a diuretic. Similarly, if a patient is already receiving a diuretic, the need for it should be carefully evaluated. In addition, any other factor found during the investigation of the patient, such as lung disease, obesity, or cigarette smoking, should be treated or modified as appropriate.

Earlier in the chapter, evidence for a positive correlation between PCV level and vascular occlusive risks in PPP and in the normal population was given. Whether the PCV should be lowered in relative and apparent polycythaemia is still debatable. This question is the central theme of the current Royal College of Physicians Research Group study (Wetherley-Mein et al, 1987) of apparent and relative polycythaemia and idiopathic erythrocytosis. The study excludes patients over 70 years, but it does provide a guide to the management of the elderly. Patients with an established PCV of 0.55 or over should be treated by venesection to lower the PCV to below 0.45. Treatment is offered to these patients, because the PCV is considerably elevated and the observed incidence of vascular occlusive events related to PCV in PPP and in the normal population would suggest that PCV values at this level are associated with a risk and that it would therefore be unethical not to treat them. The PCV of less than 0.45 was chosen as the treatment objective, based on the PCV with the minimum risk in PPP (Pearson and Wetherley-Mein, 1978) and in the normal population (Tohgi et al, 1978). Patients with PCV levels between 0.510 and 0.549 should be treated if there is a recent history of vascular occlusion, or for those who have ischaemic symptoms. The untreated patients should be kept under observation, with PCV measurement every 2–3 months to confirm that it is not rising.

As described above, the selected method of PCV reduction is venesection. This decision was based on unsuccessful long-term control with dextran and fluorocortisone in relative polycythaemia (Humphrey et al, 1980) and the demonstration that venesection was effective in the long term and led to a rise in cerebral blood flow in both apparent and relative polycythaemia (Humphrey et al, 1979).

THROMBOCYTHAEMIA

The widespread use of automated and reliable counters in haematology has increased the number of patients noted to have high platelet counts. These can be divided into two groups. In the larger group the high platelet count is secondary to some other condition and is therefore called reactive thrombocytosis, while the smaller group suffers from a myeloproliferative disorder in its own right, variously called primary thrombocythaemia, essential thrombocythaemia or haemorrhagic thrombocythaemia (Gunz, 1960). Primary thrombocythaemia (PT) is becoming the preferred term among many haematologists, and helps to bring the nomenclature into line with that for polycythaemia.

Reactive thrombocytosis

The proportions of the different underlying conditions seen vary widely. Malignant disease and chronic infections are, however, probably the commonest and are mostly seen in the elderly, while post-trauma, haemorrhage, chronic inflammatory bowel disease, postsplenectomy and rheumatoid arthritis are also common but less strongly biased towards the old. It may be, however, that the natural hyposplenism that develops with increasing age is a factor in reinforcing the numbers of reactive thrombocytoses seen among the geriatric age group. Conversely, the finding of splenomegaly in an elderly patient would support a diagnosis of PT.

Most patients with reactive thrombocytosis have only slight or moderately raised platelet counts, but counts greater than $1000 \times 10^9/l$ are not infrequently seen in the reactive group, while many patients with PT have platelet counts below this level at diagnosis.

It is generally agreed that reactive thrombocytosis is not associated with an increased incidence of thrombotic or bleeding complications (Schilling, 1980), although occasional patients with neurological dysfunction have been described (Preston et al, 1979). Another possible exception was indicated by the finding of increased thrombotic complications in a small group of young chronically anaemic patients with persistent postsplenectomy thrombocytosis (Hirsh and Dacie, 1966). Where there was no persisting anaemia, no increased incidence of vascular complications postsplenectomy was found (Boxer et al, 1978), although the thrombocytosis was transient in these patients. In any event, neither anticoagulant, nor antiplatelet or myelosuppressive therapy is generally indicated for this group of patients.

Primary thrombocythaemia

Nature: similarities and differences from PPP

Use of the G6PD locus as a marker has demonstrated that circulating red cells,

Table 2. Diagnostic criteria for primary thrombocythaemia. Adapted from Murphy et al (1986).

---

1. Platelet count > $600 \times 10^9/l$.
2. No evidence of overt polycythaemia (confirmed by RCM) or of polycythaemia masked by coexistent iron deficiency.
3. No Philadelphia chromosome (to exclude cases of chronic myeloid leukaemia).
4. Absence of reticulin pattern suggestive of myelofibrosis on bone marrow trephine.
5. No known cause for reactive thrombocytosis.

---

white cells and platelets are all derived from a single pluripotential haemo-poietic stem cell in PT (Fialkow et al, 1981; Gaetani et al, 1982) though not in reactive thrombocytosis. This establishes that PT, like PPP, is a clonal disorder.

In addition, PT and PPP have a number of clinical features in common. Both are disorders of late middle or old age, with about 50% being over the age of 60 years at diagnosis. Splenomegaly is common in both, and white count distributions are essentially similar in the two diseases (Murphy, 1983). A median survival of almost 10 years, and a 5 year survival of 80% in PT (Case, 1984; Van de Pette et al, 1986b), are comparable with those in PPP. Both show a tendency to transform into each other and into a state of myelofibrosis (Van de Pette et al, 1986b), and, irrespective of treatment, carry a small but definite risk of transformation into acute leukaemia (Geller and Shapiro, 1982).

Discussion of whether PT is a disorder in its own right or a variant of PPP sometimes hinges on the fact that pruritus and a raised NAP are much less common in the former, suggesting (though not strongly) that it could be a separate disorder. However, both conditions undoubtedly have many points of overlap, and to draw too distinct a line between them is likely to be both artificial and unfruitful. Nevertheless, exact definition of PT becomes essential in clinical trials of therapy. Therefore the diagnostic criteria for PT adopted by the Polycythaemia Vera Study Group (PVSG) are useful, particularly as a reminder that some patients who appear to have PT have in reality PPP masked by iron deficiency, induced in many cases by haemorrhagic manifestations (see Table 2). In practice the diagnosis often relies strongly on the final criterion, which is the absence of secondary causes, and on the persistence of the high platelet count.

Clinical manifestations

Vascular occlusive and haemorrhagic symptoms account for almost all the clinical manifestations of PT at presentation. However, the relative proportions of these symptoms vary widely in different series (Schafer, 1984; Murphy et al, 1986; Van de Pette et al, 1986b), depending presumably on patient selection. Patients without such manifestations at presentation are becoming commoner now that platelet counts are part of the routine blood count.

Clinical manifestations have not been formally stratified according to patient age in PT, but degenerative vascular changes are so clearly age-related that it would be quite surprising if occlusive and haemorrhagic vascular incidents were not commoner in the elderly patient with PT, both at presentation and later (Jamshidi et al, 1973). Moreover, the PVSG have already demonstrated in PPP that advanced age (> 70 years) was one of the factors which significantly contributed to the risk of thrombosis (Wasserman et al, 1981).

Numerous vascular occlusive symptoms have been described in PT. A specific microvascular syndrome presenting as erythromelalgia, purple mottling of the skin of the extremities or ischaemic changes in the digits leading to gangrene (but with normal peripheral pulses), is now well recognized (Singh and Wetherley-Mein, 1977; Walden et al, 1977). The histology (arteriolar inflammation, fibromuscular intimal proliferation with thrombotic occlusion) and probable pathogenesis as a result of platelet activation and aggregation in vivo have been elucidated (Preston et al, 1974; Michiels et al, 1984, 1985). There is no particular reason to suspect an increased incidence of this condition in the elderly, except in so far as incidental large vessel atheroma is very likely to exacerbate the problem. Microvascular thromboses or perhaps emboli (Barabas et al, 1973) have also been the suspected cause of the high incidence of neurological abnormalities in PT. Transient ischaemic attacks involving either anterior or posterior cerebral circulations, paraesthesiae, visual disturbances, including amaurosis fujax, headache, and (more rarely) epileptic fits, are the most common clinical manifestations (Preston et al, 1979; Jabaily et al, 1983) and, as discussed below, may respond dramatically to drugs which impair platelet function or reduce the count.

Occlusive vascular lesions involving the larger vessels, such as cerebrovascular accidents, mesenteric artery thrombosis and, less commonly, deep vein thrombosis and pulmonary embolism, are all described in PT but would anyway be commoner in the elderly. This also applies to myocardial infarction, though the latter has notably been described in much younger patients with PT, in the absence of other predisposing factors (Virmani et al, 1979; Douste-Blazy et al, 1984). Splenic atrophy has also been demonstrated (Marsh et al, 1966) and is probably an example of an unusual vascular occlusion occurring more commonly in PT.

The haemorrhagic symptoms of PT are particularly those associated with platelet disorders, such as bruising and mucosal bleeding (epistaxis, gastrointestinal, urological). Joint and deep tissue bleeding are unusual, except following surgery. Excessive bleeding after surgical intervention is now common knowledge (McClure et al, 1966). It is a particular hazard when the diagnosis of PT was not made before surgery. A high index of suspicion and attention to the preoperative platelet count seem mandatory.

Laboratory aspects of diagnosis

Far-reaching differences in prognosis and management make it essential to be able to distinguish between PT and reactive thrombocytosis. Sometimes diagnosis depends on unsatisfactory negative factors such as persistence of the high platelet count in the absence of conditions likely to precipitate reactive thrombocytosis. The lack of palpable splenomegaly or suggestive microvascular occlusive lesions puts the burden of diagnosis on the laboratory.

Bone marrow examination. The morphological features of bone marrow in PT are similar to those in PPP. The majority show hypercellularity involving mainly the granulocyte series and an increase in the number and mean volume of megakaryocytes, and the number of nuclear lobes (Harker and Finch, 1969; Branehög et al, 1975). Murphy et al (1986) have described a slight to moderate increase in reticulin in a quarter of cases of PT, but the situation in reactive thrombocytosis, especially the more chronic forms, is uncertain. Clearly the histological changes in PT are difficult to quantitate, and routine bone marrow examination is less helpful in diagnosis than one might have hoped. It is often difficult to obtain sufficient material for chromosome analysis, but no consistent abnormality has been found. By definition, the Ph′ chromosome is absent.

Platelet sizing. The observation of numerous large and abnormally shaped platelets on routine blood films has traditionally been associated with all the myeloproliferative disorders, including PT. Unfortunately this is not found in all cases. The parameters of platelet size – mean platelet volume (MPV) and platelet distribution width (PDW) – routinely made available by the newer electronic counters have been less helpful than expected. PDW seems the more useful parameter and values > 17.5 carry a small but significantly greater likelihood of PT (Small and Bettigole, 1981; Van der Lelie and Von dem Borne, 1986) as opposed to reactive thrombocytosis. Visual assessment by experienced observers is probably still at least as useful as PDW, but has the disadvantage of being subjective.

Platelet function tests. The finding of abnormalities of platelet function is consistent with the bleeding and thrombotic problems of PT – problems which are relatively absent in reactive thrombocytosis. Many studies have documented abnormalities of platelet function in many but not all patients with PT, but do not distinguish between symptomatic and asymptomatic patients or between those with bleeding or thrombotic problems (McClure et al, 1966; Adams et al, 1974; Walsh et al, 1977). Treatment of the PT has generally resulted in only slight or no reversal of the abnormal tests (Zucker and Mielke, 1972; Stathakis et al, 1974b). Many different tests have been used, such as platelet adhesion, aggregation, 5-hydroxytryptamine uptake and platelet factor 3 release. The most frequently found abnormality has been lack of aggregation in the presence of adrenaline. Aggregation abnormalities in response to collagen and ADP are less common (Schafer, 1984). Prolongation of the bleeding time has been found only rarely, but spontaneous platelet aggregation in vitro, or the presence of circulating platelet aggregates, has been noted in patients with PT (Wu, 1978).

   From a practical point of view, the finding of abnormal platelet function is suggestive of PT rather than reactive thrombocytosis, but negative tests are much less, if at all, helpful. This could be explained if the actual tests performed were inappropriate or the platelet abnormalities were themselves variable with time. It is also possible that some abnormalities are not intrinsic but result from platelet damage during reversible intravascular platelet aggregation (Boughton et al, 1977).

Further platelet tests. There are reports of more sophisticated tests which have demonstrated abnormalities in PT, such as lactate overproduction (Leoncini et al, 1985), reduction of platelet lifespan using indium-111 labelling (Bautista et al, 1984), reduction of nucleotides (Niskimura et al, 1979), demonstration of abnormal platelet reactivity with vessel wall subendothelium (Sacher et al, 1981), and increased metabolism of prothrombin and fibrinogen, suggesting a hypercoagulable state (Martinez et al, 1973). These tests are mainly of theoretical interest rather than being helpful diagnostically, but they do reinforce the belief that the individual platelets in PT are abnormal and that the thrombotic tendency is not just a mechanical effect of the high platelet concentration. No distinction has appeared between the platelet abnormalities of PT and those of PPP, but, since different clonal proliferations are likely to have different features, distinctions between PT and PPP, as well as between different patients with PT, might be expected.

In vitro colony studies. Abnormalities at haemopoietic stem cell level are widely studied by growing colonies in vitro. The growth of erythroid colonies 'spontaneously' in the absence of erythropoietin in the culture medium ('endogenous' erythropoietic colonies) in patients with PPP was soon followed by similar findings in other myeloproliferative disorders, including PT (Eridani et al, 1983b), but not in reactive thrombocytosis. It seems likely from these results that the stem cell abnormality in PT is back at the pluripotent stage and therefore retains ability to differentiate into the erythroid line. Megakaryocytic colony-forming units (CFU-M) are also being studied and there appears to be increased in vitro proliferative capacity in PT unassociated with any increase in a factor known as megakaryocyte colony-stimulating activity (Gewirtz et al, 1983). These data are consistent with the autonomous activity expected of neoplastic states, and contribute to the growing evidence that PT is one of this group.

Summary of laboratory diagnosis

The diagnosis of PT and its distinction from reactive thrombocytosis depends largely on the persistence of the high platelet count, and the presence of splenomegaly, typical occlusive vascular lesions and bleeding problems, or conditions known to be associated with reactive thrombocytosis. The naturally increased incidence of vascular disease in the elderly will make occlusive lesions a relatively less useful diagnostic feature. Estimation of platelet size, platelet function, and in vitro colony studies may all be helpful when positive (and are probably more useful than bone marrow examination and the NAP test). Ways of detecting lesser degrees of splenic enlargement not palpable clinically, by using isotope scanning, may also become helpful in diagnosis.

Management of primary thrombocythaemia in the elderly

Management of patients with PT depends on many factors but among the most important are age and whether the patient is symptomatic. There is considerable evidence that young patients are relatively asymptomatic (Hoagland and Silverstein, 1978; Kessler et al, 1982) and therefore a case for not treating them could be made, particularly as the risk of malignancy from some of the chemotherapeutic agents that might be used would be very worrying in the young.

The elderly *asymptomatic* patients may remain free of symptoms for many years. Although there are no published series of outcome in the untreated, survival was claimed to be less than 3 years (Case, 1984). As in PPP, however, the risk of vascular problems either due to or exacerbated by the abnormal platelets is generally felt to merit lowering of the platelet count, although not urgently. Several different chemotherapeutic regimes have been used, including melphalan, ^{32}P (Murphy et al, 1986), thiotepa and chlorambucil (Case, 1984), and hydroxyurea (Donovan et al, 1984; Murphy et al, 1986).

The use of busulphan in the treatment of PT was first described by Edgcumbe and Wetherley-Mein (1959). Van de Pette et al (1986b) reported the long-term use of low-dose busulphan in this condition. The majority of patients attained a 'controlled phase' where either none or only one short course of busulphan was required for a period of at least 1 year. The worrying incidence of leukaemia induction by ^{32}P and alkylating agents (Berk et al, 1981) has not been observed with low-dose busulphan but is a smaller anxiety in the elderly. It has been claimed (Brodsky, 1982) that the megakaryocyte characteristics approximate to the ideal cell for maximum busulphan effectiveness, and that for this reason busulphan may in theory be preferable to other alkylating agents or ^{32}P in the treatment of PT. There is no evidence at present that any one therapeutic regime is associated with longer survival than the others, and all are slow, taking weeks to lower the platelet count. Hydroxyurea appears to be effective, yet with a theoretically smaller mutagenic risk, and any unwanted myelosuppression can be rapidly reversed by stopping the drug. Overall, however, hydroxyurea is not at present particularly recommended in the elderly. It has the disadvantage of having to be taken continuously, and there is a worrying excessive 'rebound' increase in platelet count if the drug is inadvertently stopped.

There is no doubt that the *symptomatic* patient, whether young or elderly, needs to have the platelet count lowered, as the clinical benefit is well established. This can be done chronically by the chemotherapeutic agents discussed above, but in the acute ischaemic situation there are two possible additional courses of action. One is to use agents, particularly aspirin, that interfere with platelet function. There are many well-documented reports of rapid pain relief and reversal of both digital ischaemic changes and transient cerebral ischaemia by using aspirin given alone or in combination with dipyridamole (Preston et al, 1974, 1979). Various doses of aspirin have been shown to be effective, but 300–600 mg daily relieved pain more promptly than 40 mg daily (Preston, 1983) and could almost be used as a diagnostic test of ischaemic pain due to PT. An increased incidence of serious haemorrhage has been clearly documented when antiplatelet drugs are used in PPP with untreated thrombocythaemia (Tartaglia et al, 1986), and therefore they should probably be stopped once the platelet count has been lowered by myelosuppression. Aspirin and dipyridamole are at present only firmly recommended in the special situations of microvascular arterial thrombosis involving the cerebral circulation or the extremities, and should be accompanied by myelosuppressive therapy. They are contraindicated when there is a history of bleeding.

The other possible course of action in the acute situation is to lower the platelet count rapidly by plateletpheresis. This has dramatically improved not only patients with microvascular occlusive symptoms but also those with evidence of larger vascular occlusions, haemorrhage or both (Taft et al, 1977; Panlilio and Reiss, 1979). However, it has the disadvantages of an invasive procedure, and only a transient effect, and may have circulatory risks, particularly in the elderly. Its use in the uncontrolled patient requiring urgent surgery is a possibility that has not yet been documented. Acute bleeding, whether associated with surgery or not, has also been successfully treated by transfusion of fresh blood or platelet concentrates.

SUMMARY

The investigation of elderly patients presenting with raised PCV values has been described. Suitable clinical and laboratory investigation enables the separation of those with a raised red cell mass (RCM) into three groups: primary proliferative polycythaemia (PPP), secondary polycythaemia and idiopathic erythrocytosis. Those patients with a raised PCV but normal RCM either have apparent polycythaemia (normal plasma volume) or relative polycythaemia (low plasma volume).

PPP is a clonal disorder with a peak incidence in the elderly. It commonly presents with vascular occlusive symptoms/signs involving larger vessels, both arterial and venous. The microvasculature may also be involved, particularly when there is associated thrombocythaemia. Effective treatment is required to minimize the future vascular occlusive incidence and diminish the complication rate of surgery if it is ever required. Both the PCV and the platelet count, if elevated, should be adequately controlled. ^{32}P is probably the simplest treatment and is very effective, but venesection and intermittent low-dose busulphan is equally satisfactory in the co-operative patient with good peripheral veins.

Secondary polycythaemia may arise from a variety of causes, particularly from arterial hypoxaemia and renal lesions. Occasionally, more than one pathology is identified in the elderly patient. Lung disease is the most common cause of hypoxaemia. Venesection may be indicated in those patients with excessively raised PCV values.

The term idiopathic erythrocytosis should only be used for patients who have been adequately investigated. These patients most commonly present with ischaemic or vascular occlusive symptoms/signs. Relative polycythaemia may be caused by fluid loss, but generally the origin of the low plasma volume is not established. Apparent polycythaemia may represent a physiological variant or a stage before the development of a definitely raised RCM. The management of idiopathic erythrocytosis, and relative and apparent polycythaemia, should initially involve removal of known risk factors if present (e.g. hypertension) with the addition of venesection in selected patients.

Reactive thrombocytosis in the elderly is most commonly due to malignant disease or chronic infection. The high platelet count is usually asymptomatic, and antiplatelet therapy is rarely required. Primary thrombocythaemia (PT) is a clonal myeloproliferative disorder similar to PPP. The finding of splenomegaly, abnormal platelet morphology or function helps to separate PT from reactive thrombocytosis. PT most commonly presents with digital or transient cerebral ischaemia or haemorrhage. Antiplatelet drugs, notably aspirin, are valuable for those with ischaemic symptoms/signs. Myelosuppression with, for example, ^{32}P or low-dose intermittent busulphan, is effective in reducing the platelet count and usually leads to a prolonged remission.

The dominant presenting feature of both polycythaemia and thrombocythaemia is vascular occlusion, which is most commonly found in the elderly. It is therefore essential in dealing with these particular patients to perform and carefully scrutinize the results of a routine blood count.

Acknowledgements

The authors wish to thank Miss T. Passoni and Mrs P. Barnden for their assistance in documentation and secretarial work.

REFERENCES

Adams T, Schutz L & Goldberg L (1974) Platelet function abnormalities in the myeloproliferative disorders. *Scandinavian Journal of Haematology* **13:** 215–224.
Adamson JW & Fialkow PJ (1978) The pathogenesis of the myeloproliferative syndromes. *British Journal of Haematology* **38:** 299–303.
Apps MCP (1983) Sleep-disordered breathing. *British Journal of Hospital Medicine* **30:** 339–347.
Ashenhurst EM (1972) Chorea complicating polycythemia rubra vera. *Canadian Medical Association Journal* **107:** 434–437.
Barabas AP, Offen DN & Meinhard EA (1973) The arterial complications of polycythaemia vera. *British Journal of Surgery* **60:** 183–187.
Bateman S, Lewis SM, Nicholas A & Zaafran A (1978) Splenic red cell pooling: a diagnostic feature in polycythaemia. *British Journal of Haematology* **40:** 389–396.
Bautista A, Buckler P, Towler H, Dawson A & Bennett B (1984) Measurement of platelet lifespan in normal subjects and patients with myeloproliferative disease with indium oxine labelled platelets. *British Journal of Haematology* **58:** 679–687.
Begin R, Renzetti AD, Bigler AH & Watanabe S (1975) Flow and age dependence of airway closure and dynamic compliance. *Journal of Applied Physiology* **38:** 199–207.
Berk PD, Goldberg J, Silverstein M et al (1981) Increased incidence of acute leukemia in polycythemia vera associated with chlorambucil therapy. *New England Journal of Medicine* **304:** 441–447.
Berk PD, Goldberg JD, Donovan PB et al (1986) Therapeutic recommendations in polycythemia vera based on Polycythemia Vera Study Group protocols. *Seminars in Hematology* **23:** 132–143.

Berlin NI (1975) Diagnosis and classification of polycythemia. *Seminars in Hematology* 12: 339–351.

Boughton BJ, Corbett WEN & Ginsburg AD (1977) Myeloproliferative disorders: a paradox of in vivo and in vitro platelet function. *Journal of Clinical Pathology* 30: 228–234.

Boxer M, Braun J & Ellman L (1978) Thromboembolic risk of post-splenectomy thrombocytosis. *Archives of Surgery* 113: 808–809.

Branehög I, Ridell B, Swolin B & Weinfeld A (1975) Megakaryocytic quantifications in relation to thrombo kinetics in primary thrombocythaemia and allied diseases. *Scandinavian Journal of Haematology* 15: 321–332.

Brodsky I (1982) Busulphan treatment of polycythaemia vera. *British Journal of Haematology* 52 (annotation): 1–6.

Brown MM, Wade JPH & Marshall J (1985) Fundamental importance of arterial oxygen content in the regulation of cerebral blood flow in man. *Brain* 108: 81–93.

Brown SM, Gilbert HS, Krauss S & Wasserman LR (1971) Spurious (relative) polycythemia. A nonexistent disease. *American Journal of Medicine* 50: 200–207.

Burge PS, Johnson WS & Prankerd TAJ (1975) Morbidity and mortality in pseudopolycythaemia. *Lancet* i: 1266–1269.

Burris MB & Arrowsmith WK (1953) Vascular complications of polycythemia vera. *Surgical Clinics of North America* 33: 1023–1028.

Burrows B, Niden AD, Barclay WR & Kajik JE (1965) Chronic obstructive lung disease. Clinical and physiological findings in 175 patients and their relationship to age and sex. *American Review of Respiratory Disease* 91: 521–540.

Calabresi P & Meyer OO (1959) Polycythemia vera. Clinical and laboratory investigations. *Annals of Internal Medicine* 50: 1182–1216.

Calverley PMA, Leggett RJ, McElderry L & Flenley DC (1982) Cigarette smoking and secondary polycythemia in hypoxic cor pulmonale. *American Review of Respiratory Disease* 125: 507–510.

Case DC (1984) Therapy of essential thrombocythemia with thiotepa and chlorambucil. *Blood* 63: 51–54.

Chanarin I (1969) *The Megaloblastic Anaemias*, 1st edn. Oxford and Edinburgh: Blackwell Scientific Publications.

Chanarin I & Szur L (1975) Relief of intractable pruritus in polycythaemia rubra vera with cholestyramine. *British Journal of Haematology* 29: 669–670.

Charache S, Achuff S, Winslow R, Adamson J & Chervenick P (1978) Variability of the homeostatic response to altered p_{50}. *Blood* 52: 1156–1162.

Chievitz E & Thiede T (1962) Complications and causes of death in polycythaemia. *Acta Medica Scandinavica* 172: 513–523.

Clark C & Cotton LT (1968) Blood flow in deep veins of leg. Recording technique and evaluation of methods to increase flow during operation. *British Journal of Surgery* 55: 211–214.

Collier CR (1976) Oxygen affinity of human blood in presence of carbon monoxide. *Journal of Applied Physiology* 40: 487–490.

Constantinidis K (1979) Venesection fatalities in polycythaemia secondary to lung disease. *The Practitioner* 222: 89–91.

Cotes PM, Doré CJ, Liu Yin JA et al (1986) Determination of serum immunoreactive erythropoietin in the investigation of erythrocytosis. *New England Journal of Medicine* 315: 283–287.

Dawson AA & Ogston D (1970) The influence of the platelet count on the incidence of thrombotic and haemorrhagic complications in polycythaemia vera. *Postgraduate Medical Journal* 46: 76–78.

Delamore IW (1961) Vitamin B_{12} metabolism in polycythaemia vera. *Clinical Science* 20: 177–184.

Donovan PB, Kaplan ME, Goldberg JD et al (1984) Treatment of polycythemia vera with hydroxyurea. *American Journal of Hematology* 17: 329–334.

Douste-Blazy P, Taudou M, Delay M et al (1984) Essential thrombocythaemia and recurrent myocardial infarction. *Lancet* ii: 992.

Dustan HP, Tarazi RC & Bravo EL (1972) Dependence of arterial pressure on intravascular volume in treated hypertensive patients. *New England Journal of Medicine* 286: 861–866.

Edgcumbe JOP & Wetherley-Mein G (1959) Haemorrhagic thrombocythaemia treated with

Mylcran (busulphan). *Proceedings of the VII Congress of the European Society of Haematology*, London, Part II, p 324.

Edwards EA & Cooley MH (1970) Peripheral vascular symptoms as the initial manifestation of polycythemia vera. *Journal of the American Medical Association* **214:** 1463–1467.

Eisen ME & Hammond EC (1956) The effect of smoking on packed cell volume, red blood cell counts and platelet counts. *Canadian Medical Association Journal* **75:** 520–523.

Elwood PC (1971) Epidemiological aspects of iron deficiency in the elderly. *Gerontologia Clinica* **13:** 2–11.

Emery AC, Whitcomb WH & Frohlich ED (1974) 'Stress' polycythemia and hypertension. *Journal of the American Medical Association* **229:** 159–162.

England JM, Chanarin I, Petty J & Szur L (1968) Pernicious anaemia and polycythaemia vera. *British Journal of Haematology* **15:** 473–474.

Eridani S, Pearson TC, Sawyer B, Batten E & Wetherley-Mein G (1983a) Erythroid colony formation in primary proliferative polycythaemia, idiopathic erythrocytosis and secondary polycythaemia. *Clinical and Laboratory Haematology* **5:** 121–129.

Eridani S, Batten E & Sawyer B (1983b) Erythroid colony formation in primary thrombocythaemia: evidence of hypersensitivity to erythropoietin. *British Journal of Haematology* **55:** 157–161.

Fialkow P, Faquet G, Jacobson R, Vaidya K & Murphy S (1981) Evidence that essential thrombocythemia is a clonal disorder with origin in a multipotent stem cell. *Blood* **58:** 916–919.

Fjellner B & Hagermark O (1979) Pruritus in polycythaemia vera: treatment with aspirin and possibility of platelet involvement. *Acta Dermato-Venereologica (Stockholm)* **59:** 505–512.

Flenley DC (1980) Hypoxaemia during sleep. *Thorax* **35:** 81–84.

Flenley DC (1985) Disordered breathing during sleep: discussion paper. *Journal of the Royal Society of Medicine* **78:** 1031–1033.

Franzén S, Johansson B & Kaigas M (1966) Primary polycythaemia associated with multiple myeloma. *Acta Medica Scandinavica* **179** (supplement 445): 336–343.

Freeman E (1978) The respiratory system. In Brocklehurst JC (ed.) *Textbook of Geriatric Medicine and Gerontology*, 2nd edn, pp 433–451. Edinburgh, London and New York: Churchill Livingstone.

Gaetani G, Ferraris A, Galiano S, et al (1982) Primary thrombocythemia: clonal origin of platelets, erythrocytes and granulocytes in a Gd^B/Gd Mediterranean subject. *Blood* **59:** 76–79.

Gardner FH, Nathan DG, Piomelli S & Cummins JF (1968) The erythrocythaemic effects of androgens. *British Journal of Haematology* **14:** 611–615.

Geller S & Shapiro E (1982) Acute leukemia as a natural sequel to primary thrombocythemia. *American Journal of Clinical Pathology* **77:** 353–356.

Gewirtz AM, Bruno E, Elwell J & Hoffman R (1983) In vitro studies of megakaryocytopoiesis in thrombocytotic disorders of man. *Blood* **61:** 384–389.

Ghio R, Haupt E, Ratti M & Boccaccio P (1981) Erythrocytosis associated with a dermoid cyst of the ovary and erythropoietic activity of the tumour fluid. *Scandinavian Journal of Haematology* **27:** 70–74.

Gilbert HS, Warner RRP & Wasserman LR (1966) A study of histamine in myeloproliferative disease. *Blood* **28:** 795–806.

Gray AG, Boughton BJ, Burt DS & Struthers GR (1982) Basophils, histamine and gastric acid secretion in chronic myeloproliferative disorders. *British Journal of Haematology* **51:** 117–123.

Gunz FW (1960) Hemorrhagic thrombocythemia: a critical review. *Blood* **15:** 706–723.

Guthrie DL & Pearson TC (1982) PCV measurement in the management of polycythaemic patients. *Clinical and Laboratory Haematology* **4:** 257–265.

Harker LA & Finch CA (1969) Thrombokinetics in man. *Journal of Clinical Investigation* **48:** 963–974.

Harrison BDW & Stokes TC (1982) Secondary polycythaemia: its causes, effects and treatment. *British Journal of Diseases of the Chest* **76:** 313–340.

Hawkins WW, Speck E & Leonard VG (1954) Variation of the hemoglobin level with age and sex. *Blood* **9:** 999–1007.

Hirsh J & Dacie JV (1966) Persistent post-splenectomy thrombocytosis and thromboembolism: a consequence of continuing anaemia. *British Journal of Haematology* **12:** 44–53.

Hoagland HC & Silverstein MN (1978) Primary polycythemia in the young patient. *Mayo Clinic Proceedings* **53:** 578–580.

Hoffman R, Estren S, Kopel, S, Marks SM & McCaffney RP (1978) Lymphoblastic-like leukemic transformation of polycythemia vera. *Annals of Internal Medicine* **89:** 71.

Hoppin EC, Depner T, Yamuchi H & Hopper J (1976) Erythrocytosis associated with diffuse parenchymal lesions of the kidney. *British Journal of Haematology* **32:** 557–563.

Humphrey PRD, du Boulay GH, Marshall J et al (1979) Cerebral blood-flow and viscosity in relative polycythaemia. *Lancet* **ii:** 873–877.

Humphrey PRD, Michael J & Pearson TC (1980) Management of relative polycythaemia: studies of cerebral blood flow and viscosity. *British Journal of Haematology* **46:** 427–433.

Hurley PJ (1975) Red cell and plasma volumes in normal adults. *Journal of Nuclear Medicine* **16:** 46–52.

Hyde RD & Jones NF (1962) Red-cell volume and total body water. *British Journal of Haematology* **8:** 283–289.

International Committee for Standardization in Haematology (1980) Recommended method for measurement of red-cell and plasma volume. *Journal of Nuclear Medicine* **21:** 793–800.

Jabaily J, Iland H, Lazzlo J et al (1983) Neurologic manifestations of essential thrombocythemia. *Annals of Internal Medicine* **99:** 513–518.

Jacksen DV & Spurr CL (1978) Smoker's polycythemia. *New England Journal of Medicine* **298:** 972–973.

Jacobson H, Theilade K & Videbaek A (1982) Two additional cases of coexisting polycythaemia vera and chronic lymphocytic leukaemia. *Scandinavian Journal of Haematology* **29:** 405–410.

Jamshidi K, Ansari A, Windschite H & Swaim W (1973) Primary thrombocythaemia. *Geriatrics* **28:** 121–133.

Kales A, Cadieux RJ, Shaw LC et al (1984) Sleep apnoea in a hypertensive population. *Lancet* **ii:** 1005–1008.

Kaplan ME, Mack K, Goldberg JD et al (1986) Long-term management of polycythemia vera with hydroxyurea: a progress report. *Seminars in Hematology* **23:** 167–171.

Kessler CM, Klein HG & Havlik RJ (1982) Uncontrolled thrombocytosis in chronic myeloproliferative disorders. *British Journal of Haematology* **50:** 157–167.

Kiraly JF, Feldmann JE & Wheby MS (1976) Hazards of phlebotomy in polycythemic patients with cardiovascular disease. *Journal of the American Medical Association* **236:** 2080–2081.

Kligman AM, Greaves MW & Steinman H (1986) Water-induced itching without cutaneous signs. *Archives of Dermatology* **122:** 183–186.

Kolk-Vegter AJ, Bosch E & van Leeuwen AM (1971) Influence of serum hepatitis on haemoglobin levels in patients on regular haemodialysis. *Lancet* **i:** 526–528.

Kremer M, Lambert CD & Lawson N (1972) Progressive neurological deficits in primary polycythaemia. *British Medical Journal* **3:** 216–218.

Laucks SP & McLachlan MSF (1981) Aging and simple cysts of the kidney. *British Journal of Radiology* **54:** 12–14.

Lawrence JH & Berlin NI (1952) Relative polycythemia – the polycythemia of stress. *Yale Journal of Biology and Medicine* **24:** 498–505.

Leoncini G, Maresca M, Armani U & Piana A (1985) Lactate overproduction in platelets of subjects affected with myeloproliferative disorders. *Scandinavian Journal of Haematology* **35:** 229–232.

Marsh GW, Lewis SM & Szur L (1966) The use of ^{51}Cr-labelled heat-damaged red cells to study splenic function. II: Splenic atrophy in thrombocythaemia. *British Journal of Haematology* **12:** 167–171.

Martinez J, Shapiro S & Holburn R (1973) Metabolism of human prothrombin and fibrinogen in patients with thrombocytosis secondary to myeloproliferative states. *Blood* **42:** 35–46.

Master AM, Lasser RP & Jaffe HL (1958) Blood pressure in white people over 65 years of age. *Annals of Internal Medicine* **48:** 284–299.

McClure P, Ingram GIC, Stacey R, Glass U & Matchett M (1966) Platelet function tests in thrombocythaemia and thrombocytosis. *British Journal of Haematology* **12:** 478–498.

McFadzean AJS, Todd D & Tso SC (1967) Erythrocytosis associated with hepatocellular carcinoma. *Blood* **29:** 808–811.

McKennell AC & Thomas RK (1967) Adults' and adolescents' smoking habits and attitudes. A report on a survey carried out for the Ministry of Health. SS353/B. London: HMSO.

Medical Research Council Working Party (1981) Long term domiciliary oxygen therapy in chronic cor pulmonale complicating chronic bronchitis and emphysema. *Lancet* **i:** 681–686.

Messinezy M, Pearson TC, Prochazka A & Wetherley-Mein G (1985) Treatment of primary proliferative polycythaemia by venesection and low dose busulphan: retrospective study from one centre. *British Journal of Haematology* **61:** 657–666.

Michiels JJ, ten Kate FWJ, Vuzerski VD & Abels J (1984) Histopathology of erythromelalgia in thrombocythaemia. *Histopathology* **8:** 669–678.

Michiels JJ, Abels J, Steketee J, Van Vliet H & Vuzevski V (1985) Erythromelalgia caused by platelet-mediated arteriolar inflammation and thrombosis in thrombocythemia. *Annals of Internal Medicine* **102:** 466–471.

Millikan CH, Siekert RG & Whisnant JP (1960) Intermittent carotid and verterbral basilar insufficiency associated with polycythemia. *Neurology* **10:** 188–195.

Modan B & Modan M (1968) Benign erythrocytosis. *British Journal of Haematology* **14:** 375–381.

Moore-Gillon JC & Pearson TC (1986) Smoking, drinking and polycythaemia. *British Medical Journal* **292:** 1617–1618.

Moore-Gillon JC, Treacher DF, Gaminara EJ, Pearson TC & Cameron IC (1986) Intermittent hypoxia in patients with unexplained polycythaemia. *British Medical Journal* **293:** 588–590.

Morris JF, Koski A & Johnson LC (1971) Spirometric standards for healthy non-smoking adults. *American Review of Respiratory Disease* **103:** 57–67.

Murphy S (1983) Thrombocytosis and thrombocythaemia. *Clinics in Haematology* **12:** 89–106.

Murphy GP, Kenny GM & Mirand EA (1970) Erythropoietin levels in patients with renal tumours or cysts. *Cancer* **26:** 191–194.

Murphy S, Iland H, Rosenthal D & Laszlo J (1986) Essential thrombocythemia: an interim report from the Polycythemia Vera Study Group. *Seminars in Hematology* **23:** 177–182.

Nadler SB, Hidalgo JU & Bloch T (1962) Prediction of blood volume in normal human adults. *Surgery* **51:** 224–232.

Najean Y, Triebel F & Dresch C (1981) Pure erythrocytosis: reappraisal of a study of 51 cases. *American Journal of Hematology* **10:** 129–136.

Najean Y, Arrago JP, Rain JD & Dresch C (1984) The 'spent' phase of polycythaemia vera: hypersplenism in the absence of myelofibrosis. *British Journal of Haematology* **56:** 163–170.

Niskimura J, Okamoto S & Ibayashi H (1979) Abnormalities of platelet adenine nucleotides in patients with myeloproliferative disorders. *Thrombosis and Haemostasis* **41:** 787–795.

Nuki G (1983) Disorders of purine metabolism. In Weatherall DJ, Ledingham JGG & Warrell DA (eds) *Oxford Textbook of Medicine*, pp 9.70–9.80. Oxford: Oxford University Press.

Panlilio A & Reiss R (1979) Therapeutic plateletpheresis in thrombocythemia. *Transfusion* **19:** 147–152.

Pearson TC (1977) Clinical and laboratory studies in the polycythaemias. MD Thesis, University of London.

Pearson TC & Guthrie DL (1984) The interpretation of measured red cell mass and plasma volume in patients with elevated PCV values. *Clinical and Laboratory Haematology* **6:** 207–217.

Pearson TC & Wetherley-Mein G (1978) Vascular occlusive episodes and venous haematocrit in primary proliferative polycythaemia. *Lancet* **ii:** 1219–1222.

Pearson TC & Wetherley-Mein G (1979) The course and complications of idiopathic erythrocytosis. *Journal of Clinical and Laboratory Haematology* **1:** 189–196.

Pearson TC, Glass UH & Wetherley-Mein G (1978) Interpretation of measured red cell mass in the diagnosis of polycythaemia. *Scandinavian Journal of Haematology* **21:** 153–162.

Pearson TC, Botterill CA, Glass UH & Wetherley-Mein G (1984) Interpretation of measured red cell mass and plasma volume in males with elevated venous PCV values. *Scandinavian Journal of Haematology* **33:** 68–74.

Pengelly CDR (1966) Reduction of haematocrit and red-blood-cell volume in patients with polycythaemia secondary to hypoxic lung disease by dapsone and pyrimethamine. *Lancet* **ii:** 1381–1386.

Pettit JE, Lewis SM & Nicholas AW (1979) Transitional myeloproliferative disorder. *British Journal of Haematology* **43:** 167–184.

Petty TL & Finigan MM (1968) Clinical evaluation of prolonged ambulatory oxygen therapy in chronic airway obstruction. *American Journal of Medicine* **45:** 242–252.

Preston FE (1983) Aspirin, prostaglandins and peripheral gangrene. *American Journal of Medicine* **74** (supplement): 55–60.

Preston FE & Greaves M (1985) Platelet suppressive therapy in clinical medicine. *British Journal of Haematology* **60** (annotation): 589–597.

Preston FE, Emmanuel I, Winfield D & Malia R (1974) Essential thrombocythaemia and peripheral gangrene. *British Medical Journal* **3:** 548–552.

Preston FE, Martin J, Stewart R & Davies-Jones G (1979) Thrombocytosis, circulating platelet aggregates and neurological dysfunction. *British Medical Journal* **2:** 1561–1563.

Prochazka AV & Markowe HLJ (1986) The epidemiology of polycythaemia vera in England and Wales 1968–1982. *British Journal of Cancer* **53:** 59–64.

Rachmilewitz B, Manny N & Rachmilewitz M (1977) The transcobalamins in polycythaemia vera. *Scandinavian Journal of Haematology* **19:** 453–462.

Rector WG, Fortuin NJ & Conley CL (1982) Non-hematological effects of chronic iron deficiency. *Medicine* **61:** 382–389.

Sacher R, Jacobson R & McGill M (1981) Functional and morphological studies of platelet reactivity with vessel wall subendothelium in chronic myeloproliferative disease. *British Journal of Haematology* **49:** 43–52.

Sage RE (1969) Polycythemia rubra vera with pernicious anemia. Some observations on vitamin B_{12} metabolism. *Blood* **34:** 14–24.

Salem HH, Van der Weyden MB, Young IF & Wiley JS (1982) Pruritus and severe iron deficiency in polycythaemia vera. *British Medical Journal* **285:** 91–92.

Schafer AI (1984) Bleeding and thrombosis in the myeloproliferative disorders. *Blood* **64:** 1–12.

Schilling RF (1980) Platelet millionaires. *Lancet* **ii** (letter): 372–373.

Schmid-Schönbein H (1981) Interaction of vasomotion and blood rheology in haemodynamics. In Lowe GDO, Barbenel JD & Forbes CD (eds) *Clinical Aspects of Blood Viscosity and Cell Deformability*, pp 49–66. Berlin, Heidelberg, New York: Springer.

Scott GL & Horton RJ (1979) Pruritus, cimetidine and polycythemia. *New England Journal of Medicine* **300:** 434.

Shah PC, Patel AR, Dimaria F, Raba J & Vohra RM (1979) Polycythaemia in lung cancer. *Clinical and Laboratory Haematology* **1:** 329–331.

Sheridan DJ, Temperley IJ & Gatenby PBB (1974) Blood indices, serum folate and vitamin B_{12} levels in the elderly. *Journal of the Irish Colleges of Physicians and Surgeons* **4:** 39–45.

Singh AK & Wetherley-Mein G (1977) Microvascular occlusive lesions in primary thrombocythaemia. *British Journal of Haematology* **36:** 553–564.

Small BM & Bettigole RE (1981) Diagnosis of myeloproliferative disease by analysis of the platelet volume distribution. *American Journal of Clinical Pathology* **76:** 685–691.

Smith JR & Landaw SA (1978) Smokers' polycythemia. *New England Journal of Medicine* **298:** 6–10.

Sorbini CA, Grassi V, Solinas E & Muiesan G (1968) Arterial oxygen tension in relation to age in healthy subjects. *Respiration* **25:** 3–10.

Stathakis NE, Papayannis AG, Arapakis G & Gardikas C (1974a) Haemostatic defects in polycythaemia vera. *Blüt* **29:** 77–86.

Stathakis NE, Papayannis AG, Arapakis G & Gardikas C (1974b) Platelet dysfunction in essential thrombocythaemia. *Annals of Clinical Research* **6:** 198–202.

Steinman HK, Kobza-Black A, Lotti TM et al (1987) Polycythaemia rubra vera and water-induced pruritus: blood histamine levels and cutaneous fibrinolytic activity before and after water challenge. *British Journal of Dermatology* **116:** 329–333.

Stephens AD (1977) Polycythaemia and high affinity haemoglobins. *British Journal of Haematology* **36** (annotation): 153–159.

Stradling JR & Lane DJ (1981) Development of secondary polycythaemia in chronic airways obstruction. *Thorax* **36:** 321–325.

Taft E, Babcock R, Scharfman W & Tartaglia A (1977) Plateletpheresis in the management of thrombocytosis. *Blood* **50:** 927–933.

Tarazi RC, Dustan HP & Frohlich ED (1970) Long-term thiazide therapy in essential hypertension. *Circulation* **61:** 709–717.

Tartaglia AP, Goldberg JD, Berk PD & Wasserman LR (1986) Adverse effects of antiaggregating platelet therapy in the treatment of polycythemia vera. *Seminars in Hematology* **23:** 172–176.

Thomas DJ, du Boulay GH, Marshall J et al (1977) Cerebral blood flow in polycythaemia. *Lancet* **ii:** 161–163.

Thorling EB (1972) Paraneoplastic erythrocytosis and inappropriate erythropoietin production. *Scandinavian Journal of Haematology* (supplement 17).

Tohgi H, Yamanouchi H, Murakami M & Kameyama M (1978) Importance of the hematocrit as a risk factor in cerebral infarction. *Stroke* **9:** 369–374.

Van der Lelie J & Von dem Borne A (1986) Platelet volume analysis for differential diagnosis of thrombocytosis. *Journal of Clinical Pathology* **39:** 129–133.

Van de Pette JEW, Guthrie DL, Pearson TC et al (1986a) Whole blood viscosity in polycythaemia: the effect of iron deficiency at a range of haemoglobin and packed cell volumes. *British Journal of Haematology* **63:** 369–375.

Van de Pette JEW, Prochazka AV & Pearson TC (1986b) Primary thrombocythaemia treated with busulphan. *British Journal of Haematology* **62:** 229–237.

Virmani R, Popovsky MA & Roberts WC (1979) Thrombocytosis, coronary thrombosis and acute myocardial infarction. *American Journal of Medicine* **67:** 498–506.

Wade JPH (1983) Transport of oxygen to the brain in patients with elevated haematocrit values before and after venesection. *Brain* **106:** 513–523.

Wade JPH, du Boulay GH, Marshall J et al (1980) Cerebral blood flow, haematocrit and viscosity in subjects with a high oxygen affinity haemoglobin variant. *Acta Neurologica Scandinavica* **61:** 210–215.

Walden R, Adar R & Mozes M (1977) Gangrene of toes with normal peripheral pulses. *Annals of Surgery* **185:** 269–272.

Waldmann TA & Bradley JE (1961) Polycythemia secondary to a pheochromocytoma with production of an erythropoiesis stimulating factor. *Proceedings of the Society for Experimental Biology and Medicine* **108:** 425–427.

Walsh PN, Murphy S & Barry WE (1977) The role of platelets in the pathogenesis of thrombosis and haemorrhage in patients with thrombocytosis. *Thrombosis and Haemostasis* **38:** 1085–1096.

Wanless IR, Godwin TA, Allen F & Feder A (1980) Nodular regenerative hyperplasia of the liver in hematologic disorders: a possible response to obliterative portal venopathy. A morphometric study of nine cases with an hypothesis on the pathogenesis. *Medicine* **59:** 367–379.

Ward HP, Bigelow DB & Petty TL (1968) Postural hypoxemia and erythrocytosis. *American Journal of Medicine* **45:** 880–888.

Wasserman LR (1954) Polycythemia vera – its course and treatment: relation to myeloid metaplasia and leukemia. *Bulletin of the New York Academy of Medicine* **30:** 343–375.

Wasserman LR (1971) The management of polycythaemia vera. *British Journal of Haematology* **21** (annotation): 371–376.

Wasserman LR & Gilbert HS (1963) Surgery in polycythemia. *New England Journal of Medicine* **269:** 1226–1230.

Wasserman LR, Goldberg JD, Balcerzak SP et al (1981) Influence of therapy on causes of death in polycythemia vera. *Clinical Research* **29:** 573A.

Weinreb NJ & Shih C-F (1975) Spurious polycythemia. *Seminars in Hematology* **12:** 397–407.

Weisse AB, Moschos CB, Frank MJ et al (1975) Hemodynamic effects of staged hematocrit reduction in patients with stable cor pulmonale and severely elevated hematocrit levels. *American Journal of Medicine* **58:** 92–98.

Wetherley-Mein G, Pearson TC, Burney PGJ & Morris RW (1987) The Royal College of Physicians Research Unit, Polycythaemia Study. I. Objective, background and design. *Journal of the Royal College of Physicians of London* **21:** 7–16.

Willison JR, du Boulay GH, Paul EA et al (1980) Effect of high haematocrit on alertness. *Lancet* **i:** 846–848.

Wolfe JD, Tashkin DP, Holly FE, Brachman MB & Genovesi MG (1977) Hypoxemia of cirrhosis: detection of abnormal small pulmonary vascular channels by a quantitative radionuclide method. *American Journal of Medicine* **63:** 746–754.

Wrigley PFM, Malpas JS, Turnbull AL, Jenkins V & McArt A (1971) Secondary polycythaemia due to a uterine fibromyoma producing erythropoietin. *British Journal of Haematology* **21:** 551–555.

Wu K (1978) Platelet hyperaggregability and thrombosis in patients with thrombocythemia. *Annals of Internal Medicine* **88:** 7–11.

Zucker S & Mielke CH (1972) Classification of thrombocytosis based on platelet function tests: correlation with haemorrhagic and thrombotic complications. *Journal of Laboratory and Clinical Medicine* **80:** 385–394.

5

Myelodysplastic syndromes

D. G. OSCIER

Over the past decade, haematologists have become increasingly aware of patients, usually elderly, whose blood counts show anaemia, neutropenia, monocytosis and thrombocytopenia. These abnormalities may occur alone or more often in combination and usually there is no systemic illness to account for them. The bone marrow is often hypercellular and a modest increase in blast cells may be noted. The most striking features which unite these cases are characteristic morphological abnormalities in the blood and marrow of all three cell lineages.

The patients may present with symptoms of marrow failure (anaemia, infection or bleeding) or the blood count may have been performed for an incidental reason. The natural history of this condition is variable but there is a high morbidity and mortality from the complications associated with pancytopenia, and approximately 30% will undergo transformation into acute leukaemia.

A minority of younger patients have a history of prior exposure to a known mutagen such as an alkylating agent or radiotherapy, but in the majority the aetiology remains unknown. This constellation of clinical and laboratory findings is now best encompassed by the term myelodysplastic syndrome (MDS).

HISTORY

Patients who would now be recognized as having MDS have been described since the turn of the century, but evaluation of early reports is hindered by the fact that different haematologists have emphasized particular aspects of the condition and a confusing nomenclature has arisen, with some terms being synonymous and others reflecting different phases in the natural history of MDS.

In the 1930s there was much interest in patients with anaemias which were refractory to haematinics such as iron and the recently discovered vitamin B_{12} and folic acid. Rhoads and Halsey Barker (1938) described 100 cases of refractory anaemia: some were associated with and secondary to other diseases, while others were thought to be primary haematological disorders. The anaemia was often associated with leucopenia and thrombocytopenia.

Baillière's Clinical Haematology—Vol. 1, No. 2, June 1987

Hamilton Paterson (1949) described three patients who presented with refractory anaemia and subsequently developed acute myeloid leukaemia. Seven years later Bjorkman (1956) delineated a subgroup of refractory anaemia characterized by the presence of ring sideroblasts in the marrow, and one of his four cases evolved into acute myeloid leukaemia (AML).

In the 1950s and early 60s there was an increasing awareness of elderly patients with a modest increase in blast cells in the marrow in association with a peripheral cytopenia, whose illness pursued a chronic course before terminating in acute leukaemia. This condition was variously described as preleukaemic acute human leukaemia (Block et al, 1953), low percentage leukaemia (Dameshek and Gunz, 1958) and smouldering acute leukaemia (Rheingold et al, 1963).

Saarni and Linman (1973) described 132 cases of acute nonlymphocytic leukaemia. In 41 of these a preleukaemic phase was identified and was characterized by pancytopenia, a normo- or hypercellular marrow, and morphological abnormalities in all cell lines. The blast percentage in the marrow was normal or minimally increased, and since by definition all these cases subsequently evolved into acute leukaemia, the condition was called the preleukaemic syndrome. Concurrently Dreyfus et al (1970) and Dreyfus (1976) described patients with 'refractory anaemia with an excess of myeloblasts' with similar morphological abnormalities to those noted by Linman. The median survival was 20 months, and death was more often due to complications of pancytopenia than to leukaemic transformation.

The morphological classification of the acute leukaemias by the French–American–British (FAB) group (Bennett et al, 1976) included patients with an increased percentage of blasts in the marrow but to a lesser degree than that normally found in acute myeloid leukaemia, and who had a more protracted clinical course. Two categories were described, namely refractory anaemia with excess of blasts and chronic myelomonocytic leukaemia. Further study of a larger series of such patients led to the publication of the FAB criteria for the morphological criteria for MDS in 1982. Five groups were defined:

1. refractory anaemia (RA);
2. refractory anaemia with ring sideroblasts (RAS);
3. refractory anaemia with excess of blasts (RAEB);
4. refractory anaemia with excess of blasts in transformation (RAEBt);
5. chronic myelomonocytic leukaemia (CMML).

These were based on the presence of a peripheral blood monocytosis and the percentage of ring sideroblasts and blasts in the marrow. The FAB classification is considered in more detail later.

EPIDEMIOLOGY

Very little has been written about the incidence and prevalence of MDS. The main reason for this is that most of the large series of MDS patients have come from referral centres. Additional factors include the difficulty in diagnosis of some forms of MDS, especially RA, and a natural reluctance to perform a

Table 1. Number of cases of RA, RAS, CMML and RAEB for each 5-year period from age 20 upwards. Reproduced by courtesy of Dr RA Cartwright.

Age group	RAEB M	RAEB F	CMML M	CMML F	RAS M	RAS F	Total M	Total F	RA M	RA F
20–24	—	—	—	—	—	—	—	—	—	—
25–29	1	—	—	—	—	—	1	—	1	—
30–34	1	1	—	—	—	—	1	1	1	2
35–39	—	—	—	—	—	—	—	—	—	1
40–44	3	—	—	—	—	—	3	—	4	1
45–49	1	1	—	—	—	—	1	1	—	7
50–54	3	—	—	2	3	2	6	4	1	5
55–59	5	4	1	3	5	3	11	10	8	4
60–64	12	9	6	3	7	3	25	15	13	11
65–69	10	5	12	7	5	11	27	23	17	19
70–74	24	14	17	12	14	12	57	38	30	20
75–79	24	19	19	15	19	18	62	55	38	37
80–84	22	17	15	18	14	18	52	54	31	28
85–89	8	8	9	11	13	10	31	29	10	24
90–94	2	3	2	6	—	5	4	14	2	2
95+	—	—	1	—	—	1	1	1	1	—
NK	2	—	2	2	—	3	4	5	—	3
	118	81	84	79	80	86	286	250	157	164
	199		163		166		536		321	

bone marrow aspirate in an elderly person whose peripheral blood findings may be suggestive but not diagnostic of MDS.

The Leukaemia Research Fund Centre for Clinical Epidemiology at the University of Leeds has been collecting data from haematologists and histopathologists on the incidence of haematological malignancies in 26 counties in England, Scotland and Wales. The population covered in the study is 16 million people, which is approximately a third of the total population of Great Britain.

Table 1 gives the total number of male and female cases of MDS collected in 1984 and 1985 for each 5 year period from the age of 20 upwards, while Table 2 shows the age-specific rates per 100 000 people. It can be seen that in people over the age of 65 the rate rises steeply with increasing age and the disease is commoner in men than in women.

The data for RA have been analysed separately from the other FAB groups of MDS, since a marked regional variation was observed which exactly mirrored the particular interest of certain haematologists in MDS.

Similar data on acute myeloid leukaemia showed a total of 474 cases collected in 1984 alone with a rate per 100 000 of 3.0 in men and 2.7 in women. A similar trend of increasing incidence with age was noted in AML as in MDS.

Our own data on the incidence of MDS in Bournemouth, with a catchment population of 200 000, is given in Table 3. All blood samples from this population are analysed in one laboratory and no referred patients are

Table 2. Age-specific rate of RA, RAS, CMML and RAEB for each 5-year period from age 20 upwards. Reproduced by courtesy of Dr RA Cartwright.

Age group	RAEB		CMML		RAS		Total		RA	
	M	F	M	F	M	F	M	F	M	F
20–24	—	—	—	—	—	—	—	—	—	—
25–29	0.1	—	—	—	—	—	0.1	—	0.1	—
30–34	0.1	0.1	—	—	—	—	0.1	0.1	0.1	0.1
35–39	—	—	—	—	—	—	—	—	—	0.1
40–44	0.3	—	—	—	—	—	0.3	—	0.4	0.1
45–49	0.1	0.1	—	—	—	—	0.1	0.1	—	0.7
50–54	0.3	—	—	0.2	0.3	0.2	0.6	0.4	0.1	0.5
55–59	0.5	0.3	0.1	0.3	0.5	0.3	1.0	0.9	0.7	0.3
60–64	1.3	0.8	0.6	0.3	0.7	0.3	2.7	1.4	1.4	1.0
65–69	1.2	0.5	1.4	0.7	0.6	1.0	3.1	2.2	2.0	1.8
70–74	3.5	1.5	2.5	1.3	2.0	1.3	8.3	4.0	4.4	2.1
75–79	5.6	2.6	4.5	2.1	4.5	2.5	14.5	7.6	8.9	5.1
80–84	11.3	3.8	7.7	4.0	7.2	4.0	26.6	12.1	15.9	6.3
85+	11.0	3.8	13.2	5.9	14.3	5.5	39.5	15.2	14.3	9.0
All	0.6	0.4	0.5	0.4	0.4	0.4	1.6	1.3	0.9	0.8

Table 3. Newly diagnosed patients with MDS in Bournemouth.

	1981	1982	1983	1984	1985
All patients	16	24	22	28	47
RA	8	7	6	11	29
RAS	3	3	3	4	4
CMML	4	6	8	5	10
RAEB	0	7	3	7	3
RAEBt	1	1	2	1	1

included. The diagnosis of RA required the finding of morphological abnormalities in at least two cell lines but not the presence of a karyotypic abnormality.

In a further attempt to discover the prevalence of MDS, every patient over the age of 55 in a single group practice was offered the opportunity of a full blood count. From a total population of 2926, 1388 samples were obtained and the blood films critically assessed for features of MDS by a single observer. Three cases of MDS, confirmed by bone marrow examination, were diagnosed in asymptomatic people. All had RAS, and in two the only abnormality on the blood count was slight macrocytosis, although hypochromic red cells and basophilic stippling were evident on the blood film.

CLINICAL FEATURES

The presenting clinical features are those of all disorders which cause marrow failure, namely symptoms of anaemia, infection and more rarely bleeding. However, many patients, especially those with the milder form of MDS, are diagnosed on incidental blood counts. The infections are usually bacterial, reflecting both the neutropenia and neutrophil dysfunction so commonly found in MDS. In our experience the respiratory tract has been the most frequent site of infection, but we have encountered a wide range of infections, including a number of patients who have presented with pyrexia and nonspecific ill health, in whom an abdominal ultrasound or CT scan has shown a retroperitoneal abscess.

Splenomegaly is found in 10–20% of cases and almost exclusively in patients with CMML. Other presenting features also largely confined to patients with high peripheral blood monocyte counts are skin infiltration (Copplestone et al, 1986a) and serous effusions (Mufti et al, 1984). Both may resolve with lowering of the monocyte count and do not necessarily reflect leukaemic transformation.

Several groups have noted an association between MDS and lymphoid malignancies (Baumann et al, 1985; Copplestone et al, 1986b). The latter include plasma cell tumours and both B and T cell lymphomas. In some cases MDS has developed following chemotherapy for the primary lymphoproliferative disorder, but more often the two conditions have been diagnosed simultaneously.

Rare associations with MDS include urticaria pigmentosa (Vilter and Wiltse, 1985), pyoderma gangrenosum (Jacobs et al, 1985) and relapsing polychondritis (Michet et al, 1986). Schneider and Picker (1985) described the morphological features of MDS in seven patients with AIDS and one with AIDS-related complex, while Napoli et al (1986) reported a further case of AIDS-related complex with RAEBt who progressed to acute myeloid leukaemia.

LABORATORY FEATURES

Full blood count

Most patients are anaemic at presentation. Approximately half are pancytopenic, while a quarter have anaemia in combination with either leucopenia or thrombocytopenia (Saarni and Linman, 1973). Less than 5% have isolated leucopenia or thrombocytopenia. Rarely, patients may present with macrocytosis alone or an entirely normal full blood count.

Blood and marrow morphology

The ability to diagnose MDS is critically dependent on optimal staining of blood and marrow slides. We have obtained the best results with Jenner–Giemsa stain. The main morphological abnormalities found in MDS are

Table 4. Morphological abnormalities in MDS.

Lineage	Peripheral blood	Bone marrow
Erythroid	Oval macrocytosis Anisopoikilocytosis Hypochromic fragments Basophilic stippling	Erythroid hyperplasia Dyserythropoietic features Ring sideroblasts
Granulocytic	Hypogranular neutrophils Pelger neutrophils with round or bilobed nuclei	Small agranular or sparsely granular blasts Hypogranularity of promyelocytes, myelocytes and metamyelocytes
Monocytic	Monocytes agranular or with abnormal nuclear lobation Presence of promonocytes	
Megakaryocytic	Agranular or giant platelets	Micromegakaryocytes Large mononuclear megakaryocytes Large polyploid megakaryocytes with dispersed nuclei

summarized in Table 4, and some examples are shown in Figure 1. Additional features seen in a minority of patients include gross abnormalities of red cell morphology, including acanthocytosis, elliptocytosis and schistocytosis (Rummens et al, 1986), and neutrophil hypersegmentation. Eosinophil hypogranularity may also be seen.

These morphological abnormalities provide the basis for the FAB classification of MDS, which is shown in Table 5.

The term refractory anaemia (RA) is retained for historical reasons, but includes patients who may have isolated neutropenia or thrombocytopenia or may be macrocytic without anaemia. Morphological changes in RA may be confined to the erythroid series or there may be evidence of bi- or trilineage involvement. The diagnosis of RAS should be suspected in patients with an anaemia which is mildly macrocytic and whose blood film shows hypochromic red cell fragments and basophilic stippling. The definitive diagnosis rests on the finding of ring sideroblasts in the marrow. While these may be found in up to 57% of cases of primary MDS (Juneja et al, 1983), the diagnosis of RAS requires the presence of > 15% ring sideroblasts. As with RA, morphological changes may be confined to the erythroid lineage or involve the granulocytic and megakaryocytic series. Patients with RAEB and RAEBt almost invariably have features of trilineage dysplasia evident in the blood film and on marrow examination. An estimation of the marrow blast percentage may be extremely difficult in these patients, particularly when where is a concomitant increase in promyelocytes which may be morphologically abnormal. The FAB group addressed this problem by introducing precise morphological definition of the blast cells seen in MDS. They observed one population of blasts that were agranular, usually small and had one or two nucleoli (Type I blasts) and a second population of larger cells with a central nucleus and more abundant cytoplasm containing up to five azurophilic granules (Type II

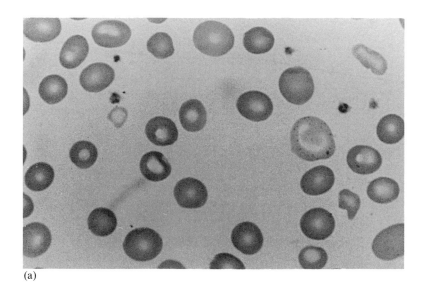

(a)

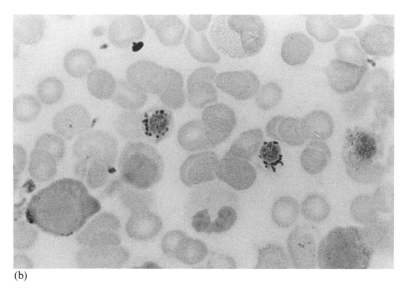

(b)

Figure 1. (a) Peripheral blood showing basophilic stippling and a hypochromic red cell fragment in a case of RAS. (b) Bone marrow stained with Perls stain for iron showing ring sideroblasts in RAS.

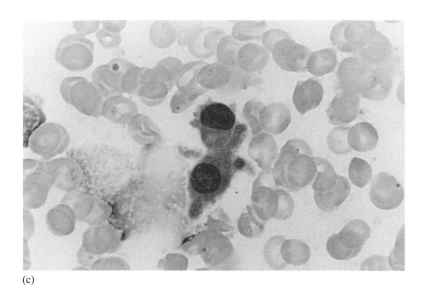

(c)

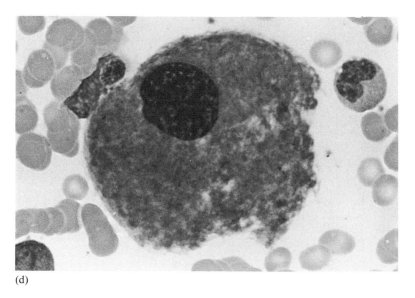

(d)

Figure 1 (*cont.*) (c) Two micromegakaryocytes. (d) Large mononuclear megakaryocyte.

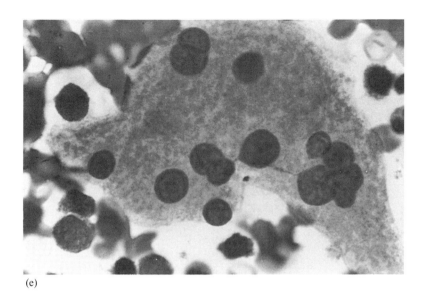

(e)

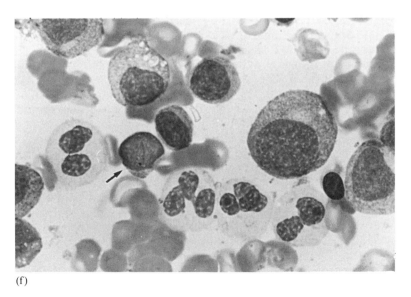

(f)

Figure 1 (*cont.*) (e) Megakaryocyte with dispersed nuclei. (f) Marrow aspirate showing hypogranular neutrophils and a type I blast (arrowed).

Table 5. The FAB subtypes.

Type	Peripheral blood	Bone marrow
Refractory anaemia (RA)	< 1% blasts	Dyshaemopoiesis in one, two or three lineages < 5% blasts
RA with ring sideroblasts (RAS)	< 1% blasts	As RA with ring sideroblasts representing at least 15% of erythroblasts
RA with excess of blasts (RAEB)	< 5% blasts	As RA with 5–20% blasts
RA in transformation (RAEBt)	As RAEB or < 5% blasts with Auer rods	As RA with 20–30% blasts or as RAEB with Auer rods
Chronic myelomonocytic leukaemia (CMML)	As any of the above with > 1 × 10^9/l monocytes	As any of the above with promonocytes

Reproduced with permission of John Wiley and Sons Ltd from Hamblin TJ & Oscier DG (1987) *Haematological Oncology* **5**.

blasts). In contrast, promyelocytes have an eccentric nucleus, Golgi zone and a moderate or increased number of azurophilic granules.

The inclusion of CMML as one of the myelodysplastic syndromes is based on the prominent trilineage dysplastic features that are frequently found in this condition. However, CMML is set apart from the other types of MDS by its proliferative features (leucocytosis, splenomegaly), and it is a source of confusion to trainees and non-haematologists that a 'leukaemia' should also be one of the myelodysplastic or 'preleukaemic' syndromes. The intention of the FAB group was to enable a more valid comparison to be made of the laboratory features, natural history, prognosis and response to treatment of an otherwise extremely heterogeneous group of patients. It is clear, however, that the arbitrary use of quantitative criteria, such as a monocyte count of > 1 × 10^9/l, to define CMML, can have little aetiological or pathogenetic significance, as attested to by the evolution of one FAB type to another, the finding of hybrid cases with features of more than one FAB type, and the lack of correlation between FAB types and particular chromosomal abnormalities.

While the morphological examination of Romanowsky stained blood and marrow films is frequently sufficient both to diagnose and categorize MDS, additional information may be obtained from cytochemical and immunocytochemical techniques. In a study of 67 patients with MDS, micromegakaryocytes were found in the peripheral blood of 34% using a monoclonal antibody against platelet glycoprotein IIIa in an immunoalkaline phosphatase technique (Erber et al, 1987). These cells superficially resemble small lymphoid cells, and in many cases were overlooked in a Romanowsky stained film.

Marrow histology

Detailed study of bone marrow histology from marrow trephines has provided additional information not obtainable from marrow aspirates alone (Tricot et al, 1984a; Frisch and Bartl, 1986). While features of dyserythropoiesis and dysgranulopoiesis are better seen in aspirates, the presence of dysmegakaryopoiesis and an assessment of megakaryocyte numbers are better determined in trephine biopsies. A more accurate indication of marrow cellularity and abnormalities of marrow topography may also be observed in a trephine. In health, granulopoiesis proceeds at the endosteal surface, while erythropoiesis and megakaryopoiesis occur in the central intertrabecular areas. The reverse pattern may be seen in MDS and the term 'abnormal localization of immature precursors' (ALIP) has been coined by Tricot et al (1984a) to describe clusters of myeloblasts and promyelocytes in the centre of the marrow. Such clusters may be found when an excess of blasts is not demonstrable in the marrow aspirate.

Abnormalities are not confined to the myeloid cells, and increased reticulin (Sultan et al, 1981), plasmacytosis, lymphoid aggregates and areas of oedema may all be found.

It should be appreciated that the FAB types of MDS cannot be readily deduced from examination of a marrow trephine alone.

Chromosomes

Karyotypic abnormalities have been detected in 30–50% of patients with MDS using conventional cytogenetic banding techniques. The success rate increases when marrow rather than blood is sampled, and when a first attempt fails, repeat testing may show an abnormality (Billstrom et al, 1986). Yunis et al (1986) investigated 56 patients with MDS using high-resolution chromosome banding techniques, and found a clonal abnormality in 44 (79%). The reported incidence of chromosomal abnormalities is therefore in part a function of the sensitivity of the method used for their detection and the number of metaphases examined. It is likely that the use of DNA probes to detect submicroscopic changes will demonstrate an even higher incidence of chromosomal abnormalities. Thein et al (1987) have used a probe to a hypervariable region on the long arm of chromosome 7 and found an abnormality in 10 out of 118 patients studied. Of these, only five had monosomy 7 or 7q− detected cytogenetically, and no patient had a cytogenetic abnormality not found by DNA analysis.

The chromosomal abnormalities found in MDS are nonrandom, the commonest being − 5, 5q−, − 7, 7q−, +8, − Y, 20q−, i.e. there is usually a loss of chromosomal material. There is no correlation between a particular abnormality and any of the FAB types, although the incidence of a chromosomal abnormality is higher in patients with RAEB and RAEBt (Knapp et al, 1985). However, certain abnormalities do have clinical and morphological correlations. Patients who have an interstitial deletion of the long arm of chromosome 5 (5q−) as the sole abnormality are frequently elderly females with RA (70%) or RAEB (30%) (Van den Berghe, 1986). They present with a macrocytic anaemia, and a normal or raised platelet count, and marrow examination shows erythroid hypoplasia and mononuclear megakaryocytes. Monosomy 7 is associated with a hypocellular bone marrow, pancytopenia and abnormal neutrophil function (Pederson-Bjergaard et al, 1982).

Patients who develop MDS following exposure to a mutagen frequently have complete or partial loss of chromosomes 5 and/or 7. A number of structural abnormalities rarely found in primary MDS also seem to be associated with secondary MDS. These include t(1;3) (p36;q21) (Bloomfield et al, 1986), t(1;7) (p11;p11) (Scheres et al, 1985) and t(2;11) (p21;q23) (de la Chapelle et al, 1986).

Marrow culture

The in vitro growth of haemopoietic progenitor cells is critically dependent on culture conditions, and in healthy individuals the normal range is wide. However, various patterns of abnormality are associated with particular haematological malignancies, e.g. greatly increased colony growth in chronic myeloid leukaemia (CML), and erythroid growth in the absence of added erythropoietin in primary proliferative polycythaemia. Abnormalities of myeloid, erythroid and megakaryocytic colony growth have all been documented in MDS. The assay most frequently studied in MDS has been the growth of granulocyte–macrophage colonies (CFU-GM). While the numbers of CFU-GM derived from bone marrow may be normal in some patients, others show a variety of abnormal patterns, including increased cluster formation and reduced or absent colony growth as found in acute myeloid leukaemia. Peripheral blood CFU-GM growth is also reduced in MDS, particularly in patients with > 5% blasts in the marrow (Tennant et al, 1986). Defective colony maturation may be found in patients both with normal and reduced colony numbers (Francis et al, 1982). Ruutu et al (1984) correlated CFU-GM growth with FAB type and found a normal growth pattern in patients with RAS and RA with the 5q − abnormality but defective growth in the other FAB types.

Increased colony and cluster numbers have been found in some patients with CMML (Sultan et al, 1974; Worsley et al, 1987), reflecting the proliferative nature of this type of MDS. Erythroid colony growth is usually depressed or absent in the majority of patients with MDS (Ruutu et al, 1984; May et al, 1985) but sufficient numbers of patients with RA have normal erythroid colony growth for this assay not to be useful in strengthening the diagnosis of MDS in those patients with minor morphological abnormalities (Worsley et al, 1987).

Similarly, reduced or absent megakaryocyte colony growth is a feature of MDS. Of 10 patients studied by Juvonen et al (1986), all had defective megakaryocytic and erythroid growth but only four had abnormal CFU-GM growth.

Table 6. Laboratory findings in MDS.

Investigation	Abnormality	Reference
Serum B$_{12}$, folate and ferritin	See text	
Red cell enzymes	Raised levels of many enzymes in glycolytic and HMP pathways. Pyruvate kinase often reduced. No clinical correlation found.	Lintula (1986)
Iron metabolism	Shortened red cell survival. Increased ineffective erythropoiesis.	May et al (1985)
Red cell antigens	Decrease in A, B, increase in i. Tn activation.	Salmon (1976)
HbF	Raised in 40%.	Newman et al (1973)
Acquired HbH disease	Occasionally found.	Annino et al (1984)
Positive Ham's test	Occasionally found.	Hauptman et al (1978)
Cytochemistry	Low NAP score.	Bendix-Hansen and Kerndrup (1985)
	Myeloperoxidase deficiency.	Scott et al (1983)
	Dual esterase positive 'paramyeloid cells'.	
Surface phenotype	Abnormal expression of FcIgG and C3b receptors.	Bynoe et al (1984)
	Persistence of mY7 on neutrophils.	Baumann et al (1986)
Granulocyte function	Reduced motility, adherence, phagocytosis and bacterial killing.	Ruutu (1986)
Serum lysozyme	Increased in CMML.	Solal-Celigny et al (1984)
Platelet function	Prolonged bleeding time with normal platelet count; reduced aggregation with adrenaline and collagen.	Rasi and Lintula (1986)
Platelet-associated immunoglobulin		Hall et al (1987)
	May be raised in the absence of immune-mediated thrombocytopenia.	
Lymphocyte populations	Reduced T4 cells.	Bynoe et al (1983)
	Reduced NK cells.	Kerndrup et al (1984)
Immunoglobulin abnormalities	Polyclonal gammopathy in 30%. Hypogammaglobulinaemia in 20%.	Economopoulos et al (1985)
		Mufti et al (1986)
	Paraprotein in 10%. Autoantibodies in 50% of CMML.	

The paradox of in vivo marrow hypercellularity and reduced or absent in vitro colony growth is also a feature of long-term marrow culture in MDS. Haemopoiesis is rarely sustained beyond 2–4 weeks and the cells retain their dysplastic morphology (Coutinho et al, 1987).

Other investigations

There is a wide range of laboratory tests which show abnormalities seen in

MDS and these are summarized in Table 6. Some are common to all or the majority of cases, while others are rare associations. While few are of practical importance in the diagnosis and management of MDS, measurement of serum B_{12} and folate is an essential investigation for a number of reasons. Firstly, megaloblastic change may be confused with the morphological features of MDS, and one group includes the failure to respond to B_{12} and folic acid as one of the diagnostic criteria for MDS (Jacobs, 1985). Secondly, megaloblastic anaemia and MDS may coexist as a result of either secondary folate deficiency in MDS or the chance combination of MDS and pernicious anaemia. Of 142 patients investigated in Bournemouth, 30% had a raised serum B_{12}, reflecting the increased transcobalamin levels associated with granulocytic hyperplasia. In the same series, the serum ferritin was increased in 25% of patients at presentation. There was a poor correlation between the ferritin level and storage iron in the marrow, and in some patients with CMML the ferritin level reflected the peripheral blood monocyte count. In those patients with a regular transfusion requirement there was good correlation between the serum ferritin and the number of units transfused.

DIFFERENTIAL DIAGNOSIS OF MDS

The diagnosis of MDS is most secure in patients with trilineage dysplasia and an abnormal karyotype. However, there are a number of situations in which diagnostic difficulties arise. The most common of these is when there are minor morphological abnormalities confined to a single lineage in patients with a normal karyotype. This applies particularly to some patients with RA and those with a slight monocytosis but minimal dysplastic features. The difficulty may be compounded if there are coexisting disorders which can affect cell morphology. While the increasing application of DNA technology such as DNA fingerprinting (Jeffreys et al, 1985) may indicate a clonal abnormality, one frequently has to rely on serial observations to determine whether the morphological changes are due to MDS or secondary to some other disorder.

It should be appreciated that the morphological abnormalities which characterize MDS are not confined to this condition. Dyserythropoiesis is a common finding and particularly prominent in megaloblastic anaemias and following the administration of cytotoxic therapy. Pelger neutrophils may rarely be found as a benign congenital anomaly or be seen in the context of de novo AML of FAB types M2 and M4. Dysplastic megakaryocytes are a feature of CML. Kuriyama et al (1986) have investigated the diagnostic significance of the morphological abnormalities associated with MDS and found that over 90% of cases had either pelger neutrophils or micromegakaryocytes or both.

Another area of diagnostic difficulty is in patients who present with high peripheral blood neutrophil and monocyte counts and show dysplastic features on the blood film. Many of these have previously been described as having Philadelphia chromosome (Ph') negative CML (Pugh et al, 1985; Travis et al, 1986). Some have the classical morphological features of CMML while others have particularly prominent dysgranulopoiesis, $> 10\%$ immature granulocytes in the peripheral blood and frequent thrombocytopenia. Patients with the latter features rarely survive beyond 18 months while patients with high count CMML may have a more protracted clinical course.

Rearrangement of the breakpoint cluster region (bcr) gene has been found in seven patients with Ph'-negative CML studied by Ganesan et al (1986). Five of these had the classical haematological features of Ph'-positive CML while two had dysplastic features. A further three cases of typical CMML had no evidence of bcr rearrangement.

A further area of interest is the number of patients who present with $> 30\%$ blasts in the marrow and who by definition have AML, yet have evolved from a preceding dysplastic phase. Brito-Babapulle (1987) reviewed 160 cases of AML in whom no previous haematological disorder was suspected and found evidence of trilineage dysplasia in 15%. Such features were invariably found in cases of M6, never in M3 and in some patients with the remaining FAB types of AML. The percentage of blasts in the marrows of patients with dysplastic features was considerably lower than that in patients with normal morphology, reflecting earlier presentation in patients with leukaemic transformation of an already compromised marrow.

This study emanated from a centre to which patients are referred for intensive chemotherapy, and it is likely that the incidence of prior dysplasia is considerably higher in more elderly patients with AML.

WHAT IS MYELODYSPLASIA?

Evidence for clonality

The frequent finding of a chromosomal abnormality in the marrow cells of patients with MDS attests to this being a clonal disorder of haemopoiesis. The question then arises as to from which stem cell the abnormal clone or clones originate. The presence of morphological abnormalities in the erythroid, myeloid and megakaryocytic series points to the target cell being a precursor of all three lineages. Amenomori et al (1986) have shown that cells from granulocyte–macrophage and from erythroid colonies grown from the marrow of a patient with CMML share a common karyotypic abnormality. However, the fact that a minority of patients with MDS develop acute leukaemias with the phenotypic and genotypic features of immature B or T cells suggests that, as in chronic myeloid leukaemia, the disease may arise in a less committed stem cell. Support for this concept comes from a case recently reported by Stark et al (1986). A 55-year-old woman developed CMML 1 year after being treated for common acute lymphoblastic leukaemia (ALL). Subsequent relapse of the ALL was associated with virtual replacement of the dysplastic marrow by blasts, but reinduction therapy with vincristine and prednisolone led to the re-emergence of the myelomonocytic clone. The same chromosomal abnormality (t(4;11)) was found in both the ALL and CMML phases of the disease, implying derivation from a common stem cell. The most compelling evidence for this concept comes from the analysis of glucose 6-

phosphate dehydrogenase (G6PD) isoenzymes in women who are hetero-zygous for this enzyme. Owing to random X chromosome inactivation, each cell only expresses one isoenzyme, but in a particular tissue there will be approximately equal expression of both isoenzymes. Prchal (1978) demon-strated the presence of a single G6PD isoenzyme in the erythroid, granulo-cytic, megakaryocytic, B and T cell lineages but not the fibroblasts from a woman with RAS. In a similar study, Raskind et al (1984) found one G6PD isoenzyme in the myeloid and B cells but not the T cells of another patient with RAS.

The analysis of restriction fragment length polymorphisms has recently been used to investigate the same question of lineage involvement in MDS. Five patients with monosomy 7 were studied with chromosome 7 specific DNA probes. Abnormalities or absence of chromosome 7 were detected in the granulocytes of four patients and in the monocytes of two of the three patients in which they were studied. No clear abnormality was found in the peripheral blood lymphocytes from any patient (Kere et al, 1987). The data therefore suggest that the target cell may vary from case to case. In some patients a multipotent stem cell appears to be involved while in others the abnormal clone arises from a more committed myeloid precursor cell. An analogous situation may exist in AML, where the disease in younger patients is often associated with the t(8;21), t(15;17) and del 11q chromosomal abnormalities and arises in a progenitor committed to granulocyte–macrophage differentia-tion. In elderly patients with AML there is an increased incidence of the same karyotypic abnormalities that are commonly found in MDS, namely -7, -5 and $+8$, and G6PD data suggest that the disease arises from a multipotent stem cell. It is apparent that AML in younger people is rarely preceded by a dysplastic phase, whereas this is commonly associated with AML in the elderly (reviewed by Layton and Mufti, 1986).

Aetiology

For most patients with MDS, the aetiology remains unknown. The major exceptions to this are those patients who develop MDS following treatment with cytotoxic drugs and/or radiotherapy. The average latent period between exposure to the mutagen and the appearance of dysplastic features is 3–4 years. Morphologically the condition differs from primary MDS in a number of respects. The marrow is often more fibrotic and less cellular, and the incidence of ring sideroblasts and mononuclear megakaryocytes is higher. Ninety per cent of cases have an abnormal karyotype, particularly monosomy or deletions of chromosomes 5 or 7. Transformation to an acute leukaemia is usual, with the median duration of the dysplastic phase being 11 months (Koeffler, 1986).

Krontiris et al (1985) suggested that a rare allele at the Ha-ras locus was linked to a susceptibility to malignancy, including MDS, but Thein et al (1986) in a larger study of 53 patients with MDS were unable to confirm this.

Pathogenesis

The pathogenesis of MDS is another area of considerable speculation but little factual information. There is much evidence to support the concept that MDS results from multiple rather than a single genetic event. Thus karyotypic

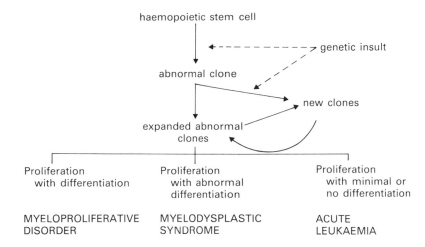

Figure 2. Hypothetical scheme to show the origin of clonal abnormalities in haematological malignancies. The nature of the disease which results depends on the properties of the abnormal clone.

evolution is a frequent accompaniment of disease progression. In the patient described by Raskind et al (1984) who was heterozygous for G6PD, two independent chromosomally abnormal clones were found in the myeloid cells, but the Epstein–Barr virus-transformed B lymphocytes, which were also of a single G6PD type, were karyotypically normal. There must therefore have been three distinct genetic events during the evolution of the patient's disease. The abnormal clone which develops as a result of genetic damage appears to have two major and distinct properties. Firstly, it has a growth advantage over normal haemopoietic stem cells, while retaining the ability to differentiate, and secondly the clone is genetically unstable (Figure 2).

The site or sites of the genetic lesions which lead to the appearance of such clones is unknown, but it is likely that they involve genes which are normally involved in the regulation of cell proliferation and differentiation. One might speculate that the abnormality may bypass the need for a growth factor or involve the production of an otherwise essential growth factor (autocrine stimulation) (Griffin and Young, 1986). It is now clear that many of the cellular oncogenes encode proteins which play a pivotal role in the way cells communicate with and respond to their environment. Point mutations of the N-ras oncogene are commonly found in AML, and in a study of 10 patients with CMML, preliminary data suggest an abnormality of N-ras in three and Ha-ras in two (Gow et al, 1987). It is intriguing that the genes which code for granulocyte–macrophage colony-stimulating factor (GM-CSF), macrophage colony-stimulating factor (M-CSF) and the C-FMS oncogene are all found on that part of the long arm of chromosome 5 which is deleted in patients with 5q− (Le Beau et al, 1986). The significance of this and the hypodiploidy which commonly accompanies MDS is unknown, but retinoblastoma provides a model for how the loss of genetic material containing putative antioncogenes may lead to malignancy (Knudson, 1985).

Myelodysplasia, preleukaemia and leukaemia

Some confusion surrounds the terms MDS and preleukaemia and their relationship to acute leukaemia. In part this is semantic but genuine difficulties arise in describing conditions in which so little is known about the aetiology and pathogenesis. The term preleukaemia is especially prone to multiple interpretations. On one hand it may be used to describe patients with a variety of disorders such as Downs syndrome or primary proliferative polycythaemia in which there is an increased risk of subsequently developing acute leukaemia. On the other it may describe a phase in an illness in which progression to acute leukaemia is inevitable if the patient survives long enough. Such a term may be appropriate to patients who develop a dysplastic phase secondary to exposure to a mutagen, but since so many patients die without ever undergoing leukaemic transformation it is generally better avoided. Conceptual problems may also arise when considering leukaemic transformation in MDS, depending on whether one uses the clinically useful but arbitrary definition of acute leukaemia as a marrow containing > 30% blasts, or a biological definition reflecting the appearance of a myeloid clone capable of proliferation but not differentiation (Galton, 1986). It is apparent that a patient who presents with trilineage dysplasia and 25% blasts in the marrow does not develop a new disease when some weeks later the marrow blast count reaches 30%.

NATURAL HISTORY

Various patterns of evolution have been observed in patients with MDS (Figure 3). The morphological changes that may occur are listed in Figure 4. New or additional karyotypic abnormalities may arise during the course of the disease and these have been correlated with the morphological changes in a series of 46 patients studied by Tricot et al (1985b). Some patients, comprising 48% of Tricot's series, and shown as group C in Figure 3, have a stable course over many years. The initial FAB diagnosis is RA, RAS or CMML, and the majority are ALIP-negative. Additional chromosomal abnormalities rarely occur during the course of their disease, and many die from incidental causes. Patients in group D have a gradual increase in blasts in the marrow and may therefore evolve from the FAB group RA through RAEB and RAEBt to AML. This pattern was observed in 24% of Tricot's cases, and in a series of 101 consecutive cases of MDS Vallespi et al (1985) documented four cases of RA and one of RAS which evolved through other

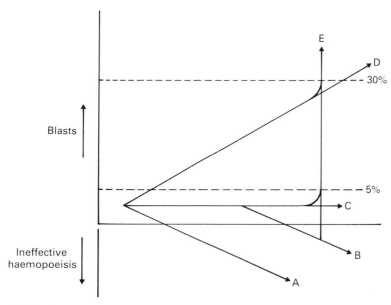

Figure 3. Hypothetical scheme of the various patterns of evolution in MDS. The ordinate above the origin shows the percentage of blasts in the marrow. Below the origin is represented an arbitrary scale of increasingly ineffective haemopoiesis without an increase in blasts. Modified from Tricot et al (1985b).

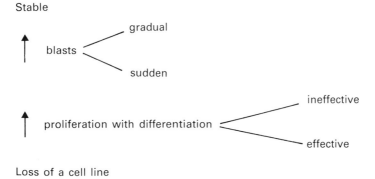

Figure 4. Morphological evolution of MDS.

FAB groups before progressing to an acute leukaemia. Patients in this group are often ALIP-positive and rarely show karyotypic evolution. They frequently succumb to infections or haemorrhagic complications with or without evolution to acute leukaemia.

A further type of evolution (groups A and B) is characterized by increasing pancytopenia without an increase in marrow blasts. Dysplastic changes become more pronounced, and occasionally, increasing anaemia may be due to red cell aplasia. The incidence of new karyotypic abnormalities in this group is uncertain, and the morphological changes may reflect clonal expansion rather than clonal evolution.

In any of the previous groups there may be a rapid increase in blast cells and an abrupt transformation to an acute leukaemia. The risk is highest in those patients who already have an increase in marrow blasts. This pattern (group E) was found in 28% of Tricot's cases. Eighty-two per cent were ALIP-positive and 61.5% developed additional chromosomal abnormalities.

The majority of the acute leukaemias which develop in patients with MDS are myeloid in phenotype. Most of these are M2 or M4 but some cases have a megakaryoblastic component (Ruiz-Arguelles, 1987). However, acute lymphoblastic leukaemias of T cell (Pereira et al, 1985) and B cell origin (Berneman et al, 1985; Bonati et al, 1986) as well as biphenotypic cases (Eridani et al, 1985) have all been described.

Fohlmeister et al (1985a,b) have drawn attention to a group of patients who present with pancytopenia and hypocellular marrows containing foci of cells with dysplastic features, most noticeable in the megakaryocytes. Of 111 patients initially considered to have aplastic anaemia, 21 had dysplastic features and 14 of these developed an acute leukaemia compared to six from the nondysplastic group. Serial marrows from these patients showed an evolution from hypocellularity to erythroid hyperplasia and finally to myeloid hyperplasia with leukaemic transformation.

Rarely, patients with MDS who present with hypercellular marrows and peripheral cytopenia develop a proliferative phase with predominantly mature cells in the peripheral blood (Economopoulos et al, 1984). Evolution to a myelofibrotic phase is another unusual finding (Williams et al, 1985). While karyotypic evolution usually involves the acquisition of additional chromosomal changes, sometimes a previously documented abnormal clone may disappear (Miller et al, 1985; Mecucci et al, 1986) with no obvious concomitant morphological change.

PROGNOSTIC FACTORS

The median survival of patients with MDS is approximately 2 years (Table 7). However, some patients succumb from the complications of pancytopenia or leukaemic transformation soon after diagnosis, while others have a stable and benign course for many years and may die of an unrelated cause. Much effort has been expended in finding factors of prognostic significance, and these are listed in Table 8. They may be considered in two main groups. Firstly there are those which depend on an assessment of quantitative and qualitative changes

Table 7. Median survival of patients with MDS.

Number of patients	Median survival (months)	Author
193	21	Coiffier et al (1983)
162	28	Teerenhovi and Lintula (1986)
141	24	Mufti et al (1985)
101	7.4	Vallespi et al (1985)
85	15	Tricot et al (1985)
69	27	Weisdorf et al (1983)

Table 8. Prognostic features in MDS.

Haemoglobin, neutrophil, monocyte and platelet counts
Percentage of blasts in blood and marrow
Presence of ALIPs
FAB classification
Scoring system (Mufti et al, 1985; Varela et al, 1985; Fenaux et al, 1987)
Chromosomes
In vitro marrow culture
DNA ploidy

in the peripheral blood and bone marrow, and secondly those parameters such as chromosomal status, in vitro colony growth and DNA ploidy which are independent of cell numbers and morphology.

Individual blood and marrow parameters

The majority of patients who die from MDS do so because of bleeding or infection as a consequence of ineffective haemopoiesis or leukaemic transformation. It is therefore not surprising to discover that the haemoglobin, neutrophil count, platelet count and the percentage of blasts in the peripheral blood and bone marrow each have prognostic significance when analysed separately. The relative importance and absolute levels of these parameters which are of most predictive value have varied among series. Coiffier et al (1983) found a haemoglobin of < 8 g/dl and a neutrophil count of $< 1.4 \times 10^9/l$ to be the best discriminant of short survival, while Teerenhovi and Lintula (1986) showed a haemoglobin of < 10 g/dl and a platelet count of $< 50 \times 10^9/l$ to be predictive of a poor prognosis. The degree of monocytosis and the granulocyte count are both of prognostic significance in patients with CMML. In a study of 53 patients, a monocyte count of $> 2.6 \times 10^9/l$ and a neutrophil count of $> 15 \times 10^9/l$ were both associated with short survival and an increased risk of leukaemic transformation (Worsley et al, 1987).

Many groups have confirmed that the finding of $> 5\%$ blasts in the marrow is a strong prognostic indicator of both leukaemic transformation and short survival. Tricot et al (1986b) found that the minority of patients who present with > 5% blasts in the blood have a median survival of only 2–5 months. The significance of Auer rods in blast cells is uncertain. Neither Seigneurin and Audhuy (1983) nor Weisdorf et al (1981) found them to be an adverse prognostic factor, while in the FAB classification their presence alters the category from RAEB to RAEBt.

Tricot et al (1984b) have shown that the presence of ALIPs also correlates with survival. All patients who have a demonstrable increase in blast cells in a marrow aspirate are ALIP-positive, but for those patients in the RA and RAS FAB groups the median survival of ALIP-negative cases was 1465 days compared to 416 days for those who were ALIP-positive.

Combined blood and marrow parameters

Increased predictive value may be obtained by combining the information derived from the blood count, blood film and bone marrow.

Table 9. Median survival of the FAB subtypes of MDS.

Series	No. of points	Survival (months)				
		RA	RARS	CMML	RAEB	RAEBt
Weisdorf et al (1983)	69	52	29	2	12	11
Coiffier et al (1983)	193	40	52	11	10	
Vallespi et al (1985)	101	20	14	4	13	2.5
Tricot et al (1985a)	85	18	21	10	10	4.5
Foucar et al (1985)	109	64	71	18	7	5
Varela et al (1985)	56	38	53	17	13	3
Mufti et al (1985)	141	32	76	22	10.5	5
Jacobs et al (1986)	49	> 60	> 60	25	21	16
Teerenhovi and Lintula (1986)	162	48	41	16	21	13
Kerkhofs et al (1987)	237	50	> 60	> 60	9	6

Many series (Table 9) have confirmed the predictive value of the FAB classification. All series show the enhanced survival of patients with RA and RAS compared to those with RAEB and RAEBt. The survival of patients with CMML varies considerably among series and lends support to the view that this is a heterogeneous group.

The survival of patients within the other FAB types is by no means uniform. Thus patients with RAS and trilineage dysplasia have a shorter survival and increased risk of leukaemic transformation than those patients in whom the morphological abnormalities appear confined to the erythroid series (Hast, 1986).

A number of scoring systems with prognostic significance have been devised. The FAB score of Varela et al (1985) combines the qualitative changes of dysgranulopoiesis and dysmegakaryopoiesis with quantitative blood and marrow abnormalities and is predictive of both survival and leukaemic transformation. A simpler system is the Bournemouth score (Mufti et al, 1985). One point is allocated for each of the following:

Haemoglobin < 10 g/dl
Neutrophil count $< 2.5 \times 10^9/l$
Platelet count $< 100 \times 10^9/l$
Marrow blast count $> 5\%$

In a series of 141 patients, the median survival of patients scoring 0 or 1 was 62 months, for those scoring 2 or 3 it was 22 months, and for those scoring 4 it was 8.5 months. This system has prognostic value within the FAB group and its value has been independently confirmed by Kerkhofs et al (1987). It is, however, of little value in patients with CMML, since even those patients with clinically aggressive disease have neutrophilia rather than neutropenia. The allocation of 1 point for a neutrophil count of $> 15 \times 10^9/l$ restores the predictive value (Worsley et al, 1987).

In a similar study, Fenaux et al (1987) have used a discriminant score based on the haemoglobin, degree of peripheral blood monocytosis and percentage of marrow blasts, to divide patients with CMML into two groups: one with a median survival of 8.5 months and a high risk of leukaemic transformation and the other with a median survival of 49 months.

Chromosomes

The impact of an abnormal karyotype on prognosis is unclear. Whereas Todd and Pierre (1986) and Jacobs et al (1986) found a shorter survival in those patients with an abnormal karyotype, neither Tricot et al (1985a) nor Borgstrom (1986) were able to confirm this. A number of possible explanations exist to explain these differences. An abnormal karyotype is more commonly found in patients with secondary MDS who have a high rate of leukaemic transformation, and this group was excluded from Tricot's series. The particular chromosomal abnormalities observed and whether they are single or complex and involve some (AN) or all metaphases (AA) also appears to have prognostic significance. There is general agreement that those patients who have a complex karyotypic abnormality or show karyotypic evolution have both a shorter survival and an increased incidence of leukaemic transformation. Kerkhofs et al (1987) found that patients who were NN and AN had a longer survival and lower risk of developing acute leukaemia than those who were AA. The 5q$-$ abnormality alone is associated with a benign clinical course, whereas patients with -7 or 7q$-$ have a rapid clinical evolution and high risk of leukaemic transformation.

An isodicentric X chromosome idic(X)(q13) has been observed in five patients with RAS, and three of these have progressed to AML (Dewald et al, 1982).

Of 56 patients studied by Yunis et al (1986), 12 with a normal karyotype were alive at 49 months, while the median survival of patients with an abnormal chromosome 7 was 12 months and that of patients with a complex karyotypic abnormality was only 4 months. It is of particular interest that the prognostic significance of the karyotypic change was independent of the FAB type.

In vitro culture

Greenberg (1986) has recently collected data from six studies on 179 patients with MDS in whom the clinical course has been correlated with CFU-GM growth patterns. Those patients with nonleukaemic growth patterns had a 20–40% incidence of leukaemic transformation and a median survival of 9–50 months. Patients with leukaemic growth patterns had a 50–80% incidence of progression to leukaemia and a median survival of only 5–10 months. Thus while a leukaemic growth pattern generally signifies a poor prognosis, the outcome of patients with normal colony growth is too varied to be of clinical value.

DNA content

The DNA content of bone marrow cells from patients with MDS has been measured by flow cytometry and found to be abnormal in about 50% of cases. Clark et al (1986) showed that patients who were hypodiploid had a significantly shorter survival than those who were diploid or hyperdiploid.

Summary

It is now possible to assess with reasonable accuracy the likely prognosis of a patient with MDS at presentation. The single parameter which gives the clearest guide to prognosis is the percentage of blasts in the marrow. However, additional information is readily obtained by applying the FAB classification and/or the Bournemouth score. The predictive value of chromosomal abnormalities in relation to information more easily obtainable from the blood count, blood film and examination of the bone marrow, requires further study. There are, however, limitations which apply to all of the prognostic factors currently available. Anyone familiar with the management of patients with MDS will be aware that for a given degree of pancytopenia some patients may remain well for prolonged periods while others may suffer from recurrent infective and/or bleeding problems. This discrepancy may reflect differences in the immune status of patients with MDS or differing degrees of neutrophil and platelet functional abnormalities.

As in chronic lymphatic leukaemia, the rate of disease progression may vary in a way which is not wholly predictable, and for these reasons there should be, wherever possible, a period of observation prior to initiating treatment.

MANAGEMENT OF MDS

The possibility of cure is confined to the tiny minority of young patients with HLA-compatible siblings for whom allogeneic bone marrow transplantation is the treatment of choice (Appelbaum et al, 1987). Since the majority of patients are elderly, management decisions must reflect the patient's physical and mental health, social situation and his or her own expectations and wishes. Accordingly, management options range through observation only,

Table 10. Treatment of MDS.

Supportive	
Intensive	Chemotherapy
	BMT
Hormonal	Steroids
	Androgens
	Danazol
'Differentiating' agents	Low-dose cytosine arabinoside
	13-*cis*-retinoic acid
	1,25-dihydroxyvitamin D_3
	α-interferon
Oral cytotoxics	Idarubicin
	Etoposide
	Hydroxyurea

supportive care, a variety of chemotherapeutic agents (Table 10) and symptomatic relief only for those patients whose general health is so poor that they could derive no benefit from an improvement in their haematological status.

Supportive care

The mainstay of supportive care has traditionally been and continues to be the use of red cell transfusions in patients who are symptomatically anaemic. Transfusion because the haemoglobin has fallen below a particular arbitrary level is to be strongly discouraged. Cardiac dysfunction in elderly sideroblastic patients who may have coexisting ischaemic heart disease is occasionally a problem but the use of subcutaneous desferrioxamine is usually confined to younger patients.

Platelet transfusions are clearly indicated in thrombocytopenic patients in the treatment of acute bleeding episodes or as prophylaxis prior to surgery or following chemotherapy, but have little role in the long-term management of persistent thrombocytopenia. The potential clinical importance of platelet and neutrophil dysfunction in patients whose platelet and neutrophil counts may be normal or minimally depressed should not be forgotten when deciding, for example, on the need for platelet support prior to surgery or the choice between oral and intravenous antibiotics in an infected patient.

Intensive treatment

It is the general, though largely anecdotal, experience of haematologists treating elderly patients with MDS that they respond poorly to intensive chemotherapy. This view is supported by the results of two small studies.

Armitage et al (1981) compared the survival of 13 patients with RAEB and seven patients with CMML given intensive chemotherapy with that of 15 similar patients treated with supportive care only. Only three treated patients (aged 23, 48, 68) achieved complete remission, and the median survival of the treated group was less than the supported group.

Tricot and Boogaerts (1986a) treated 15 patients with MDS intensively and found that while six out of seven (86%) patients under the age of 50 achieved a complete remission, only two of the eight patients over 50 remitted. The median duration of remission was 12 months. While high-dose chemotherapy has a role in the management of young patients with MDS, there is little to commend its use in the elderly.

Hormonal treatment

Bagby et al (1980) treated 34 patients with preleukaemia with prednisolone, having previously documented the effect of corticosteroids on in vitro CFU-GM growth. Of the five patients who showed enhanced in vitro colony growth, three had a clinical response. None of the other 29 patients responded and eight developed serious side effects attributable to steroid therapy. Thus, although steroids may benefit a minority of patients, their use should logically be confined to patients showing improved CFU-GM growth in vitro.

Najean and Pecking (1979) randomized 58 patients with MDS to receive supportive care only or a combination of the androgen metenolone and cytosine arabinoside. There was no survival difference between the two groups, and no convincing data exist to support the use of androgens in MDS.

Danazol has been used successfully in three patients with thrombocytopenia and MDS (Cines et al, 1985). It is not possible to deduce the FAB type of the patients, all of whom had raised levels of platelet-associated immunoglobulin. Our own experience of danazol in five patients with MDS, in whom thrombocytopenia due to ineffective megakaryopoiesis has been the main clinical problem, has not been promising.

Agents which induce differentiation in vitro

In the 1970s it was realized that a variety of compounds of widely differing structure could induce the differentiation of myeloid leukaemic cell lines (Lotem and Sachs, 1974). The HL60 cell line derived from a patient with acute promyelocytic leukaemia has been extensively studied, and some agents, such as dimethylsulphoxide and retinoic acid, are able to induce granulocytic differentiation, while others, such as tetradecanoyl phorbol 13-acetate (TPA) and 1,25-dihydroxycholecalciferol ($1,25\text{-}(OH)_2\text{-}D_3$) induce monocytic differentiation. A number of drugs, such as the anthracyclines and cytosine arabinoside, currently used as cytotoxic agents, also act in low dose as differentiating agents in vitro.

Their dramatic in vitro effects, coupled with the disappointing results obtained with conventional high-dose chemotherapy, have led to the widespread use of some of these drugs, particularly cytosine arabinoside, in patients with MDS. The rationale for their use is the differentiation of immature nonfunctional cells into functionally competent mature cells. This might produce two added benefits: firstly the removal of an inhibitory effect on residual normal haemopoietic cells, and secondly of the differentiating agent acting on all the clonogenic dysplastic cells, leading to extinction of the abnormal clone.

Some drugs, such as retinoic acid and $1,25\text{-}(OH)_2\text{-}D_3$, appear to act as true differentiating agents, by increasing the rate of cell differentiation without inhibiting the proliferation of cells not involved in the differentiation process. On the other hand, all the in vitro differentiators which are cytotoxic at high doses are DNA synthesis inhibitors. They may, therefore, be able to switch off the synthesis of those factors which induce a cell to continue to proliferate without hindering the action of naturally occurring or endogenous differentiating agents. If this were so it should follow that true differentiators and DNA synthesis inhibitors should act synergistically and that treatment would have to be prolonged to enable the differentiators to act on cells as they enter the cell cycle (Bloch, 1984). Synergism has been demonstrated in vitro by Francis et al (1985), who showed that a combination of a differentiator and a DNA synthesis inhibitor greatly increased the maturation of CFU-GM grown from patients with MDS compared to the effect of either agent alone. This and similar evidence has stimulated the clinical use of combinations of 'differentiating agents'.

Low-dose cytosine arabinoside (LDAC)

Since the first successful report by Baccharani and Tura (1979) of the use of LDAC in MDS, this agent has been used extensively (Table 11), but no randomized trial demonstrating improved survival has yet been published. Evaluation of the role of LDAC in MDS has been hampered by the differing doses, duration, and routes of administration, together with varying criteria of response. In addition, most reports have concentrated on the initial reponse to LDAC, and questions such as which subgroup of patients are most likely to benefit, and how long treatment should continue, remain unanswered. However, enough patients have been treated to draw some tentative conclusions.

It is clear that responses may be observed with a variety of dose regimens. The most commonly used regimen has been 10 mg/m² s.c. 12 hourly for 21 days. Marrow hypocellularity is almost invariable with this treatment, but is not usually as profound as that following intensive chemotherapy. Some degree of peripheral cytopenia always occurs and on occasions may be as severe and long-lasting as with high-dose chemotherapy (Mufti et al, 1983). Such treatment should not be initiated unless there is both the capability and willingness to provide full inpatient haematological support. It is, however,

Table 11. Treatment of MDS with low-dose cytarabine: results from 11 series.

Series	No. of patients	Dose	Duration (days)	No. showing favourable response (CR + PR)	
Baccarani et al (1983)	12	20–30 mg/m²/day i.v. or i.m.	7–10	4	(33%)
Tricot et al (1984c)	26	30–50 mg/day s.c.	14–28	15	(58%)
Mufti et al (1984)	17	10 mg/m²s.c. bd	21	7	(41%)
Roberts et al (1985)	4	10 mg/m²s.c. bd	14 (mean)	2	(50%)
Griffin et al (1985)	16	20 mg/m²day i.v.	14–21	11	(68%)
Winter et al (1985)	16	10 mg/m²s.c. bd	14–21	9	(56%)
Inbal et al (1985)	6	10 mg/m²s.c. bd	14	4	(67%)
Degos et al (1985)	38	10 mg/m²s.c. bd	19 (median)	15	(39%)
Alessandrino et al (1985)	15	10 mg/m²s.c. bd	14	2	(13%)
Worsley et al (1986)	6	3 mg/m²s.c. bd	21	4	(67%)
Pesce et al (1986)	11	5–10 mg/m² bd	21	2*	(18%)
	11	3 mg/m²s.c. bd	21	0*	(0%)
Total	178			75	(42%)

* CR only

Reproduced with permission from John Wiley and Sons Ltd from Hamblin TJ & Oscier DG (1987) *Haematological Oncology* **5**

well-documented that a minority of patients will respond dramatically without the need for supportive care and without nonhaematological side effects. Such patients may receive their treatment at home, with the LDAC being administered by themselves, a relative, or a district nurse, with obvious social and economic benefits.

In an attempt to reduce the degree and duration of cytopenia we have used a dose of 3 mg/m² SC 12 hourly for 21 days in eight patients, with three complete and three partial responses (Worsley et al, 1986). The peripheral blood counts fell in all cases but only three required platelet support and two developed infections which responded to treatment. An alternative approach employed by Griffin et al (1985) has been the use of a continuous IV infusion of LDAC at a dose of 20 mg/m²/day for 14–21 days. Of 16 patients treated, 11 responded, but considerable myelosuppression was observed. All patients required platelet support, and 17 of the 28 courses administered were associated with fevers requiring antibiotic treatment.

The overall response rate with LDAC is about 40%, and responses have been observed in all FAB types of MDS. The response rate in patients who have transformed to AML is lower but it is likely that the response to treatment will differ between those patients whose marrow blast count has gradually risen to 30% and those in whom a sudden leukaemic transformation has occurred.

Response to treatment may be complete or partial, and can be defined as follows:

Complete response   < 5% blasts in marrow and normal peripheral blood count.

Partial response   Increase in haemoglobin by > 2 g/dl.
Increase in platelet count by $> 50 \times 10^9/l$.
Decrease in marrow blasts:
(a) 50% fall in those whose initial blast count exceeded 10%.
(b) < 3% in those whose initial blast count was 5–10%.

Where pre- and post-treatment blood and marrow morphology and karyotype have been compared in those patients achieving a complete response, two patterns emerge. Some patients retain the morphological features of dysplasia and retain an abnormal karyotype, while others show normal cellular morphology and revert to a normal karyotype. The first type of response supports the view that LDAC acts by causing cell differentiation, whereas the latter lends support to the argument that it has a primary cytotoxic effect. An understanding of the mechanism of action is further complicated by the recent demonstration that remission blood and marrow in AML which is morphologically and karyotypically normal may still be of clonal origin (Fearon et al, 1986). It is quite likely that LDAC may act differently when given s.c. 12 hourly, thereby producing an initial peak but an unsustained serum level compared to its administration by continuous i.v. infusion.

When maintenance treatment is given, the duration of response seems to be prolonged, and in our experience the median response is about 1 year. In the series of Griffin et al (1985), where no maintenance was offered, the median duration of response was 3–5 months, but five relapsed patients were retreated and all responded.

In our limited experience, those patients who have developed acute leukaemia while on maintenance therapy have not subsequently responded to intensive chemotherapy with a combination of high-dose cytosine arabinoside and mitozantrone.

13-*cis*-retinoic acid

There have been a number of uncontrolled studies on the use of 13-*cis*-retinoic acid in MDS, and the results are summarized in Table 12. Increases in one or more cells in the peripheral blood are not seen for at least 3 weeks after starting treatment and have been documented in approximately one-third of cases. However, the responses have been minimal, temporary and of little clinical significance. In the patients treated by Picozzi et al (1986) there was good correlation between an increase in circulating neutrophils and an improvement in CFU-GM growth in vitro.

A further drawback to the use of 13-*cis*-retinoic acid is that at doses of 100 mg/m²/day (which achieve serum levels comparable to those which induce granulocytic differentiation of HL60 cells), side effects such as dryness of the skin, mucositis, nausea, lethargy and joint pains may necessitate drug withdrawal or dose reduction.

Table 12. Treatment of MDS with 13-*cis*-retinoic acid.

Study	Dosage/day	No. of patients	No. responding
Gold et al (1983)	20–125 mg/m²	15	5
Greenberg et al (1985)	1–3 mg/kg	18	3
Besa et al (1985)	100 mg/m²	24	7
Kerndrup et al (1986)	20–100 mg/m²	6	2
Picozzi et al (1986)	2.5–4 mg/kg	15	8
Total		78	25

A recent study has suggested that continuous treatment for at least 1 year with a lower dose of 13-*cis*-retinoic acid (20 mg/day) is well tolerated and may improve survival in patients with RA (Clark et al, 1987).

Other agents and combination therapy

Three uncontrolled trials using 1,25-$(OH)_2$-D_3 at doses of 1.0–2.5 μg daily have shown no evidence of haematological improvement (Mehta et al, 1984; Koeffler et al, 1985; Richard et al, 1986). The dose in vivo which would mirror that required to induce in vitro differentiation causes severe hypercalcaemia, and further trials must await the introduction of analogues which do not cause hypercalcaemia (Koeffler, 1986).

A single patient with RAEB reported by Galvani et al (1987) was treated with three megaunits of interferon (Wellferon) daily. After an initial period of worsening cytopenia, there was a marked improvement in the haemoglobin and neutrophil count, and a marrow aspirate at 6 weeks showed the features of RA.

Robert et al (1987) randomized 62 patients with primary MDS and 18 patients with AML to receive either LDAC alone, interferon, 13-*cis*-retinoic acid and 1,25-$(OH)_2$-D_3, or all four drugs. Preliminary results on 51 evaluable patients showed complete remission in six and partial remission in 10. No significant differences between the regimes has been seen so far. Ho et al (1987) treated 14 patients with a combination of LDAC 5 mg/m²/12 hourly SC and 13-*cis*-retinoic acid 60 mg/m²/day, and obtained ony partial responses in two patients.

The superiority of combination over single-agent treatment remains to be shown, as does the optimal combination of drugs. The benefit of newer agents such as γ interferon and recombinant GM-CSF remains to be evaluated, but only agents which are simple to administer and are devoid of serious side effects are likely to enter widespread clinical use.

Oral cytotoxic chemotherapy

Cytotoxic drugs such as hydroxyurea, 6-mercaptopurine, 6-thioguanine, razoxane and etoposide, given orally, may all be effective in controlling the peripheral blood leucocytosis in patients with high-count CMML. Our preference has been for etoposide, which in doses as low as 50 mg once or twice weekly may lead to the resolution of leukaemic skin infiltration, normalization of blood counts and disappearance of splenomegaly. However, not all patients respond and some may acquire resistance to one agent but still be responsive to another. Whether these agents are more effective than LDAC and whether their use prolongs survival remains to be established.

Preliminary data on the use of an oral anthracycline Idarubicin (4-demethoxydaunorubicin) has produced encouraging results. Johnson and Parapia (1986) have treated five patients with a single dose of 50 mg/m² repeated every 2–6 weeks. Three patients with RAEB achieved a complete response after three or four courses, while one with RAEBt and one who had undergone leukaemic transformation each had a partial response. The attractions of an effective oral treatment are obvious, and Idarubicin warrants further study.

A therapeutic strategy in MDS

There are some patients with MDS whose management is relatively straightforward. Patients who are well, with good prognostic features, require careful and regular follow-up only. This group would include many patients with RA, RAS and low-count CMML, particularly if they are ALIP-negative. Similarly, patients who are symptomatically anaemic and yet have normal granulopoiesis and megakaryopoiesis may have prolonged survival with regular red cell transfusions.

At the other extreme are patients in whom one can confidently predict short survival. Such patients are those whose disease has already transformed to acute leukaemia, those with RAEBt, those with high-count CMML and those with a Bournemouth score of 4 or a complex abnormal karyotype. A minority of patients in other groups who may already have experienced one or more episodes of life-threatening infection or bleeding should also be included in this category, for whom a response to treatment is the only way of prolonging survival. No treatment has yet been shown to be more effective than LDAC. It should be appreciated, however, that the demise of some patients will be hastened by this approach.

There remains a substantial number of patients for whom there is little information to suggest the most appropriate management. This group will include the majority of patients with RAEB and some with RA, RAS and CMML who have bi- or trilineage involvement. As no treatment is devoid of possible complications, one approach is to observe these patients until they enter the high-risk group. An alternative view is that early treatment is likely to be less toxic when peripheral blood counts are higher, and if it is successful the progresssion of the disease may be halted or at least delayed. It is to be hoped that controlled trials will resolve this dilemma.

REFERENCES

Alessandrino EP, Orlandi E, Brusamolino E, Lazzarino M & Bernasconi C (1985) Low-dose arabinosyl cytosine in acute leukaemia after a myelodysplastic syndrome and in elderly leukaemia. *American Journal of Hematology* **20**: 191–193.

Amenomori T, Tomonaga M, Yoshida Y et al (1986) Cytogenetic evidence for partially committed myeloid progenitor cell origin of chronic myelomonocytic leukaemia and juvenile chronic myeloid leukaemia: both granulocyte–macrophage precursors and erythroid precursors carry identical marker chromosome. *British Journal of Haematology* **64:** 539–546.

Annino L, Di Giovanni S, Tentori L Jr et al (1984) Acquired hemoglobin H disease in a case of refractory anemia with excess of blasts (RAEB) evolving into acute nonlymphoid leukemia. *Acta Haematologica* **72:** 41–44.

Appelbaum FR, Storb R, Ramberg RE et al (1987) Treatment of preleukemic syndromes with marrow transplantation. *Blood* **69:** 92–96.

Armitage JO, Dick FR, Needleman SW & Burns CP (1981) Effect of chemotherapy for the dysmyelopoietic syndrome. *Cancer Treatment Reports* **65:** 601–605.

Baccarani M & Tura S (1979) Differentiation of myeloid leukaemic cells. New possibilities for therapy. *British Journal of Haematology* **42:** 485–490.

Baccarani M, Zaccaria A, Bandini G et al (1983) Low dose arabinosyl cytosine for treatment of myelodysplastic syndromes and subacute myeloid leukemia. *Leukemia Research* **7**(4): 539–545.

Bagby GC Jr, Gabourel JD & Linman JW (1980) Glucocorticoid therapy in the preleukemic syndrome (hemopoietic dysplasia). *Annals of Internal Medicine* **92:** 55–58.

Baumann MA, Libnoch JA, Hansen RM, Heckman MG & Hanson GA (1985) Concurrent myelodysplasia and lymphoproliferation: a disorder of the true pluripotential stem cell. *Quarterly Journal of Medicine*, New Series 55, **218:** 199–211.

Baumann MA, Keller RH, McFadden PW, Libnoch JA & Patrick CW (1986) Myeloid cell surface phenotype in myelodysplasia: evidence for abnormal persistence of an early myeloid differentiation antigen. *American Journal of Hematology* **22:** 251–257.

Bendix-Hansen K & Kerndrup G (1985) Myeloperoxidase-deficient polymorphonuclear leucocytes (V): relation to FAB-classification and neutrophil alkaline phosphatase activity in primary myelodysplastic syndromes. *Scandinavian Journal of Haematology* **35:** 197–200.

Bennett JM, Catovsky D, Daniel M-T et al (1976) Proposals for the classification of the acute leukaemias. *British Journal of Haematology* **33:** 329–331.

Bennett JM, Catovsky D, Daniel M-T et al (1982) Proposals for the classification of the myelodysplastic syndromes. *British Journal of Haematology* **51:** 189–199.

Berneman ZN, Van Bockstaele D, De Meyer P et al (1985) A myelodysplastic syndrome preceding acute lymphoblastic leukaemia. *British Journal of Haematology* **60:** 353–354.

Besa EC, Hyzinskin NK & Abrahm JL (1985) High dose prolonged *cis* retinoic acid (RA) is required for clinical response in myelodysplastic syndrome (MDS). *Blood* **66** (5) (supplement) (abstract 663).

Billstrom R, Nilsson P-G & Mitelman F (1986) Cytogenetic analysis in 941 consecutive patients with haematologic disorders. *Scandinavian Journal of Haematology* **37:** 29–40.

Bjorkman SE (1956) Chronic refractory anaemia with sideroblastic bone marrow. A study of four cases. *Blood* **11:** 250–259.

Bloch A (1984) Induced cell differentiation in cancer therapy. *Cancer Treatment Reports* **68:** 199–205.

Block M, Jacobson LO & Bethard WF (1953) Preleukemic acute human leukemia. *Journal of the American Medical Association* **152:** 1018–1029.

Bloomfield CD, Garson OM, Volin L, Knuutila A & de la Chapelle A (1986) t(1;3)(p36;q21) in acute nonlymphocytic leukemia: a new clinicopathologic association. *Blood* **68:** 320–322 (letter).

Bonati A, Delia D & Starich R (1986) Progression of a myelodysplastic syndrome to pre-B acute lymphoblastic leukaemia with unusual phenotype. *British Journal of Haematology* **64:** 487–491.

Borgstrom G (1986) Cytogenetics of the myelodysplastic syndromes. *Scandinavian Journal of Haematology* **36:** 74–77.

Brito-Babapulle F, Catovsky D & Galton DAG (1987) De novo acute myeloid leukaemia with trilineage dysplasia: I. Clinical and laboratory features. *Blood* (in press).

Bynoe AG, Scott CS, Ford P & Roberts BE (1983) Decreased T-helper cells in the myelodysplastic syndromes. *British Journal of Haematology* **54:** 97–101.

Bynoe AG, Scott CS, Hough D & Roberts BE (1984) Granulocyte Fc-IgG and C3b receptor expression in the primary myelodysplastic syndromes (MDS): relationship with dysgranulopoiesis and evidence for heterogeneity of morphological subgroups. *Clinical and Experimental Immunology* **55:** 183–188.

Cines DB, Cassileth PA & Kiss JE (1985) Danazol therapy in myelodysplasia. *Annals of Internal Medicine* **103:** 58–60.

Clark RE, Hoy TG & Jacobs A (1984) Granulocyte and monocyte surface membrane markers in the myelodysplastic syndromes. *Journal of Clinical Pathology* **38:** 301–304.

Clark RE, Jacobs A, Lush CJ & Smith SA (1987) Effect of 13 *cis* retinoic acid on survival of patients with myelodysplastic syndrome. *Lancet* **i:** 763–765.

Clark R, Peters S, Hoy T et al (1986) Prognostic importance of hypodiploid hemopoetic precursors in myelodyplastic syndrome. *New England Journal of Medicine* **314:** 1472–1475.

Coiffier B, Adeleine P, Viala JJ et al (1983) Dysmyelopoietic syndromes. A search for prognostic factors in 193 patients. *Cancer* **52:** 83–90.

Copplestone JA, Oscier DG, Mufti GJ & Hamblin TJ (1986a) Monocytic skin infiltration in chronic myelomonocytic leukaemia. *Clinical and Laboratory Haematology* **8:** 115–119.

Copplestone JA, Mufti GJ, Hamblin TJ & Oscier DG (1986b) Immunological abnormalities in myelodysplastic syndromes. II. Coexistent lymphoid or plasma cell neoplasms: a report of 20 cases unrelated to chemotherapy. *British Journal of Haematology* **63:** 149–159.

Coutinho L, Geary CG, Testa N et al (1987) Long term bone marrow culture studies in patients with myelodysplasia (MDS). *British Journal of Haematology* (abstract) (in press).

Dameshek W & Gunz FW (1958) *Leukemia*, p 16. New York: Grune and Stratton.

Degos L, Castaigne S, Tilly H, Sigaux F & Daniel MT (1985) Treatment of leukemia with low-dose Ara-C: a study of 160 cases. *Seminars in Oncology* **12** (supplement 3): 196–199.

de la Chapelle A, Knuutila W & Elonen E (1986) Translocation (2;11)(p21;q23) in acute non-lymphocytic leukaemia: a non-random association. *Scandinavian Journal of Haematology* **36** (supplement 45): 91–97.

Dewald GW, Pierre RV & Phyliky RL (1982) Three patients with structurally abnormal X chromosomes, each with Xq13 breakpoints and a history of idiopathic acquired sideroblastic anemia. *Blood* **59:** 100–105.

Dreyfus B (1976) Preleukemic states. I. Definition and classification. II. Refractory anemia with excess of myeloblasts in the bone marrow (smoldering acute leukemia). *Blood Cells* **2:** 33–35.

Dreyfus B, Rochant H, Sultan C, Clauvel JP & Chesneau AM (1970) Les anemies refractaires avec exces de myeloblastes dans la moelle. Etude de onze observations. *Nouveau Presse Médecine* **78:** 359–364.

Economopoulos T, Papageorgiou E & Hadjioannou J (1984) Refractory anaemia with excess of blasts terminating as Ph¹ negative chronic myeloid leukaemia. *Scandinavian Journal of Haematology* **32:** 493–495.

Economopoulos T, Economidou J, Giannopoulos G et al (1985) Immune abnormalities in myelodysplastic syndromes. *Journal of Clinical Pathology* **38:** 908–911.

Erber WN, Jacobs A, Oscier DG, O'Hea AM & Mason DY (1987) Circulating micromegakaryocytes in myelodysplasia. *Journal of Clinical Pathology* (in press).

Eridani S, Chan LC, Halil O & Pearson TC (1985) Acute biphenotypic leukaemia (myeloid and nul-ALL type) supervening in a myelodysplastic syndrome. *British Journal of Haematology* **61:** 525–529.

Fearon ER, Burke PJ, Schiffer CA, Zehnbauer BA & Vogelstein B (1986) Differentiation of leukemia cells to polymorphonuclear leukocytes in patients with acute nonlymphocytic leukemia. *New England Journal of Medicine* **315:** 15–24.

Fenaux P, Jouet JP, Zandecki M et al (1987) Chronic and subacute myelomonocytic leukaemia in the adult: a report of 60 cases with special reference to prognostic factors. *British Journal of Haematology* **65:** 101–106.

Fohlmeister I, Fischer R, Modder B, Rister M & Schaefer HE (1985a) Aplastic anaemia and the hypocellular myelodysplastic syndrome: histomorphological, diagnostic and prognostic factors. *Journal of Clinical Pathology* **38:** 1218–1224.

Fohlmeister I, Fischer R & Schaefer HE (1985b) Preleukemic myelodysplastic syndromes (MDS): pathogenetical considerations based on retrospective clinicomorphological sequential studies. *Anticancer Research* **5:** 179–188.

Foucar K, Langdon RM, Armitage JO, Olson DB & Carrol TJ Jr (1985) Myelodysplastic syndromes. A clinical and pathologic analysis of 109 cases. *Cancer* **56:** 553–561.

Francis GE, Guimaraes JE, Berney JJ et al (1982) T lymphocyte subsets and partial uncoupling of granulocyte macrophage progenitor cell differentiation and proliferation in normal cells. *Experimental Haematology Review* (supplement 12): 179–193.

Francis GE, Guimaraes JET, Berney JJ & Wing MA (1985) Synergistic interaction between differentiation inducers and DNA synthesis inhibitors: a new approach to differentiation induction in myelodysplasia and acute myeloid leukaemia. *Leukaemia Research* **9:** 573–582.

Frisch B & Bartl R (1986) Bone marrow histology in myelodysplastic syndromes. *Scandinavian Journal of Haematology* **36** (supplement 45): 21–37.

Galton DAG (1986) The myelodysplastic syndromes. Part I. What are they? Part II. Classification. *Scandinavian Journal of Haematology* **36:** 11–20.

Galvani et al (1987) Alpha interferon in myelodysplasia. *British Journal of Haematology* **66:** 145.

Ganesan TS, Rassool F, Guo A-P et al (1986) Rearrangement of the bcr gene in Philadelphia chromosome-negative chronic myeloid leukemia. *Blood* **68:** 957–960.

Gold EJ, Mertelsmann RH, Itrl LM et al (1983) Phase 1 clinical trial of 13-*cis*-retinoic acid in myelodysplastic syndromes. *Cancer Treatment Reports* **67:** 981–986.

Gow JW, Oscier DG & Padua RA (1987) Detection of mutated c-Ha-ras in chronic granulocytic and chronic myelomonocytic leukaemias. *British Journal of Haematology* (abstract) (in press).

Greenberg BR, Durie BGM, Barnett TC & Meyskens FL (1985) Phase I-II study of 13-*cis*-retinoic acid in myelodysplastic syndrome. *Cancer Treatment Reports* **69:** 1369–1374.

Greenberg PL (1986) In vitro culture techniques defining biological abnormalities in the myelodysplastic syndromes and myeloproliferative disorders. *Clinics in Haematology* **15:** 973–995.

Griffin JD & Young DC (1986) The role of colony stimulating factors in leukaemogenesis. *Clinics in Haematology* **15:** 995–1002.

Griffin JD, Spriggs D, Wisch JS & Kufe DW (1985) Treatment of preleukemic syndromes with continuous intravenous infusion of low-dose cytosine arabinoside. *Journal of Clinical Oncology* **3:** 982–991.

Hall AG, Proctor SJ & Saunders PWG (1987) Increased platelet associated immunoglobulin in myelodysplastic syndromes. *British Journal of Haematology* **65:** 245–246.

Hamilton-Paterson JL (1949) Preleukaemic anaemia. *Acta Haematologica* **2:** 309–316.

Hast R (1986) Sideroblasts in myelodysplasia: their nature and clinical significance. *Scandinavian Journal of Haematology* **36:** 53–55.

Hauptman GM, Sondag D, Lang JM & Oberling F (1978) False positive acidified serum lysis test in a preleukaemic dyserythropoiesis. *Acta Haematologica* **59:** 73–79.

Ho AD, Martin H, Knauf W et al (1987) Combination of low-dose cytosine arabinoside and 13-*cis*-retinoic acid in the treatment of myelodysplastic syndromes. *Leukaemia Research* (in press).

Inbal A, Januszewick E, Rabinowictz M & Shaklai M (1985) A therapeutic trial with low-dose cytarabine in myelodysplastic syndromes and acute leukemia. *Acta Haematologica* **73:** 71–74.

Jacobs A (1985) Myelodysplastic syndromes: pathogenesis, functional abnormalities, and clinical implications. *Journal of Clinical Pathology* **38:** 1201–1217.

Jacobs P, Palmer S & Gordon-Smith EC (1985) Pyoderma grangrenosum in myelodysplasia and acute leukaemia. *Postgraduate Medical Journal* **61:** 689–694.

Jacobs RH, Cornbleet MA, Vardiman JW et al (1986) Prognostic implications of morphology and karyotype in primary myelodysplastic syndromes. *Blood* **67:** 1765–1772.

Jeffreys AJ, Wilson V & Thein SL (1985) Hypervariable minisatellite regions in human DNA. *Nature* **314:** 67–73.

Johnson E & Parapia IA (1986) Successful oral chemotherapy with idarubicin in refractory anaemia with excess blasts (RAEB). *Proceedings of the Combined British and Netherlands Society of Haematology*, Antwerp.

Juneja SK, Imbert M, Sigaux F, Jouault H & Sultan C (1983) Prevalence and distribution of ringed sideroblasts in primary myelodysplastic syndromes. *Journal of Clinical Pathology* **36:** 566–569.

Juvonen E, Partanen S, Knwutila S & Ruutu T (1986) Megakaryocyte colony formation by bone marrow progenitors in myelodysplastic syndromes. *British Journal of Haematology* **63**: 331–334.

Kere J, Ruutu T & de la Chapelle A (1987) Monosomy 7 in granulocytes and monocytes in myelodysplastic syndrome. *New England Journal of Medicine* **316**: 499–503.

Kerkhofs H, Hermans J, Haak HL & Leeksma CHW (1987) Utility of the FAB classification for myelodysplastic syndromes. Investigation of prognostic factors in 256 cases. *British Journal of Haematology* **65**: 73–81.

Kerndup G, Mayer K, Ellegard J & Hokland P (1984) Natural killer (NK) activity and antibody-dependent cellular cytotoxicity (ADCC) in primary preleukaemic syndrome. *Leukaemia Research* **8**: 239–247.

Kerndrup G, Bendix-Hansen K, Pedersen B, Ellegaard J & Hokland P (1986) Primary myelodysplastic syndrome. Treatment of 6 patients with 13-*cis* retinoic acid. *Scandinavian Journal of Haematology* **36** (supplement 45): 128–132.

Knapp RH, Dewald GW & Pierre RV (1985) Cytogenetic studies in 174 consecutive patients with preleukemic or myelodysplastic syndromes. *Mayo Clinic Proceedings* **60**: 507–516.

Knudson AG (1985) Hereditary cancer, oncogenes and antioncogenes. *Cancer Research* **45**: 1437–1443.

Koeffler HP (1986) Myelodysplastic syndromes (preleukemia). *Seminars in Hematology* **23**: 284–299.

Koeffler HP, Hirji K & Itri L (1985) 1,25-hydroxy vitamin D₃: in vivo and in vitro effects on human preleukaemic and leukaemic cells. *Cancer Treatment Reports* **69**: 1399–1407.

Krontiris TG, DiMartino NA, Colb M & Parkinson DR (1985) Unique allelic restriction fragments of the human Ha-ras locus in leukocyte and tumour DNAs of cancer patients. *Nature* **313**: 369–374.

Kuriyama K, Tomonaga M, Matsuo T, Ginnai I & Ichimaru M (1986) Diagnostic significance of detecting pseudo-Pelger–Huet anomalies and micro-megakaryocytes in myelodysplastic syndrome. *British Journal of Haematology* **63**: 665–669.

Layton DM & Mufti GJ (1986) Myelodysplastic syndromes: their history, evolution and relation to acute myeloid leukaemia. *Blüt* **53**: 423–436.

Le Beau MM, Westbrook CA, Diaz MO et al (1986) Evidence for the involvement of GM-CSF and FMS in the deletion (5q) in myeloid disorders. *Science* **231**: 984–987.

Lintula R (1986) Red cell enzymes in myelodysplastic syndromes: a review. *Scandinavian Journal of Haematology* **36** (supplement 45): 56–59.

Lotem J & Sachs L (1974) Different blocks in the differentiation of myeloid leukaemic cells. *Proceedings of the National Academy of Science USA* **71**: 3507–3511.

May SJ, Smith SA, Jacobs A et al (1985) The myelodysplastic syndrome: analysis of laboratory characteristics in relation to the FAB classification. *British Journal of Haematology* **59**: 311–319.

Mecucci C, Rege-Cambrin G, Michaux J-L, Tricot G & Van den Berghe H (1986) Multiple chromosomally distinct cell populations in myelodysplastic syndromes and their possible significance in the evolution of the disease. *British Journal of Haematology* **64**: 699–706.

Mehta AB, Kumaran TO & Marsh GW (1984) Treatment of advanced myelodysplastic syndrome with alfacalcidol. *Lancet* **ii**: 761.

Michet JC, McKenna CH, Luthra HS & O'Fallon WM (1986) Relapsing polychondritis. Survival and predictive role of early disease manifestations. *Annals of Internal Medicine* **104**: 74–78.

Miller BA, Weinstein HJ, Nell M et al (1985) Sequential development of distinct clonal chromosome abnormalities in a patient with preleukaemia. *British Journal of Haematology* **59**: 411–418.

Mufti GJ, Oscier DG, Hamblin TJ & Bell AJ (1983) Low doses of cytarabine in the treatment of myelodysplastic syndrome and acute myeloid leukaemia. *New England Journal of Medicine* **309**: 1653–1654.

Mufti GJ, Oscier DG, Hamblin TJ, Nightingale A & Darlow S (1984) Serous effusions in monocytic leukaemias. *British Journal of Haematology* **58**: 547–552.

Mufti GJ, Stevens JR, Oscier DG, Hamblin TJ & Machin D (1985) Myelodysplastic syndromes: a scoring system with prognostic significance. *British Journal of Haematology* **59**: 425–433.

Mufti GJ, Figes AN, Hamblin TJ, Oscier DG & Copplestone JA (1986) Immunological abnormalities in myelodysplastic syndromes. I. Serum immunoglobulins and autoantibodies. *British Journal of Haematology* **63**: 143–147.

Najean Y & Pecking A (1979) Refractory anaemia with excess of myeloblasts in the bone marrow: a clinical trial of androgens in 90 patients. *British Journal of Haematology* **37:** 25–33.

Napoli VM, Stein SF, Spira TJ & Raskin D (1986) Myelodysplasia progressing to acute myeloblastic leukemia in an HLTV-III virus-positive homosexual man with AIDS-related complex. *American Journal of Clinical Pathology* **86:** 788–791.

Newman DR, Pierre RV & Linman JW (1973) Studies on the diagnostic significance of hemoglobin F levels. *Mayo Clinic Proceedings* **48:** 199–202.

Pedersen-Bjergaard J, Vindelov L, Philip P et al (1982) Varying involvement of peripheral granulocytes in the clonal abnormality − 7 in bone marrow cells in preleukemia secondary to treatment of other malignant tumours: cytogenetic results compared with results of flow cytometric DNA analysis and neutrophil chemotaxis. *Blood* **60:** 172–179.

Pereira AM, De Castro JT, Santos EG, Perloiro MC & Catovsky D (1985) T lymphoblastic transformation of refractory anaemia with excess of blasts. *Clinical and Laboratory Haematology* **7:** 89–95.

Pesce A, Cassuto JP, Bayle J et al (1986) Very-low-dose cytarabine for elderly patients. *Lancet* **ii:** 1436.

Picozzi VJ, Swanson G, Morgan R, Hecht F & Greenberg PL (1986) 13-*cis* retinoic acid for myelodysplastic syndromes. *Journal of Clinical Oncology* **4:** 589–595.

Prchal JT, Trockmorton DW, Carrol AJ et al (1978) A common progenitor for myeloid and lymphoid cells. *Nature* **274:** 590–591.

Pugh WC, Pearson M, Vardiman JW & Rowley JD (1985) Philadelphia chromosome-negative chronic myelogenous leukaemia: a morphological reassessment. *British Journal of Haematology* **60:** 457–467.

Rasi V & Lintula R (1986) Platelet function in the myelodysplastic syndromes. *Scandinavian Journal of Haematology* **36** (supplement 45): 71–73

Raskind WH, Tirumali N, Jacobson R, Singer J & Fialkow J (1984) Evidence for a multistep pathogenesis of a myelodysplastic syndrome. *Blood* **63:** 1318–1323.

Rheingold JJ, Kaufman R, Adelson E & Lear A (1963) Smoldering acute leukemia. *New England Journal of Medicine* **268:** 812–815.

Rhoads CP & Barker WH (1938) Refractory anaemia: analysis of 100 cases. *Journal of the American Medical Association* **110:** 794–796.

Richard C, Mazo E, Cuadrado MA et al (1986) Treatment of myelodysplastic syndrome with 1,25-dihydroxy-vitamin D₃. *American Journal of Haematology* **23:** 175–178.

Robert K-H, Hellstrom E, Gahrton G et al (1987) Acute myelogenous leukemia and myelodysplastic syndromes treated with retinoic acid, 1,25-dihydroxy vit D3, alpha interferon, and low dose cytosine arabinoside. *4th International Symposium on Therapy of Acute Leukemias*, Rome.

Roberts JD, Ershler WB, Tindle BH & Stewart JA (1985) Low-dose cytosine arabinoside in the myelodysplastic syndromes and acute myelogenous leukemia. *Cancer* **56:** 1001–1005.

Ruiz-Arguelles GJ (1987) Immunologic classification of blast cells in RAEB. *British Journal of Haematology* **65:** 124.

Rummens JL, Verfaillie C, Criel A et al (1986) Elliptocytosis and schistocytosis in myelodysplasia: report of two cases. *Acta Haematologica* **75:** 174–177.

Ruutu T (1986) Granulocyte function in the myelodysplastic syndromes. *Scandinavian Journal of Haematology* **36** (supplement 45): 66–70.

Ruutu T, Partanen S, Lintula R, Teerenhovi L & Knuutila S (1984) Erythroid and granulocyte–macrophage colony formation in myelodysplastic syndromes. *Scandinavian Journal of Haematology* **32:** 395–402.

Saarni MJ & Linman JW (1973) The haematologic syndrome preceding acute myeloid leukemia. *American Journal of Medicine* **55:** 38–48.

Salmon A (1976) Blood group changes in preleukaemic states. *Blood Cells* **2:** 211–220.

Scheres JMJC, Hustinx TWJ, Geraedts JPM et al (1985) Translocation 1;7 in hematologic disorders: a brief review of 22 cases. *Cancer Genetics and Cytogenetics* **18:** 207–213.

Schneider DR & Picker LJ (1985) Myelodysplasia in the acquired immune deficiency syndrome. *American Journal of Clinical Pathology* **84:** 144–152.

Scott CS, Cahill A, Bynoe AG et al (1983) Esterase cytochemistry in primary myelodysplastic syndromes and megaloblastic anaemias: demonstration of abnormal staining patterns associated with dysmyelopoiesis. *British Journal of Haematology* **55:** 411–418.

Seigneurin D & Audhuy B (1983) Auer rods in refractory anemia with excess of blasts: presence and significance. *American Journal of Clinical Pathology* **80:** 359–362.

Solal-Celigny P, Desaint B, Herrera A et al (1984) Chronic myelomonocytic leukemia according to FAB classification analysis of 35 cases. *Blood* **63:** 634–638.

Stark AN, Scott CS, Bhatt B & Roberts BE (1986) Myelodysplastic syndrome coexisting with acute lymphoblastic leukaemia. *Journal of Clinical Pathology* **39:** 728–730.

Sultan C, Marquet M & Joffroy Y (1974) Etude de certaines dysmyelopoieses acquises idiopathiques et secondaires par culture de moelle in vitro. *Annales de Médicine Interne* **125:** 599.

Sultan C, Sigaux F, Imbert M & Reyes F (1981) Acute myelodysplasia with myelofibrosis: a report of eight cases. *British Journal of Haematology* **49:** 11–16.

Teerenhovi L & Lintula R (1986) Natural course of myelodysplastic syndromes—Helsinki experience. *Scandinavian Journal of Haematology* **36:** 102–106.

Tennant GB, Jacobs A & Bailey-Wood R (1986) Peripheral blood granulocyte–macrophage progenitors in patients with the myelodysplastic syndromes. *Experimental Hematology* **14:** 1063–1068.

Thein SL, Oscier DG, Flint J & Wainscoat JS (1986) Ha-ras hypervariable alleles in myelodysplasia. *Nature* **321:** 84–85.

Thein SL, Oscier DG, Jeffreys AJ et al (1987) Detection of chromosome 7 loss in myelodysplasia using an extremely polymorphic DNA probe (submitted for publication).

Todd WM & Pierre RV (1986) Pre-leukaemia: a long term prospective study of 326 patients. *Scandinavian Journal of Haematology* **36:** 114–120.

Travis LB, Pierre RV & Dewald GW (1986) Ph′ negative chronic granulocytic leukaemia: a nonentity. *American Journal of Clinical Pathology* **85:** 186–193.

Tricot G & Boogaerts MA (1986) The role of aggressive chemotherapy in the treatment of the myelodysplastic syndromes. *British Journal of Haematology* **63:** 477–483.

Tricot G, De Wolf-Peeters C, Hendrickx B & Verwilghen RL (1984a) Bone marrow histology in myelodysplastic syndromes. I. Histological findings in myelodysplastic syndromes and comparison with bone marrow smears. *British Journal of Haematology* **57:** 423–430.

Tricot G, De Wolf-Peeters C, Vlietinck R & Verwilghen RL (1984b) Bone marrow histology in myelodysplastic syndromes. II. Prognostic value of abnormal localization of immature precursors in MDS. *British Journal of Haematology* **58:** 217–225.

Tricot G, De Bock R, Dekker AW et al (1984c) Low dose cytosine arabinoside (Ara C) in myelodysplastic syndromes. *British Journal of Haematology* **58:** 231–240.

Tricot G, Vlietinck R, Boogaerts MA et al (1985a) Prognostic factors in the myelodysplastic syndromes: importance of initial data on peripheral blood counts, bone marrow cytology, trephine biopsy and chromosomal analysis. *British Journal of Haematology* **60:** 19–32.

Tricot G, Boogaerts MA, De Wolf-Peeters C, Van den Berghe H & Verwilghen RL (1985b) The myelodysplastic syndromes: different evolution patterns based on sequential morphological and cytogenetic investigations. *British Journal of Haematology* **59:** 659–670.

Tricot G, Vlietinck R & Verwilghen RL (1986) Prognostic factors in the myelodysplastic syndromes: a review. *Scandinavian Journal of Haematology* **36:** 107–113.

Vallespi T, Torrabadella M, Julia A et al (1985) Myelodysplastic syndromes: a study of 101 cases according to the FAB classification. *British Journal of Haematology* **61:** 83–92.

Van den Berghe H (1986) The 5q− syndrome. *Scandinavian Journal of Haematology* **36:** 78–81.

Varela BL, Chuang C, Woll JE & Bennett JM (1985) Modifications in the classification of primary myelodysplastic syndromes: the addition of a scoring system. *Hematological Oncology* **3:** 55–63.

Vilter RW & Wiltse D (1985) Preleukemia and urticaria pigmentosa followed by acute myelomonoblastic leukemia. *Archives of Internal Medicine* **145:** 349–352.

Weisdorf DJ, Oken MM, Johnson GJ et al (1981) Auer rod positive dysmyelopoietic syndrome. *American Journal of Haematology* **11:** 397–402.

Weisdorf DJ, Oken MM, Johnson GJ & Rydell RE (1983) Chronic myelodysplastic syndrome: short survival with or without evolution to acute leukaemia. *British Journal of Haematology* **55:** 691–700.

Williams MD, Shinton NK & Finney RD (1985) Primary acquired sideroblastic anaemia and myeloproliferative disease: a report on three cases. *Clinical and Laboratory Haematology* **7:** 113–118.

Winter JN, Variakojis D, Gaynor ER, Larson RA & Miller KB (1985) Low-dose cytosine arabinoside (Ara-C) therapy in the myelodysplastic syndromes and acute leukemia. *Cancer* **56:** 443–449.

Worsley A, Mufti GJ, Copplestone JA, Oscier DG & Hamblin TJ (1986) Very-low-dose cytarabine for myelodysplastic syndromes and acute myeloid leukaemia in the elderly. *Lancet* **i:** 966.

Worsley A, Mufti GJ, Stevens J, Oscier DG & Hamblin TJ (1987a) Chronic myelomonocytic leukaemia: a scoring system with prognostic significance. *British Journal of Haematology* (submitted for publication).

Worsley A, Darlow S, Figes A, Hamblin TJ & Oscier DG (1987b) Erythroid and granulocyte-macrophage colony formation in myelodysplastic syndromes. *British Journal of Haematology* (in press).

Yunis JJ, Rydell RE, Oken MM et al (1986) Refined chromosome analysis as an independent prognostic indicator in de novo myelodysplastic syndromes. *Blood* **67:** 1721–1730.

6

The management of leukaemia in the elderly

MICHAEL A. BAKER

The management of all patients with leukaemia raises a number of issues that centre around the toxicity of specific treatment compared to the benefits of therapy. Management decisions are more difficult in leukaemia occurring over the age of 65 because of the apparent increase in toxicity of current chemotherapy in this population, and the resulting decrease in benefit to the patient's duration and quality of life.

Leukaemias occurring in this age group may be intrinsically different; for example, the acute myeloblastic leukaemia that follows myelodysplasia in the elderly (Table 1). There is an increased likelihood of concurrent disease accompanied by medication that may interact with antileukaemic therapy. There is clinical evidence to suggest that the resilience of normal haematopoietic stem cells following cytotoxic chemotherapy is reduced in the elderly, leading to prolonged pancytopenia (Lipschitz, 1985). Infections and haemorrhagic complications of leukaemia and of chemotherapy are less well tolerated than in younger patients. Intravenous access is often more difficult in elderly patients, although the tendency to use indwelling, centrally-placed lines has improved access for all patients. Very aggressive treatment regimens that require haematologic rescue by allogeneic marrow transplant or autologous marrow infusion, are at present sufficiently toxic that patients over the age of 50 are almost universally excluded at the present time.

Future therapeutic developments, such as the clinical availability of haematopoietic growth factors, may render cytotoxic chemotherapy safer in the elderly patient with leukaemia. At the present time, however, the management of leukaemia in patients over 65 requires that difficult and sometimes controversial decisions be addressed. This chapter explores the current management alternatives for elderly patients with leukaemia.

INCIDENCE

The annual incidence of leukaemia in the general population is about 9 per 100 000 population (Wintrobe, 1981) (Table 2). The annual, age adjusted incidence of leukaemia in the population aged 65 and over is 69 per 100 000

Table 1. Problems associated with the management of leukaemia in the elderly.

Leukaemias may be intrinsically different
High incidence of preceding myelodysplasia
Increased likelihood of coincident disease
Decreased resilience of normal haematopoiesis
Lower tolerance to toxic complications
Intravenous access more difficult
Ineligibility for marrow transplants

---

population (Baranovsky, 1986). The prevalence of leukaemia (i.e. the number of people alive with a history of leukaemia) is about 40 per 100 000 in the general population, but 203 per 100 000 in the population over age 70 (Feldman, 1986). The incidence and prevalence of leukaemia continue to rise after age 65, so that over 50% of all leukaemias occur in the elderly.

Men have a slightly higher incidence and prevalence of leukaemia in all age groups (a ratio of about 4:3), but in the elderly, the incidence of leukaemia in men is double that in women (79 versus 41 per 100 000). The incidence of leukaemia in the elderly has been stable over the decade of the 1970s (Baranovsky, 1986). For all leukaemias, the five year survival rate is 32% for men aged 45–64 and 25% for men over age 65, with women surviving slightly better (33% and 29%).

It is important to note that over 50% of leukaemias occur after the age of 65. If subtypes of leukaemia are analysed, this holds true for all categories except for acute lymphoblastic leukaemia (Baranovsky, 1986). As discussed later in the chapter, reports that discuss the management of leukaemia often exclude patients over 65, and hence the majority of patients may not be considered.

Table 2. Incidence of leukaemia in the elderly.

Leukaemia	Incidence per 100 000 population age 65 & over		Percent of all cases that are 65 or over	
	Males	Females	Males	Females
All patients	69.0	34.2	53	57
Acute leukaemia				
myeloblastic	16.4	8.5	52	51
lymphoblastic	1.8	0.7	13	10
Chronic leukaemia				
myelogenous	8.5	4.7	54	59
lymphocytic	24.6	12.3	64	75
Other leukaemias*	17.6	8.0	58	66

* Other leukaemias include largely those that are not specified.
Adapted from Baranovsky & Myers (1986).

MYELODYSPLASTIC SYNDROMES (PRELEUKAEMIA)

Clinicians have long appreciated that leukaemia, especially in the elderly, may follow a prolonged period of refractory anaemia. Other patients were considered 'smouldering' leukaemias or oligoleukaemias because of their low numbers of blast cells and the prolonged time interval to the development of frank acute leukaemia. These conditions share features of abnormal haematopoiesis and do not always progress to leukaemia, and have therefore recently been renamed the myelodysplastic syndromes. The mean age of patients with myelodysplastic syndromes is 65 to 70. Many patients progress to acute leukaemia and there are several agents under clinical trial for treatment of these conditions. It is therefore important to include the myelodysplastic syndromes when considering the management of leukaemia in the elderly.

Myelodysplastic syndromes are discussed in greater detail in Chapter 5, but since the principles of management depend on an understanding of the prognosis of these diseases some repetition is necessary here.

Most patients with a myelodysplastic syndrome will not develop acute leukaemia (Koeffler, 1986). Refractory anaemia with ringed sideroblasts (RARS) progresses to acute leukaemia in only 10% of patients, refractory anaemia (RA) in 15%, chronic myelomonocytic leukaemia (CMML) in 30%, refractory anaemia with excess blasts (RAEB) in 40% and refractory anaemia with excess blasts in transformation (RAEB-T) in 60%. The pancytopenia associated with the primary myelodysplastic disease may also lead to fatality from infection or haemorrhage. A scoring system has recently been proposed for predicting prognosis in myelodysplastic syndromes based on blood and bone marrow findings (Mufti, 1985). The percentage of bone marrow blasts and the peripheral blood haemoglobin, neutrophil and platelet counts were used to divide 141 patients into three groups with significant differences in median survival (62 months, 22 months and 8 months). Cytogenetic changes are commonly seen in myelodysplastic syndromes, particularly deletions of the long arm of chromosomes 5, 7 or 20, or the acquisition of an additional chromosome X (Yunis, 1986). Both the extent and the pattern of evolution of chromosome changes predict for the likelihood of conversion to acute leukaemia (Tricot, 1985), particularly in RAEB. Studies of in-vitro growth of granulocyte–macrophage colonies from marrow aspirates generally reveal decreased numbers of colonies compared to normal marrow (Greenberg, 1979). Progressive decrease in cloning efficiency, or an increase in the large cluster pattern have been associated with progression to leukaemia and poor prognosis (Buzaid, 1986). Patients developing myelodysplasia after exposure to chemotherapy or radiotherapy generally carry a worse prognosis than patients with de novo disease (Michels, 1985).

Using the French–American–British (FAB) morphological classification, the myelodysplastic syndromes fall into two main prognostic groups (Koeffler 1986). RA and RARS are similar in prognostic parameters and have a median survival of 65 to 70 months. CMML, RAEB and RAEB-T also form a group with similar prognostic features and have a median survival of 5 to 10 months.

Management

Management decisions in the elderly patient with a myelodysplastic syndrome must first take into account the natural history and prognosis of the individual patient's disease. A period of observation is usually indicated with red cell transfusions given as necessary. Determination of the prognostic indicators and the course of the individual disease may allow a long period of symptomatic management and support without specific therapeutic agents being introduced.

A number of agents given alone or in combination have been used to treat myelodysplastic syndromes, but most treatments are either toxic, generally ineffective or both, especially in the elderly patient (Editorial, 1984; Buzaid, 1986). Pyridoxine, pyridoxal-5-phosphate and folic acid have been used primarily in sideroblastic anaemias with some case reports of improvement in haemoglobin levels and decrease in transfusion requirement (Meier, 1982). It is not clear whether responsive patients have primary refractory anaemia or are in fact pyridoxine or folate deficient. Since both drugs are inexpensive and non-toxic, an 8 to 12 week trial of pyridoxine 200 mg per day and folate 5 mg per day may be warranted in RARS, but most patients will not respond.

Corticosteroids have been reported to show improved peripheral blood counts in a small number of patients with RA and RARS (Daniak, 1980). The toxicity of steroid treatment is high, particularly in the elderly and should probably not be used in this setting. Stimulation of marrow colonies in vitro may be used to select the few patients who may show a transient response to steroids. Androgens have been tested in RAEB and in other myelodysplastic syndromes and found to be ineffective (Najean, 1977). Danazol has apparently led to improvement in platelet count and haemoglobin in a small number of patients, but they may have had immune mechanisms active and are not typical cases (Cines, 1985; Buzaid, 1986).

There are a large number of drugs and chemicals that induce the differentiation of leukaemia cells in vitro. Two of these, 13-*cis*-retinoic acid and 1,25-dihydroxyvitamin D_3, have been tested in the treatment of myelodysplastic syndromes. The hypothesis is that differentiation of the affected pluripotent stem cell will lead to increased production of mature blood cells. Retinoic acid treatment was associated with partial responses in a few patients with RAEB, RARS and CMML. The responses were delayed, transient and associated with toxicity that included cheilosis, hyperkeratosis, stomatitis and hepatotoxicity (Greenburg, 1985). Vitamin D_3 was less successful and also associated with significant toxicity (Koeffler, 1985). These differentiating agents require further study and are not generally recommended at present.

Aggressive cytotoxic combination chemotherapy has been studied in the myelodysplastic syndromes that have a poor prognosis. Response rates of 50% have been obtained in RAEB and CMML with a median duration of response of 6 to 8 months; however, the responding patients had a median age of under 55 years (Mertelsmann, 1980). Aggressive combination chemotherapy for the elderly patient with a myelodysplastic syndrome is likely to do more harm than good.

Cytosine arabinoside has been shown to be both a cytotoxic and a differentiating agent in studies of leukaemic cells and cell lines in vitro. There have been a number of trials of cytosine arabinoside using various low dose regimens for the treatment of myelodysplastic syndromes. Although a response is seen in about half the patients treated with various regimens, the duration of response is short and the toxicity is high, particularly in elderly patients (Wisch, 1983; Tricot, 1984; Winter, 1985). Very low dose cytosine arabinoside, 3 mg/m² twice daily for 21 days, has shown promise of producing a response in patients with RAEB and RAEB-T in elderly patients in some clinics (Worsley, 1986), but not others (Pesce, 1986), and further studies are in progress. Bone marrow transplants have been studied in the myelodysplastic syndromes but are not suitable for elderly patients.

Management of myelodysplastic syndromes in the elderly requires judgment and patience. Determination of prognostic indicators, follow-up observations, transfusions and supportive care may constitute the optimum therapy for this group of patients. More specific therapy must be considered unsuccessful to date and the results of further studies will be awaited with interest.

ACUTE MYELOBLASTIC LEUKAEMIA

Acute myeloblastic leukaemia (AML) is a devastating illness that has world-wide distribution. Important strides have been made in understanding the pathogenesis of this disease and treatments are now available where none existed 20 years ago. Unfortunately, most patients with AML still die of their disease in less than two years; the treatment carries a high morbidity, and more than half of the patients are elderly. Considerable judgment must be exercised in managing this type of leukaemia.

Discussions of treatment modalities for AML have often paid insufficient attention to the age distribution of the affected population. The incidence of AML in the general population is about 3 per 100 000 population with the ratio of men:women being 3:2 (Wintrobe, 1981). Several recent studies from Denmark, Canada and the United States have provided detailed information on the age distribution of AML determined in a large population base (Brincker, 1985; The Toronto Leukaemia Study Group, 1986; Baranovsky, 1986; Feldman, 1986). The median age of patients with AML is 60 to 65 years. The incidence of the disease rises continuously with age, from about 1 per 100 000 under age 20 to about 15 per 100 000 over age 80. The incidence in males over 65 (16.4 per 100 000) is double that for females over 65 (8.5 per 100 000). The prevalence of the disease, the number of patients alive with AML, also rises sharply with age in both sexes.

Classification

The classification of AML has been largely dependent on morphology by light microscopy (Bennett, 1985) (Table 3). The FAB classification recognizes the probable lines of differentiation of the leukaemic blast cells. The M1 type has largely undifferentiated blasts with a few granules or Auer rods; M2 cells show early granular differentiation; M3 cells are promyelocytes, but multilobed nuclei and microgranular forms are recognized; M4 cells are myelomonocytic; M5 cells are monoblastic or monocytic; M6 is erythroleukaemia; and the recently described M7 type has megakaryoblasts and abnormal platelets. The FAB classification has been important in standardizing diagnoses for comparison of treatment results, but has not defined important differences in prognosis or treatment selection. Exceptions to this rule would include identification of M3 subtypes that have coagulation abnormalities at presentation, and the recognition that M4 and M5 subtypes have an increase in invasion of tissues including the central nervous system.

The homogeneity of prognosis and treatment response amongst the various morphologic subtypes has stimulated a search for more clinically helpful classifications. New technological developments have led to proposals for classification systems that might supplement if not replace strict morphological criteria. These techniques are chromosome banding and cell surface marker analysis. High resolution chromosome banding, using quinacrine or Giemsa staining has permitted abnormalities to be detected in most AML patients (Yunis, 1984). Many of the chromosome changes seen are frequently and specifically associated with AML as differentiated from the apparent random chromosome changes seen in malignant cell lines, for example. Some of the cytogenetic changes are associated with morphological subtypes, such as the reciprocal translocation between the long arms of chromosomes 15 and 17, t(15;17), in M3 leukaemias. Most non-random cytogenetic changes cross morphological lines and have been shown to have independent clinical relevance (Keating, 1987). The translocation t(8;21) and inversion of chromosome 16 were found to have favourable prognosis. The translocation t(15;17) and the deletion of the Y chromosome were of intermediate prognosis. Other translocations, abnormalities and deletions were associated with poor prognosis. It is noteworthy that the favourable chromosome changes are seen less commonly and other changes more commonly in elderly patients, suggesting that chromosome changes themselves may explain the poor response rate of leukaemia in elderly patients (Li, 1983; Keating, 1987).

Table 3. FAB classification of acute myeloblastic leukaemia.

FAB nomenclature	Predominant cell type
M1, undifferentiated myelocytic	Myeloblasts
M2, myelocytic	Myeloblasts, promyeloblasts, myelocytes
M3a, promyelocytic	Hypergranular promyelocytes
M3b, microgranular	Microgranular promyelocytes, bilobed nuclei
M4, myelomonocytic	Promyelocytes, myelocytes, promonocytes, monocytes
M5a, monoblastic	Monoblasts
M5b, monocytic	Monoblasts, promonocytes, monocytes
M6, erythroleukaemia	Erythroblasts
M7, megakaryocytic	Megakaryocyte precursors

Adapted from Bennett et al (1985), and Gale and Foon (1987).

Bone marrow and peripheral blood cells express surface molecules that are characteristic of their lineage and stage of maturation. Leukaemic blast cells express similar surface molecules that probably indicate the lineage of the leukaemia and the maturation of a majority of the blasts. The development of a large array of monoclonal antibodies that specifically recognize the lineage and differentiation antigens has led to attempts at classification of leukaemias by surface marker expression. This approach has become clinically important in the lymphoid leukaemias but has only recently been investigated in AML (Ball, 1983; Griffin, 1986). Myeloid antigens MY4 and MY7 predicted for a low rate of complete remission. Expression of antigens HLA-DR, MY8 and Mol was associated with decreased continuous complete remission and expression of MY8 was associated with decreased survival. The expression of MY4 and MY7 was independent of age, but the other antigens were not specifically studied for this parameter. Future classifications of AML are likely to be based on cytogenetics and surface markers in addition to morphology.

AML in the elderly may have characteristics that are intrinsically distinctive. The number of patients with AML that have a preceding myelodysplastic disorder is difficult to determine, but it is likely that the percentage is higher in the elderly. Beguin et al (1985) noted a significantly lower tumour mass in elderly AML patients, as well as a decrease in Auer rods in this age group. In-vitro growth characteristics of blast cells are different in the elderly (Giannoulis, 1984). Chromosomal changes are generally more frequent in elderly patients as discussed above, and the correlation of cell kinetics with chromosomal changes is quite different in older and younger patients (Kantarjian, 1985a).

Management

The management of AML in the elderly raises controversial issues. Interpretation of recent studies suggests in some cases that patients over 65 should receive aggressive combination chemotherapy regimens, whereas other studies suggest they should not. Studies of low dose and very low dose chemotherapy regimens suggest benefit in some studies but not others. A review of recent publications in this field may be helpful in formulating management policies and designing future studies.

Reviews of AML treatment up to the mid-70s acknowledged a generally poor prognosis for older patients. Controversy centred around whether AML in the elderly should remain untreated, should be treated conservatively or with intensive chemotherapy (Peterson, 1977). A number of studies have since been published to suggest that elderly patients should receive intensive combination chemotherapy. Peterson and Bloomfield (1977) reported remissions in seven of fourteen patients aged 61 to 70 and recommended intensive therapy with daunorubicin and cytosine arabinoside in this age group. Reiffers et al (1980) treated 29 patients from age 60 to 83 with intensive combination chemotherapy obtaining similar results to younger patients and advised that elderly patients were not exposed to a higher risk of death than younger patients. Foon et al (1981a, 1981b) reported identical complete remission rates and survival for 33 patients aged 60 to 82 as for 74 patients aged 15 to 59 treated with daunorubicin, cytosine arabinoside and thioguanine. These authors conclude that response rates in elderly patients and their duration and quality of remission are such that intensive chemotherapy should be used in this age group. Keating et al (1981) studied 91 patients over age 50 with AML and concluded that treatment with an anthracycline and cytosine arabinoside leads to a good quality complete remission in one-half of older patients. Torti et al (1983) have shown that anthracycline endomyocardial injury is independent of increasing age. Three consecutive older patients with AML following myelodysplasia reported by Murray et al (1983) achieved stable complete remission after uncomplicated intensive induction regimens. Beguin et al (1985) analysed 95 consecutive patients with AML, 25 of whom were over age 70. Most elderly patients were untreated and had short survivals, so they feel that this group should be treated with full dose combination chemotherapy regimens. Ohno et al (1986) treated 51 consecutive AML patients with behenoyl cytosine arabinoside, daunorubicin, 6-mercaptopurine and prednisolone and noted that five of six patients aged 60 to 74 achieved complete remission so that age was not a significant prognostic variable. Preisler et al (1987) also found that age was not a significant variable in the outcome of 67 patients with poor-risk AML treated with high dose cytosine arabinoside. Of 23 patients over age 70, 10/17 treated with 2 g/m^2 achieved complete remissions.

Conservative options

Consideration of the above studies would lead to the conclusion that elderly patients with AML should be treated with the intensive combination chemotherapy regimens that are now standard for younger patients. Other reports, however, need to be considered. Bern et al (1981) described the treatment of 14 patients, aged 50 to 72 with a regimen previously reported to be very successful in patients under 50. Only two of the 14 older patients achieved complete remission, and the median survival was 3.2 months compared to over 17 months in younger patients. Lonnqvist et al (1982) reported that only 13 of 67 patients with AML over age 60 achieved complete remission with cytosine arabinoside, 6-thioguanine, prednimustine and vincristine.

Brincker (1985) has conducted an epic review of several thousand AML patients using cancer registries in Denmark and the United States, as well as published studies of cooperative groups and prominent cancer institutes. He stresses the age distribution of AML, noting that 54% to 59% of patients are over age 60. He combines age-specific incidence data with age-specific data on complete remission rates to estimate an overall remission rate of 35% to 49% in AML. He estimates the complete remission rate to be 30% for all patients aged 65 to 69 and 22% for all patients age 75 to 79. The Toronto Leukaemia Study Group (1986) analysed the course of 272 patients with AML, 79 of whom were aged 70 and over. Of the 79 elderly patients, 15 were not treated, six were partially treated and 58 received a full induction therapy. Only 13 patients achieved complete remission, representing 16% of all the elderly patients, or 22% of the fully treated patients. The best figures could be obtained by considering 29 elderly patients who received full treatment with the most recent regimen, ten of whom attained a complete remission (34%). Similar results have been obtained in Southampton (Copplestone, 1986). The Medical Research Council's 8th AML trial reports that age at presentation and performance status were the factors most strongly associated with poor survival in a trial of daunorubicin, cytosine arabinoside and 6-thioguanine in 1127 patients (Rees, 1986). The complete remission rate was 58% for patients 60 to 69, 39% for patients 70 to 74, and 22% for patients 75 and over. Kahn et al (1984) have suggested that this chemotherapy regimen is more effective in the elderly if used at lower doses.

Although some elderly patients with AML will achieve complete remission and good quality of life with intensive combination chemotherapy, it is clear that most patients in this age group will not be so fortunate. There is evidence from in-vitro studies that low doses of cytosine arabinoside may induce differentiation of leukaemic blast cells to mature forms rather than cause cell death (Sachs, 1978). Low dose cytosine arabinoside has therefore been used in clinical trials for treatment of AML particularly in the elderly. Harousseau et al (1984) observed complete remissions in 15 of 30 elderly patients with AML (mean age 73) treated with cytosine arabinoside 10 mg/m^2 every 12 hours for 7 to 21 days. Remissions had a median duration of 10 months. Most patients had cytopenias but gastrointestinal side effects and life-threatening infections were less common than observed in elderly patients treated with intensive chemotherapy. Tilley et al (1985) reported very similar results in 30 patients aged 65 to 85 and noted that six of the patients who achieved complete remission had no post-therapeutic bone marrow aplasia.

Other groups studying low dose cytosine arabinoside in elderly AML patients have found very poor response rates. Alessandro et al (1985) reported no complete remissions in six patients, and Mufti et al (1983) noted severe bone marrow suppression with death from bleeding or infection in some patients. Cheson et al (1986) have recently reviewed 53 publications reporting 751 patients with haematologic malignancies treated with 5–20 mg/m^2/day of cytosine arabinoside. He estimates a complete remission rate of 32% in 237 patients with primary AML but notes that myelotoxicity was high in those reports that presented toxicity data. They conclude that further studies are necessary and that low dose cytosine arabinoside should not be routinely used in clinical practice at the present time. Worsley et al (1986) report the use of very low dose (3 mg/m^2 twice daily for 21 days) cytosine arabinoside with good response in four elderly patients with AML. Pesce et al (1986) noted complete remissions in four of 16 AML patients at this dose but also notes a high frequency of marrow toxicity.

The management of AML in elderly patients remains unsatisfactory. Most patients do not respond to intensive combination chemotherapy, and those who do, may not always enjoy a good quality of life. Low dose and very low dose cytosine arabinoside require further investigation. Newer drugs such as aclarubicin (Takahashi 1986), mitoxantrone (Paciucci 1984) and others (Gale 1987) may have a better therapeutic index in the elderly but studies are still in progress. Treatment decisions in this group of patients must be made after consultation with the patient and the patient's family with full disclosure of realistic remission rates and drug toxicities. Patients under 75 with good performance status and the will to receive treatment should be given standard intensive combination chemotherapy or entered into clinical trials of low dose cytosine arabinoside or new agents.

CHRONIC LYMPHOCYTIC LEUKAEMIA

Chronic lymphocytic leukaemia (CLL) is the commonest form of leukaemia, accounting for about one-third of patients with leukaemia in the general population (Wintrobe, 1981). Almost all patients are over age 40, and about two-thirds of patients are over age 65, so that CLL is by far the most common form of leukaemia in the elderly (Baranovsky, 1986). The average annual incidence rate for men over age 65 is about 25 per 100 000 and for women over age 65 is about 12 per 100 000. The relatively long survival of patients with CLL leads to a high prevalence rate in the elderly population that may be estimated at about 100 patients per 100 000 population for men over age 70 (Feldman, 1986). CLL is fully discussed in Chapter 7.

Management decisions in CLL in the elderly require a detailed understanding of prognostic variables. The asymptomatic patient with good prognostic indicators will live for several years and may well succumb to an unrelated illness. The advanced patient with poor prognostic indicators will be constantly symptomatic and may benefit from one of several therapeutic options. Although there is no evidence that treatment of CLL prolongs life, it is apparent that many patients with advanced disease will have improved quality of life with specific therapy. In addition, a Spanish study (cited by Gale, 1985) has suggested that even untreated patients with early disease will have a shorter lifespan than controls, although this point is controversial (The French Co-operative Group, 1986). A number of investigators have, therefore, devised scoring systems and multivariate analyses, in an attempt to predict which patients might benefit most from specific therapy.

The Rai (1975) and Binet (1981) staging systems, are very helpful in making management decisions, but each category tends to encompass large and heterogeneous groups of patients. Half the patients in the Rai system are of intermediate prognosis (stages I and II), and half the patients in the Binet system are in Group A. Lee et al (1987) have conducted a multivariate regression analysis of 325 untreated CLL patients and identified a number of clinical, haematologic and biochemical parameters associated with survival. They demonstrated that the combination of age, lymphadenopathy, uric acid, alkaline phosphatase and lactic dehydrogenase had the strongest predictive relation to survival time. This technique will be most useful in assigning different risk categories within each Rai stage or Binet group.

Recent studies have suggested that cytogenetic findings may be a significant factor in determining prognosis (Han 1984a, Pittman 1984). Patients with complex cytogenetic changes have a poor prognosis. Detection of Trisomy 12 was an indication of the need for early therapy in some series, but not others. The 14 q+ abnormality was often associated with prolymphocytic or lymphomatous transformation, advanced staging, or refractoriness to therapy.

Stage 0 disease of the Rai staging system clearly carries a very good prognosis. In several series, there is no documented progression of disease with follow up for 6 to 24 years (Han 1984b). Patients with monoclonal B-cell lymphocytosis, benign clinical course, normal hormonal and cellular immunity and normal karyotype have been designated as a benign variant of CLL. Chanarin et al (1984) have reported that 8 of 19 patients with persistent lymphocytosis, but neither lymphadenopathy, hepatomegaly nor splenomegaly had a T-lymphocytosis that was likely to be reactive rather than neoplastic in nature. Carstairs et al (1985) have reported a persistent polyclonal B lymphocytosis induced by cigarette smoking that subsides when smoking is discontinued. Granulated T-cell lymphocytosis has been reported in association with neutropenia and in some cases polyarthritis. Although some cases have clonal chromosome abnormalities suggesting neoplasia, other patients have had spontaneous regressions of disease suggesting a chronic reactive or immunoregulatory disorder (McKenna 1985).

Management

Specific treatment for CLL has not changed substantially in over 30 years. The mainstay of therapy for symptomatic patients is chlorambucil with or without prednisone. Chlorambucil therapy is well tolerated in the elderly as therapy is given orally without nausea and vomiting and can be titrated on a daily or biweekly dose schedule. A dose of chlorambucil of 0.1 to 0.2 mg/kg/day will produce clinical and haematological improvement in 40 to 60% of patients (Gale 1985). Prednisone may be associated with an initial paradoxical lymphocytosis but will generally have a rapid lympholytic effect with clinical improvement. The side effects of prednisone may be exacerbated in the elderly and special attention should be paid to monitoring blood sugar, blood pressure and fluid retention. Prednisone may be used alone as initial treatment in patients with advanced disease but is otherwise used in combination with chlorambucil. Other alkylating agents, in particular cyclophosphamide, are probably equally effective. Combinations of alkylating agent and prednisone have produced response rates of up to 80% in patients with advanced disease (Han 1973). Responders live longer than non-responders, but this does not provide convincing evidence that these chemotherapy regimens alter the natural history of the disease.

Chemotherapy with more aggressive combinations has been studied in advanced disease. Drugs such as cyclophosphamide, vincristine, prednisone, Adriamycin, BCNU and melphalan have been used in various combinations with some possible benefit seen in uncontrolled trials. The French Cooperative Group on CLL (1986) has published the first interim results of a large randomized clinical trial of several drug regimens for treatment of CLL. Randomization of 60 stage C (advanced) patients to cyclophosphamide, vincristine and prednisone (COP) or to the same drugs plus Adriamycin

(CHOP) showed a significant improvement in survival at two years for CHOP (44% with COP and 77% with CHOP, $p = 0.0013$). It is noteworthy that there was no difference in survival in 455 stage A (good prognosis) patients randomized to chlorambucil or to no treatment. There was also no difference in survival in 224 stage B (intermediate prognosis) patients randomized to chlorambucil or to COP.

Other treatments for CLL either provide no improvement on the above chemotherapy regimens, or are still under investigation. Whole body irradiation, splenic irradiation and extracorporal irradiation have all been studied in the past but have not appeared to be superior to chemotherapy. Combinations of chemotherapy and total body irradiation are still under study but may be poorly tolerated in the elderly patient. Splenectomy may be indicated in patients with refractory haemolytic anaemia, refractory immune thrombocytopenia or massive splenic infarction but is otherwise not helpful in managing the disease. Repeated leukapheresis using modern apheresis equipment may help reduce tumour burden in refractory patients with high white count, but is not indicated in routine management. The success of recombinant α-interferon in hairy cell leukaemia has stimulated interest in interferon treatment of CLL, but so far no useful therapeutic response has been documented. Monoclonal anti-lymphocyte antibodies have produced a transient decrease in some patients with T-cell CLL but have otherwise not proven to be clinically beneficial.

Hypogammaglobulinaemia affects 50% of CLL patients and may play a role in increasing bacterial infections in affected patients. Intramuscular gammaglobulin has been ineffective in raising serum immunoglobulins to significant levels, but intravenous gammaglobulin may be more effective. The role of this modality in the elderly patient is unclear, but is not generally recommended. Patients with immune mediated haemolytic anaemia or thrombocytopenia will usually respond to steroids combined with an alkylating agent to treat the underlying disease. Splenectomy may be necessary in refractory patients.

The prolymphocytic variety of CLL is poorly responsive to any of the chemotherapy regimens studied (Hollister 1982). The French Cooperative Group on CLL (1986) excluded patients with prolymphocytic leukaemia from its randomized chemotherapy studies. Chlorambucil and prednisone may be tried in this group of patients, but short survival will be the rule. Two cases of T-cell prolymphocytic leukaemia have responded to deoxycoformycin (El Agnaf 1986).

In coming to management decisions for the elderly patient with CLL, investigations should be undertaken that allow classification, staging and cytogenetic analysis of the individual patient's illness. Patients with good and probably intermediate prognosis disease may be best left untreated in the over 65 age group. Chlorambucil and prednisone would be the first line of therapy for patients with poor prognosis but combination chemotherapy with CHOP may be helpful in very advanced or refractory disease. The success of α-interferon in hairy cell leukaemia has raised hopes for the future development of other relatively non-toxic therapy in this common affliction of the elderly.

HAIRY CELL LEUKAEMIA

Hairy cell leukaemia (HCL) is a relatively new disorder that represents less than 2% of all leukaemias. Elderly patients are affected by HCL, as the mean age is about 50 and the range of reported cases extends into the 80s and undoubtedly occurs in older patients than those reported. The main reason for devoting a separate section to this rare disorder is the remarkable advances in systemic therapy that have very recently occurred.

The malignant cell in HCL has been difficult to define, as hairy cells have phagocytic capabilities suggestive of monocytes and receptors for sheep cell rosettes and interleukin-2 suggestive of T-lymphocytes. The cells are most likely B-lymphocytes, however, since they express surface immunoglobulins and B-cell antigens, and most importantly, the genes coding for immunoglobulin light and heavy chains are rearranged in the same fashion as other B-cell neoplasms (Korsmeyer 1983). T-cell variants of HCL have been described and the human retrovirus HTLV-II has been isolated from two such cases.

Clinical presentation

There is a male predominance of 4:1 in HCL that is accentuated in elderly patients. About 10% of patients, particularly elderly men, are essentially asymptomatic and do not have splenomegaly. Up to 25% of all patients have minimal symptoms and are discovered during investigations for other reasons. More typically, patients present with weakness, lethargy or fatigue (Golomb, 1978). Other patients may present with fever or bruising secondary to cytopoenias. Splenomegaly is a feature in 90% of patients. HCL patients do not manifest peripheral lymphadenopathy, skin lesions from leukaemia, central nervous system involvement or lytic bone lesions. Most patients are pancytopoenic with a small number of circulating hairy cells. The marrow and spleen, however, are infiltrated with hairy cells. The malignant cells are mononuclear with a slightly indented central nucleus, a single nucleolus, abundant gray cytoplasm with hair-like projections. They characteristically stain with tartrate-resistant acid phosphatase (Golde, 1986).

The median survival of patients with HCL is 4 to 5 years but 40% of patients survive more than 8 years after diagnosis, particularly elderly males. A staging system has been proposed by Jansen et al (1982) based on haemoglobin level and spleen size at the time of diagnosis in 291 patients from an international collaborative study group. This staging system has not been widely used to date, perhaps because of the retrospective nature of the analysis and the introduction of new therapy since the staging system was devised. Infection is a major complication of HCL with bacterial infections and opportunistic agents both posing serious clinical problems. Vasculitis and polyarthritis can complicate HCL in a minority of patients.

Management

Management of the elderly patient with HCL requires judgment and discretion based on an understanding of the natural history of the disease, as with other forms of leukaemia discussed in this chapter. In addition, new effective forms of systemic therapy have become available very recently (Golomb, 1987). We will be obliged to monitor carefully the results of clinical trials of these new agents over the next few years as the current management approach may evolve accordingly. Up to 25% of elderly patients will be asymptomatic at presentation, and a majority of the remaining patients may require only initial supportive care such as red cell transfusions or treatment of infection. Most patients, therefore, will benefit from a period of observation of several weeks or months. Patients with severe pancytopenia, frequent infections and prominent splenomegaly may require therapeutic intervention early on.

Splenectomy has formed the mainstay of therapy for many years (Golomb, 1983). Approximately 75% of patients have a response to splenectomy, and perhaps 50% will require no further treatment for many years (Golde, 1986). The reason for the effectiveness of splenectomy is unknown, but is has been postulated that the spleen provides a unique environment for the proliferation of hairy cells and in addition contributes to pancytopenia through hypersplenism. Patients who progress following splenectomy, were previously treated with low dose alkylating agents but had a low response rate and a high infection rate.

Both interferon and pentostatin (deoxycoformycin) have now been shown to be effective in hairy cell leukaemia. Several groups have studied the role of interferon in HCL patients with progressive disease. Recombinant α-interferon is very effective in reducing the tumour burden in HCL. Quesada et al (1986) reported nine complete and 17 partial remissions in 30 patients, most of whom were previously treated. Five of seven previously untreated patients had a complete remission in this series. Using a dose of 3×10^6 interferon units given by intramuscular or subcutaneous injection daily and then three times weekly, side-effects were minimal consisting largely of fatigue, malaise and low grade fever in some patients. Tumour remissions with a decrease in transfusion requirements and infections resulted in an improved quality of life in most patients reported in all series (Golomb, 1987). The duration of therapy is not yet clear, as discontinuation of therapy after one year resulted in clinical relapse of one third of patients. Remissions were reinduced with further therapy, so that intermittent treatment may be acceptable.

The second effective treatment is deoxycoformycin (pentostatin). Spiers et al (1987) have reported that 16 of 27 patients receiving deoxycoformycin achieved complete remissions and ten had partial remissions for an overall response rate of 96%. The one unresponsive patient had previously been splenectomized and received α-interferon as well. Using 5 mg/m^2/day intravenously for two days followed by 12 days rest, a mean of 11 doses were required to achieve complete remission. None of the patients has yet relapsed during a nine-month median follow up and no maintenance therapy has been given. Most patients had myelosuppression, one died of multiple opportunistic infections and some renal and hepatic toxicity was observed.

Further clinical trials and long term follow up are required before the role of interferon or deoxycoformycin will be clearly established in HCL. At the

Table 4. Treatment options for elderly patients with hairy-cell leukaemia.

Treatment	Reference
Observation alone	Golde et al (1986)
Splenectomy	Golomb & Vardiman (1983)
Interferon	Quesada et al (1986)
Deoxycoformycin	Spiers et al (1987)
Chlorambucil	Golomb (1981)

present time, Golomb and Ratain (1987) and Golde et al (1986) have recommended that patients who have adequate blood counts and a nonpalpable spleen not be treated at all, and that patients with cytopenias, a large spleen and patchy bone marrow infiltration still receive a splenectomy as first line therapy. Patients with diffusely involved marrow and a nonpalpable spleen (as well as splenectomy failures) should receive systemic therapy and at present this should be α-interferon. Deoxycoformycin is currently recommended for patients who fail splenectomy and interferon, but with longer follow up of patients in clinical trials, deoxycoformycin might replace interferon as the systemic drug of choice because of its higher complete remission rate.

In the elderly HCL patient, α-interferon offers a particularly attractive treatment alternative to splenectomy or deoxycoformycin for patients who require specific treatment. It would appear that interferon can produce clinical remissions with minimal toxicity and maximum benefit to quality of life. The effectiveness of this biological product in HCL should provide a standard for the therapeutic index of other treatments for leukaemia in the elderly.

CHRONIC MYELOGENOUS LEUKAEMIA

Chronic myelogenous leukaemia (CML) has an incidence of 1.4 per 100 000 in the general population, but as with acute myeloblastic and chronic lymphocytic leukaemia, the incidence rises markedly in the elderly. The average annual incidence rate for men over 65 is 8.5 per 100 000 and for women is 4.7 per 100 000 (Baranovsky 1986). As a result of this increasing incidence with age, over half of CML patients are now over age 65. Although there have been several recent developments that have improved our understanding of the fundamental nature of CML (Griffin, 1986), the therapy for this disorder has not improved in many years. The management of CML in the elderly is not controversial at present.

Clinical presentation

Most patients with CML present in the stable or chronic phase with symptoms of weakness, fatigue and weight loss, and prominent splenomegaly without lymphadenopathy. There is a marked leukocytosis with granulocytes and all precursor forms including blast cells represented in the peripheral blood. The marrow is packed with granulocyte precursors. Neutrophil alkaline phosphatase is absent in stains of peripheral blood films. Granulocyte function and membrane biochemistry are abnormal (Baker, 1986) but recurrent infections are not a problem.

Cytogenetic studies of bone marrow or peripheral blood granulocyte precursors reveal a reciprocal translocation between the long arms of chromosomes 9 and 22. The resulting small chromosome 22 is the Ph[1] chromosome that is seen in over 90% of CML patients. New information in recent years has suggested a functional role for the Ph[1] translocation in the pathogenesis of CML (Canaani, 1983). The c-*abl* proto-oncogene is situated at the breakpoint on chromosome 9 and translocated intact to the breakpoint cluster region (*bcr*) on chromosome 22. The translocated and altered c-*abl-bcr* gene is expressed in CML and the resulting mRNA is larger than normal. The protein product has tyrosine kinase activity but the target for this enzyme has not been identified. Studies of Ph[1] negative CML cells have revealed rearranged *bcr* genes and altered expression of c-*abl* suggesting that these changes are involved in the pathogenesis of the disease (Griffin 1986). Fialkow et al (1981) have documented the clonal nature of CML by studying the X chromosome linked enzyme glucose-6-phosphate dehydrogenase. Women heterogeneous for this enzyme expressed only one isotype in malignant white cells and either of two isotypes in non-malignant skin fibroblasts. Similar techniques were used in culture studies to suggest that formation of the neoplastic clone precedes development of the Ph[1] chromosome.

Patients in the chronic or stable phase of CML are relatively easy to manage. Most patients will ultimately transform to an accelerated or blastic phase of CML at which time the disease becomes almost refractory to treatment. Several studies have attempted to define prognostic factors in patients with CML (Champlin, 1985). After the first year, there is a relatively constant risk of 25% per year of developing blast crisis in the following year. The median survival is about three years. Factors present at diagnosis that carry a higher risk of early blast crisis include a high leukocyte count, a large proportion of immature cells, large spleen or liver, basophilia, eosinophilia, anaemia, thrombocytopenia and lack of a typical Ph[1] chromosome. Kantarjian et al (1985b) have found that age 60 years or older was associated with shorter survival in a multivariate analysis of over 300 CML patients.

Management

The mainstay of treatment for patients in the stable phase is intermittent busulfan or hydroxyurea. Busulphan is an oral alkylating agent that acts on an early myeloid precursor resulting in a prolonged duration of effect. Careful monitoring of blood counts is necessary to avoid severe pancytopenia. Non-haematopoietic toxicity is uncommon and includes pulmonary fibrosis, skin pigmentation, dryness of mucous membranes and cataracts. Hydroxyurea on the other hand is more useful than busulphan in rapidly lowering a very high white cell count, and is relatively non-toxic.

Clinical remissions are easily produced with either oral agent, but true marrow remissions are rarely obtained. Symptoms are easily relieved and a good quality of life is attainable in elderly patients. More aggressive strategies have been studied in younger patients but are not appropriate in the patient over age 65. Splenectomy and high dose combination chemotherapy have briefly eradicated the Ph[1] clone in some patients, but the morbidity and mortality are unacceptably high without clear benefit to overall survival. Allogeneic marrow transplantation has also been studied and may be of benefit to younger patients but is inappropriate in the elderly population (Goldman 1986).

The use of interferon in CML is of interest because of the unique success of this agent in hairy cell leukaemia. Talpaz et al (1986) have recently reported that recombinant α-interferon was active in 13 of 14 patients with CML in stable phase and that six of these patients had suppression of the Ph[1] chromosome. Further experience and follow-up of interferon therapy is indicated before general use is recommended because of the utility of chemotherapy. The relatively low toxicity of interferon and the possibility of completely suppressing the Ph[1] positive clone make this a therapy worthy of further study.

Blast crisis of CML in the elderly patient is very difficult to treat. Most patients develop a syndrome resembling acute myeloblastic leukaemia, but 30% will have blast cells with apparent lymphoblastic lineage. Treatment of the myeloid blast crisis is unsatisfactory at any age, with the median survival of all patients in the range of two months (Griffin 1986). The lymphoid blast crisis may be identified by a combination of morphological and surface marker studies. Remissions are obtained in about half the patients treated with vincristine and prednisone, but remission durations are brief. Intensive regimens designed for adult acute lymphoblastic leukaemia have not been shown to be more effective in CML lymphoid blast crisis and are probably inappropriate in the elderly patient.

CML in the elderly patient is easily managed with good quality of life in the stable chronic phase. Busulphan or hydroxyurea is well tolerated and effective in controlling symptoms. Interferon may introduce a new strategy but requires further study. Blast crisis of CML is not easy to manage in the elderly patient. A trial of vincristine and prednisone is warranted in lymphoid blast crisis but otherwise, at present, palliative care alone would be optional.

ACUTE LYMPHOBLASTIC LEUKAEMIA

Acute lymphoblastic leukaemia (ALL) is predominantly a disease of childhood that is relatively uncommon in adults. Recent attention has focused on adult ALL because of improved results with very aggressive treatment in the adult population (Jacobs 1984). The average age of patients reported in these treatment series ranges from 25 to 35 and no patients over 65 are included. Increasing age beyond 30 was a negative prognostic indicator. It is of interest, however, that the American National Cancer Institute, Surveillance, Epidemiology and End Results Programme notes an incidence of ALL in the elderly of 1 per 100 000 with about 10% of all cases of ALL occurring in this age group (Baranovsky 1986). There is no literature to suggest how these few patients fare and certainly no clinical trials to evaluate management strategies. Elderly patients with ALL are probably best managed with vincristine and prednisone induction regimens. If a complete remission were obtained, maintenance with 6-mercaptopurine and methotrexate should be considered. Patients with good performance status might be considered for more intensive therapy, but this would have to be weighed against the negative prognostic impact of age in this disease and considerations of quality of life.

SUMMARY

Leukaemia is relatively common in the elderly compared to the general population, with over half of all cases of leukaemia occurring in patients aged 65 and over. Special problems are associated with treating patients in this age group. The leukaemias may be intrinsically different, in part because of the high incidence of preceding myelodysplasia. There is increased likelihood of coincident disease. There is lower tolerance to toxic complications, such as infection and bleeding, associated with a decreased resilience of normal haematopoiesis. There is more difficulty in obtaining intravenous access in elderly patients. These problems render patients ineligible for marrow transplants.

Myelodysplastic syndromes occur predominantly in the elderly. There are a number of myelodysplastic syndromes now identified, each with its character-istic natural history. Management decisions are based on accurate diagnosis of the specific syndrome, consideration of prognostic features, a period of observation, and conservative treatment principles. More than half the cases of acute myeloblastic leukaemia also occur in the elderly. Prognostic factors must be examined and the literature carefully scrutinized for results pertinent to the elderly patient. In some patients treatment may be justifiably withheld, others may benefit from low dose cytosine arabinoside and some patients should receive aggressive combination chemotherapy.

Management of the chronic leukaemias in the elderly is a less controversial area. Chronic lymphocytic leukaemia is the most common of the leukaemias in this age group. Prognostic factors can be determined using staging criteria. Observation alone is indicated in many patients. Chlorambucil and predni-sone are the most widely used drugs for symptomatic disease. Aggressive combination chemotherapy may benefit a few patients with advanced or refractory CLL. Hairy cell leukaemia is a rare disorder but many of the patients are over age 65. The elderly male patient may have a particularly benign course and require no therapy. Splenectomy is the standard first line of therapy, but recombinant α-interferon is sufficiently effective and non-toxic that it should be the treatment of choice in some patients. Deoxycoformycin is also effective in preliminary trials and may soon be routinely indicated.

It is not often appreciated that half of all patients with chronic myelogenous leukaemia are aged 65 and over. Treatment in the chronic phase consists of intermittent busulphan or hydroxyurea. The accelerated or blastic phase in

CML may respond to vincristine and prednisone if the blasts have lymphoid characteristics, but myeloid blast crisis is essentially untreatable. Clinical trials of interferon in the chronic phase will be watched with interest. Acute lymphoblastic leukaemia is very uncommon in the elderly. The new aggressive, long-term combination chemotherapy regimens are probably not appropriate in this age group and more conservative regimens are usually employed.

Acknowledgements

The author has been supported by grants from the National Cancer Institute of Canada and the Medical Research Council of Canada. I wish to thank Mrs Claire Guiver-Bond for preparation of the manuscript. I am indebted to Dr John H. Crookston for the inspiration to study leukaemia.

REFERENCES

Alessandrino EP, Orlandi E, Brusamolino E et al (1985) Low dose arabinosyl cytosine in acute leukaemia after a myelodysplastic syndrome and in elderly leukaemia. *American Journal of Haematology* **20:** 191–193.

Baker MA, Kanani A, Hindenburg A & Taub RN (1986) Changes in the granulocyte membrane following chemotherapy for chronic myelogenous leukaemia. *British Journal of Haematology* **62:** 431–438.

Ball ED & Fanger MW (1983) The expression of myeloid specific antigens on myeloid leukaemia cells: correlations with leukaemia subclasses and implications for normal myeloid differentiation. *Blood* **61:** 456–460.

Baranovsky A & Myers MH (1986) Cancer incidence and survival in patients 65 years of age and older. *CA – A Cancer Journal for Clinicians* **36:** 26–41.

Beguin Y, Bury J, Fillet G & Lennes G (1985) Treatment of acute nonlymphocytic leukaemia in young and elderly patients. *Cancer* **56:** 2587–2592.

Bennett JM, Catovsky D, Daniel MT et al (1985) Proposed revised criteria for the classification of acute myeloid leukaemia: A report of the French–American–British Co-operative Group. *Annals of Internal Medicine* **103:** 620–625.

Bern MM, Cloud LP, Corkery JC et al (1981) Age and treatment of acute nonlymphoblastic leukaemia. *New England Journal of Medicine* **305:** 642–643.

Binet JL, Auquier A, Dighiero G et al (1981) A new prognostic classification of chronic lymphocytic leukaemia derived from a multivariate survival analysis. *Cancer* **48:** 198–206.

Brincker H (1985) Estimate of overall treatment results in acute nonlymphocytic leukaemia based on age-specific rates of incidence and of complete remission. *Cancer Treatment Reports* **69:** 5–11.

Buzaid AC, Garewall HS & Greenberg BR (1986) Management of myelodysplastic syndromes. *American Journal of Medicine* **80:** 1149–1157.

Canaani E, Gale RP, Steiner-Saltz D et al (1984) Altered transcription of an oncogene in chronic myeloid leukaemia. *Lancet* **i:** 593–595.

Carstairs KC, Francombe WH, Scott JG & Gelfand EW (1985) Persistent polyclonal lymphocytosis of B lymphocytes, induced by cigarette smoking? *Lancet* **i:** 1094.

Champlin RE & Golde DW (1985) Chronic myelogenous leukaemia: Recent advances. *Blood* **65:** 1039–1047.

Chanarin I, Harrisingh D, Tidmarsh E & Skacel PO (1984) Significance of lymphocytosis in adults. *Lancet* **ii:** 897–899.

Cheson BD, Jasperse DM, Simon R & Friedman MA (1986) A critical appraisal of low-dose cytosine arabinoside in patients with acute non-lymphocytic leukaemia and myelodysplastic syndromes. *Journal of Clinical Oncology* **4:** 1857–1864.

Cines DB, Cassileth PA, & Kiss JE (1985) Danazol therapy in myelodysplasia. *Annals of Internal Medicine* **103:** 58–60.

Copplestone JA, Smith AG, Oscier DG & Hamblin TJ (1986) True outlook in acute myeloblastic leukaemia. *Lancet* **i:** 1104.

Daniak N, Hoffman R, Ritchey AK et al (1980) In vitro steroid sensitivity testing: a possible means to predict response to therapy in primary hypoproliferative anaemia. *American Journal of Haematology* **9:** 401–402.

Editorial (1984) Treatment for preleukaemia? *Lancet* **ii:** 943–944.

El-Agnaf MR, Enniz KE, Morris RCM et al (1986) Successful remission induction with deoxycoformycin in elderly patients with T-helper prolymphocytic leukaemia. *British Journal of Haematology* **63:** 93–104.

Feldman AR, Kessler L, Myers MH & Naughton MD (1986) The prevalence of cancer. Estimates based on the Connecticut Tumour Registry. *New England Journal of Medicine* **315:** 1394–1397.

Fialkow PJ, Martin PJ, Najfield V et al (1981) Evidence for a multistep pathogenesis of chronic myelogenous leukaemia. *Blood* **58:** 158–163.

Foon KA & Zighelboim J (1981a) Treatment of acute myelogenous leukaemia in older patients. *New England Journal of Medicine* **305:** 1470.

Foon KA, Zighelboim J, Yale C & Gale RP (1981b) Intensive chemotherapy is the treatment of choice for elderly patients with acute myelogenous leukaemia. *Blood* **58:** 467–471.

French Cooperative Group on Chronic Lymphocytic Leukaemia (1986) Effectiveness of "CHOP" regimen in advanced untreated chronic lymphocytic leukaemia. *Lancet* **i:** 1346–1350.

Gale RP & Foon KA (1985) Chronic lymphocytic leukaemia. Recent advances in biology and treatment. *Annals of Internal Medicine* **103:** 101–120.

Gale RP & Foon KA (1987) Therapy of acute myelogenous leukaemia. *Seminars in Haematology* **24:** 40–54.

Giannoulis N, Ogier C, Hast R et al (1984) Difference between young and old patients in characteristics of leukaemic cells: older patients have cells growing excessively in vitro, with low antigenicity despite high HLA-DR antigens. *American Journal of Haematology* **16:** 113–121.

Golde DW, Jacobs AD, Glaspy JA & Champlin RE (1986) Hairy-cell leukaemia: Biology and treatment. *Seminars in Hematology* **23:** Suppl. 1: 3–9.

Goldman JM, Apperley JF, Jones L et al (1986) Bone marrow transplantation for patients with chronic myeloid leukaemia. *New England Journal of Medicine* **314:** 202–207.

Golomb HM, Catovsky D & Golde DW (1978) Hairy cell leukaemia. A clinical review based on 71 cases. *Annals of Internal Medicine* **89:** 677–683.

Golomb HM (1981) Progress report on chlorambucil therapy in postsplenectomy patients with progressive hairy cell leukaemia. *Blood* **57:** 464–467.

Golomb HM & Ratain MJ (1987) Recent advances in the treatment of hairy-cell leukaemia. *New England Journal of Medicine* **316:** 870–872.

Golomb HM & Vardiman JW (1983) Response to splenectomy in 65 patients with hairy-cell leukaemia: An evaluation of spleen weight and bone marrow involvement. *Blood* **61:** 349–352.

Greenberg BR, Durie BG, Co-Barnett T & Meyskins FL Jr (1985) Phase I-II study of 13-*cis*-retinoic acid (isotretinoin) in myelodysplastic syndromes. *Cancer Treatment Reports* **69:** 1369–1374.

Greenberg PL & Mara B (1979) The preleukaemic syndrome, correlation of in vitro parameters of granulopoiesis with clinical features. *American Journal of Medicine* **66:** 951–958.

Griffin JD (1986) Management of chronic myelogenous leukaemia. *Seminars in Haematology* **23:** Suppl 1: 20–26.

Griffin JD, Davis R, Nelson DA et al (1986) Use of surface markers analysis to predict outcome of adult acute myeloblastic leukaemia. *Blood* **68:** 1232–1241.

Han T, Ezdinli EZ, Shimaoka KS & Desai DV (1973) Chlorambucil vs combined chlorambucil-corticosteroid therapy in chronic lymphocytic leukaemia. *Cancer* **31:** 502–508.

Han T, Ozer H, Sadamori N et al (1984a) Prognostic importance of cytogenetic abnormalities in patients with chronic lymphocytic leukaemia. *New England Journal of Medicine* **310:** 298–292.

Han T, Ozer H, Garrigan M et al (1984b) Benign monoclonal B cell lymphocytosis—A benign variant of CLL: clinical, immunologic, phenotypic, and cytogenetic studies in 20 patients. *Blood* **64:** 244–252.

Harousseau JL, Castaigne S, Milpied N et al (1984) Treatment of acute non-lymphoblastic leukaemia in elderly patients. *Lancet* **ii**: 288.

Hollister D & Coleman M (1982) Treatment of prolymphocytic leukaemia. *Cancer* **50**: 1687–1689.

Jacobs AD & Gale RP (1984) Recent advances in the biology and treatment of acute lymphoblastic leukaemia in adults. *New England Journal of Medicine* **311**: 1219–1231.

Jansen J & Hermans J (1982) Clinical staging system for hairy-cell leukaemia. *Blood* **60**: 571–577.

Kahn SB, Begg CS, Mazza JJ et al (1984) Full dose versus attenuated dose of daunorubicin, cytosine arabinoside, 6-thioguanine in the treatment of acute non lymphocytic leukaemia in the elderly. *Journal of Clinical Oncology* **2**: 865–870.

Kantarjian HM, Barlogie B, Keating MJ et al (1985a) Pretreatment cytokinetics in acute myelogenous leukaemia. *Journal of Clinical Investigation* **76**: 319–324.

Kantarjian HM, Smith TL, McCredie KB et al (1985b) Chronic myelogenous leukaemia: A multivariate analysis of the associations of patient characteristics and therapy with survival. *Blood* **66**: 1326–1335.

Keating MJ, McCredie KB, Benjamin RS et al (1981) Treatment of patients over 50 years of age with acute myelogenous leukaemia with a combination of rubidazone and cytosine arabinoside, vincristine and prednisone (ROAP). *Blood* **58**: 584–590.

Keating MJ, Cork A, Broach Y et al (1987) Toward a clinically relevant cytogenetic classification of acute myelogenous leukaemia. *Leukaemia Research* **11**: 119–133.

Koeffler HP (1986) Myelodysplastic syndromes (preleukaemia). *Seminars in Haematology* **23**: 284–299.

Koeffler HP, Hirji K & Itri L (1985) 1, 25-dehydroxyvitamin D_3: In vitro and in vivo effects on human preleukaemic and leukaemic cells. *Cancer Treatment Reports* **69**: 1399–1407.

Korsmeyer SJ, Greene WC, Cossman J et al (1983) Rearrangement and expression of immunoglobulin genes and expression of Tac antigen in hairy-cell leukaemia. *Proceedings of the National Academy of Sciences USA* **80**: 4522–4526.

Lee JS, Dixon DO, Kantarjian HM et al (1987) Prognosis of chronic lymphocytic leukaemia: a multivariate regression analysis of 325 untreated patients. *Blood* **69**: 929–936.

Li YS, Khalid G & Hayhoe FGJ (1983) Correlation between chromosomal pattern, cytological subtypes, response to therapy, and survival in acute myeloid leukaemia. *Scandinavian Journal of Haematology* **30**: 265–277.

Lipschitz DA, Goldstein S, Reis R et al (1985) Cancer in the elderly: Basic science and clinical aspects. *Annals of Internal Medicine* **102**: 218–228.

Lonnquist B, Andersson B, Bjorkholm M et al (1982) Prednimustine and vincristine compared with cytosine arabinoside and thioguanine for treatment of elderly patients with acute nonlymphoblastic leukaemia. *Cancer Chemotherapy and Pharmacology* **9**: 89–92.

McKenna RW, Arthur DV, Gajl-Peczalska KH et al (1985) Granulated T cell lymphocytosis with neutropoenia: malignant or benign chronic lymphoproliferative disorder? *Blood* **66**: 259–266.

Meier PJ, Fehr J & Meyer UA (1982) Pyridoxine responsive primary acquired sideroblastic anaemia. *Scandinavian Journal of Haematology* **29**: 421–424.

Mertelsmann R, Thaler HT, To L et al (1980) Morphological classification, response to therapy, and survival in 263 adult patients with acute nonlymphocytic leukaemia. *Blood* **56**: 773–781.

Michels SD, McKenna RW, Arthur DC & Brunning RD (1985) Therapy related acute myeloid leukaemia and myelodysplastic syndrome: a clinical and morphologic study of 65 cases. *Blood* **65**: 1364–1372.

Mufti GJ, Oscier DG, Hamblin TJ et al (1983) Low doses of cytarabine in the treatment of myelodysplastic syndrome and acute myeloid leukaemia. *New England Journal of Medicine* **309**: 1653–1654.

Mufti G, Stevens JR, Oscier D et al (1985) Myelodysplastic syndromes: A scoring system with prognostic significance. *British Journal of Haematology* **59**: 425–433.

Murray C, Cooper B & Kitchens LW (1983) Remission of acute myelogenous leukaemia in elderly patients with prior refractory dysmyelopoietic anaemia. *Cancer* **52**: 967–970.

Najean Y & Pecking A (1977) Refractory anaemia with excess of myeloblasts in the bone marrow: a clinical trial of androgens in 90 patients. *British Journal of Haematology* **37**: 25–33.

Ohno R, Kato Y, Nagura E et al (1986) Behenoyl cytosine arabinoside, daunorubicin, 6-mercaptopurine and prednisolone combination therapy for acute myelogenous leukaemia in adults and prognostic factors related to remission duration and survival length. *Journal of Clinical Oncology* **4:** 1740–1747.

Paciucci PA, Cuttner J & Holland JF (1984) Mitoxantrone in patients with refractory acute leukaemia. *Seminars in Oncology* **11:** 36–40.

Pesce A, Cassuto JP, Bayle J et al (1986) Very low dose cytarabine for elderly patients. *Lancet* **i:** 1436.

Peterson BA & Bloomfield CD (1977) Treatment of acute nonlymphocytic leukaemia in elderly patients. A prospective study of intensive chemotherapy. *Cancer* **40:** 647–652.

Pittman S & Catovsky D (1984) Prognostic significance of chromosome abnormalities in chronic lymphocytic leukaemia. *British Journal of Haematology* **58:** 649–660.

Preisler HD, Raza A, Barcos M et al (1987) High dose cytosine arabinoside as the initial treatment of poor-risk patients with acute nonlymphocytic leukaemia: A leukaemia intergroup study. *Journal of Clinical Oncology* **5:** 75–82.

Quesada Jr, Hersh EM, Manning J et al (1986) Treatment of hairy-cell leukaemia with recombinant alpha-interferon. *Blood* **68:** 493–497.

Rai KR, Sawitsky A, Cronkite EP et al (1975) Clinical staging of chronic lymphocytic leukaemia. *Blood* **46:** 219–234.

Rees JKH, Swirsky D, Gray RG & Hayhoe FGJ (1986) Principal results of the Medical Research Council's 8th acute myeloid leukaemia trial. *Lancet* **ii:** 1236–1241.

Reiffers J, Raynal F & Broustet A (1980) Acute myeloblastic leukaemia in elderly patients. Treatment and prognostic factors. *Cancer* **45:** 2816–2820.

Sachs L (1978) The differentiation of myeloid leukaemic cells: new possibilities for therapy. *British Journal of Haematology* **40:** 509–517.

Spiers ASD, Moore D, Cassileth PA et al (1987) Remission in hairy-cell leukaemia with pentostatin (2'-deoxycoformycin). *New England Journal of Medicine* **316:** 825–830.

Takahashi I, Yorimitsu S, Hara M et al (1986) Aclarubicin in the treatment of elderly patients with acute nonlymphocytic leukaemia. *Acta Medica Okayama* **40:** 175–177.

Talpaz M, Kantarjian HM, McCredie K et al (1986) Haematologic remission and cytogenetic improvement induced by recombinant human interferon alpha-A in chronic myelogenous leukaemia. *New England Journal of Medicine* **314:** 1065–1069.

Tilley H, Castaigne S, Bordessoule D et al (1985) Low dose cytosine arabinoside treatment for acute nonlymphocytic leukaemia in elderly patients. *Cancer* **55:** 1633–1636.

The Toronto Leukaemia Study Group (1986) Results of chemotherapy for unselected patients with acute myeloblastic leukaemia: Effect of exclusions on interpretation of results. *Lancet* **i:** 786–788.

Torti FM, Bristow MR, Howes AE et al (1983) Reduced cardiotoxicity of doxorubicin delivered on a weekly schedule. Assessment by endomyocardial biopsy. *Annals of Internal Medicine* **99:** 745–749.

Tricot G, Boogaers MA, De Wolf-Peeters C et al (1985) The myelodysplastic syndromes: Different evolution patterns based on sequential morphological and cytogenetic investigations. *British Journal of Haematology* **59:** 659–670.

Tricot G, De Bock R, Dekker AW et al (1984) Low dose cytosine arabinoside (ARA-C) in myelodysplastic syndromes. *British Journal of Haematology* **58:** 231–240.

Winter JM, Variakojis D, Gaynor ER et al (1985) Low dose cytosine arabinoside (ARA-C) therapy in the myelodysplastic syndromes and acute leukaemia. *Cancer* **56:** 443–449.

Wintrobe MM, Lee DR, Boggs DR et al (1981) *Clinical Haematology*. Philadelphia: Lea & Febiger.

Wisch JS, Griffin JD & Kufe DW (1983) Response of preleukaemic syndromes to continuous infusion of low-dose cytarabine. *New England Journal of Medicine* **309:** 1599–1602.

Worsley A, Mufti GJ, Copplestone JA et al (1986) Very low dose cytarabine for myelodysplastic syndromes and acute myeloid leukaemia in the elderly. *Lancet* **i:** 966.

Yunis JJ, Brunning RD, Howe RB & Labell M (1984) High resolution chromosomes as an independent prognostic indicator in adult acute nonlymphocytic leukaemia. *New England Journal of Medicine* **311:** 812–815.

Yunis JJ, Rydell RE, Oken MM et al (1986) Refined chromosome analysis as an independent prognostic indicator in de novo myelodysplastic syndromes. *Blood* **67:** 1721–1730.

7

Chronic lymphocytic leukaemia

T. J. HAMBLIN

Chronic lymphocytic leukaemia (CLL) is a name used with varying degrees of precision for a number of conditions in which there is a progressive accumulation of small, morphologically mature lymphocytes in the blood, bone marrow, lymph nodes and spleen. Careful study of lymphocyte morphology and cell markers has enabled these diseases to be subclassified (Table 1). The term CLL is usually applied to a tumour of small B lymphocytes, the form of the disease commonest in Europe and North America.

EPIDEMIOLOGY

CLL is the commonest leukaemia seen in old age. The annual incidence varies with the age and sex structure of the population, and figures between 0.6 and 3.7 per 100 000 have been quoted for various areas of the USA (Young et al, 1981). In Bournemouth, where 30% of the population is over 60, the annual incidence is 10 per 100 000. The disease is very rare below the age of 50 but after this there is a relatively rapid rise in incidence. Most authors suggest that the disease is approximately twice as common in men as in women (Court-Brown and Doll, 1959; Fraumeni and Miller, 1967). However, the disease occurs approximately 6 years later in women than in men (Young et al, 1981), so that, although at any given age it is twice as common in men, the greater longevity of women means that this sex difference will be obscured in any series that contains large numbers of the old and very old. Thus, of the 200 patients seen in Bournemouth between 1972 and 1985, there were 104 men and 96 women (Hamblin et al, 1987). There is no evidence to suggest that the disease is more benign in older age groups. Age-specific survival curves simply reflect the fact that younger people have more of their lives remaining than old people (Figure 1).

There are no differences in the age-specific incidences between black and white Americans, but among Chinese, Japanese, Philipinos and American Indians, the incidence is about five times less (Weiss, 1978). Among Jews, the rate is twice that of non-Jewish North Americans (MacMahon and Koller, 1957).

Table 1. Subclassification of CLL.

Disease	Cases seen in Bournemouth 1972–1985	Overall incidence %*
B cell tumours		
B-CLL	200	69
B-PLL	2	6.5
WM with lymphocytosis	2	1
NHL spillover	18	13
HCL	8	6
T cell tumours		
T-CLL	7	1
T-PLL	0	1.5
Sezary's syndrome	1	2
ATLL	0	

* Catovsky (1984) based on 1000 patients studied at the Hammersmith Hospital.

Abbreviations:
CLL: chronic lymphocytic leukaemia
PLL: prolymphocytic leukaemia
WM: Waldenstrom's macroglobulinaemia
NHL: non-Hodgkin's lymphoma
ATLL: adult T lymphoma/leukaemia
HCL: hairy cell leukaemia

It is difficult to assess how accurate the reported prevalence figures are. It is known that trivial disease will remain undiagnosed unless a blood count happens to be performed, and low-grade lymphocytoses are often uninvestigated. Our study of 1388 blood counts from individuals over the age of 55 in a single general practice uncovered three previously unknown cases of CLL, which suggests that for every known case in the community there are many others that have not drawn attention to themselves.

AETIOLOGY

The cause of CLL is unknown. In contrast to other leukaemias there is no evidence that ionizing radiation is involved (Bizzozero et al, 1967). Nor do the drugs known to induce myelodysplasia and acute leukaemia give rise to CLL. Immunodeficiency syndromes are commonly followed by other types of lymphoid tumour but not by CLL (Kersey et al, 1973).

No virus has been seriously implicated in the cause of CLL. The discovery of antibodies to HTLV I in three out of five patients with CLL in Jamaica (Hendriks, 1985) is almost certainly an incidental finding.

It is likely that host factors are at least as important in the cause as environmental factors. The low rate among Japanese does not increase when they migrate to America (Nishiyama et al, 1969). Furthermore, there have

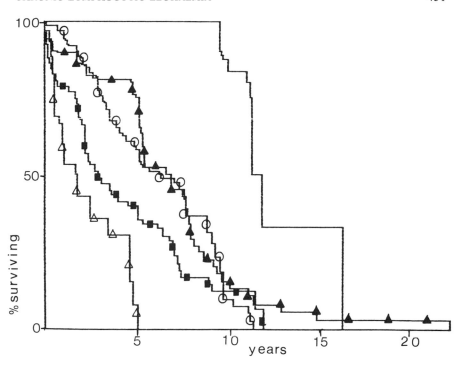

Figure 1. Actuarial survival curves for patients with CLL presenting at various ages: ———, < 55; ▲–▲–▲, 55–64; ○–○–○, 65–74; ■–■–■, 75–84; △–△–△, 85 and over.

been several reports of multiple cases of CLL among siblings and other family members (Blattner et al, 1976; Catovsky, 1984). Although a high level of consanguinity has been reported in familial CLL (Kurita et al, 1974), no obvious pattern of inheritance can be distinguished.

CLINICAL FEATURES

Textbooks and the older literature tend to give a more aggressive picture of the disease than is encountered in practice. There are three reasons for this: (1) in the past, distinctions between CLL and prolymphocytic leukaemia (PLL) and spillover from non-Hodgkin's lymphoma (NHL) were not always made; (2) most reported series are from referral centres, but the most benign cases are less likely to be referred; and (3) modern diagnostic methods are capable of recognizing the disease when there is minimal evidence of its presence.

Thus, in Bournemouth, of 200 elderly patients with CLL seen between 1972 and 1985, 143 (71.5%) presented on an incidental blood count (Hamblin et al, 1987). This contrasts with 25% detected in this way at the Royal Marsden Hospital prior to 1966 (Galton, 1966). When discussing clinical features, therefore, I shall make reference to the Bournemouth series, contrasting the findings with those reported elsewhere.

Of the remaining 57 Bournemouth patients, 17 presented with symptoms of anaemia, 16 noticed enlarged lymph nodes, and 15 presented with an infection, three with weight loss and two with bruising or purpura. Two noticed an enlarged spleen, and one presented with acute gout and one with prostatic obstruction due to leukaemic infiltration.

The commonest clinical finding was lymphadenopathy, which was present in 116 (58%) patients. Lymph nodes are usually palpable in the neck (anterior and posterior triangles and supraclavicular areas), in the axillae and in the groins. They are generally small, discrete and nontender. Epitrochlear nodes are occasionally found, but mediastinal widening on the chest x-ray is seldom seen and para-aortic nodes rarely looked for. However, when lymphograms are performed, more than 50% of patients show abdominal lymph node enlargement (Auclerc et al, 1984).

Splenomegaly was seen in 50 patients (25%) at presentation and developed later in a further 34 (17%). Four patients had splenomegaly without lymphadenopathy, a group believed to have a particularly benign prognosis (Dighiero et al, 1979). Massive splenic enlargement is rare, and symptoms related to splenomegaly seldom amount to more than early satiety after meals. Splenic pain occurs much less frequently than in chronic myeloid leukaemia or myelofibrosis.

Hepatomegaly was seen in 43 patients (21.5%) and later developed in a further 15 (7.5%). Ascites was found in three patients, and was in each case a feature of an accompanying disease.

Other clinical features were rare. B symptoms are seldom a presenting feature although weight loss occurs in advanced cases, as with any malignant disease. Night sweats were a feature in only three patients. However, leg cramps were surprisingly common. When questioned specifically, 57 out of 111 patients admitted to cramps in the legs at night sufficient to wake them at least once a month, compared to 18 out of 78 hospital inpatients of similar age and sex.

Earlier workers claim that the skin is involved in more than 50% of cases (Sweet et al, 1977). However, in the Bournemouth series, apart from 11 patients in whom purpura was seen at some stage in their illness, there were only seven patients with skin lesions: two with leukaemia cutis, two with exfoliative dermatitis, two with extensive psoriasis and one with pityriasis lichenoides. It is unlikely that the last two conditions were related to the leukaemia.

Gastrointestinal complications of CLL are exceedingly rare (Tuckel and Cachia, 1986) and none were seen in this series. However, extensive leukaemic involvement of the small and large bowel has been reported (Cornes and Jones, 1962; Prolia and Kirsner, 1964), although these reports date from the era before the diagnosis was so clearly delineated and may well have been cases of diffuse centrocytic lymphoma with blood spillover.

Similarly, reports of pulmonary infiltrates and pleural effusions (Green and Nichols, 1959) may relate to NHL spillover. We have not seen them in CLL, although during the same period several cases of follicular lymphoma (centroblastic/centrocytic) have been complicated by pleural effusions and a leukaemic phase, and we have seen two cases of diffuse, well-differentiated, lymphocytic lymphoma (the usual histological picture seen in CLL), which have been confined to lung parenchyma without a blood or marrow phase. We have seen mediastinal obstruction producing a superior vena caval syndrome once, in association with a PLL transformation of CLL.

Neurological disease is reportedly rare. Sweet et al (1977) listed leukaemic meningitis, cranial nerve palsies, spinal cord syndromes, nerve root compression and peripheral nerve involvement, all due to leukaemic infiltrates. In our experience these are much less likely to occur than in other lymphoid tumours. However, 32 patients in the Bournemouth series did have evidence of pre-existing or developing neurological disease (Table 2). The cases of anosmia

Table 2. Cases of neurological disease occurring in patients with CLL.

Neurological disease	Number of cases
Parkinson's disease	11
Motor shingles	4
Bell's palsy	4
Peripheral neuropathy	3
Anosmia	3
Multiple sclerosis	2
Von Recklinghausen's disease	1
Motor neurone disease	1
Medial rectus palsy	1
Meningioma	1
Total	32

and medial rectus palsy responded to treatment with antileukaemic drugs but the other diseases may not be directly related to the CLL. However, two of our patients had pre-existing multiple sclerosis (MS). A recent epidemiological study has found a higher than expected incidence of MS among family members of patients with CLL (Bernard et al, 1987).

Leukaemic infiltration of the kidneys is a common postmortem finding (Norris and Weiner, 1961) but does not usually cause clinical problems. Nephrotic syndrome has been reported on several occasions (Dathan et al, 1974; Feehally et al, 1981; Seney et al, 1986) and was seen once in our series. It responded rapidly to treatment with cyclophosphamide and plasma exchange. Leukaemic infiltration of the prostate gland has been seen twice in our series (once as a presenting feature), and in addition we have twice seen diffuse, well-differentiated, lymphocytic lymphoma apparently confined to the prostate without a detectable blood or bone marrow phase.

Skeletal lesions are rare. There is no evidence for the secretion of tumour necrosis factor by CLL cells. Hypercalcaemia occurs infrequently (McMillan et al, 1980). We have seen it on six occasions, always preterminally.

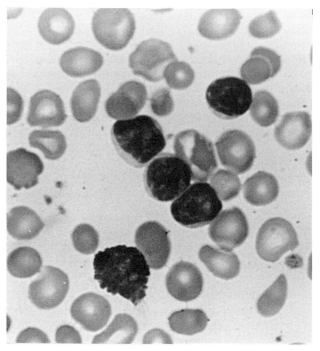

Figure 2. The morphology of B-CLL cells showing small round cells with clumped basophilic chromatin and occasional 'smudge' cells.

HAEMATOLOGICAL FEATURES

CLL is characterized by a persistent lymphocytosis in blood and bone marrow. Various authors give lymphocyte counts of $> 5 \times 10^9/l$ (Sweet et al, 1977), $> 10 \times 10^9/l$ (Catovsky, 1984) and $> 15 \times 10^9/l$ (Skarin, 1985) as criteria for diagnosis, but what is more important is evidence of monoclonality and the characteristic morphology. Monoclonality has been recognized by the finding of a single glucose 6-phosphate dehydrogenase isotype (Fialkow et al, 1978), a unique pattern of immunoglobulin idiotype specificity (Hamblin et al, 1980), clonal chromosomal abnormalities (Gahrton et al, 1980) and a single immunoglobulin gene rearrangement (Korsmeyer et al, 1981). However, it is usually sufficient to demonstrate the expression of a single immunoglobulin light-chain type on the cell surface. Very high lymphocyte counts are occasionally seen. Counts over $500 \times 10^9/l$ may be associated with a hyperviscosity syndrome (Baer et al, 1985). One group has found lymphopenia in a preleukaemic phase of CLL (Brandt and Nilsson, 1980) but others have not confirmed this (Bjorkholm et al, 1984).

   The leukaemic lymphocytes are small round monomorphic cells with a high nuclear/cytoplasm ratio (Figure 2). The nucleus contains heavily clumped, basophilic chromatin, and sometimes an indistinct nucleolus may be discerned. The cytoplasm is scanty and apparently fragile since 'smudge' cells are usually plentiful in blood films. Usually, a small percentage of the CLL cells are large with a prominent nucleolus (prolymphocytes).

Anaemia carries a poor prognosis in CLL, but only when it is a consequence of marrow failure. In the Bournemouth series 30 patients presented with anaemia due to marrow infiltration (15%) and another seven developed it during the course of their illness. A further 23 patients suffered from anaemia from other causes: 10 with autoimmune haemolytic anaemia, four with iron deficiency, five with myelodysplasia, three with other cancers and one with pernicious anaemia.

Similarly, thrombocytopenia only carries a poor prognosis when caused by marrow failure. Thirty-nine patients of the Bournemouth series (19.5%) had platelet counts of less than $100 \times 10^9/l$ from this cause, and in addition two had immune thrombocytopenia and three hypersplenism. Two patients developed thrombocytopenia due to the appearance of, respectively, refractory anaemia with excess of blasts, and acute myeloblastic leukaemia.

HISTOLOGY

Although in most centres bone marrow trephine examination is seldom performed in CLL, it does provide diagnostic and prognostic information. Marrow infiltration tends to be within the central marrow space, whereas in most forms of NHL it is paratrabecular. Four patterns of infiltration may be recognized in CLL: interstitial, nodular, mixed nodular and interstitial, and diffuse (Rozman et al, 1981). The last two of these are associated with a poor prognosis.

Lymph nodes are seldom biopsied but lymph node histology helps in the diagnosis of transformation of CLL (see below) and in distinguishing CLL from NHL. In most instances the histological picture of CLL is of sheets of small lymphocytes with occasional immature cells replacing the normal nodal architecture, and is indistinguishable from diffuse, well-differentiated, lymphocytic lymphoma (WDLL). The confusion engendered by the plethora of histological classifications for lymphoma is justly famous. The WDLL group in the Rappaport classification include both the tissue phase of CLL and that of Waldenstrom's macroglobulinaemia, although these are usually distinguishable histologically. Also included is a group histologically resembling CLL in which neither blood nor marrow lymphocytosis is seen during the course of the illness (Pangalis et al, 1977).

CHROMOSOMES

Cytogenetic studies in CLL have appeared more recently than for other leukaemias because the cells divide infrequently and respond poorly to phytohaemagglutinin. However, pokeweed mitogen, lipopolysaccharide, Epstein–Barr virus, and, most successfully, tetradecanoly phorbol acetate (TPA), have been effective in stimulating CLL cells to produce analysable metaphases. In a number of papers, abnormal karyotypes have been found in

30–60% of patients (Sadamoii et al, 1983; Pittman and Catovsky, 1984; Juliusson and Gahrton, 1985).

The commonest abnormality has been trisomy 12, but also found commonly has been 14q + (breakpoint q32), sometimes as part of a reciprocal translocation t(11;14)(q13;q32) and sometimes involved in the reciprocal translocation t(14;18)(q32;q13) commonly seen in low-grade follicular lymphomas. Also seen fairly frequently by a number of authors has been 6q −, and our own group has described a high incidence of structural abnormalities of the long arm of chromosome 13 (Oscier et al, 1985).

The significance of chromosome abnormalities in CLL is not fully established, especially as most large series contain patients from whom no analysable metaphases can be obtained, and it is not always clear whether the normal karyotypes found represent the tumour cells or an accompanying normal cell population.

Juliusson and Gahrton (1985) have demonstrated a poorer actuarial survival for patients with abnormal karyotypes in all or most of the cells analysed compared to those with normal karyotypes in most or all of their cells. Conflicting findings have made it unclear whether or not certain karyotypes may be found in association with more benign disease. Although Juliusson et al (1985) found trisomy 12 to be associated with more aggressive disease, the reverse has been reported by Han et al (1984b), who found that isolated trisomy 12 was associated with the same survival curve as that of a normal karyotype. This conflict may be resolved by the finding that trisomy 12 is often the basis for karyotypic evolution (Ohtaki et al, 1986) and that such cases have a poor survival.

In our experience, patients with complex karyotypic abnormalities have a high incidence of progressive disease which requires treatment, but 42% of patients with Binet stage A disease (Table 5) had an abnormal karyotype, and complex karyotypes were found in some patients with very low grade nonprogressive stage A disease (Oscier et al, 1985).

The molecular importance of these chromosomal abnormalities is largely unknown. The oncogene c-*ras*-Kirsten occurs on chromosome 12 but no information concerning the gene product in CLL is yet available. The t(11;14) translocation involves the juxtaposition of the heavy-chain locus with a postulated transforming gene, *bcl*-1 (Tsujimoto et al, 1984). Involvement of a similar gene, *bcl*-2, has been postulated for the t(14;18) translocation (Tsujimoto et al, 1985).

LYMPHOCYTE MARKERS

The characteristic membrane marker of CLL cells is surface immunoglobulin. In most cases IgM is found either alone or in combination with IgD; both classes show the same light-chain type (Hamblin and Hough, 1977). IgG is often seen on the surfaces of CLL cells but in most cases this is an artefact caused by cytophilic binding to Fcγ receptors (Stevenson et al, 1981). However, a small proportion of patients express endogenous surface IgG (3% in the Bournemouth series). Surface IgA is also very occasionally found

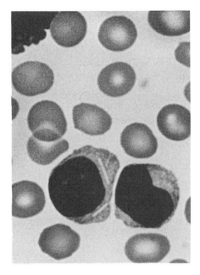

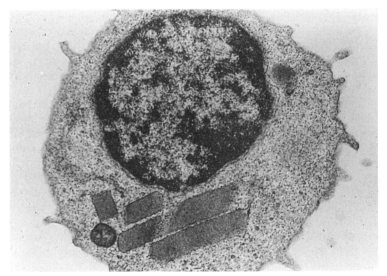

Figure 3. Crystalline inclusions of IgA in a case of CLL: (a) Romanowsky stain; (b) FITC staining; (c) EM.

(Rudders and Ross, 1975). It was seen only once in the Bournemouth series. Surface immunoglobulin is present in relatively small amounts on most CLL cells; it has been estimated at about 9000 molecules/cell (Ternynck et al, 1974). In some cases no surface Ig can be detected by immunofluorescence, although it may be detectable by more sensitive methods (Dhaliwhal et al, 1978). In some surface negative cases, cytoplasmic Ig is present, often in the form of crystalline inclusions (Figure 3) (Cawley et al, 1976). It has been suggested that surface negative cells accumulate as the disease progresses (McLaughlin et al, 1973).

In most cases CLL cells have a receptor for mouse red blood cells, and since this receptor is rarely found on the cells from other B cell tumours it has diagnostic importance (Catovsky et al, 1976). In contrast a range of monoclonal antibodies against CD19, CD20, CD22, CD24 and CD37 react with both CLL cells and most other B cells (Foon et al, 1986b). Other markers of diagnostic value are CD21, the C3d receptor, which is characteristically present on relatively immature B cells (Ross and Polley, 1975), and the CD5 antigen, which is mainly confined to T cells but is also present on B-CLL cells (Foon et al, 1982).

Other T cell antigens are absent in CLL, although a small proportion of patients (3% in the Bournemouth series) have cells forming anomalous sheep red blood cell rosettes. In these cases it is believed that the surface immunoglobulin has antisheep red blood cell activity (Mills et al, 1985).

THE NATURE OF THE CLL CELL

Phenotypic analysis suggests that, despite its apparently mature morphology, the CLL cell has been 'frozen' at an early stage of differentiation. Both the C3d receptor (CD21) and weak surface immunoglobulin are transient features seen early in maturation. In an attempt to discover the normal cellular counterpart of CLL cells, Caligaris-Capio et al (1982) identified a small population (2–3%) of B cells bearing both CD5 and mouse red cell receptor in normal tonsil and lymph nodes around the margins of germinal centres. These cells also expressed scanty surface Ig. This population appears early in ontogeny, being present in primary lymph node nodules in fetuses of 17 weeks gestation and by 22 weeks in the fetal spleen clustered around dentritic cells (Bofil et al, 1985). In normal peripheral blood, 1–10% of B cells bear mouse red cell receptors and CD5 (Plater-Zyberk et al, 1985) but they are increased following bone marrow allograft (Ault et al, 1985) and in active rheumatoid arthritis (Youinou et al, 1978). The CD5 antigen is highly conserved. A similar molecule on mouse lymphocytes is detected by the Ly-1 antibody. Observations on tumours derived from Ly-1-positive B cells (Mercolino et al, 1986) has led to speculation that the normal counterpart of the CLL cell is a primitive B cell which expresses germ line immunoglobulin genes coding primarily for autoantibodies, including idiotypic and anti-idiotypic specificities, and that these cells 'set up' the repertoire of the immune system (Lydyard et al, 1987).

Although CLL cells are poorly reactive with most mitogens, TPA induces the cells to differentiate into activated cells similar to PLL cells. Under these conditions secretion of IgM or class switching to surface IgG may occur (Juliusson et al, 1983). The cells lose the mouse red cell receptor but express CD5 in increased quantities (Miller and Gralow, 1984). Under certain circumstances cells resembling hairy cells appear (Caligaris-Cappio et al, 1984). The cells react with FMC7, a marker for PLL and hairy cell leukaemia.

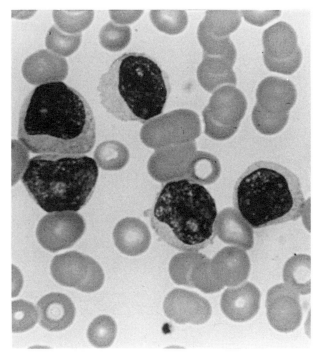

Figure 4. PLL cells showing moderately condensed chromatin and a prominent nucleolus.

DIFFERENTIAL DIAGNOSIS

Any cause of a peripheral blood lymphocytosis must be distinguished from CLL. A number of virus infections may give rise to a transitory lymphocytosis, and lymphocyte counts of the order of $50 \times 10^9/l$ may be occasionally seen in pertussis. Most of these infections occur in children. Their spontaneous resolution and if necessary marker studies will distinguish them from CLL. A number of other lymphoid tumours produce a similar but distinguishable blood picture.

Prolymphocytic leukaemia

PLL was first described by Galton et al (1974). It occurs in the same aged population as CLL, with a similar male preponderance. The characteristic clinical feature is splenomegaly in the absence of lymphadenopathy. The lymphocyte count is frequently greater than $100 \times 10^9/l$, and anaemia and thrombocytopenia are present in over 50% of cases.

The prolymphocyte is larger than the characteristic CLL cell. The round nucleus has moderately condensed chromatin and a prominent central nucleolus. Cytoplasm is relatively abundant (Figure 4). Smudge cells are not usually seen. If the blood film is examined at the thick end, the cells are often

Table 3. Surface phenotypes of cells from CLL and variants.

	B-CLL	B-PLL	HCL	NHL cb/cc	NHL dcc	T-CLL	WM
CD2	−	−	−	−	−	+	−
CD3	−	−	−	−	−	+	−
CD4	−	−	−	−	−	−	−
CD5	+	+	−	−	+	−	−
CD8	−	−	−	−	−	+	−
CD10	−	−	−	+	−	−	−
CD19	+	+	+	+	+	−	+
CD20	+	+	+	+	+	−	+
CD21	+	−	−	−	−	−	−
CD22	+	+	+	+	+	−	+
CD24	+	+	+	+	+	−	+
CD37	+	+	+	+	+	−	+
SIg	+	+++	++	++	++	−	++
MRBC	+	±	±	−	−	−	−
FMC7	−	+	+			−	−
HNK-1	−	−	−	−	−	+	−
Leu11	−	−	−	−	−	−	−
DR	+	+	+	+	+	−	+
PCA-1	−	−	+	−	−	−	+

mistaken for those of CLL. In a proportion of the patients the disease appears to arise from a transformation of CLL, and for this reason in a minority of patients the cell markers resemble those of CLL. However, in the majority the pattern is distinctive (Table 3). A monoclonal band is found in the serum in 30%, and a characteristic chromosomal translocation, t(6;12) has been described (Sadamori et al, 1983). The disease is always progressive, with a median survival of 24 months. The treatment of choice, especially in elderly patients, is low-dose splenic irradiation (Oscier et al, 1981). Other cases have responded to CHOP chemotherapy (Sibbald and Catovsky, 1979). A minority of patients have T-PLL (Catovsky, 1982). In a third of these there are skin lesions, and in two-thirds lymphadenopathy. The cell markers are those of CD4-positive T helper cells and the median survival is 7 months.

Hairy cell leukaemia

This condition is also commoner in elderly males and is characterized by splenomegaly without lymphadenopathy (Golomb et al, 1978). Lymphocytosis is rare, being seen in less than 20%. The majority, who have pancytopenia of varying degree, may present diagnostic difficulties but are unlikely to be confused with CLL. Hairy cells are of moderate size and have an oval nucleus containing spongy chromatin and abundant pale blue cytoplasm with fine thread-like cytoplasmic projections (Figure 5). The cells are phagocytic for latex particles and show acid phosphatase activity which is tartrate-resistant (isoenzyme 5). In most cases they are B cells with characteristic surface

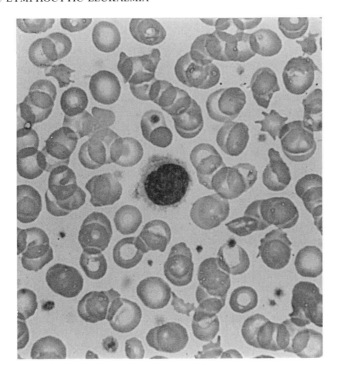

Figure 5. A hairy cell. The chromatin is described as spongy. There are fine thread-like cytoplasmic projections.

markers (Table 3) but a rare T cell type has been described. Success has attended treatment by splenectomy, and with interferon α and deoxycorfomy-cin.

Waldenstrom's macroglobulinaemia (WM)

A peripheral lymphocytosis is seen in a minority of patients with WM. Although the lymphocytes present in the peripheral blood may resemble CLL cells, plasmacytoid cells are usually present (Figure 6). Distinction between CLL with an IgM paraprotein and WM with a peripheral lymphocytosis may be difficult but can usually be resolved on histological grounds (WM has greater numbers of plasmacytoid and plasma cells) or by cell surface markers (Table 3).

Non-Hodgkin's lymphoma spillover

In low and intermediate grade NHL there is frequently a spillover of cells into the peripheral blood which may be detected immunologically, but a frank lymphocytosis is rarer. In the past this phenomenon was known as lymphosarcoma cell leukaemia, but this term is now archaic. Two types of

NHL, follicular lymphoma, centroblastic/centrocytic, nodular (cb/cc), and diffuse centrocytic lymphoma (dcc), are most likely to occur in a leukaemic phase and thus to present diagnostic difficulty. Cb/cc lymphoma is the commonest lymphoma in Europe and North America, and when a leukaemic phase is present there is usually widespread lymphadenopathy involving cervical, axillary and inguinal regions as well as retroperitoneal lymph nodes. Hepatosplenomegaly is also frequently present. In dcc lymphoma, although splenomegaly is frequently present, lymphadenopathy is less likely, perhaps signifying an origin for the malignant cell other than the follicular centre. Lymphoma cells are generally larger than CLL cells (Figure 7). A proportion of the cells have a notched or cleaved nucleus, the chromatin is less condensed than in CLL and a nucleolus is frequently visible. Cytoplasm is usually minimal. In cb/cc there is usually a small proportion of larger cells with round nuclei with more open chromatin and one or more peripheral nucleoli (centroblasts). Bone marrow trephine histology may show diffuse infiltration, but when it is focal it is usually paratrabecular rather than in the central marrow spaces. Lymph node histology is diagnostic but in a number of cases is unavailable, either because no enlarged lymph nodes are present or because the physician is reluctant to subject the patient to a major abdominal operation to obtain lymph node histology.

Diagnosis must therefore be made in a sizeable number of patients on the basis of finding cleaved cells in the blood. Cell markers may be helpful (Table 3) in that lymphoma cells usually have more surface immunoglobulin than

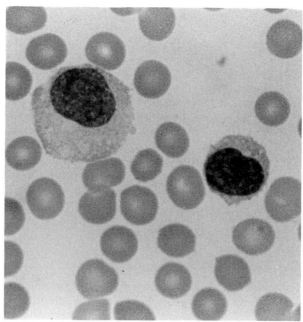

Figure 6. Waldenström's macroglobulinaemia. Note the lymphoplasmacytoid cell.

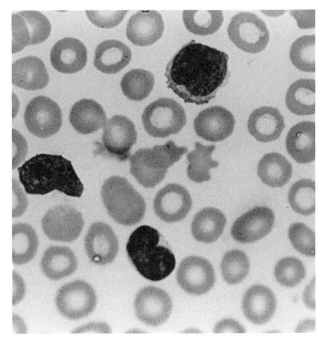

Figure 7. Non-Hodgkin's lymphoma. Nuclei have prominent clefts.

CLL cells, and cb/cc cells frequently express the CD10 antigen, while dcc cells usually express the CD5 antigen but not the mouse red blood cell receptor. However, anomalies are found quite frequently and we have a number of patients who resemble CLL clinically and have characteristic CLL markers but for whom we have been reluctant to make that diagnosis because of the cleaved cell morphology. Further investigation of this subgroup is warranted.

The distinction between CLL and low-grade lymphoma is necessary since the latter has a worse prognosis and is more likely to require treatment.

T cell CLL

The term T cell CLL has been used quite widely to encompass a variety of conditions, including Sézary syndrome and adult T-lymphoma/leukaemia (ATLL). The cellular morphology of the second of these two conditions is so different from B-CLL that it hardly forms part of the differential diagnosis. However, small Sézary cells may be extremely difficult to distinguish from B-CLL cells. (Figure 8).

Some of the earlier reports of T-CLL may have referred to patients with B-CLL whose cells formed anomalous rosettes with sheep red blood cells, but there is now common consent that T-CLL refers to a condition in which there is a proliferation of large granular lymphocytes, frequent splenomegaly and neutropenia (Newland et al, 1984). The characteristic cells have mature nuclei

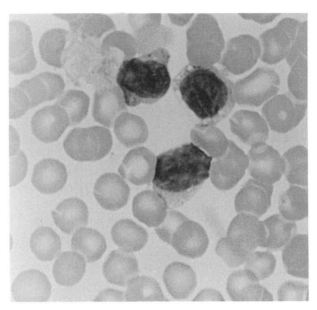

Figure 8. Sézary cells. Small Sézary cells may be difficult to distinguish from B-CLL. Careful examination reveals nuclear convolutions.

and abundant cytoplasm with azurophil granules (Figure 9). The lymphocytosis is moderate (5–20 × 10^9/l) and frequently nonprogressive. The cells show a membrane phenotype of considerable heterogeneity but most commonly they are CD8-positive, HNK-1 positive (Table 3). Occasionally they have a helper cell phenotype (Spiers et al, 1986). Functionally they behave as cytotoxic/suppressor cells (Pandolfi et al, 1982) and only seldom act as natural killer cells (Schlimok et al, 1982).

A number of patients give a history of rheumatoid arthritis (Newland et al, 1984) and this needs to be distinguished from Felty's syndrome. Other reactive conditions may give rise to a proliferation of CD8-positive T cells, and evidence of clonality is necessary before the diagnosis of T-CLL is made. This may be in the form of chromosomal abnormality, or by the finding of a rearrangement of the TCrβ gene (Knowles et al, 1985). An unusual feature of the T cell receptor structure is that there are few variable region segments that can be used to make up the β-chain, and unlike the immunoglobulin idiotype they are rarely, if ever, altered by somatic mutation. Monoclonal antibodies which identify such variable region segments react with 3–5% of normal T cells, and therefore between 20 and 30 such antibodies would encompass the whole T cell repertoire. The prospects are therefore good for identifying clonal expansion of T cells using a panel of their antibodies (Clark et al, 1986).

Most patients run a benign, stable course, although infections may be troublesome because of neutropenia. Transformation to a high grade T cell lymphoma has been reported (Oscier et al, 1986).

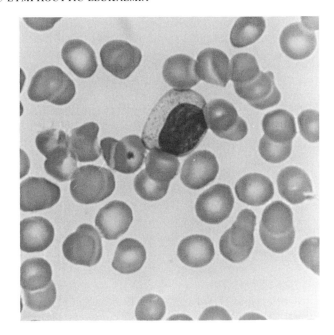

Figure 9. T-CLL. There is abundant cytoplasm with azuraphil granules.

NATURAL HISTORY, STAGING AND PROGNOSIS

The natural history of CLL is extremely variable. Some patients have survived for up to 36 years with minimal disease and little or no evidence of disease progression (Marlow and Evans, 1977). On the other hand, other patients may present with a low white count and a single enlarged lymph node, yet within months develop bone marrow failure and massive lymphadenopathy and hepatosplenomegaly. These are, however, the minority and the normal pattern of progression is for a slow increase in white count, degree of marrow infiltration, and size of lymph nodes and spleen, with eventual marrow failure. In the elderly it is extremely likely that the patient will die from an incidental cause. Of 81 deaths in the Bournemouth series, 42 were from causes unrelated to CLL.

There are three factors which affect the prognosis in CLL: (1) the tumour mass; (2) the rate of progression; and (3) the sensitivity of the tumour to chemotherapy.

Table 4. Staging criteria of Rai et al (1975).

Stage 0	Lymphocytosis of blood and bone marrow only
Stage I	Lymphocytosis plus lymphadenopathy
Stage II	Lymphocytosis plus splenomegaly or hepatomegaly
Stage III	Lymphocytosis plus anaemia (Hb < 11 g/dl)
Stage IV	Lymphocytosis plus thrombocytopenia (platelets $< 100 \times 10^9/l$)

Two fairly widely used methods of clinical staging are thought to be good indices of the tumour mass. The Rai staging system (Table 4) (Rai et al, 1975) certainly correlates with survival, but probably contains too many subtypes. It is not possible to detect a prognostic difference between groups I and II or between III and IV. On average, patients in groups III and IV have a median survival of 12 months, groups I and II a median survival of 7 years, and group 0 a median survival of greater than 12 years (Rai et al, 1975).

Table 5. Criteria of Binet staging system (Binet et al, 1981).

Stage A	< 3 involved sites, Hb > 10 g/dl, platelets > $100 \times 10^9/l$
Stage B	> 3 involved sites, Hb > 10 g/dl, platelets > $100 \times 10^9/l$
Stage C	Hb < 10 g/dl or platelets < $100 \times 10^9/l$

Cervical, axillary, inguinal nodes, spleen and liver each count as one involved site.

The Binet prognostic groups (Binet et al, 1981) are limited to three (Table 5) and also give useful prognostic information. In describing individual patients it is sometimes helpful to use a combination of the two systems; A0, BII, CIV and so on.

Neither system specifies that anaemia or thrombocytopenia should be the result of marrow failure, but this is an important stipulation. Anaemia or thrombocytopenia with autoimmune or other causes does not carry the same grave prognosis (Phillips et al, 1977).

Actuarial survival of the Bournemouth series grouped according to the Binet series shows group A apparently doing worse than group B until 8 years have passed (Figure 10). This illustrates one of the difficulties of looking at survival figures in elderly populations—patients die of other diseases. Since most patients in group A are diagnosed because of an incidental blood test, such patients may be more likely to die from the illness for which the blood test was performed. Patients with groups B and C CLL are more likely to be diagnosed because of the clinical effects of the disease. Many of these patients—especially in group B—will respond satisfactorily to treatment.

The total blood lymphocyte count is a crude measure of tumour mass. Some workers have found that a lymphocyte count of $> 50 \times 10^9/l$ is also a feature carrying a poor prognosis, and a white count of this level may delineate the long survivors and the rather shorter survivors in Rai groups I and II (Baccarani et al, 1982; Rozman et al, 1982). However, in the Bournemouth series we are unable to allocate a poorer prognosis to those with lymphocyte counts greater than $50 \times 10^9/l$.

The degree of bone marrow infiltration is a better measure of tumour mass. Patients with diffuse infiltration or mixed nodular and interstitial infiltration have a worse prognosis that those with either interstitial or nodular infiltration (Rozman et al, 1981).

The rate of progression in CLL may be hard to gauge. Although the white blood count may be static for many years, at the same time the gradual

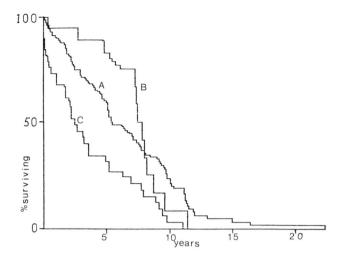

Figure 10. Actuarial survival of 200 CLL patients according to Binet stage A, B and C.

obliteration of the marrow spaces may be silently taking place. In other patients the major proliferation of the tumour appears to occur in the lymph nodes or spleen. Since in all series there is a proportion of early deaths in the 'good prognosis' groups and a number of long survivors in the 'poor prognosis' groups, it is important to try to assess the rate of progression of the disease, and any treatment schedule should include a period of observation to determine whether the patient has 'stable' or progressive disease (Galton, 1984), unless end-stage disease with marrow failure is already present, when treatment may be urgent.

In the Bournemouth series, disease progression was defined as the movement of the patient from one Binet class to another or a doubling of the lymphocyte count within 12 months. Using these criteria and excluding early deaths (most of which will have been in patients with 'progressive' disease) there was no difference in actuarial survival between those who had 'stable' and those who had 'progressive' disease. However, the exclusion of early deaths probably invalidates this analysis.

In most cases of CLL the disease is extremely susceptible to treatment with corticosteroids or alkylating agents. Those few patients who are totally resistant to these agents are likely to have a poor prognosis. In vitro cytotoxicity assays have not yet been developed to such a degree as to help in selecting patients whose disease will be resistant to therapy. Developing resistance to chemotherapy may be a feature of transformation of the disease.

While the staging systems for CLL are in widespread use, it will be appreciated that their major limitation is that they tell the physician nothing of the biology of the disease. With observation, factors such as rate of progression and susceptibility to treatment emerge, but attempts have been made to diagnose in advance which patients ought to be treated early, and which can be safely left untreated.

In trying to evaluate these attempts the difficulty is in ensuring that we are looking at B-CLL and not simply separating variants such as T-CLL, PLL and NHL spillover. Thus there have been a number of attempts to correlate prognosis with variations in cell morphology or size. Some of these reports appear to be in conflict, but these conflicts can probably be resolved if allowance is made for the use of different technical methods.

Early results which suggested a poorer prognosis for patients with larger cells (Zacharski and Linman, 1969; Gray et al, 1974), were undoubtedly separating patients with PLL or NHL spillover, but the study by Dubner et al (1978), which recognized a poorer prognosis for patients with greater numbers of large nucleolated cells in their peripheral blood films, was probably looking at the tendency for increasing numbers of prolymphocytes to appear as the disease progresses. On the other hand, Peterson et al (1980) found a better prognosis for patients with larger cells on the blood film. A close reading of the text, however, reveals that these were not prolymphocytes but almost certainly residual T cells.

Interpretation of studies which use electronic means to estimate cell size (Kuse et al, 1985) is difficult since it is usually not clear whether the techniques are measuring whole cell volume or that of the nucleus only. However, the results of these studies are consistent with the idea that accumulation of prolymphocytes carries a poor prognosis while retention of normal T cells carries a better one.

Since the ontogeny of B cells is associated with changes in surface markers, we had the idea that subclassifying CLL according to the class of surface immunoglobulin might reveal tumours of differing biological behaviour. Our original study (Hamblin and Hough, 1977) suggested that patients whose tumour cells expressed scanty IgMk had a more benign variety of CLL than patients whose cells expressed surface IgMλ, IgM+Dk, IgM+Dλ or no detectable surface immunoglobulin. We also suggested that this was a particular characteristic of elderly females.

Support for these observations came from Jayaswel et al (1977), who suggested that patients with surface IgM+D provided fewer long-term survivors than patients with surface IgM alone, while patients with undetectable surface Ig had more extensive disease. In a smaller group of patients, Mellstedt et al (1978) found that patients with surface λ chains had more active disease than those with surface κ chains.

However, neither Foa et al (1979) nor Flanagan et al (1981) could find any significant differences between patients whose cells expressed different classes of surface Ig, and Baldini et al (1984) found that patients whose cells expressed surface IgM+D survived for longer than those expressing surface IgM alone. Unfortunately, this group did not analyse the surface IgMκ group separately. The study of Ligler et al (1983) is hard to interpret since it used flow cytometry rather than microscopy, and double staining cells were not determined. Their finding that patients whose cells express predominantly surface IgG had less advanced disease than those whose cells expressed predominantly either surface IgM or IgD is puzzling in view of the very low incidence of CLL cells expressing intrinsic IgG.

Table 6. Clinical characteristics of CLL patients related to surface Ig class.

	Mκ	Mλ	M+Dκ	M+Dλ	Null	G or A
Binet stage						
A	54	8	34	18	23	5
B	3	0	6	3	6	5
C	2	1	15	9	11	2
Total	59	9	55	30	40	7
WBC $> 50 \times 10^9/l$	14	3	25	19	24	2
Progressive disease	12	3	22	18	23	2
Required treatment	14	4	25	18	22	2

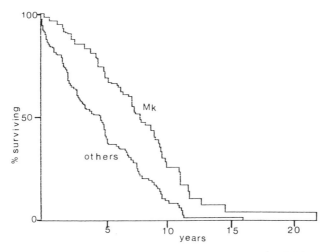

Figure 11. Actuarial survival of CLL patients whose cells express surface IgMκ compared with other groups.

In order to resolve these discrepancies we have extended our series to 200 patients, taking care to exclude cases of PLL, hairy cell leukaemia, and NHL spillover from analysis, but taking similar care to include all cases of CLL diagnosed at a single district general hospital (Hamblin et al, 1987). This study confirmed most of the findings of our earlier paper. There were significantly more patients with Binet stage A disease in those whose cells showed surface IgMκ than in any other group (Table 6). In addition, patients with surface IgMκ were significantly less likely to have progressive disease, to have a total lymphocyte count of $< 50 \times 10^9/l$ or to require treatment (Table 6). Patients with surface IgMκ also survived significantly longer than other groups (Figure 11), and this was also true when patients of 75 and over were excluded from analysis or when the analysis was confined to patients presenting with stage A disease.

However, in this extended series we did not find that the benign subtype was confined to elderly women. The sex ratio and age distribution among those patients whose cells expressed surface IgMk was the same as for other groups.

Other workers have suggested that benign subgroups of CLL exist. Caligaris-Cappio et al (1984) suggested that a group of patients with a distinctive membrane phenotype (CD5-positive, RFA-4-positive) had a more benign course. We have seen this phenotype in five out of 70 patients tested. Not all have had benign disease but this group does include our longest survivor (21 years), as does the group identified by Baccarani et al (1982), who suggested that stage A patients with isolated splenomegaly were long survivors. We have had four such patients in our series who have survived respectively 1060, 3617, 4278 and 8083 days from diagnosis.

Han et al (1984a) also recognized a benign variant of CLL which they designated benign monoclonal B-cell lymphocytosis. The characteristic features of the 20 cases that they described were a nonprogressive course over 6.5–24 years, Rai stage 0, and lymphocyte count $< 50 \times 10^9/l$. The following characteristics were also noted in some of the patients: mostly normal serum Ig levels, positive delayed hypersensitivity reactions in at least one of five skin test antigens, low levels of [^{3}H]thymidine uptake, normal response to PHA stimulation.

We have seen 18 patients with stage A0 nonprogressive disease who have survived from 6 to 21 years from diagnosis. In addition, there are seven stage A1 and five stage A2 patients with nonprogressive disease who have survived for more than 6 years. Of these 30, only six had normal immunoglobulins. In six out of the 15 in whom chromosomes were analysed, an abnormal karyotype was found. In this benign group, which approximates to the benign monoclonal B cell lymphocytosis of Han et al (1984a), 20 expressed surface IgMκ, six IgM + Dκ, one IgMλ, and one IgM + D, and two had no detectable surface Ig.

COMPLICATIONS

Immunodeficiency

Recurrent infections are among the most important complications in CLL, and in one series 46% of the patients died from an infective cause (Boggs et al, 1966). Improvements in antibiotics and supportive care may have lessened their impact, but infections were still responsible for 26% of the 81 deaths in our own series. Bacterial infections, including recurrent bronchopneumonia, urinary tract infections, sinusitis, staphylococcal abscesses and skin infections are particularly common (Sweet et al, 1977).

Viral infections may be difficult to document because poor antibody responses invalidate the usual serological criteria for diagnosis. A rare and often fatal haemophagocytic syndrome resembling histiocytic medullary phagocytosis is probably virally induced (Manoharan et al, 1981b). However, the most commonly reported viral infection is herpes zoster. In the Bournemouth series, 40 patients out of the 140 for whom a history was available gave a story of shingles, five of them on two occasions. Only 18 of the attacks occurred after the diagnosis of CLL, but of the 27 attacks occurring before the diagnosis of CLL, 16 occurred in the 5 years prior to diagnosis. The implication of this finding is that the existence of CLL or at least its associated immunodeficiency precedes the formal diagnosis by several years.

In some patients the course of the illness was particularly severe. There were four cases of motor shingles, 10 cases of severe and persistent post-herpetic neuralgia and one case of disseminated zoster. In one patient the shingles scars failed to heal and continued to break down and discharge until her death 6 years later. This patient developed Parkinson's disease at the same time as the attack of shingles, an association we have also seen in two elderly patients with Hodgkin's disease. Of group A patients, 19.1% gave a history of shingles, compared to 41% of group B and 50% of group C.

The cause of the immunodeficiency is multifactorial. Neutropenia secondary to chemotherapy, impaired natural killer cell activity (Foa et al, 1984), treatment with corticosteroids, and defective complement activity (Heath and Cheson, 1985), all play a minor part, but the major element is hypogammaglobulinaemia, which has been reported to occur in 50–75% of patients, becoming more severe as the disease advances (Boggs and Fahey, 1960). Serum IgA is reported to be the first class reduced (Foa et al, 1979), followed by IgM and then IgG.

Of 196 Bournemouth patients who had serum immunoglobulins measured at presentation, IgA was reduced in 117, IgM in 87 and IgG in 99. A polyclonal rise in IgA was seen in five, in IgM in three and in IgG in seven. Normal levels of IgA were found in 76, of IgM in 97 and of IgG in 87. In only 34 patients were all three serum immunoglobulins normal. In 55, all three classes were reduced. In 32 patients a single class of immunoglobulin was reduced. This was IgA on 18 occasions, IgM on seven occasions and IgG on seven occasions.

There was a tendency for lower levels of serum immunoglobulins to be found in more advanced disease, but even advanced disease may have all three classes within the normal range (Table 7). Although there was a trend for patients with a reduction of all three immunoglobulin classes at presentation to survive for a shorter period, this did not quite reach statistical significance.

There were 74 (37.8%) patients who gave a history of more than one infection requiring antimicrobial treatment in the previous 12 months. Of these, 35 had all three classes reduced (63.3%), five had all classes of Ig normal (14.7%), five had a paraprotein (38.5%), 12 had one class of Ig reduced (37.5%), 12 two classes of Ig reduced (25.5%), and five had raised immunoglobulins (33.3%).

The risk of recurrent infection correlated better with serum IgG levels. Seventeen out of thirty-nine with IgG levels less than 5 g/l (43.5%) had recurrent infections, 12/22 with IgG levels less than 4 g/l (54.5%) and 10/10 with levels less than 3 g/l (100%). Patients with recurrent infections had a significantly shorter survival than those without infections.

The cause of the hypogammaglobulinaemia is unclear. It is unlikely that it is simply a 'crowding out' of normal lymphoid tissue by the tumour population. Even in patients with minimal evidence of CLL there is complete abrogation

Table 7. Binct stage related to serum immunoglobulins in 196 patients with CLL (percentages in brackets).

Immunoglobulin levels	Binet stage				
	A0	A1	A2	B	C
IgG					
Low	40 (42.1)	17 (54.8)	8 (50.0)	15 (68.2)	24 (75.0)
Normal	51 (53.6)	13 (41.9)	7 (43.8)	5 (22.7)	6 (18.7)
High	3 (3.2)	1 (3.2)	1 (6.3)	0 (0.0)	2 (6.3)
Paraprotein	1 (1.1)	0 (0.0)	0 (0.0)	2 (9.1)	0 (0.0)
IgA					
Low	45 (47.3)	14 (45.1)	11 (68.8)	20 (90.9)	26 (81.3)
Normal	46 (48.4)	17 (54.8)	5 (31.2)	2 (9.1)	5 (15.6)
High	4 (4.2)	0 (0.0)	0 (0.0)	0 (0.0)	1 (3.2)
Paraprotein	0 (0.0)	0 (0.0)	0 (0.0)	0 (0.0)	0 (0.0)
IgM					
Low	37 (38.9)	13 (41.9)	7 (43.8)	16 (72.7)	18 (56.3)
Normal	53 (55.7)	7 (54.8)	7 (43.8)	5 (22.7)	10 (31.2)
High	2 (2.1)	0 (0.0)	1 (6.3)	0 (0.0)	0 (0.0)
Paraprotein	4 (4.2)	1 (3.2)	1 (6.3)	1 (4.6)	3 (9.4)
All three classes normal	19 (20.0)	10 (31.2)	2 (12.5)	1 (4.5)	2 (6.3)
Total	95	31	16	22	32

of the primary antibody response to a new antigen injected intravenously (Hamblin et al, 1975).

At least one report has correlated the degree of hypogammaglobulinaemia with decreases in numbers of T helper cells, and increases in T suppressor cells (Plastoucus et al, 1982). Several studies have confirmed the reduction in T helper cells and the increase in T suppressor cells (Chiorazzi et al, 1979; Lauria et al, 1980; Kay, 1981). Functional studies have been less clear, and to a degree contradictory, but in general they suggest decreased T helper function and increased T suppressor function (Han et al, 1981; Kay et al, 1983). These abnormalities of T cell function are probably reactive to the B cell proliferation. Chromosomal analysis and G6PD heterozygosity demonstrate that the T cells are not part of the malignant clone (Prchal et al, 1979), nor is there usually rearrangement of the TcRβ gene. Although a recent study has demonstrated TcRβ rearrangement in the B cells of two cases of CLL (O'Connor et al, 1985), this is probably an example of lineage infidelity.

Monoclonal proteins

Contrary to the general view of the CLL cell as an inert, nonsecretory cell (Fu et al, 1974), it does secrete both whole immunoglobulin (Stevenson et al, 1980) and free light chains (Gordon et al, 1978) in small but readily detectable amounts. Conventional cellulose acetate electrophoresis of serum detects a monoclonal protein in 5–10% of patients (Alexanian, 1975). Thus in the Bournemouth series 10 had IgM and three IgG paraproteins. However, more sensitive detection methods such as isoelectric focusing with immunofixation demonstrate monoclonal proteins in the serum (Sinclair et al, 1984) and urine (Pierson et al, 1980) of the majority of patients. Using a radioimmunoassay, Stevenson et al (1980) were able to show that in patients with low serum immunoglobulins, up to 95% of the IgM and 65% of the IgD in the serum was idiotypic. Furthermore, the IgM was present as the secreted pentameric form rather than as the 7S monomer and therefore could not have arisen by membrane dissolution.

Autoimmunity

Although hypogammaglobulinaemia is the most prominent immunological abnormality in patients with CLL, paradoxically the incidence of autoimmune disease is also high. Autoimmune haemolytic anaemia has been reported to occur in 10–20% of patients at some time during the disease (Sweet et al, 1977), although I believe that this is an overestimate produced by the assembly of the more severe cases. Autoimmune thrombocytopenia occurs in 1–2% of cases of CLL (Ebbe et al, 1962), and autoimmune neutropenia is rarer still (Rustagi et al, 1983). Pure red cell aplasia is commoner in T-CLL than B-CLL but when it occurs in the latter it may be associated with autoantibodies to developing erythroblasts (Abeloff and Waterbury, 1974). Reports of the association of CLL with systemic lupus erythematosus, rheumatoid arthritis, Sjogren's syndrome, ulcerative colitis, allergic vasculitis, nephrotic syndrome, pernicious anaemia and bullous pemphigoid have appeared in the literature (Miller, 1962; Damashek, 1967; Goodnough and Muir, 1980; Feehally et al, 1981).

Of 195 patients tested in Bournemouth, there were 15 with positive direct antiglobulin tests (Hamblin et al, 1986). Of these one had an anti-I monoclonal IgM cold agglutinin which was presumed to be the product of the tumour. Of the other 14, 10 had an overt haemolytic anaemia. Four patients had evidence of immune thrombocytopenia. In this series we also saw one patient with pure red cell aplasia and one with isolated neutropenia, both of which were possibly immune-mediated.

Tissue autoantibodies were present in 42 patients and also in 42 of 194 age- and sex-matched elderly controls (Table 8). Two of the patients had myxoedema, one had thyrotoxicosis, and one had pernicious anaemia. Other possibly autoimmune diseases found in association with CLL in this series but not associated with the autoantibodies detailed in Table 8 were two cases each of rheumatoid arthritis, cryptogenic cirrhosis and immune vasculitis, and one case each of interstitial pulmonary fibrosis, nephrotic syndrome, polymyositis and polymyalgia rheumatica.

The lower than expected number of cases of autoimmune haemolytic anaemia in this series was related to the large number of stage A cases in this series. The incidence of positive antiglobulin tests among stable group A cases was 2.9%, whereas among group A cases that showed disease progression it was 18%, among group B, 9%, and among group C, 11%. The likelihood of

Table 8. Autoantibodies in sera of 195 patients with CLL and 194 age-matched controls.

Antibodies	CLL	Controls
Antinuclei	12	7
Antimitochondria	1	3
Anti-smooth muscle	8	4
Anti-skeletal muscle	2	0
Anti-salivary duct	1	0
Anti-parietal cells	10	18
Antithyroid	13	9
Antikeratin	1	2
Antireticulin	3	6

stable group A patients not being referred to specialized centres probably accounts for the higher incidence of haemolytic anaemia in reported series.

Although isolated cases of nonhaematological autoimmune disease have been reported in association with CLL, these are rare and for the most part may have occurred by chance. Any explanation for the high incidence of autoimmune disease in CLL must take account of the fact that the autoimmunity is almost always directed against blood cells. The other clue to the association is the frequent induction of autoimmune haemolysis following treatment with cytotoxic drugs (Lewis et al, 1966). Despite these two clues and the obvious evidence of destruction of normal immunity by the tumour, no-one has a convincing explanation for the autoimmune haemolytic anaemia of CLL.

Transformation of CLL

Three types of transformation are recognized in B-CLL: (1) prolymphocytoid transformation (Enno et al, 1979); (2) immunoblastic transformation or Richter's syndrome (Richter, 1928); and (3) transformation to acute lymphoblastic leukaemia (Brouet et al, 1973).

Prolymphocytoid transformation

The existence of variable proportions of 'atypical' larger cells among the small monomorphic cells of B-CLL has long been recognized (Zacharski and Linman, 1969), but the accumulation of such cells accompanied by progressive clinical deterioration and refractoriness to treatment was described by Enno et al (1979) as a prolymphocytoid transformation of the CLL (Figure 12). Melo et al (1986a) have examined the relationship between CLL and PLL by studying 164 cases of typical CLL submitted to the first Medical Research Council trial on CLL together with 146 cases sent in as atypical CLL or PLL. They separated them on the basis of the percentage of prolymphocytes on the blood film. One hunded and seventy-four with < 10% prolymphocytes were

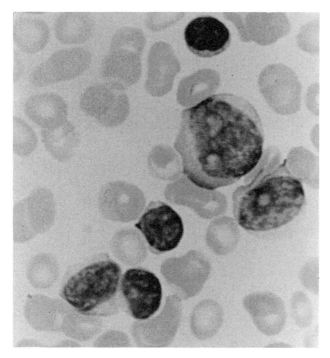

Figure 12. Prolymphocytoid transformation of B-CLL.

designated CLL, 84 with 11–55% prolymphocytes were called CLL/PLL, and 42 with > 55% prolymphocytes were recognized as PLL. In many respects the CLL/PLL group were intermediate between CLL and PLL. They resembled the CLL group, and differed from the PLL group in having more lymphadenopathy, a younger age of presentation, and cells which have reacted with mouse red blood cells and anti-CD5 antibodies but reacted poorly with the monoclonal antibody FMC7. However, they resembled PLL in having larger spleens and cells with dense surface immunoglobulin. Response to treatment was similar to that of the group with CLL.

Possession of large numbers of prolymphocytes does imply progression (Melo et al, 1986b). Half of the patients in the CLL/PLL group had stable numbers of prolymphocytes, and patients with typical CLL had transient increases in prolymphocytes during the course of their disease. A small population of patients had a sustained progression to a PLL-like blood picture, but in only two did the cell markers change to resemble PLL. However, the group with sustained progression responded poorly to single-agent chemotherapy. Survival in the CLL/PLL group correlated with the prolymphocyte count: those with < 15% prolymphocytes had the same outlook as typical CLL, whereas those with > 15% prolymphocytes survived as poorly as PLL (Melo et al, 1987).

Our own experience is similar to that of the Hammersmith workers (Hamblin et al, 1985) and gives some indication of the frequency of this change. Among the 200 patients we have studied, 11 have fallen within the CLL/PLL group, seven have remained with stable disease, and four have progressed to a PLL-like blood picture, but in only one did the cell markers change to resemble PLL. In an unpublished study in which we separated small and large cells on a percol gradient and examined the cell-discriminating cell markers, CD5, mouse rosettes and SIg density on large and small cells, in most cases both lots of cells had the same markers but there were individual exceptions. Interestingly, two of the patients in this group also developed a myeloid malignancy, both having received much chemotherapy.

Richter's syndrome

In Richter's syndrome the patient with CLL experiences a sudden clinical deterioration associated with rapidly enlarging lymph nodes, often with hepatosplenomegaly, in the face of an unchanged or even falling white cell count. 'B' symptoms are often present. The histological nature of the developing lymphoma was originally designated reticulum cell sarcoma, and more recently diffuse histiocytic lymphoma. The use of these archaic terms has tended to obscure the pathological process, and imprecise diagnosis has allowed some cases of centroblastic transformation of centroblastic/centrocytic lymphoma with spillover to be included as cases of Richter's syndrome.

It is, however, now clear that true Richter's syndrome represents an immunoblastic transformation of CLL in which the immunoblasts express the same class of surface Ig light chain as the original CLL (Foucar and Rydell, 1980; Kruskall, 1983), but also have strong cytoplasmic immunoglobulin staining and may secrete enough Ig to produce a serum monoclonal band.

In two cases in which more extensive cell markers were performed there was a class switch from IgM to IgG in one patient, and both lost the CD5 antigen on transformation (Chan and Dekmezian, 1986).

Richter's syndrome responds poorly to chemotherapy, and the median survival time is 4 months (Trump et al, 1980).

In the Bournemouth series, Richter's syndrome has been seen only once.

Acute lymphoblastic leukaemia

Acute leukaemia supervening in CLL was first recognized by Lawrence et al (1949), but the report of Pisciotta and Hirschboeck (1957) was the first recognizably acute lymphoblastic transformation. In one of the cases described by Brouet et al (1973), not only was the surface Ig of both CLL and acute leukaemia of the same class (IgMk), but Ig from both types of cell had rheumatoid factor activity—thus demonstrating a common origin.

Blast transformation of CLL is undoubtedly very rare. It is not usually associated with a rapid increase in size of lymph nodes or spleen, but the leukaemic cells are probably similar to the immunoblasts seen in Richter's syndrome. Marker studies have given conflicting information. In at least one case, retention of the CD5 antigen was noted (Miller et al, 1984), and in another the blast cells were Tdt-positive (Januszewicz et al, 1983).

The patients do not seem to improve on conventional treatment for acute lymphoblastic leukaemia.

No case of acute lymphoblastic transformation has been seen in the Bournemouth series.

Other haematological malignancies

Myeloma

There are only 21 documented cases where CLL and multiple myeloma (MM) coexisted (Jeha et al, 1981; Pines et al, 1984). Only six cases have been investigated immunologically, and in four of these the light-chain type of the two tumours differed. In an early case (Preud'homme and Seligmann, 1972) both tumours expressed IgAλ, and more recently a patient was described who developed a plasmacytoma secreting IgMk 8 years after being diagnosed as CLL expressing surface IgMk (Pines et al, 1984). In neither of these cases was idiotypic identity established.

We have seen two patients with coincident CLL and MM. In neither case was the Ig light chain the same.

Myelodysplasia

There have been a number of reports of the coexistence of refractory sideroblastic anaemia (RSA) and CLL (Papayannis et al, 1974; Copplestone et al, 1986). It is probably true that other forms of myelodysplasia have not generally been reported in association with CLL because of the difficulty of making the diagnosis in patients with bone marrows heavily infiltrated with small lymphocytes. In the Bournemouth series there have been four cases of coexistent RSA and one case of refractory anaemia. One of the cases of RSA also underwent a prolymphocytoid transformation and had been heavily pretreated before the appearance of either complication.

Chronic granulocytic leukaemia

Chronic granulocytic leukaemia (CGL) has been reported to coexist with CLL on seven occasions (Carcassone and Gascard, 1968; Whang-Peng et al, 1974; Vilpo et al, 1980; Faguet et al, 1983; Schreiber et al, 1984; Hashimi et al, 1986). No evidence has been presented to suggest that the two malignant clones were in any way linked.

Acute myeloblastic leukaemia

Acute myeloblastic leukaemia (AML) has been associated with CLL on rather more occasions. Zarrabi et al (1977), when reviewing the world literature, found an overall incidence in 11 large series of 1.7%. In many cases the AML was presumably secondary to treatment with radiotherapy (Osgood, 1964) or chemotherapy (Catovsky and Galton, 1971), but there are 10 cases in the literature in which the AML appeared before chemotherapy was administered (Lawlor et al, 1979; Manoharan et al, 1981a). To these numbers we can add one of our own, a 92-year-old woman who died on admission having presented with a white cell count of $452 \times 10^9/l$, of which approximately half were myeloblasts and half typical CLL cells.

We have seen one other case with coexistent CLL and AML but she had been treated with chlorambucil over a prolonged period. Interestingly, she had also developed a prolymphocytoid transformation.

The evidence that the association of CLL and other haematological disorders is more than a chance occurrence is difficult to obtain. From our epidemiological study we are aware that CLL has a prevalence in the elderly community of 1 in 500 and that MDS is about as common, so that the discovery of five cases with both diseases in a catchment population of 200 000 studied for 13 years would not be excessive. Apart from the known risk of developing AML following treatment with alkylating agents, and the supposed role of an impaired immune system in failing to control nascent tumours, there are no biological reasons to link the separate tumours. In almost all studies there have been no characteristics to link the two malignant clones, and indeed the aetiological factors of most haematological malignancies studied do not play a part in the cause of CLL.

Nonhaematological cancers

Nonhaematological malignancies are common in patients with CLL. Several studies have reported greater numbers than expected (Beresford, 1952; Hansen, 1973; Manusow and Weinerman, 1975; Greene et al, 1978; Davis et al, 1987).

Although one study has suggested that when patients are adequately matched for sex and age the true incidence is no higher than expected (Lopaciuk et al, 1977), most studies conclude that there is a real increased risk of developing subsequent cancer in CLL. The increased risk does not seem to be confined to a single type of cancer—in various series, excess numbers of skin, lung, colorectal and soft tissue tumours were reported.

Table 9. Nonhaematological tumours occurring in patients with CLL.

Skin cancers	18
Carcinoma of bladder	12
Carcinoma of bronchus	9
Carcinoma of breast	5
Colorectal carcinomas	4
Carcinoma of prostate	4
Carcinomas of stomach, pancreas, vulva, cervix and larynx, and fibrosarcoma	1 each

In the Bournemouth series, 52 of the 200 patients had 58 subsequent cancers (Table 9).

The presumed cause for the increased numbers is a lack of immunosurveillance, although the precise mechanism is poorly worked out.

TREATMENT

Opinions on how to treat CLL have varied considerably, from those who recommended active treatment for symptomless patients with minimal disease, to those who withheld it from all but those with symptoms or obviously progressing disease. Osgood was the pioneer of radiotherapy in the treatment of CLL (Osgood, 1951) and he believed that systematic reduction of the tumour load would benefit all patients. However, this view finds little favour today. It is clear that many long-term survivors have received no treatment whatsoever, and since no effective treatment is without side effects it needs to be clearly established which patients would benefit.

The staging systems of Rai et al (1975) and Binet et al (1981) are attempts to preselect patients who would benefit from treatment. The survival of Rai stage 0 and Binet stage A patients is so good, being close to that of age- and sex-matched controls (French Cooperative Group, 1986), that many physicians have the prejudice that specific treatment would be unwise, whereas patients with Rai stages III and IV and Binet stage C have such a poor prognosis that most agree that treatment must be attempted. For intermediate groups there are intermediate opinions.

In making a decision on whether to treat, a further factor needs to be taken into consideration. Some patients with widespread disease show no progression, whereas some with minimal disease are rapidly progressive. For this reason many authors build a period of observation and assessment into their treatment protocols (Rai and Sawitsky, 1985).

Treatment modalities

Alkylating agents

Chlorambucil has been the most widely used agent in the treatment of CLL in recent times. It is lympholytic in the great majority of cases and consequently reduces the white count and the size of lymph nodes and spleen. An increase in haemoglobin and platelet count may be expected in the long term, and systemic symptoms are usually relieved. However, complete abolition of the disease is never acheived. Even patients with 'complete remissions' (no lymphadenopathy or splenomegaly, normal blood count and marrow aspirates) will have focal collections of small lymphocytes on bone marrow trephine biopsy.

Formerly, chlorambucil was usually given as a continuous daily oral dosage of 0.05–0.15 mg/kg, more or less indefinitely, but more recently it has become fashionable to give it intermittently in a dose of 0.8–2.5 mg/kg over 1–4 days in divided doses, repeating the course every 4 weeks.

In low doses, chlorambucil is well-tolerated, although in doses of greater than 0.5 mg/kg it may cause nausea or abdominal pain. A small proportion of patients develop a widespread drug rash, sometimes with eyelid oedema. Chlorambucil is both myelosuppressive and immunosuppressive. Anaemia, neutropenia and thrombocytopenia are particular problems in patients beginning treatment with heavily infiltrated bone marrows. In a few patients, autoimmune haemolytic anaemia is precipitated by chlorambucil treatment (Lewis et al, 1966). The hypogammaglobulinaemia of CLL is not improved by chlorambucil and is probably made worse (Galton, 1984). Intermittent dosage regimes may be less toxic in this respect. Chlorambucil is undoubtedly leukaemogenic, especially if given according to a continuous low-dose schedule. A 10% incidence of AML among 5 year survivors who have received continuous chlorambucil for 3 years has been predicted (Galton, 1984).

Other aklylating agents, especially cyclophosphamide or melphalan, are probably equally as effective as chlorambucil, but are seldom used alone in CLL except in cases of chlorambucil hypersensitivity.

Corticosteroids

Since corticosteroids are lympholytic but not myelosuppressive, they are useful agents at the start of treatment in patients with heavily involved bone marrows. It is usual to see a rise in lymphocyte count when steroids are first used. This undoubtedly represents a redistribution between body compartments, and with continued administration the count falls. Corticosteroids are also indicated in the treatment of autoimmune haemolytic anaemia, neutropenia and thrombocytopenia.

Long-term steroids should be avoided in CLL. Not only are the usual corticosteroid complications of diabetes mellitus, hypertension and osteoporosis particularly likely to occur in the elderly, but the immunodeficiency of CLL will be intensified. However, in at least one trial the combination of intermittent chlorambucil and prednisolone was superior to chlorambucil alone (Han et al, 1973).

Combination chemotherapy

There has been a great reluctance to introduce combination chemotherapy for CLL. It is axiomatic that cure is impossible in CLL, and therefore, since palliation is the aim, *primum non procere* has been the guiding aphorism. However, the relatively nontoxic COP regime (cyclophosphamide, vincristine, prednisolone) has been used in a number of centres. In the large multicentre French study it had no advantage over chlorambucil alone in Binet group B CLL when the trial was analysed at 4 years (Chastang et al, 1986).

The use of doxorubicin-containing regimes such as CHOP (cyclophosphamide, doxorubin, vincristine, prednisolone) has been discouraged (Galton, 1984) because of their toxicity in a frail and elderly population. Nevertheless, the French Cooperative Group have found this regime to be markedly more effective in group C CLL than COP (Chastang et al, 1986). Even with these regimes, long-term survival of transformed CLL (to PLL or Richter's syndrome) has not been reported.

Radiotherapy

In the past, radiophosphorus (Osgood, 1951) or whole body irradiation (Johnson, 1977) were popular treatments for CLL, but they have been largely replaced by chemotherapy. However, CLL cells are usually radiosensitive, and repeated exposure to low doses of ionizing radiation of any part of the body through which lymphocytes circulate causes a fall in lymphocyte count and a reduction in the size of lymph nodes and spleen. The modern practice of splenic irradiation by the Padua method (Oscier et al, 1981) makes use of this principle. One hundred centiGrays administered to an enlarged spleen at weekly intervals has proved very successful in reducing the lymphocytosis, and this treatment is incorporated into the current MRC trial.

Experimental treatments

Leucapheresis. Although it is cumbersome, time-consuming and expensive, the use of a continuous-flow cell separator to remove lymphocytes is an effective way of reducing the total lymphocyte mass. It is possible to remove up to 2×10^{11} cells/day, depending on the white cell count. In patients refractory to chemotherapy it may provide long-term control of the disease (Goldfinger et al, 1980).

Interferon. Despite its well-known effectiveness in hairy cell leukaemia, interferon α has had only a minimal effect in CLL (O'Connell et al, 1986). It appears that brief and partial responses are occasionally seen, but acceleration of the disease has also been described (Foon et al, 1986a).

Monoclonal antibodies. Treatment with monoclonal antibodies directed against surface immunoglobulin idiotype has produced only transient responses (Hamblin et al, 1980). Examination of this system has demonstrated numerous escape mechanisms (Gordon et al, 1984), the chief of which is antigenic modulation. The construction of a univalent antibody bearing a human Fcγ region has given encouraging results in overcoming these inhibitions (Hamblin et al, 1987a).

The CD5 antigen has also been used as a target for monoclonal antibody attack (Dillman et al, 1982) but this molecule is also subject to antigenic modulation (Schroff et al, 1984). The conjugation of monoclonal antibody to drugs or toxins remains an interesting idea whose time has not yet come.

Supportive care

Early treatment of infection is mandatory in CLL. This especially applies to herpes zoster infections, which may be extremely severe in this disease. Early

treatment with intravenous acyclovir is effective and should not be denied the
patient. Prophylactic immunization is useless in CLL, and the use of live
vaccines is hazardous. They should never be used.

Intravenous immunoglobulin

Several clinical trials are evaluating the effect of regular infusions of
immunoglobulin (Besa, 1984). Since recurrent infections correlate well with
low serum levels of IgG, it is to be hoped that the group of patients with this
complication will benefit from this treatment. No study has yet reported an
advantage of the more expensive but more convenient intravenous preparations over intramuscular γ-globulin.

Splenectomy

Dramatic improvement in anaemia, thrombocytopenia and neutropenia may
be achieved by splenectomy in patients with large spleens (Christensen et al,
1977) but it is difficult to establish an effect on long-term survival (Ferrant et
al, 1986). The operative mortality (Christensen et al, 1970) and increased risk
of infection make this a less attractive option unless there is unresponsive
haemolysis or thrombocytopenia.

Treatment recommendations

In my view, treatment should be withheld from patients with Binet stage A
disease unless or until they show clear signs of progression. Those with an
overwhelming urge to treat stage A disease should be encouraged to enter
their patients into a prospective trial comparing treatment with no treatment.

At first patients should be reviewed at monthly intervals, when most elderly
patients will be found to have stable disease. Once this is established, a 6
monthly interval between reviews is appropriate. A rising lymphocyte count is
not in itself an indication for treatment. A falling haemoglobulin or platelet
count should be investigated. Autoimmune haemolysis or thrombocytopenia
is more likely to occur in late stages of the disease, but at any stage they should
be treated with prednisolone and chlorambucil. A falling haemoglobin which
is caused by increasing marrow failure is an indication for treatment with
chlorambucil. It is not necessary for the haemoglobin to fall below 10 g/dl
before treatment starts. If treatment is not delayed it may be possible to avoid
the use of corticosteroids with their attendant side effects in elderly,
immunodeficient patients.

In the group of patients with isolated splenomegaly who otherwise have
stage A disease and reportedly a good prognosis (Dighiero et al, 1979), there is
no indication for treatment unless troublesome hypersplenism supervenes. In
this case the choice of treatment is between chlorambucil and low-dose splenic
irradiation. The relative values of these are currently being assessed by an
MRC trial.

In stage B, CLL treatment should certainly be offered to patients with B
symptoms and to those with distressing or uncomfortable organomegaly. The

treatment of choice is intermittent chlorambucil, although in patients with spleens larger than 5 cm below the costal margin a case can be made for low-dose intermittent splenic irradiation. Other patients in stage B should be observed at intervals, and action taken as appropriate, as for stage A.

Patients with stage C disease merit treatment. It must be clear that anaemia or thrombocytopenia is indeed a consequence of marrow failure, but once this is established immediate treatment with prednisolone 40 mg/m^2 for 3 weeks should be followed by intermittent chlorambucil. For patients who respond poorly to this protocol, consideration should be given to the use of CHOP. This may require admission to hospital and intensive haematological support, and will not be appropriate for every patient.

In patients unresponsive to conventional treatment, experimental treatments may be tried, but the dignity of the patient must be respected.

Acknowledgements

I am grateful to my many colleagues for their help in my studies of CLL. I would particularly like to thank Professor George Stevenson, Dr Freda Stevenson, Dr John Smith and Dr David Oscier.

This work has been supported by the Leukaemia Research Fund and Tenovus.

I am grateful to Mrs Keyna Avery for typing the manuscript.

REFERENCES

Abeloff MD & Waterbury MD (1974) Pure red cell aplasia and chronic lymphocytic leukemia. *Archives of Internal Medicine* **134:** 721–724.

Alexanian R (1975) Monoclonal gammapathy in lymphoma. *Archives of Internal Medicine* **135:** 62–66.

Auclerc MF, Desprez-Cyrely JP, Maral J et al (1984) Prognostic value of lymphograms in chronic lymphocytic leukemia. *Cancer* **53:** 888–895.

Ault KA, Antin JH, Ginsberg D et al (1985) Phenotype of recovering cell populations after marrow transplantation. *Journal of Experimental Medicine* **161:** 1483–1502.

Baccarani M, Cavo M, Gobbi M, Lauria F & Tura S (1982) Staging of chronic lymphocytic leukemia. *Blood* **59:** 1191–1196.

Baer MR, Stein RS & Dessypris EN (1985) Chronic lymphocytic leukemia with hyperleukocytosis: the hyperviscosity syndrome. *Cancer* **56:** 2865–2969.

Baldini L, Mozzana R, Cesana B et al (1984) Clinical stage and immunological findings in chronic lymphocytic leukemia. *Bolletino Istitut Sieroterapia Milan* **63:** 50–56.

Beresford OD (1952) Chronic lymphatic leukaemia associated with malignant disease. *British Journal of Cancer* **6:** 339–344.

Bernard SM, Cartwright RA, Darwin RM et al (1987) A possible association between multiple sclerosis and lymphoma/leukaemia. *British Journal of Haematology* **65:** 122–123.

Besa EC (1984) Use of intravenous immunoglobulin in chronic lymphocytic leukemia. *American Journal of Medicine* **7**(3A): 209–218.

Binet JL, Catovsky D, Chandra P et al (1981) Chronic lymphocytic leukaemia: proposals for a revised prognostic staging system. *British Journal of Haematology* **48:** 365–367.

Bizzozero OJ Jr, Johnson KG, Ciocco A et al (1967) Radiation related leukemia in Hiroshima and Nagasaki 1946–1964. II. Observations on type-specific leukemia, survivorship and clinical behaviour. *Annals of Internal Medicine* **66:** 522–530.

Bjorkholm M, Grimfors G, Kimby E & Holm G (1984) No evidence of a lymphocytopenic state before manifestation of chronic lymphocytic leukemia. *Acta Medica Scandinavica* **215:** 371–374.

Blattner WA, Strober W, Muchmore AV et al (1976) Familial chronic lymphocytic leukemia. Immunologic and cellular characterisation. *Annals of Internal Medicine* **84:** 554–557.

Bofil M, Janossy G, Janossa M et al (1985) The fetal development of the B lymphoid system in man. *Journal of Immunology* **136:** 1531–1538.

Boggs DR & Fahey JL (1960) Serum protein changes in malignant disease. II. The chronic leukemias, Hodgkin's disease, and malignant melanoma. *Journal of the National Cancer Institute* **25:** 1381–1390.

Boggs DR, Sofferman SA, Wintrobe MM & Cartwright GE (1966) Factors influencing the duration of survival in chronic lymphocytic leukemia. *American Journal of Medicine* **40:** 243–254.

Brandt L & Nilsson PG (1980) Lymphocytopenia preceding chronic lymphocytic leukemia. *Acta Medica Scandinavica* **208:** 13–16.

Brouet JC, Preud'homme JL, Seligmann M & Bernard J (1973) Blast cells with monoclonal surface immunoglobulin in two cases of acute blast crisis supervening on chronic lymphocytic leukaemia. *British Medical Journal* **4:** 23–24.

Caligaris-Cappio F, Gobbi M, Bofill M & Janossy G (1982) Infrequent normal B-lymphocytes expressed features of B-chronic lymphocytic leukaemia. *Journal of Experimental Medicine* **155:** 623–628.

Caligaris-Cappio F, Janossy G, Campana D et al (1984) Lineage relationship of chronic lymphocytic leukemia and hairy cell leukemia: studies with TPA. *Leukemia Research* **8:** 567–578.

Carcasonne Y & Gascard E (1968) Leucémie myéloide succedant à une leucémie lymphoide. *Marseille Médical* **105:** 339–341.

Catovsky D (1982) Prolymphocytic leukaemia. *Nouvelle Révue Francaise d'Hématologie* **24:** 343–347.

Catovsky D (1984) Chronic lymphocytic, prolymphocytic and hairy cell leukaemias. In Goldman JM & Preisler HD (eds) *Haematology. 1. Leukaemias*, pp 266–298. London: Butterworths.

Catovsky D & Galton DAG (1971) Myelomonocytic leukaemia supervening on chronic lymphocytic leukaemia. *Lancet* **i:** 478–479.

Catovsky D, Cherchi M, Okos A, Hegde U & Galton DAG (1976) Mouse red-cell rosettes in B-lymphoproliferative disorders. *British Journal of Haematology* **33:** 173–177.

Cawley JC, Smith JL, Goldstone AH et al (1976) IgA and IgM cytoplasmic inclusions in a series of cases with chronic lymphocytic leukaemia. *Clinical and Experimental Immunology* **23:** 78–80.

Chan WC & Dekmezian R (1986) Phenotype changes in large cell transformation of small cell lymphoid malignancies. *Cancer* **57:** 1971–1978.

Chastang C, Travade P, Benichou J, Dighiero G & Binet J-L (1986) Patient accrual and interim statistical analysis in long-term clinical trials: the French chronic lymphocytic leukemia CLL 80 protocol as a case study. *Statistics in Medicine* **5:** 465–473.

Chiorazzi N, Fu SM, Ghodrat M et al (1979) T cell helper defect in patients with chronic lymphocytic leukemia. *Journal of Immunology* **122:** 1087–1090.

Christensen BEN, Kuld Hansen L, Kvist Kristensen J & Videbaek A (1970) Splenectomy in haematology. Indications, results, and complications in 41 patients. *Scandinavian Journal of Haematology* **7:** 247–260.

Christensen BEN, Hansen MM & Videbaek A (1977) Splenectomy in chronic lymphocytic leukaemia. *Scandinavian Journal of Haematology* **18:** 279–287.

Clark DM, Boylston AW, Hall PA & Carrel S (1986) Antibodies to T cell antigen receptor beta chain families detect monoclonal T cell proliferation. *Lancet* **ii:** 835–837.

Copplestone JA, Mufti GJ, Hamblin TJ & Oscier DG (1986) Immunological abnormalities in myelodysplasia. II: Coexistent lymphoid or plasma cell neoplasms. A report of 20 cases unrelated to chemotherapy. *British Journal of Haematology* **63:** 149–159.

Cornes JS & Jones TG (1962) Leukaemic lesions of the gastrointestinal tract. *Journal of Clinical Pathology* **15:** 305–313.

Court-Brown WM & Doll R (1959) Adult leukaemia: trends in mortality in relation to aetiology. *British Medical Journal* **1:** 1063–1069.

Damashek W (1967) Chronic lymphocytic leukemia—an accumulative disease of immunologically incompetent lymphocytes. *Blood* **29:** 566–584.

Dathan JRE, Heyworth MF & MacIver AG (1974) Nephrotic syndrome in chronic lymphocytic leukaemia. *British Medical Journal* **3:** 655–657.

Davis JW, Weiss NS & Armstrong BK (1987) Second cancers in patients with chronic lymphocytic leukemia. *Journal of the National Cancer Institute* **78:** 91–94.

Dhaliwal HS, Ling NR, Bishop S & Chapel H (1978) Expression of immunoglobulin G on blood lymphocytes in chronic lymphocytic leukaemia. *Clinical and Experimental Immunology* **31:** 226–236.

Dighiero G, Charron D, Debre P et al (1979) Identification of a pure splenic form of chronic lymphocytic leukaemia. *British Journal of Haematology* **41:** 169–176.

Dillman RO, Shawler DL, Sobol RE et al (1982) Murine monoclonal antibody therapy in two patients with chronic lymphocytic leukemia. *Blood* **59:** 1036–1045.

Dubner HN, Crowley JJ & Schilling RF (1978) Prognostic value of nucleoli and cell size in chronic lymphocytic leukemia. *American Journal of Hematology* **4:** 337–341.

Ebbe S, Wittels B & Damashek W (1962) Autoimmune thrombocytopenic purpura ('ITP type') with chronic lymphocytic leukemia. *Blood* **19:** 23–27.

Enno A, Catovsky D, O'Brien M et al (1979) 'Prolymphocytoid' transformation of chronic lymphocytic leukaemia. *British Journal of Haematology* **41:** 9–18.

Faguet GB, Little T, Agee JF & Garver FA (1983) Chronic lymphatic leukemia evolving into chronic myelocytic leukemia. *Cancer* **52:** 1647–1652.

Feehally J, Hutchinson RM, Hackay EG & Walls J (1981) Recurrent proteinuria in chronic lymphocytic leukaemia. *Clinical Nephrology* **16:** 51–54.

Ferrant A, Michaux J-L & Sokal G (1986) Splenectomy in advanced chronic lymphocytic leukemia. *Cancer* **58:** 2130–2135.

Fialkow PJ, Najfeld V, Reddy A, Singer J & Steinmann L (1978) Chronic lymphocytic leukemia: clonal origin in a committed B lymphocyte progenitor. *Lancet* **ii:** 444–446.

Flanagan NG, Ridway JC, Kozlowski CL & Copsey PC (1981) Clinical and immunological features in patients with chronic lymphocytic leukaemia presenting in an area of high incidence. *Clinical and Laboratory Haematology* **4:** 343–349.

Foa R, Catovsky D, Brozovic M et al (1979) Clinical staging and immunological findings in chronic lymphocytic leukemia. *Cancer* **44:** 483–487.

Foa R, Lauria F, Lusso P et al (1984) Discrepancy between phenotypic and functional features of natural killer T-lymphocytes in B-cell chronic lymphocytic leukaemia. *British Journal of Haematology* **58:** 509–516.

Foon KA, Schroff RW & Gale RP (1982) Surface markers on leukemia and lymphoma cells. *Blood* **60:** 1–19.

Foon KA, Bottino G, Abrams PG et al (1985) Phase II trial of recombinant leucocyte A interferon in patients with advanced chronic lymphocytic leukemia. *American Journal of Medicine* **78:** 216–220.

Foon KA, Roth MS & Bunn PA Jr (1986a) Alpha interferon treatment of low grade B-cell non-Hodgkin's lymphomas, cutaneous T-cell lymphomas and chronic lymphocytic leukemia. *Seminars in Oncology* **13**(supplement 2): 35–42.

Foon KA, Gale RP & Todd RF (1986b) Recent advances in the immunologic classification of leukemia. *Seminars in Hematology* **23**(4): 257–283.

Foucar K & Rydell RE (1980) Richter's syndrome in chronic lymphocytic leukemia. *Cancer* **46:** 118–134.

Fraumeni JR Jr & Miller RW (1967) Epidemiology of human leukaemia: recent observations. *Journal of the National Cancer Institute* **38:** 593–605.

French Cooperative Group (1986) Effectiveness of 'CHOP' regimen in advanced untreated chronic lymphocytic leukemia. *Lancet* **i:** 1346–1349.

Fu SM, Winchester RJ, Feizi T, Walzer PD & Kunkel HG (1974) Idiotypic specificity of surface immunoglobulin and the maturation of leukemic bone-marrow-derived lymphocytes. *Proceedings of the National Academy of Sciences USA* **71:** 4487–4490.

Gahrton G, Robert K-H, Friberg K, Zech L & Bird AG (1980) Nonrandom chromosomal aberrations in chronic lymphocytic leukemia revealed by polyclonal B-cell mitogen stimulation. *Blood* **56:** 640–647.

Galton DAG (1966) The pathogenesis of chronic lymphocytic leukaemia. *Canadian Medical Association Journal* **94:** 1005–1010.

Galton DAG (1984) Chronic lymphocytic leukaemia: treatment. In Goldmann JM & Preisler HD (eds) *Haematology. 1. Leukaemias,* pp. 299–321. London: Butterworths.

Galton DAG, Goldman JM, Wiltshaw E et al (1974) Prolymphocytic leukaemia. *British Journal of Haematology* **27:** 7–23.

Goldfinger D, Capostagno V, Lowe C, Sacks HJ & Gatti RA (1980) Use of long term leukapheresis in the treatment of chronic lymphocytic leukemia. *Transfusion* **20:** 450–454.

Golomb HM, Catovsky D & Golde DW (1978) Hairy cell leukemia. A clinical review based on 71 cases. *Annals of Internal Medicine* **89:** 677–683.

Goodnough LT & Muir A (1980) Bullous pemphigoid as a manifestation of chronic lymphocytic leukaemia. *Archives of Internal Medicine* **140:** 1526–1527.

Gordon J, Abdul-Ahad A & Smith JL (1978) Free light chain synthesis by neoplastic cells in chronic lymphocytic leukaemia and non-Hodgkin's lymphoma. *Immunology* **34:** 397–403.

Gordon J, Abdul-Ahad A, Hamblin TJ, Stevenson FK & Stevenson GT (1984) Barriers to successful immunotherapy with anti-idiotype antibody. *British Journal of Cancer* **49:** 547–557.

Gray JL, Jacobs A & Block M (1974) Bone marrow and peripheral blood lymphocytosis in the prognosis of chronic lymphocytic leukemia. *Cancer* **33:** 1169–1178.

Green RA & Nichols NJ (1959) Pulmonary involvement in leukemia. *American Review of Respiratory Disease* **80:** 833–840.

Greene MH, Hoover RN & Fraumeni JF Jr (1978) Subsequent cancer in patients with chronic lymphocytic leukemia—a possible immunological mechanism. *Journal of the National Cancer Institute* **61:** 337–340.

Hamblin TJ & Hough D (1977) Chronic lymphatic leukaemia: correlation of immunofluorescent characteristics with clinical features. *British Journal of Haematology* **36:** 359–365.

Hamblin TJ, Verrier Jones J & Peacock DB (1975) The immune response to ϕx 174 in man: iv. Primary and secondary antibody production in patients with chronic lymphatic leukaemia. *Clinical and Experimental Immunology* **21:** 101–108.

Hamblin TJ, Abdul-Ahad AK, Gordon J, Stevenson FK & Stevenson GT (1980) Preliminary evidence in treating lymphocytic leukaemia with antibody to immunoglobulin idiotypes on the cell surfaces. *British Journal of Cancer* **42:** 495–502.

Hamblin TJ, Oscier DG, Gregg EO & Smith JL (1985) Cell markers in a large single centre series of chronic lymphocytic leukaemia: the relationship between CLL and PLL. *British Journal of Haematology* **61:** 556.

Hamblin TJ, Oscier DG & Young BJ (1986) Autoimmunity in chronic lymphocytic leukaemia. *Journal of Clinical Pathology* **39:** 713–716.

Hamblin TJ, Cattan AR, Glennie MJ et al (1987a) Initial experience in treating human lymphoma with a chimeric univalent derivative of monoclonal anti-idiotype antibody *Blood* **69:** 790–797.

Hamblin TJ, Oscier DG, Stevens JR & Smith JL (1987b) Long survival in B-CLL correlates with surface IgMk phenotype. *British Journal of Haematology* **66:** 21–26.

Han T, Ezdinli EZ, Shimoaka K & Desai DV (1973) Chlorambucil vs combined chlorambucil-corticosteroid therapy in chronic lymphocytic leukemia. *Cancer* **31:** 502–508.

Han T, Ozer H, Henderson ES et al (1981) Defective immunoregulatory T-cell function in chronic lymphocytic leukemia. *Blood* **58:** 1182–1189.

Han T, Ozer H, Gavigan M et al (1984a) Benign monoclonal B-cell lymphocytosis—a benign variant of CLL: clinical, immunologic, phenotypic and cytogenetic studies in 20 patients. *Blood* **64:** 244–252.

Han T, Ozer H, Sadamori N et al (1984b) Prognostic importance of cytogenetic abnormalities in patients with chronic lymphocytic leukemia. *New England Journal of Medicine* **310:** 288–292.

Hansen MM (1973) Chronic lymphocytic leukaemia. Clinical studies based on 189 cases followed for a long time. *Scandinavian Journal of Haematology* **18** (supplement 1): 216.

Hashimi L, Al-Katib A, Mertelsmann R, Mahamed AN & Koziner B (1986) Cytofluorometric detection of chronic myelocytic leukemia supervening in a patient with chronic lymphocytic leukemia. *American Journal of Medicine* **80:** 269–275.

Heath ME & Cheson BD (1985) Defective complement activity in chronic lymphocytic leukemia. *American Journal of Hematology* **19**: 63–73.

Hendriks J (1985) A possible association between HTLV-I and B-cell chronic lymphocytic leukemia in Jamaica. *Acta Haematologica* **74**: 55–57.

Januszewicz E, Cooper IA, Pilkington G & Jose D (1983) Blastic transformation of chronic lymphocytic leukemia. *American Journal of Hematology* **15**: 399–402.

Jayaswel U, Roath S, Hyde RD, Chisolm DM & Smith JL (1977) Blood lymphocyte surface markers and clinical findings in chronic lymphoproliferative disorders. *British Journal of Haematology* **37**: 207–215.

Jeha T, Hamblin TJ & Smith JL (1981) Coincident chronic lymphocytic leukemia and osteosclerotic multiple myeloma. *Blood* **57**: 617–619.

Johnson RE (1977) Radiotherapy as primary therapy for chronic lymphocytic leukemia. *Clinics in Haematology* **6**(1): 237–244.

Juliusson G & Gahrton G (1985) Abnormal/normal metaphase ratio in chronic B-lymphocytic leukemia. *Cancer Genetics and Cytogenetics* **18**: 307–323.

Juliusson G, Robert K-H, Hammerstrom L et al (1983) Mitogen-induced switching of heavy-chain class secretion in chronic B-lymphocytic leukemia and immunocytoma cell populations. *Scandinavian Journal of Immunology* **17**: 51–59.

Juliusson G, Robert K-H, Ost A et al (1985) Prognostic information from cytogenetic analysis in chronic B-lymphocytic leukemia and leukemic immunocytoma. *Blood* **65**: 135–141.

Kay NE (1981) Abnormal T-cell subpopulation function in CLL: excessive suppressor (Tγ) and deficient helper (Tμ) activity with respect to B-cell proliferation. *Blood* **57**: 418–420.

Kay NE, Oken MM & Perri RT (1983) The influential T cell in B cell neoplasms. *Journal of Clinical Oncology* **1**: 810–816.

Kersey JH, Spector BD & Good RA (1973) Primary immunodeficiency diseases and cancer: the immunodeficiency-cancer registry. *International Journal of Cancer* **12**: 333–347.

Knowles DM, Dalla-Favera R & Pelicci P-G (1985) T-cell receptor β-chain rearrangements. *Lancet* **ii**: 159–160.

Korsmeyer SJ, Hieter PA, Ravetch JV et al (1981) Developmental hierarchy of immunoglobulin gene rearrangements in human leukemic pre-B-cells. *Proceedings of the National Academy of Sciences USA* **78**: 7096–8100.

Kruskall MS (1983) Case records of the Massachusetts General Hospital. *New England Journal of Medicine* **309**: 297–305.

Kurita S, Kamei Y & Ota K (1974) Genetic studies on familial leukemia. *Cancer* **34**: 1098–1101.

Kuse R, Schuster S, Schubbe H, Dix S & Haysmann K (1985) Blood lymphocyte volumes and diameters in patients with chronic lymphocytic leukemia and normal controls. *Blut* **50**: 243–248.

Lauria F, Foa R & Catovsky D (1980) Increase in T-gamma lymphocytes in B-cell chronic lymphocytic leukemia. *Scandinavian Journal of Haematology* **24**: 187–190.

Lawlor E, McCann SR, Whelan A, Greally J & Temperley IJ (1979) Acute myeloid leukaemia occurring in untreated chronic lymphocytic leukaemia. *British Journal of Haematology* **43**: 369–373.

Lawrence JH, Low-Beer BVA & Carpender JWJ (1949) Chronic lymphocytic leukemia: a study of 100 patients treated with radioactive phosphorus. *Journal of the American Medical Society* **140**: 585–588.

Lewis FB, Schwartz RS & Damashek W (1966) X-radiation and alkylating agents as possible 'trigger' mechanisms in the autoimmune complications of malignant lymphoproliferative disease. *Clinical and Experimental Immunology* **1**: 3–11.

Ligler FS, Kettman JR, Smith G & Frankel EP (1983) Immunoglobulin phenotype on B-cells correlates with clinical stage of chronic lymphocytic leukemia. *Blood* **62**: 256–263.

Lopaciuk HZ, Wieczorek AJ, Romejko M et al (1977) Occurrence of malignant neoplasms in patients with chronic lymphatic leukaemia. *Haematologia* **11**: 279–287.

Lydyard PM, Youinou PY & Cooke A (1987) CD-5 positive B cells in rheumatoid arthritis and chronic lymphocytic leukaemia. *Immunology Today* **8**(2): 37–39.

MacMahon B & Koller EK (1957) Ethnic differences in the incidences of leukemia. *Blood* **12**: 1–10.

Manoharan A, Catovsky D, Clein P et al (1981a) Simultaneous or spontaneous occurrence of lympho- and myeloproliferative disorders: a report of four cases. *British Journal of*

Haematology **48:** 111–116.

Manoharan A, Catovsky D, Lampert IA et al (1981b) Histiocytic medullary reticulosis complicating chronic lymphocytic leukaemia: malignant or reactive? *Scandinavian Journal of Haematology* **26:** 5–13.

Manusow D & Weinerman BH (1975) Subsequent neoplasia in chronic lymphocytic leukemia. *Journal of the American Medical Association* **232:** 267–269.

Marlow AA & Evans ER (1977) Chronic lymphocytic leukemia. First pathological sign after 22 years. *Western Journal of Medicine* **126:** 408–409.

McLaughlin H, Wetherly-Mein G, Pitcher C & Hobbs J (1973) Non-immunoglobulin-bearing B-lymphocytes in chronic lymphatic leukaemia? *British Journal of Haematology* **25:** 7–14.

McMillan P, Mundy G & Mayer P (1980) Hypercalcaemia and osteolytic bone lesions in chronic lymphocytic leukaemia. *British Medical Journal* **281:** 1107.

Mellstedt H, Petterson D & Holm G (1978) Lymphocyte subpopulations in chronic lymphocytic leukaemia. *Acta Medica Scandinavica* **204:** 485–489.

Melo JV, Catovsky D & Galto DAG (1986a) The relationship between chronic lymphocytic leukaemia and prolymphocytic leukaemia. I. Clinical and laboratory features of 300 patients and characterisation of an intermediate group. *British Journal of Haematology* **63:** 377–387.

Melo JV, Catovsky D & Galton DAG (1986b) The relationship between chronic lymphocytic leukaemia and prolymphocytic leukaemia. II. Patterns of evolution of 'prolymphocytoid' transformation. *British Journal of Haematology* **64:** 77–86.

Melo JV, Catovsky D, Gregory WM & Galton DAG (1987) The relationship between chronic lymphocytic leukaemia and prolymphocytic leukaemia. IV. Analysis of survival and prognostic features. *British Journal of Haematology* **65:** 23–29.

Mercolino TJ, Arnold LN & Haughton G (1986) Phosphatidyl choline is recognised by a series of Ly-1 + murine B cell lymphomas specific for erythrocyte membranes. *Journal of Experimental Medicine* **163:** 155–165.

Miller ALC, Habershaw JA, Dhaliwhal HS & Lister TA (1984) Chronic lymphocytic leukaemia presenting as a blast cell crisis. *Leukemia Research* **8:** 905–912.

Miller DG (1962) Patterns of immunological deficiency in leukemias and lymphomas. *Annals of Internal Medicine* **57:** 703–715.

Miller RA & Gralow J (1984) The induction of leu-1 antigen expression in human malignant and normal B-cells by phorbol myristic acetate (PMA). *Journal of Immunology* **133:** 3408–3414.

Mills LE, O'Donnell JF, Guyre PM et al (1985) Spurious E rosette formation in B cell chronic lymphocytic leukemia due to monoclonal anti-sheep RBC antibody. *Blood* **65:** 270–274.

Nath I, Curtis J, Mangalik A & Talwar GP (1975) Lymphocytes devoid of T and B cell markers in chronic lymphatic leukemia. *Acta Haematologica* **53:** 37–43.

Newland AC, Catovsky D, Linch D et al (1984) Chronic T cell lymphocytosis: a review of 21 cases. *British Journal of Haematology* **58:** 433–446.

Nishiyama H, Mokuno J & Inoue T (1969) Relative frequency and mortality rate of various types of leukemia in Japan. *Gann* **60:** 71–81.

Norris HJ & Weiner M (1961) The renal lesions in leukemia. *American Journal of Medical Sciences* **241:** 512–524.

O'Connell MJ, Colgan JP, Oken MM (1986) Clinical trial of recombinant leucocyte A interferon as initial therapy for favorable histology non-Hodgkin's lymphomas and chronic lymphocytic leukemia: an Eastern Cooperative Oncology Group pilot study. *Journal of Clinical Oncology* **4:** 128–136.

O'Connor NTJ, Wainscoat JS, Weatherall DJ et al (1985) Rearrangement of the T-cell receptor β-chain gene in the diagnosis of lymphoproliferative disorders. *Lancet* **i:** 1295–1297.

Ohtaki K, Han T & Sandberg AA (1986) Sequential chromosomal abnormalities in B cell chronic lymphocytic leukemia: a study of 13 cases. *Cancer Genetics and Cytogenetics* **20:** 73–87.

Oscier DG, Catovsky D, Errington RD et al (1981) Splenic irradiation in B-prolymphocytic leukaemia. *British Journal of Haematology* **48:** 577–584.

Oscier DG, Mufti GM, Fitchett M, Hamblin TJ & Seabright M (1985) Chromosomal analysis of 52 cases of B-CLL. *British Journal of Haematology* **61:** 573.

Oscier DG, Mufti GM, Hamblin TJ, Jones DB & Smith JL (1986) Evolution of terminal deoxynucleotidyl transferase-positive lymphoma from a chronic T cell lymphocytosis. *Scandinavian Journal of Haematology* **36:** 221–228.

Osgood EE (1951) Titrated regularly spaced radioactive phosphorus or spray roentgen therapy of leukemias. *Archives of Internal Medicine* **87:** 329–348.

Osgood EE (1964) Treatment of chronic leukemias. *Journal of Nuclear Medicine* **5:** 139–153.

Pandolfi F, Semenzato G, de Rossi G et al (1982) Heterogeneity of T-CLL defined by monoclonal antibodies in nine patients. *Clinical Immunology and Immunopathology* **24:** 330–341.

Pangalis GA, Northwani BN & Rappaport H (1977) Malignant lymphoma, well differentiated lymphocytic: its relationship with chronic lymphocytic leukemia and macroglobulinaemia of Waldenström. *Cancer* **39:** 999–1010.

Papayannis AG, Stathakis NE, Kyrkoy K, Panani A & Gardikas C (1974) Primary acquired sideroblastic anaemia associated with chronic lymphocytic leukaemia. *British Journal of Haematology* **28:** 125–129.

Peterson LC, Bloomfield CD & Brunning RD (1980) Relationship of clinical staging and lymphocyte morphology to survival in chronic lymphocytic leukemia. *British Journal of Haematology* **45:** 563–567.

Phillips EA, Kempin S, Passe S, Mike V & Clarkson B (1977) Prognostic factors in chronic lymphocytic leukaemia and their implications for therapy. *Clinics in Haematology* **6**(1): 203–222.

Pierson J, Darley T, Stevenson GT & Virji M (1980) Monoclonal immunoglobulin light chains in the urine of patients with lymphoma. *British Journal of Cancer* **41:** 681–688.

Pines A, Ben-bassat I, Selzer G & Ramot B (1984) Transformation of chronic lymphocytic leukemia to plasmacytoma. *Cancer* **54:** 1904–1907.

Pisciotta AV & Hirschboeck JS (1957) Therapeutic considerations in chronic lymphocytic leukemia. *Archives of Internal Medicine* **99:** 334–345.

Pittman S & Catovsky D (1984) Prognostic significance of chromosomal abnormalities in chronic lymphocytic leukaemia. *British Journal of Haematology* **58:** 649–660.

Plastoucas CD, Galinksi M, Kempin S et al (1982) Abnormal T lymphocyte subpopulations in patients with B cell chronic lymphocytic leukemia: an analysis by monoclonal antibodies. *Journal of Immunology* **129:** 2305–2312.

Plater-Zyberk C, Maini RN, Lam K et al (1985) A rheumatoid arthritis B cell expresses a phenotype similar to that of chronic lymphocytic leukemia. *Arthritis and Rheumatism* **28:** 971–976.

Prchal J, Lucivero G, Carroll AJ, Lawton AR & Scott CW (1979) A study of a patient with chronic lymphocytic leukemia (CLL) which demonstrates that proliferation of the lymphocyte clone in CLL does not include T lymphoctes. *Clinical Immunology and Immunopathology* **13:** 231–236.

Preud'homme JL & Seligmann M (1972) Surface bound immunoglobulin as a cell marker in human lymphoproliferative disease. *Blood* **40:** 777–794.

Prolla JC & Kirsner JB (1964) The gastrointestinal lesions and complications of the leukaemias. *Annals of Internal Medicine* **61:** 1084–1104.

Rai KR & Sawitsky A (1985) Diagnosis and treatment of chronic lymphocytic leukemia. In Wiernik PH, Canellos GP, Kyle RA & Schiffer CA (eds). *Neoplastic Diseases of the Blood*, pp. 105–120. New York: Churchill Livingstone.

Rai KR, Sawitsky A, Cronkite EP et al (1975) Clinical staging of chronic lymphocytic leukemia. *Blood* **46:** 219–234.

Richter MN (1928) Generalised reticular cell sarcoma of lymph nodes associated with lymphatic leukemia. *American Journal of Pathology* **3:** 285–292.

Ross GD & Polley MJ (1975) Specificity of human lymphocyte complement receptors. *Journal of Experimental Medicine* **141:** 1163–1180.

Rozman C, Hernandez-Nieto L, Montserrat E & Brugues R (1981) Prognostic significance of bone marrow patterns in chronic lymphocytic leukaemia. *British Journal of Haematology* **47:** 529–537.

Rozman C, Montserrat E, Feliu E et al (1982) Prognosis of chronic lymphocytic leukemial. A multivariate survival analysis of 150 cases. *Blood* **59:** 1001–1005.

Rudders RA & Ross R (1975) Partial characterisation of the shift from IgG to IgA synthesis in the clonal differentiation of human leukemic bone marrow-derived lymphocytes. *Journal of Experimental Medicine* **142:** 549–559.

Rustagi P, Han T, Ziolkowski L, Currie M & Logue D (1983) Anti-granulocyte antibodies in chronic lymphocytic leukemia and other chronic lymphoproliferative disorders. *Blood* **62**(supplement 1): 106.

Sadamori N, Han T, Minowada J, Cohen E & Sandberg AA (1983) Chromosome studies in stimulated lymphocytes of B-cell chronic lymphocytic leukemia. *Hematological Oncology* **1**: 243–250.

Schlimok G, Theil E, Rieber EP et al (1982) Chronic leukemia with a hybrid surface phenotype (T lymphocytic/myelononcytic): leukemic cells displaying natural killer activity and antibody dependent cellular cytotoxicity. *Blood* **59**: 1157–1162.

Schreiber ZA, Azelrod MR & Ababe LS (1984) Coexistence of chronic myelogenous leukemia and chronic lymphocytic leukemia. *Cancer* **54**: 697–701.

Schroff RW, Farrell MM, Klein MM, Oldham RK & Foon KA (1984) T65 antigen modulation in phase I monoclonal antibody trial with chronic lymphocytic leukemic patients. *Journal of Immunology* **133**: 1641–1648.

Seney FD Jr, Federgreen WR, Stein H & Kashgarian M (1986) A review of nephrotic syndrome associated with chronic lymphocytic leukemia. *Archives of Internal Medicine* **146**: 137–141.

Sibbald R & Catovsky D (1979) Complete remission in prolymphocytic leukaemia with the combination chemotherapy CHOP. *British Journal of Haematology* **42**: 488–490.

Sinclair D, Dagg JH, Mowat AM, Parrott DMV & Stott DI (1984) Serum paraproteins in chronic lymphocytic leukaemia. *Journal of Clinical Pathology* **37**: 463–466.

Skarin AT (1985) Pathology and morphology of chronic leukemias and related disorders. In Wiernik PH, Canellos GP, Kyle RA & Schiffer CA (eds) *Neoplastic Diseases of the Blood*, pp 19–50. New York: Churchill Livingstone.

Spiers ASD, Lawrence DA, Levine M & Weitzman H (1986) T-cell chronic lymphocytic leukaemias and T-cell lymphoma-leukaemia: heterogeneity and anomalous cell markers. *Scandinavian Journal of Haematology* **37**: 421–424.

Stevenson FK, Hamblin TJ, Stevenson GT & Tutt AC (1980) Extracellular idiotypic immunoglobulin arising from human leukemic B lymphocytes. *Journal of Experimental Medicine* **152**: 1484–1496.

Stevenson FK, Hamblin TJ & Stevenson GT (1981) The nature of IgG on the surface of B lymphocytes in chronic lymphocytic leukemia. *Journal of Experimental Medicine* **154**: 1965–1969.

Sweet DL Jr, Golomb HM & Ultmann JE (1977) The clinical features of chronic lymphocytic leukaemia. *Clinics in Haematology* **6**(1): 185–202.

Ternynck T, Diaghiero G, Follezou J & Binet JL (1974) Comparison of normal and CLL lymphocyte surface Ig determinants using peroxidase-labelled antibodies: I. Detection and quantitation of light chain determinants. *Blood* **43**: 789–795.

Trump DL, Mann RB, Phelps R, Roberts H & Conley CL (1980) Richter's syndrome: diffuse histiocytic lymphoma in patients with chronic lymphocytic leukaemia. *American Journal of Medicine* **68**: 539–548.

Tsujimoto Y, Yunis J, Onorato-Showe L et al (1984) Molecular cloning of the chromosomal breakpoint of B-cell lymphomas and leukemias with the t(11;14) translocation. *Science* **224**: 1403–1406.

Tsujimoto Y, Cossman J, Jaffe E et al (1985) Involvement of *bcl-2* gene in human follicular lymphoma. *Science* **228**: 1140–1143.

Tucker J & Cachia PG (1986) Gastrointestinal bleeding due to large bowel infiltration by chronic lymphocytic leukaemia. *Postgraduate Medical Journal* **62**: 45–46.

Vilpo JA, Klemi P, Lassila O & de la Chapelle A (1980) Concomitant presentation of two chronic leukemias: evidence for independent clonal evolution. *American Journal of Hematology* **8**: 205–211.

Weiss NS (1978) Geographical variation in the incidence of the leukemias and the lymphomas. *National Cancer Institute Monograph* **53**, p 139. NIH publication No. 79-1864.

Whang-Peng J, Gralnik HR, Johnson RE, Lee EC & Lear A (1974) Chronic granulocytic leukemia (CGL) during the course of chronic lymphocytic leukemia (CLL): correlation of blood, marrow and spleen morphology and cytogenetics. *Blood* **43**: 333–339.

Youinou P, Le Goff P, Saleun JP et al (1978) Familial occurrence of monoclonal gammapathies. *Biomedicine* **28**: 226–232.

Young JL, Percy CL & Asire AJ (eds) (1981) SEER: Incidence and mortality data: 1973–1977. *National Cancer Institute Monograph* **57**. NIH Publication No. 81-2330.
Zacharski LR & Linman JW (1969) Chronic lymphocytic leukemia versus chronic lymphosar-coma cell leukemia. *American Journal of Medicine* **47**: 75–81.
Zarrabi MH, Grunwald HW & Rosner F (1977) Chronic lymphocytic leukemia terminating in acute leukemia. *Archives of Internal Medicine* **137**: 1059–1064.

8

Malignant lymphoma in the elderly

JOHN W. SWEETENHAM
CHRISTOPHER J. WILLIAMS

A large proportion of patients presenting with Hodgkin's disease and non-Hodgkin's lymphomas are aged 65 or more and they pose an important problem for physicians involved in their care. Unfortunately, the management of this group of patients has been the subject of few clinical studies. Most of the studies that have been reported have been retrospective and were not designed specifically to address the problems of older patients. As a result, uncertainties still exist regarding their appropriate management. Most clinical trials in the management of lymphomas exclude patients over 65 years of age. In those studies where such patients are not systematically excluded, median ages of the study populations are usually well below 65 years. This presumably reflects a referral bias into specialist centres.

It is important to examine this bias in referral before discussing the lymphomas in depth. Carbone (1985) has shown that elderly patients with cancer are usually offered fewer treatment options than their younger counterparts. This is largely because their physicians believe them to be unable to withstand intensive chemotherapy or radiotherapy. Furthermore, the probable outcome for these patients was felt not to justify the toxicity of their treatment. Both of these apparent prejudices have been the subject of several studies.

DO ELDERLY PATIENTS TOLERATE TREATMENT FOR CANCER LESS WELL THAN THEIR YOUNGER COUNTERPARTS?

There are many physiological and pharmacological reasons why this might be the case. Changes in organ function, especially of the liver and kidneys, may alter drug metabolism and excretion and thereby produce enhanced toxicity in elderly patients. Ageing tissues may be less capable of repair after treatment-induced changes. The physical and psychological tolerance of chemotherapy in elderly patients has been investigated by several groups, but with conflicting results.

The Eastern Cooperative Oncology Group (ECOG) in the United States has retrospectively examined data from randomized trials of chemotherapy in various malignancies (Begg and Carbone, 1983). Elderly patients were entered into 19 trials; these included disease at eight primary sites. Lymphomas were not included in this analysis since patients over 70 were not eligible for their trials in lymphoma. Five thousand four hundred and fifty nine patients were entered into these trials, 780 (13%) of them being 70 years or over. The authors suggested that there was little bias for entry of patients into these trials. However, hidden bias in referral may well have existed, with only the 'fittest' elderly being referred and this may have influenced tolerance for chemotherapy in this group. Several drug-related toxicities were reviewed including haematological, gastro-intestinal and neurological. Only haematological toxicity was more common in those over 70 than in younger patients. The authors found this to be significant for only two drugs, semustine (methyl CCNU) and methotrexate, perhaps due to an age-related fall in renal clearance.

In contrast to these results, age has been shown to be a risk factor for anthracycline cardiotoxicity (Bristow et al, 1978) and bleomycin-induced pulmonary fibrosis (Blum et al, 1973). As will be discussed later, Armitage and Potter (1984) have shown increased treatment-related complications with advancing age.

The psychosocial consequences of chemotherapy in elderly patients have been examined in a study of 238 patients undergoing treatment for lymphoma or breast cancer (Nerenz et al, 1986). No trend for a greater incidence of side-effects in older patients was seen. In fact, the over 76 age group experienced fewer side-effects overall than younger patients. Less emotional distress, and less life disruption were apparent in older patients.

IS THE OUTCOME FOR ELDERLY PATIENTS TREATED FOR CANCER SIGNIFICANTLY WORSE THAN FOR YOUNGER PATIENTS?

This is clearly an extremely difficult problem to answer. The elderly are more likely to have serious pre-existing diseases which may affect outcome and the biology of cancer may vary with age.

The ECOG study mentioned previously showed no difference in response rate or survival for any malignancy when comparing patients aged 70 or more with those under 70 years. Although a trend for poorer survival was evident in some tumours, this did not achieve statistical significance.

Data from studies of the non-Hodgkin lymphomas have shown variable results with respect to the importance of age as a prognostic factor (vide infra). In some studies, however, an undoubted trend for poorer survival with increasing age exists.

Both of the above questions must therefore remain unanswered. This is largely because of patient selection which makes it difficult to draw reliable conclusions. However, the data suggest that there may be a group of elderly patients with cancer, in good general health, who are able to withstand the rigours of intensive treatment and who have a favourable outcome.

The remainder of this chapter reviews the characteristics of elderly patients with non-Hodgkin's lymphoma and Hodgkin's disease.

NON-HODGKIN'S LYMPHOMAS

Age-related incidence

Except for a few uncommon subtypes of non-Hodgkin's lymphoma (NHL), the incidence of these diseases tends to increase with advancing age, reaching a plateau in the 8th decade (Newell et al, 1987). This is true both for low grade, and most intermediate grade NHLs classified according to the Working Formulation of the National Cancer Institute (National Cancer Institute sponsored study, 1982) (Figure 1). As a result of this trend, the proportion of elderly patients presenting with NHL is high. In Southampton, a retrospective study between 1977 and 1982 of an unselected group of patients (except by referral bias) showed that 38 patients of 203 (18.7%) were 65 years or over (Mead et al, 1984).

In a study from the South West Oncology Group in the USA (Dixon et al, 1986) of chemotherapy in advanced diffuse histiocytic lymphoma, patients of 65 years or older formed 26% of the study population. Similar figures are available from other studies, many of which will almost certainly be affected by referral bias.

Changes in the nature of non-Hodgkin's lymphomas with advancing age

It is difficult to obtain consistent data on this subject but some studies have revealed a trend for the nature of the NHLs to change with increasing age. In general, the elderly appear to present with more factors suggesting an unfavourable prognosis. This makes assessment of the influence of age or subsequent management very difficult.

Changes in histology with age

Many studies have shown that intermediate or high grade lymphomas are the predominant sub-types of NHL in the elderly. The study of Carbone et al (1986) comprised 50 patients, of whom 42 (84%) had intermediate or high grade histology in the Rappaport classification. Analysis of patient groups from other studies confirms this trend though some studies have produced conflicting data. For example, in a series by Nathwani et al (1978) of 77 patients aged 60 and over with NHL, nodular lymphoma, poorly differentiated (NLPD) was the commonest sub-type with diffuse histiocytic lymphoma the second most frequent.

A recent study from the Yorkshire Regional Health Authority (Barnes et al, 1987) has shown a marked trend for an increase in diffuse v. follicular histology with advancing age (Figure 2).

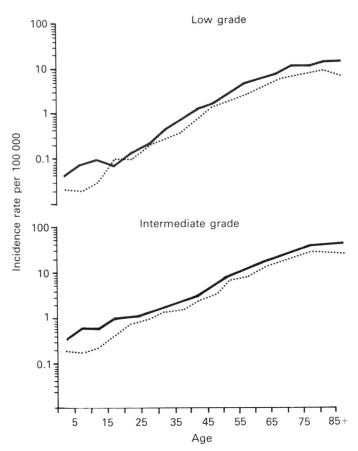

Figure 1. Age-specific incidence per 100 000 cases of low grade and intermediate grade lymphoma amongst 13 600 patients reported to the Surveillance, Epidemiology and End Results program of the National Cancer Institute, USA ——— = male; ······· = female. Taken from Newell et al (1987).

Changes in stage according to age at presentation

No obvious change in stage at presentation according to age has been documented in the follicular lymphomas. For diffuse lymphomas Elias (1979) has suggested that stage III and IV disease is more common in elderly patients. Three hundred and thirty seven patients presenting to Stanford from 1971 to 1977 formed the basis of this report. A lower median age group for patients with stages I and II disease was demonstrated compared with those with stages III and IV disease (43.16 v. 51.27 years, $p = 0.0001$). When subdivided into nodular or diffuse histologies (Rappaport classification), this trend was significant only for diffuse NHLs. A definite trend for advanced stage with advancing age was seen. In the study of Foucar et al (1983), diffuse mixed NHL (Rappaport) was the histological sub-type most common in the elderly,

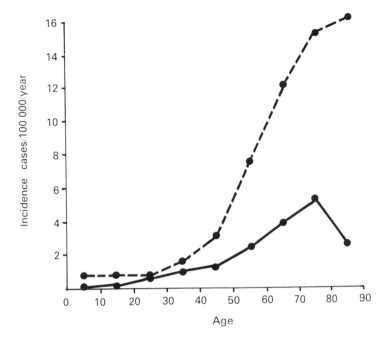

Figure 2. Age-specific incidence of major groups of NHL: ———— follicular; – – – – diffuse, in the Yorkshire Health Region between 1978 and 1982. Taken from Barnes et al (1987).

many of these patients having advanced disease. Twenty-one of the patients were aged 65 or over, and 14 (66%) of these had stage III or IV disease. In the study of 38 elderly patients with unfavourable prognosis NHL in Southampton, 23 (61%) had stage III or IV disease (Mead et al, 1984).

Frequency of extranodal nodal disease with advancing age

Two of the above-mentioned studies have documented a high frequency of extranodal disease amongst elderly patients with diffuse NHL and a similar trend was seen in a study from Sheffield, UK (Hancock et al, 1983). It should be noted that the role of extranodal disease as a prognostic variable is unclear and its influence in the elderly is therefore uncertain.

Performance status and age

Some studies have demonstrated a fall in performance status with advancing age. Performance status at presentation has been identified as having prognostic significance in some studies.

Thus elderly patients, particularly those with diffuse NHL, have a number of associated disease characteristics which may explain in part their poorer outcome after treatment, and which confuse the role of age as an independent prognostic factor, as will be discussed below.

Problems of investigation and staging

Prejudices regarding the outcome for older patients with NHL may well influence the degree to which these patients are investigated. In one post-mortem series, 38 patients were identified as dying of lymphoma in a Japanese geriatric hospital from 1972 to 1983 (Fukayama et al, 1985). In seven of these cases, the diagnosis was missed despite highly suggestive clinical and laboratory data. Five of those cases had extranodal disease and all were stage IV, suggesting perhaps that the patients' general state had precluded intensive investigation.

The problem of adequacy of staging of NHL has not been specifically addressed in the elderly in any study of which we are aware. One study of follicular lymphoma (early stage) at Stanford (Paryani et al, 1983) showed an advantage in terms of freedom from relapse for patients staged by laparotomy, but no survival benefit was demonstrated. Such improved relapse free survival may merely reflect selection of good risk patients for surgical staging.

Though it is possible that inadequately staged patients have a poorer outlook, this may simply reflect the poor condition at presentation of a group in whom adequate staging was not felt to be appropriate. Staging laparotomy is rarely used in NHL, has no obvious impact on survival and is inappropriate in the elderly. Other staging procedures have little associated morbidity (bone marrow examination, ultrasonography, computed tomography) and there is little justification for not performing these in elderly patients who are to be offered treatment.

The outcome for elderly patients – age as a prognostic factor

For reasons already discussed above, the role of age as an independent factor for prognosis is difficult to discover from published data. The effect of age on outcome is unclear and results from trials are conflicting.

Low grade NHL

No specific studies in elderly patients exist, Paryani et al (1983) have reviewed their experience at Stanford University Hospital of patients with stage I and II NHL with nodular and favourable histology. In this study, multivariate analysis revealed age as the most powerful prognostic factor, in terms of overall survival and freedom from relapse ($p = 0.0001$). Rudders et al (1979) reported 86 consecutive patients with nodular NHL. Age was identified as having prognostic significance. In contrast to this, a recent study from St. Bartholomew's Hospital, London, which included 148 patients with follicular lymphoma of all stages (age range 23–79) failed to demonstrate a trend for poorer survival with increasing age (Gallagher et al, 1986). Two studies from the M.D. Anderson Hospital, one of early stage and one of all stages of follicular NHL, with 109 patients also failed to show age to have prognostic importance (McLaughlin et al, 1986; Cabanillas et al, 1979).

Intermediate and high grade NHL

As with studies in low grade lymphomas, results are conflicting and it is difficult to draw any firm conclusions.

In early (stage I and II) disease, very few data are available. Kaminski et al (1986) have reviewed data from 148 patients with stage I and II large cell lymphoma treated by primary radiation therapy. The median age of this group was 51 (range 16–88) with about one-third of the patients being over 60 years of age. Standard staging procedures were used with about 60% of patients having a laparotomy for diagnostic or staging purposes. Forty seven per cent had a formal staging laparotomy. In this study, age was identified as a prognostic indicator for survival (five year survival ≥ 60 year $= 30\%$ v. ≤ 60 years $= 63\%$). Unfortunately the paper does not give details of which patients had adequate staging with lymphangiography (88%) and bone marrow biopsy (95%), or staging laparotomy. If the older patients were those who were not adequately staged, then the significance of these results is questionable.

Armitage et al (1982) have studied a series of 75 patients with diffuse histiocytic (Rappaport) lymphomas of all stages. These patients had received CHOP (cyclophosphamide, Adriamycin (doxorubiun hydrochloride), vincristine, prednisone) chemotherapy between 1975 and 1980. The median age of the group was 64 years (range 33–94). Complete remission rates were similar for patients of less than 64 years of age when compared with those more than 64 years (49% v. 53%). In a multivariate analysis, age did not affect survival. A later report from the same group showed a tendency for poor survival with age, but this did not achieve statistical significance.

Several studies of diffuse large cell lymphomas have produced similar conclusions (Bloomfield et al, 1971; Cabanillas et al, 1978; Fisher et al, 1981). A National Cancer Institute study of 157 patients with diffuse large cell lymphoma showed no trend for reduced survival with age. Nineteen per cent of the patients in this study were over 60 years of age. A study from the Memorial Sloan Kettering Hospital showed no difference in complete remission rate or survival for patients greater than or less than 45 years of age, treated with chemotherapy for stage III and IV diffuse large cell lymphoma (Koziner et al, 1982).

One hundred and twenty-one patients were treated in Boston, USA with m- or M-BACOD (methotrexate, bleomycin, Adriamycin, cyclophosphamide, vincristine, dexamethasone) for stage II–IV large cell lymphoma (Shipp et al, 1986). Although the complete remission rate was less in patients over 60 years, age had no effect on survival.

In contrast to all these studies, the South West Oncology Group (SWOG) in the USA have reviewed 307 cases of stage III/IV diffuse histiocytic lymphoma to assess the role of age on therapeutic outcome (Dixon et al, 1986). All patients received CHOP chemotherapy with and without other agents, primarily bleomycin, BCG and levamisole. Twenty-six per cent of patients in this series were aged 65 years or older.

Both complete remission rates and overall survival fell significantly with increasing age in this study (Figure 3). Furthermore, age was not associated

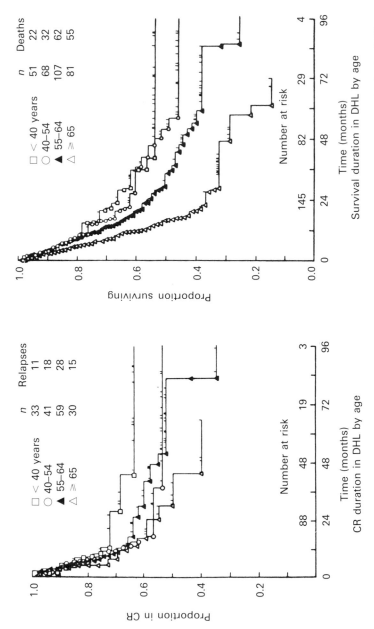

Figure 3. Duration of complete remission and overall survival according to age for 307 patients with DHL treated by the South West Oncology Group USA. From Dixon et al (1986).

with changes in the distribution of other factors such as performance status or B symptoms. Thus, age appeared to be of independent prognostic importance. In their discussion of this paper, the authors suggest that the decline in survival may have resulted from less intensive chemotherapy in older patients, since intended dose reductions were not always followed. They analysed their data excluding patients whose initial doses were low, and the effect of age on oucome was much reduced. However, the outcome for patients may well be related to the *reasons* for initial dosage reduction rather than the effect of more intensive treatment.

Hancock et al (1983) studied NHL of all grades and stages in Sheffield from 1971 to 1980 and showed a decline in survival with increasing age in 342 patients. The trend for poor survival is especially marked for those over 65 (five year survival = 21% v. 51% for those less than 35). Retrospective data on 61 patients with stage IV diffuse large cell lymphoma from the M.D. Anderson Hospital all treated with CHOP–bleomycin show poorer survival for patients older than 56 years.

In summary, data on the role of age as a prognostic factor are very variable. This is probably a result at least in part, of varying criteria for selection of patients in different centres and in individual trials. It is difficult to draw any definite conclusions except to say that in those studies where patients have been treated uniformly, age has been of less prognostic importance.

Toxicity of treatment for NHL in the elderly

There are reasonable theoretical grounds for suspecting toxicity might be more marked in elderly patients and several studies have addressed the problem of toxicity from chemotherapy in elderly patients with NHL.

In the SWOG trial, treatment protocols specified an initial dose reduction for elderly patients, although in many cases this was not carried out. Overall, a slight tendency for more severe leukopenia was found with age, although this was not significant, even for the 23 patients of 65 years or older who received full starting doses of chemotherapy. Despite this, four of these patients had severe leukopenia (white cell count nadir less than $1.0 \times 10^9/l$).

In support of this, 62 patients with NHL of 65 years or older were studied for myelotoxicity at Idaho, USA (Montgomery et al, 1982). No significant trend for increased toxicity was seen with advancing age for this group of patients over 65.

Armitage and Potter (1984) have, however, recorded increasing treatment-related complications with advancing age. Of a total of 75 patients, 20 were aged 70 or older, and all stages of disease were included. No initial dosage adjustment was made for older patients. Patients over 70 tended to have a poorer survival, although the trend was not statistically significant. However, death within the first two cycles of treatment occurred in five of these 20 elderly patients compared with one of 55 younger patients. Causes of death included bowel perforation, sepsis and acute tumour lysis. The authors list a number of factors in elderly patients which might have contributed to the increased complication rate, including fall in the relative weight of the liver, and declining renal clearance of cyclophosphamide, with reduced hepatic clearance of Adriamycin and vincristine. Increased end organ sensitivity, particularly changes in lymphocyte function was also implicated. They conclude that it may be appropriate to reduce drug dosage in the elderly and recommend active use of supportive measures.

In summary, treatment-related complications seem to be somewhat more common in the elderly and an initial dosage reduction, perhaps by 25% seems reasonable. Drug dosage can be escalated in subsequent courses if the treatment is tolerated well. SWOG data suggest that there is a sub-group of elderly patients who can be treated at full dose from initiation of treatment with no ill effects. It is unclear how these patients can be recognized, though they probably have a high performance status at the outset of treatment.

Specific studies of NHL in the elderly

Most of these have already been mentioned, but some studies have been concerned specifically with elderly populations and have devised treatment protocols for the elderly.

A retrospective review of 38 patients from Southampton of 65 years and over with poor prognosis NHL compared treatments of varying intensities from simple symptomatic measures to intensive combination chemotherapy depending upon stage and general condition (Mead et al, 1984).

This study included patients of all stages. Patients aged over 65 comprised 36.5% of the total of those with poor prognosis NHLs who presented to this single institution during the study period. Radiotherapy was effective when used with curative intent in fully staged stage I patients, but responses to palliative radiotherapy were poor and short-lived. Single agent chemotherapy was given to two patients, who failed to respond. Four patients who received CVP chemotherapy (cyclophosphamide, vincristine and prednisone) had all died at the time of the report.

Twenty-two patients were treated with more intensive chemotherapy, including VAP (vincristine, Adriamycin, prednisone); VAMP (vincristine, Adriamycin, methotrexate, prednisone), VAMP and CHOP, achieved complete remission and eight were disease free with a median follow up of 19 months (range 12–48). Two patients died of other causes, with no evidence of lymphoma. The authors comment that intensive treatment was well tolerated in the elderly patients and only one case of treatment-related toxicity was found.

The conclusions of this study were that survival was short if patients were treated with palliative intent, and that, when considered clinically appropriate, patients should be adequately staged and treated intensively. Elderly patients who received intensive treatment tolerated chemotherapy well and had an outcome comparable with younger patients.

Carbone et al (1986) from Avanio, Italy retrospectively studied 50 patients aged 65 or older (median 71.5) with all grades and all stages of NHL. Treatment was considered to be 'conservative' in 19 (single agent chemotherapy, e.g. with vincristine, vinblastine, teniposide) or 'aggressive' (CVP,

CHOP, ABVD – Adriamycin, bleomycin, vinblastine, dacarbazine) in 26. Five patients did not receive chemotherapy. Overall, 19 patients (42%) had complete remission and 11 achieved partial remission. Median survival was 2.2 years. Patients with stage I or II disease did significantly better than those with stage III or IV disease. No significant difference in response or survival was seen between those treated aggressively or conservatively, although it should be emphasized that treatments were not randomized. The authors of this study concluded that most of the NHL which they saw in the elderly was diffuse large cell, most was of advanced stage, and aggressive treatment did not improve their survival.

We are aware of only one group who have published data on chemotherapy regimens specifically designed for NHL in elderly patients. The group from Avanio have reported their experience with a total of 71 unselected patients of 70 years or older, treated either with teniposide 100 mg/m² i.v. weekly (42 patients) or etoposide and prednimustine both 100 mg/m² by mouth for five days in every 21 days (29 patients) (Zagonel et al, 1986). Most were stage III or IV and 72% were intermediate or high grade according to the Working Formulation. Fifteen patients were of diffuse large cell sub-type and a complete remission rate of 53% (eight patients) was recorded for these patients. They reported little treatment related toxicity.

Unfortunately they were only able to compare these results with historical controls and it is not therefore possible to assess the relative efficacy or toxicity of such a treatment with more aggressive combination chemotherapy such as CHOP. Randomized trials are clearly required.

CONCLUSIONS

Problems of patient selection and a lack of prospective trials make conclusions difficult. However, some points do seem reasonably well established for this group of patients:

1. The elderly form a very significant proportion of patients developing non-Hodgkin's lymphoma and thereby present a very difficult management problem.
2. The nature of NHL in the elderly differs from their younger counterparts – unfavourable histology is more common in most series, as is advanced stage (for the diffuse NHLs), extranodal disease and poor performance status. All of these factors may contribute to an overall tendency for poorer outcome in the elderly.
3. Most staging procedures commonly used in NHL have a very low morbidity. Whilst there can be no justification for staging laparotomy in these patients, other procedures such as bone marrow biopsy, lymphangiography and computed tomography should be performed, unless there are compelling clinical reasons for not doing so.
4. For elderly patients with low grade non-Hodgkin's lymphoma, there is little evidence that this group have a worse prognosis. Since treatment when

indicated is relatively non-toxic, we feel that they should be treated in the same way as younger patients.

5. Conclusions are difficult to draw in patients with intermediate and high grade lymphoma. The available data suggest that there is a sub-group of elderly patients who are able to withstand intensive treatment and who therefore should receive exactly the same treatment regimens as younger counterparts. Certainly patients with good general health and a high performance status at presentation should be offered such treatment.

6. Amongst elderly patients who have been treated aggressively (and who are therefore a highly selected group) tolerance of treatment has been very good. Most centres commence chemotherapy in elderly patients at attenuated dosage – usually around 75% for drugs with significant haematological or other toxicities. This practice seems reasonable although if patients tolerate treatment well, dosage escalation should be considered.

7. More prospective studies which address questions in the elderly patients are required, since these are such a common and challenging group of patients. Few studies are currently available and it is essential that more are conducted preferably in a randomized fashion so that efficacy and toxicity can be compared with standard regimens such as CHOP chemotherapy.

HODGKIN'S DISEASE

Age-related incidence

Hodgkin's disease has a bimodal age distribution. In developed countries, the first peak in incidence occurs in the late 20s. The incidence then declines to about 45 years and thereafter, it increases steadily with age. This had led to the suggestions that Hodgkin's disease in the older age group may be a different disease with a separate aetiology, especially since some pathological features of the disease vary with age (see below).

A large proportion of patients with Hodgkin's disease fall within the 'elderly' age group. In a review of 6314 patients with all stages of Hodgkin's disease seen at 473 hospitals in the USA, over 20% were 60 years or older (Kennedy et al, 1985). Several other studies have shown a similar proportion of patients in this age group. By contrast, of 1169 patients seen at Stanford University Hospital, USA between 1968 and 1981, only 52 (4%) were over 60, emphasizing the degree of referral bias which can affect interpretation of many studies in specialist centres (Austin-Seymour et al, 1984). Comparison of the age at presentation of Stanford patients with epidemiology data for the NCI (Figure 4) confirms this selection bias.

Changes in features of Hodgkin's disease with advancing age

As in the non-Hodgkin's lymphomas, epidemiological evidence suggests that elderly patients tend to present with features which carry a poor prognosis. B symptoms and advanced stage (Ann Arbor III or IV) have been shown to be

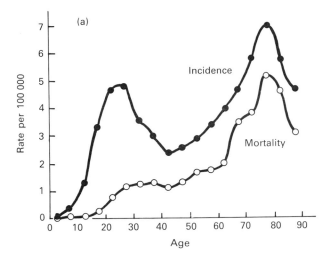

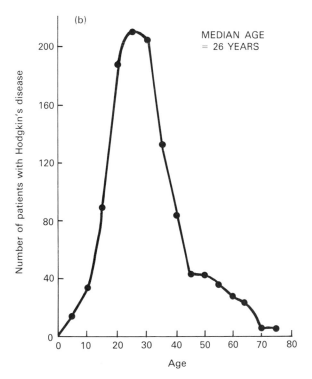

Figure 4a. Incidence and mortality rate for patients with Hodgkin's disease by age group as reported by the Surveillance, Epidemiology and End Results program of the Biometry Branch of the NCI. **4b.** Histogram of age at presentation of patients with Hodgkin's disease at Stanford University from 1968 to 1987. Reproduced with permission from Austin-Seymour et al (1984).

more common with increasing age. For example, in the study of Lokich et al (1974) from Harvard, 38 of 47 patients aged 60 or over had stage III or IV disease. In addition, the nodular sclerosing sub-type of Hodgkin's disease, which carries a relatively favourable prognosis, is less common with advancing age.

The outcome for elderly patients with Hodgkin's disease – age as a prognostic factor

Most studies in Hodgkin's disease of all stages have identified age as an important prognostic factor. In the study of Kennedy et al (1985) 6314 patients with all stages of Hodgkin's disease were reviewed. A sharp decline in five year and ten year survival was seen with advancing age (Figure 5). This trend remained, although was slightly less marked, when deaths from causes other than Hodgkin's disease were excluded.

The Cancer and Leukaemia Group B (CALG B) in the USA have studied the effect of age on therapeutic outcome for patients with advanced Hodgkin's disease treated with two combination chemotherapy regimens (Peterson et al, 1982). A total of 385 patients were seen, 73 of whom (19%) were aged 60 or over. Both the complete remission rate and overall survival in this study fell with age. For the age group less than 40, 90% were alive at one year, compared with 78% and 53% for the 40–59, and 60 years or more age groups respectively. Furthermore, within the group over 60, this trend was maintained. The median survival for patients of 60–69 was 21 months, compared with only nine months for those over 70 years. In a multivariate analysis, age maintained its prognostic significance.

The SWOG experience in stage III and IV Hodgkin's disease treated with MOPP chemotherapy shows a significant decline in survival with age when comparing groups of patients older than or younger than 40 (Coltman, 1980). In this study, patients of 60 years and older did better than those aged 40–60 but the number of patients is small and this difference only just achieves statistical significance ($p = 0.05$). Similar effects of age on survival have been reported by Sutcliffe et al (1978), Fabian et al (1984), and Farber et al (1980). Lokich et al (1974) studied 47 patients with all stages of Hodgkin's disease aged 60 or over. Their median survival was poor. For stage I and II disease, median survival was 27 months, compared with only 15 months for stage III and three months for stage IV disease.

The experience of Stanford University Medical Center of Hodgkin's disease in patients over 60 has been reviewed (Austin-Seymour et al, 1984). Of a total of 1169 patients referred during the study period, 52 (4%) were 60 years or older. A significant decline in both freedom from relapse and survival was seen with age. The overall median survival for this study group is 48 months and compares favourably with most other studies of elderly patients. However, these patients were much more aggressively staged and more importantly, the over 60 age group comprised only 4% of the Stanford referrals compared with much higher percentages in the other studies, e.g. 19% in the CALG B. Clearly, therefore, this group of elderly patients is highly selected.

The studies of the British National Lymphoma Investigation (BNLI) in

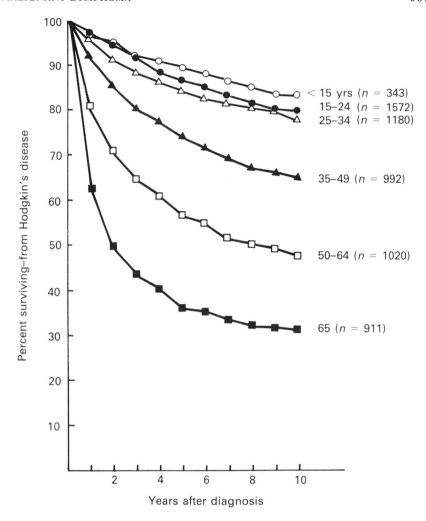

Figure 5. Survival care for 6314 patients with Hodgkin's disease reported to the Cancer Commission of the American College of Surgeons by age. From Kennedy et al (1985).

Hodgkin's disease of all stages, treated with a variety of chemotherapy and radiotherapy regimens have associated increasing age with poorer survival in multivariate analysis (Haybittle et al, 1985). They have developed a prognostic index for Hodgkin's disease, incorporating age at presentation with other factors including sex and mediastinal involvement.

Occasional studies have failed to attribute any prognostic significance to age. Most of these, such as the study of Hoppe et al (1980) have, however, included only small subsets of patients who were aggressively staged and with low median ages.

Most studies recognize the importance of age in the prognosis of Hodgkin's disease and it would appear that, irrespective of stage, elderly patients have a poorer outcome.

Problems of staging in Hodgkin's disease

The role of staging laparotomy in Hodgkin's disease in any age group is unclear. Despite strong intellectual arguments for its use, there is little evidence that the more precise staging by laparotomy has had a significant impact on survival in Hodgkin's disease. In elderly patients, co-existing diseases can potentially add to the post-operative complication rate for staging laparotomy. (In the Stanford study 22 of 52 patients over 60 years of age had other serious disease such as ischemic heart disease and diabetes mellitus.) Most studies make no mention of the problems of staging. In the Stanford study, 46 of 52 patients over 60 had bipedal lymphangiography and 25 (48%) had a formal staging laparotomy and splenectomy. Only one surgical complication was noted in this group.

Thirteen patients in this study were clinical stage I–IIIA and were considered to have been inadequately staged. Their survival was poor (35% at five years). The laparotomy-staged group with pathological stage I–IIIA disease had a substantially improved five year survival of 86% (15 patients, $p = 0.006$).

In their discussion, the authors conclude that one of the reasons for the improved survival of their group compared with the groups in Harvard (Lokich et al, 1974) and Stockholm (Wedelin et al, 1982) is their more meticulous staging. However, as already discussed, the patient population is highly selected, and the patients in the Stanford group who underwent staging laparotomy were younger than non-laparotomy patients. Thirteen of 15 were between 60 and 65 years of age. Thus, their improved outcome may well be a result of selection rather than a true contribution from staging laparotomy.

In summary, staging laparotomy is a morbid procedure and cannot be recommended for elderly patients on the basis of published data.

Toxicity of treatment for Hodgkin's disease

Only two studies give details about treatment toxicity, according to age, both relating primarily to chemotherapy.

In the Cancer and Leukaemia Group B study (Peterson et al, 1982) drug-related toxicity was shown to increase in frequency and severity with age. This was particularly true for haematological toxicity which was described as severe or life-threatening in only 14% of patients less than 40 years of age, compared with 33% of those over 60. In a multivariate analysis, increasing age was the major prognostic factor for drug-induced myelotoxicity ($p = <0.001$). Neurotoxicity from vinca alkaloids was more common in patients over 40 years old.

The increased haematological toxicity is presumably reflected in the amounts of drug given to elderly patients. The dosages were significantly lower with increasing age. For example, with mechlorethamine/nitrosoureas, 47% of those aged < 40 received full dosage at cycle five, compared with only 19% of those aged 60 or over. A similar trend is seen for vinca alkaloids, although it is not apparent for procarbazine. However, these dosage reductions did not appear to affect the attainment of complete remission. For patients who received 90% or more of the planned dose in the first three cycles of treatment, the complete remission rate was 50% (11 of 22) compared to 48% (16 of 33) for those who received less than 90% total planned dose.

The Stanford series does not quote comparative toxicity data by age. Nevertheless 21 (40%) of the 52 patients aged 60 or more years suffered from weight loss of 10% or more, neutropenia or thrombocytopenia. Thirty three patients in this study were adequately staged by current standards and aggressively treated for all stages of disease. Treatments included sub-total, or total lymphoid irradiation (TLI), TLI with hepatic irradiation and combination chemotherapy. Half this group had the complications listed above. In addition, three patients had radiation induced problems (two pneumonitis, one duodenitis). Six patients in this study developed second malignancies. Two of these were acute leukaemias, one non-Hodgkin's lymphoma, two carcinomas and one melanoma. The last three are unlikely to be related to treatment and reflect the elderly nature of the population.

CONCLUSIONS

Once again, a lack of adequate published evidence, together with major patient selection problems make it difficult to draw conclusions. Some points do, however, emerge:

1. Hodgkin's disease in the elderly is a relatively common problem accounting for about 20% of all cases. Unfortunately, such an age distribution is not found in those major series which have influenced our thinking on this disease.
2. As with NHL, Hodgkin's disease differs in its nature in elderly patients. Favourable histology is less common, whereas advanced disease and B symptoms occur more frequently than in younger patients.
3. As with NHL, most staging procedures carry a low morbidity and should be undertaken. However, staging laparotomy cannot generally be recommended in this group where it may have significant morbidity and mortality.
4. Most published series show that age is an adverse factor in Hodgkin's disease of all stages. As with NHL, some subsets of elderly patients probably have an outcome similar to younger patients. These patients are difficult to select on the basis of available data.
5. Treatment toxicity appears to increase in elderly patients, presumably because of the use of alkylating agents in higher doses than are used in NHL. Initial dosage modification, particularly for vinca alkaloids and alkylating agents, is prudent. There is no evidence that this adversely affects outcome and dose escalation can be used if tolerance is good.

6. As with NHL, current information is inadequate and further studies are required in unselected populations, particularly to investigate the tolerance of current therapies in elderly patients.

REFERENCES

Armitage JO, Dick FR, Corder MP et al (1982) Predicting therapeutic outcome in patients with diffuse histiocytic lymphoma treated with cyclophosphamide, adriamycin, vincristine and prednisolone (CHOP). *Cancer* **50:** 1695–1702.

Armitage JO & Potter JF (1984) Aggressive chemotherapy for diffuse histiocytic lymphoma in the elderly: increased complications with advancing age. *Journal of the American Geriatric Society* **32:** 269–273.

Austin-Seymour MM, Hoppe RT & Cox RS (1984) Hodgkin's disease in patients over sixty years old. *Annals of Internal Medicine* **100:** 13–18.

Barnes N, Cartwright RA, O'Brien C et al (1987) Variation in lymphoma incidence within Yorkshire Health Region. *British Journal of Cancer* **55:** 81–84.

Begg CB & Carbone PP (1983) Clinical trials and drug toxicity in the elderly: the experience of the Eastern Cooperative Oncology Group. *Cancer* **52:** 1986–1992.

Bloomfield CD, Goldman A, Dick F et al (1971) Multivariate analysis of prognostic factors in the non-Hodgkin's malignant lymphomas. *Cancer* **33:** 870–879.

Blum RH, Carter SK & Agre K (1973) A clinical review of bleomycin – a new antineoplastic agent. *Cancer* **31:** 903–913.

Bristow MR, Mason JW, Billingham ME et al (1978) Doxorubicin cardiomyopathy: evaluation by phonocardiography, endomyocardial biopsy and cardiac catheterisation. *Annals of Internal Medicine* **88:** 168–175.

Cabanillas F, Burke S, Smith TL et al (1978) Factors predicting for response and survival in adults with advanced non-Hodgkin's lymphoma. *Archives of Internal Medicine* **138:** 413–418.

Cabanillas F, Smith T, Bodey GP et al (1979) Nodular malignant lymphomas: factors affecting complete response rate and survival. *Cancer* **44:** 1983–1989.

Carbone A, Tirelli U, Volpe R et al (1986) Non-Hodgkin's lymphoma in the elderly: a retrospective clinicopathologic study of 50 patients. *Cancer* **57:** 2185–2189.

Carbone PP, Begg C & Moorman J (1985) Cancer in the elderly: clinical and biological considerations. In Pullman B et al (eds) *Inter-relationships among ageing, cancer and differentiation*, pp 313–323. Dordrecht: Reidel.

Coltman CA (1980) Chemotherapy of advanced Hodgkin's disease. *Seminars in Oncology* **VII:** 155–173.

Dixon DO, Neilan B, Jones SE et al (1986) Effect of age on therapeutic outcome in advanced diffuse histiocytic lymphoma. The South West Oncology Group experience. *Journal of Clinical Oncology* **4:** 295–305.

Elias L (1979) Differences in age and sex distributions among patients with non-Hodgkin's lymphoma. *Cancer* **43:** 2540–2546.

Fabian C, Sayre R, Dixon D et al (1984) Response rates as a function of age in Hodgkin's disease: A SWOG study. *Proceedings of the American Society of Clinical Oncology* **25:** 240.

Farber LR, Prosnitz LR & Cadman EC (1980) Curative potential of combined modality therapy for advanced Hodgkin's disease. *Cancer* **46:** 1509–1517.

Fisher RI, Hubbard SM, DeVita VT et al (1981) Factors predicting long-term survival in diffuse mixed, histiocytic or undifferentiated lymphoma. *Blood* **58:** 45–51.

Foucar K, Armitage JO & Dick FR (1983) Malignant lymphoma, diffuse mixed small and large cell. A clinicopathologic study of 47 cases. *Cancer* **51:** 2090–2099.

Fukayama M, Murai T, Ikebuchi K et al (1985) Malignant lymphoma of the elderly. Evaluation of undiagnosed cases. *Japanese Journal of Geriatrics* **22**(6): 564–567.

Gallagher CJ, Gregory WM, Jones AE et al (1986) Follicular lymphoma: prognostic factors for response and survival. *Journal of Clinical Oncology* **4:** 1470–1480.

Hancock BW, Aitken M, Ross CMD et al (1983) Non-Hodgkin's lymphoma in Sheffield 1971–1980. *Clinical Oncology* **9**: 109–119.

Haybittle JL, Easterling MJ, Bennett MH et al (1985) Review of British National Lymphoma Investigation studies of Hodgkin's disease and development of prognostic index. *Lancet* **i**: 967–995.

Hoppe RT, Rosenberg SA, Kaplan HS et al (1980) Prognostic factors in pathological stage IIA Hodgkin's disease. *Cancer* **46**: 1240–1246.

Kaminski MS, Coleman CN & Colby TV (1986) Factors predicting survival in adults with stage I and II large cell lymphoma treated with primary radiation therapy. *Annals of Internal Medicine* **104**: 747–756.

Kennedy BJ, Loeb V, Peterson VM et al (1985) National survey of patterns of care for Hodgkin's disease. *Cancer* **56**: 2547–2556.

Koziner B, Little C, Passe S et al (1982) Treatment of advanced diffuse histiocytic lymphoma: an analysis of prognostic variables. *Cancer* **47**: 1571–1579.

Lokich JJ, Pinkus GS & Moloney WC (1974) Hodgkin's disease in the elderly. *Oncology* **29**: 484–500.

McLaughlin P, Fuller LM, Velasquez WS et al (1986) Stage I–II follicular lymphoma. Treatment results for 76 patients. *Cancer* **58**: 1596–1602.

Mead GM, MacBeth FR, Williams CJ et al (1984) Poor prognosis non-Hodgkin's lymphoma in the elderly: clinical presentation and management. *Quarterly Journal of Medicine* **211**: 381–390.

Montgomery P, Beck TM, Smith CE et al (1982) Chemotherapy in the elderly. *Proceedings of the American Society of Clinical Oncology* **23**: 56.

Nathwani BN, Kim H, Rappoport H et al (1978) Non-Hodgkin's lymphomas: a clinicopathological study comparing two classifications. *Cancer* **41**: 303–325.

National Cancer Institute sponsored study of classification of non-Hodgkin's lymphomas (1982) Summary and description of a working formulation for clinical usage. *Cancer* **49**: 2112–2135.

Nerenz DR, Love RR, Leventhal H et al (1986) Psychosocial consequences of cancer chemotherapy for elderly patients. *Health Services Research* **20**(6): 961–974.

Newell GR, Cabanillas FG, Hagemeister FJ et al (1987) Incidence of lymphoma in the US classified by the Working Formulation. *Cancer* **59**: 857–861.

Paryani SB, Hoppe RT, Co RS et al (1983) Analysis of non-Hodgkin's lymphomas with nodular and unfavourable histologies, stages I and II. *Cancer* **52**: 2300–2307.

Peterson BA, Pajak TE, Cooper MR et al (1982) Effect of age on therapeutic response and survival in advanced Hodgkin's disease. *Cancer Treatment Report* **66**: 889–898.

Rudders RA, Kaddis M, Delellis RA et al (1979) Nodular non-Hodgkin's lymphoma (NHL): factors influencing prognosis and indicators for aggressive treatment. *Cancer* **43**: 1643–1651.

Shipp MA, Harrington DP, Klatt MM et al (1986) Identification of major prognostic sub-groups of patients with large cell lymphoma treated with m-BACOD and M-BACOD. *Archives of Internal Medicine* **104**: 757–765.

Sutcliffe SB, Wrigley PPM, Peto J et al (1978) MVPP chemotherapy regimen for advanced Hodgkin's disease. *British Medical Journal* **i**: 679–683.

Wedelin M, Bjorkholm M, Ogenstad B et al (1982) Prognostic factors in Hodgkin's disease with special reference to age. In Wedelin C (ed) *On the prognosis of Hodgkin's disease: a clinical and immunological study*, pp 1–18. Stockholm: Karolinska Institute.

Zagonel V, Tirelli U & Carbone A (1986) Treatment of non-Hodgkin's lymphoma in the elderly. *Journal of Clinical Oncology* **3**: 1866–1867.

9

The disposition of cytotoxic drugs in the elderly

H. WYNNE
K. W. WOODHOUSE

Although malignant disease is a common problem in the ageing population, there is a widespread reluctance among many clinicians to treat patients in this age group with chemotherapeutic agents. In large part this is due to the propensity of elderly patients to suffer adverse reactions to cancer chemo-therapy, both haematological and organ-specific (Woodhouse and Blain, 1983). While it is likely that the ageing marrow and other organs are inherently more susceptible to adverse drug reactions, differences in drug disposition in this population may also be responsible for differing toxicities.

The purpose of this chapter is to discuss the disposition of the cytotoxic drugs, with particular emphasis on the elderly patient.

DRUG DISPOSITION IN THE ELDERLY: GENERAL PRINCIPLES

A detailed review of all aspects of drug disposition in geriatric patients is beyond the scope of this chapter. However, a few important points are worthy of note.

Absorption

Drug absorption is probably not affected to any great extent by age. Experiments using drugs such as practolol and digoxin have revealed that although absorption may be slightly slower in the old, it tends to be just as complete (Castleden et al, 1977; Cusack et al, 1979; Fulton et al, 1979).

Presystemic elimination

Studies of hepatic presystemic elimination have given contradictory results. Plasma concentrations of propranolol are higher in hospitalized geriatric patients than in young adults following oral dosing (Castleden and George, 1979). However, studies using metoprolol in healthy geriatric individuals have failed to demonstrate impaired first-pass metabolism (Regardh et al, 1983). It seems likely that frailty, rather than fundamental ageing changes, is responsible for the reduced presystemic elimination of highly extracted drugs that has been reported in some studies.

Distribution

A number of changes in body composition occur with ageing. These include an increase in body fat and a fall in lean body mass (Novak, 1972), and a 10–15% fall in body water between the ages of 20 and 90 years (Vestal et al, 1975; Shock et al, 1963). These alterations may result in changes in drug distribution; for example, the fall in the distribution volumes of antipyrine (Vestal et al, 1975) and ethanol (Vestal et al, 1977) probably reflect decreased body water. Although these changes are very interesting, and are important in interpreting pharmacokinetic data, the clinical importance remains unclear.

Protein binding

Several authors have reported age-related changes in the levels of plasma proteins responsible for drug binding. For example, serum albumin falls with age (Hale et al, 1983), whereas α_1-acid glycoprotein tends to rise (although these alterations are less marked than with albumin). Studies of age-related changes in protein binding may be complicated by coexistent disease which tends to depress serum albumin and raise serum α_1-acid glycoprotein. Once more the clinical significance of these changes in protein binding is controversial.

Renal excretion

The elimination of renally excreted drugs decreases with advancing years, consequent on a reduction in glomerular filtration rate (falling by 10% per 10 years after the fourth decade (Wilkinson, 1983)). This is particularly important for drugs with a narrow therapeutic index, such as aminoglycoside antibiotics (Kampmann and Molholm-Hansen, 1979), and, of course, anticancer drugs.

Liver metabolism

Several morphological and physiological changes which may modify drug metabolism occur in the liver with ageing. These have recently been reviewed (James, 1983; Woodhouse, 1985). The most important features include a reduction in size, from 2.5% body weight at the age of 50 to 1.6% body weight at the age of 90, and a reduction in liver blood flow from 1400 ml/min at the age of 30, to 800 ml/min at the age of 75. Age may also affect hepatic drug metabolism itself.

The exact extent to which age affects this variable is controversial, and conflicting studies have appeared in the literature. Even in normals there is considerable inter-individual variation in liver metabolism. This is due to genetics (Eichelbaum, 1982), caffeine and cigarette consumption (Vestal et al, 1975), disease (Woodhouse et al, 1984a), nutritional and vitamin status (Smithard and Langman, 1978), and ageing. In general, studies have shown that oxidized drugs tend to show decreased clearance with age (although not invariably so), whereas conjugated drugs tend to have unimpaired clearance in the elderly (Mooney et al, 1985). The explanation for reduced drug oxidation with age is unclear. While the specific activity of microsomal mono-oxygenase enzymes tends to fall with ageing in animals (Wynne et al, 1987), no similar reduction has been demonstrated in humans (Woodhouse et al, 1984b).

Conclusion

A large number of changes occur with ageing which are likely to influence the disposition of drugs. Perhaps the most important of all is the age-related decline in renal function. However, it must be understood that studies of drug disposition in the elderly are confounded by coexisting disease and debility as well as other drug therapy, and these factors are likely to be extremely important in patients with malignant disease. The discussion of the disposition of cytotoxic drugs in the elderly which follows should be interpreted with this caveat in mind.

ALKYLATING AGENTS

Anti-tumour antibiotics

Doxorubicin
Doxorubicin is an antibiotic preparation from *Streptomyces peucetius* var. *caesius*. The drug has a wide spectrum of activity in both haematological and solid malignancy. In common with all anthracyclines it intercalates between adjoining nucleotide pairs in the DNA helix, interfering with further synthesis (Di Marco et al, 1971). The drug is administered intravenously. Following this it is rapidly dispersed throughout the plasma and tissues, with an initial mean distribution $t_\frac{1}{2}$ of around 30 min. An intermediate $t_\frac{1}{2}$ of 3 h represents extensive liver extraction and subsequent release of drug and metabolites, including adriamycinol (active), adriamycinone (inactive), and several inactive agly-cones (Benjamin, 1975). In a third phase, lasting hours to 7–10 days, levels of drug and metabolites decline only slowly (Creasey et al, 1976). Relatively little drug is excreted into the urine (5–6% by 5 days). Biliary excretion probably accounts for a large part of drug elimination (Bachur et al, 1975).

The single acute dose-limiting toxicity of doxorubicin is bone marrow suppression, whereas cardiotoxicity is a cumulative dose restraint at around 550 mg/m^2 for young adults (a total, lifetime dose). Children have been noted to tolerate higher doses than adults, whereas patients treated with other cytotoxics, as well as elderly patients, with a lower bone marrow reserve, become more rapidly intoxicated, sometimes after a few doses (Bonadonna et al, 1970).

Age (>70 years) has been shown to be a significant risk factor for cardiotoxicity, and it has been recommended that the total dose be limited to 300 mg/m^2 in this age group (Bristow et al, 1978; Von Hoff et al, 1978). Anthracycline cardiotoxicity has also been described after only the first or second dose of the drug in elderly patients (Bristow et al, 1979).

The increased cardiotoxicity of doxorubicin in the elderly may partly be explained by an apparent age-related decline in the clearance of the drug: Robert and Hoerni (1983) observed a highly significant correlation ($p < 0.0005$) between the early clearance of doxorubicin and the age of the patient. Since a close relationship between peak plasma levels, clinical short-term response (Robert et al, 1982), and uptake and activity of the drug in stem cells (Andersson et al, 1982), has been reported, it has been proposed that the dose of doxorubicin be adjusted according to the age of the patient. Young subjects require higher doses in order to obtain the same drug exposure as older patients during the critical distribution phase of the drug.

The origin of the age dependence of the early clearance of doxorubicin is still a matter of conjecture. It may be that uptake of drugs into cells is higher in younger patients, or that hepatic extraction and biliary excretion is less efficient in elderly patients.

Daunorubicin

Daunorubicin is an anthracycline antibiotic obtained from *Streptomyces peucetius*. It is used almost exclusively as an antileukaemic agent. Like doxorubicin, it tightly binds to nucleic acid molecules, interfering with both DNA and RNA synthesis (Theologides et al, 1968).

Daunorubicin is usually given as a single intravenous dose. After administration, the drug is rapidly distributed and cleared with a short initial $t_{\frac{1}{2}}$ of 40 min (Huffman et al, 1972), followed by a later phase with a mean $t_{\frac{1}{2}}$ of 46–55 h (Alberts et al, 1971). The major step in daunorubicin metabolism involves reduction to daunorubicinol by aldo–keto reductases (Bachur, 1975). Following this, the major step is reduction to form 7-deoxyaglycones. Urinary excretion of daunorubicin accounts for around 23% of the administered dose, the primary urinary species being daunorubicinol. The cytoplasmic enzyme, daunorubicin reductase, which converts daunorubicin to daunorubicinol, is present in normal mammalian tissues, as well as in human leukaemic myeloblasts; intracellular levels of this enzyme have been reported to relate to clinical response (Huffman and Bachur, 1972). Interestingly, a poor clinical response was noted among the more elderly patients, with a significant negative correlation ($p < 0.05$) between age and response. Further study suggested that lower levels of daunorubicin reductase were present in the leukaemic cells of the older age groups.

Like doxorubicin, daunorubicin causes cardiotoxicity. This may be more of a risk in the elderly, and may occur after only one or two doses (Bristow et al, 1979; Woodhouse and Blain, 1983).

Bleomycin

The bleomycins are a highly water-soluble group of complex glycopeptides produces from *Streptomyces verticillus*. The commercially available preparation consists of 13 different bleomycin species, and is used particularly for the chemotherapy of squamous cell carcinoma, lymphoma, and testicular tumours.

Bleomycin may be given by a variety of systemic routes. After intravenous administration, the drug disappears from the serum with a mean initial $t_{\frac{1}{2}}$ of 10–20 min and a terminal phase $t_{\frac{1}{2}}$ of 2.5 h (Alberts et al, 1978).

Peak blood levels after intramuscular injection are obtained in 30–60 min and are one-third that of a similar intravenous dose. $t_{\frac{1}{2}}$ is similar after both IV and IM dosing (Oken et al, 1981).

Approximately 50% of the drug is renally excreted over the first 24 h, and dosage adjustments are necessary when severe renal dysfunction is present (Crooke et al, 1977). Clearance of bleomycin correlates fairly well with creatinine clearance in individual patients, and it has been recommended that the dose is reduced to 75% when glomerular filtration rate (GFR) is between 10 and 50 ml/min, and to 50% when GFR is less than 10 ml/min (Bennett et al, 1980).

Bleomycin also undergoes metabolic biotransformation in many tissues, high enzyme activity being present in liver, bone marrow, and lymph nodes, and low activity being present in lung and skin. It is not known whether bleomycin metabolites possess significant antitumour activity.

Age-dependent changes in bleomycin kinetics have been noted, with longer half-lives in older populations ($t_{\frac{1}{2}}\alpha = 24$ min; $t_{\frac{1}{2}}\beta = 4$ h; Evans et al, 1981). This is likely to reflect decreased renal function in the older patient, as urinary recovery of the drug declines with age, only 45% of the dose being recovered in the urine of elderly patients (Alberts et al, 1978), whereas the corresponding urinary recovery in a younger group of testicular carcinoma patients was 68% (Crooke et al, 1977).

Pulmonary toxicity is the most serious long-term complication of bleomycin therapy, with a possible incidence of 5–10%, and a mortality rate of 10% in patients with clinically apparent toxicity. Elderly patients (> 70 years) are particularly likely to be affected (Blum et al, 1973). The higher incidence of bleomycin toxicity in the elderly may be related to reduced urinary excretion of the drug, or to lower enzyme activity in the elderly lung, with corresponding reduced conversion to inactive metabolites.

Mitomycin

Mitomycin, an antitumour antibiotic isolated from *Streptomyces caespitosus*, is composed of quinone, urethane and aziridine groups, and has activity against a variety of tumours, including transitional cell, squamous and adenocarcinomas. The drug acts through bioreductive alkylation and seems to be selectively toxic to hypoxic cells (Kennedy et al, 1980).

After intravenous administration, mitomycin is rapidly cleared from the plasma with an initial mean $t_{\frac{1}{2}}$ of around 5 min and terminal $t_{\frac{1}{2}}$ of 50 min.

Elimination is largely by hepatic metabolism, some excretion occurring in the bile, and 10–30% of administered dose appearing unchanged in the urine within 8 h of injection. Volume of distribution is approximately 18 $1/m^2$, and clearance is 18 $1/h/m^2$ (den Hartigh et al, 1983). However, considerable interindividual variation in pharmacokinetic parameters has been noted. Attempts to correlate this with the clinical status of the patient have not been successful, with no relationship being demonstrated between the pharmacokinetic variables and the type of disease, presence of metastases, renal failure, or hepatic failure. Furthermore, no significant correlation between pharmacokinetic variables and age has been noted.

Classic alkylating agents

Cyclophosphamide

Cyclophosphamide is one of the most frequently used alkylating agents because of its wide spectrum of activity against human tumours. It is often used in combination regimes, e.g. the induction therapy of non-Hodgkin's lymphoma.

Cyclophosphamide may be administered orally or intravenously. After an oral dose, however, 31–66% is present in the stools (Bagley et al, 1973). The parent compound is inactive but undergoes hepatic oxidation to produce the active metabolites 4-hydroxycyclophosphamide and phosphoramide mustard. Detoxification to 4-ketocyclophosphamide and carboxycyclophosphamide, which undergo urinary excretion, accounts for 85% of an administered dose (Juma et al, 1979).

Apparent volume of distribution of cyclophosphamide approximates body water at 0.74 1/kg, and mean $t_{\frac{1}{2}}$ is approximately 9 h (Juma et al, 1980). The $t_{\frac{1}{2}}$ of phosphoramide mustard is similar to that of cyclophosphamide, whereas that of nor-nitrogen mustard is significantly shorter, around 3 h.

The disposition of cyclophosphamide has been noted to change during the course of repetitive treatments. Increased clearance and volume of distribution of cyclophosphamide, combined with lower plasma concentrations of alkylating activity, has been noted during the third course of treatment compared to the first, although this trend was not maintained when the seventh course of treatment was studied (Edwards et al, 1980). The observations did not, however, correlate with clinical and biochemical estimates of renal and hepatic function, or plasma protein status in the few patients studied.

Renal insufficiency (creatinine clearances of 0–51 ml/min) have been shown to significantly increase the mean $t_{\frac{1}{2}}$ of cyclophosphamide, from values of 8–10 h, with a corresponding reduction in total body clearance from 59 ml/kg/h to 49 ml/kg/h. The plasma $t_{\frac{1}{2}}$ of phosphoramide mustard showed a parallel increase (Juma et al, 1981). Total plasma alkylating activity has also been shown to increase with renal failure. These data suggest that a reduction in dose may be necessary in patients with renal impairment. A large interindividual variation in the rate of activation of cyclophosphamide has been noted, but this is unrelated to the age of the patient (Mouridsen et al, 1974).

Although liver failure, with clinical evidence of encephalopathy, jaundice and flap, significantly increases mean cyclophosphamide $t_{\frac{1}{2}}$ (from 7.6 to 12.5 h) and reduces total body clearance (from 45 to 63 ml/kg/h) (Juma, 1984), the relatively minor changes in hepatic function which occur with ageing are unlikely to have a major influence on the kinetics of the drug.

Melphalan

Melphalan, the L-isomer of the synthetic product formed from the amino acid phenylalanine, and nitrogen mustard, is used extensively in the treatment of malignant disease, especially multiple myeloma and ovarian carcinoma.

Although melphalan may be given intravenously, it is more often administered by mouth. The oral bioavailability, however, is very variable between individuals both when it is given in high ($56\% \pm 20\%$) (Alberts et al, 1979) and in low ($78\% \pm 16\%$) (Woodhouse et al, 1983) doses. Absorption after fasting is rapid, peak concentrations being reached approximately 1 h after dosing. The elimination half-life of around 67 min is similar after the oral and intravenous routes (Woodhouse et al, 1983). Melphalan biotransformation is probably primarily by spontaneous degradation to monohydroxy- and dihydroxymelphalan. Both are subsequently excreted in the urine.

A significant negative correlation exists between glomerular filtration rate and both the terminal $t_{\frac{1}{2}}$ of melphalan (Bosanquet and Gilby, 1982) and the area under the melphalan plasma concentration/time curve (Adair et al, 1986a). This suggests that renal function rather than age is of importance when melphalan therapy is being planned, particularly in view of the frequent occurrence of renal impairment in myeloma patients.

Thio-TEPA

Thio-TEPA, an ethylenimine-type compound, is an alkylating agent, chemically related to nitrogen mustard. It has been used in the treatment of carcinomas of breast and ovary, but one of its most widespread applications today is in topical treatment of bladder papillomas (Burnand et al, 1976).

After intravenous administration, plasma concentrations of thio-TEPA decline in a biexponential manner with a distribution $t_{\frac{1}{2}}$ of around 8 min and a mean elimination half-life of 125 min. Steady-state apparent volume of distribution has been calculated to approximate body water at 0.7 l/kg, while total body clearance is approximately 186 ml/min/m^2 (Cohen et al, 1986).

Thio-TEPA metabolic pathways have not been fully characterized. Evidence suggests that the major metabolic clearance is by conversion of thio-TEPA to TEPA by oxidative desulphuration, as well as to other unknown metabolites, prior to urinary excretion. Unfortunately the effects of age on the pharmacokinetics of this drug have not been completely evaluated. The major dose-limiting toxicity is bone marrow suppression (Bruce and Edgcomb, 1967).

Busulphan

Busulphan is an agent used in the palliative treatment of chronic myelocytic leukaemia (Galton, 1953). It has now been used for more than 30 years.

Busulphan is an alkylating agent which has less reactivity towards guanine in DNA than do mustards and epoxides, but which interacts more avidly with nucleophilic thiol groups (Roberts and Warwick, 1961). Busulphan has a lower overall toxicity than mustards, producing a reduction in circulating granulocyte count with much less effect on peripheral lymphocyte count (Elson, 1958).

Busulphan is normally administered intermittently by the oral route. Analytical methods for the quantitation of busulphan and its metabolites in blood and tissue are unsatisfactory, and most pharmacokinetic studies have used a radiolabelled drug. Following administration, busulphan is readily absorbed from the gastrointestinal tract and rapidly eliminated from the plasma. Multiple metabolites are produced and 12 have been isolated, including methanesulphonic acid and 3-hydroxytetrahydrothrophene-1,1-dioxide. About 10–50% of a dose is excreted as urinary metabolites within 24 h.

Because of the difficulty in assay, and the incomplete knowledge of metabolic profile, detailed information on the kinetics of this drug in the elderly is unfortunately not available.

Chlorambucil

Chlorambucil is an alkylating agent which has been in clinical use for more than two decades. It is of the mustard type, producing DNA crosslinking. It is used in the treatment of chronic lymphocytic leukaemia, Hodgkin's disease, and non-Hodgkin's lymphoma as well as ovarian carcinoma.

The intravenous preparation is unstable and spontaneously hydrolyses rapidly. The drug is therefore usually given by the oral route. Peak plasma concentrations occur 40–70 min after dosing (McLean et al, 1979). Mean plasma $t_{\frac{1}{2}}$ is approximately 90 min. Chlorambucil is almost completely metabolized to two main products, partly by oxidation to an aminophenyl acetic acid derivative; the second metabolite has not yet definitely been identified. More than 95% of the drug is excreted in the urine as metabolites.

Food significantly delays drug absorption and tends to reduce peak plasma levels, although the effect of these changes on tumour response and tòxicity remains open to debate (Adair et al, 1986b).

Regression analysis of kinetic data reveals that chlorambucil elimination is independent of renal function, as would be expected, and although no specific age-related data is available it would seem unlikely that age is a major determinant of chlorambucil pharmacokinetics.

Nitrosoureas

The nitrosoureas developed as a result of the observation that 1-methyl-1-nitroso-3-nitrosoguanidine (MNNG) had antitumour activity, that its nitroso group was responsible for cytotoxicity, and that this was increased by substitution of a chloroethyl group for the methyl group. Although over 200 nitrosoureas were eventually synthesized, only a few were developed for clinical use, including carmustine (BCNU), lomustine (CCNU), and strepto-zotocin.

Carmustine and lomustine

These drugs, which have activity against a wide range of human tumours, produce delayed and cumulative bone marrow toxicity, which has seriously limited their clinical applications.

Both drugs apparently spontaneously decompose in physiological conditions, including in plasma, with a $t_{\frac{1}{2}}$ of under 2 h (Schein, 1978), and as a result of this a series of alkylating moieties are formed. Metabolism by hepatic oxygenases to hydroxylated products also occurs, and 75% of an administered dose of CCNU appears as these products in plasma, mediating its therapeutic and toxic effects (Walker and Hilton, 1976). While the elderly may experience more myelotoxicity, little specific information is available on the effect of age on the disposition of these drugs. Spontaneous biotransformation is unlikely to be an age-related event.

Miscellaneous alkylator-like agents

Cisplatin

Cisplatin is a platinum complex which is used in the treatment of bladder, ovarian, testicular, bronchial, and head and neck tumours (Prestayko et al, 1980). It inhibits DNA synthesis, perhaps as a result of the formation of intrastrand and interstrand crosslinks in DNA (Zwelling and Kohn, 1979).

Cisplatin is not absorbed orally and is therefore given by intravenous injection. Although the parent drug is eliminated from plasma in a biphasic manner with an initial $t_{\frac{1}{2}}$ of less than 1 h and a slower terminal $t_{\frac{1}{2}}$ of 1–3 days, platinum itself may be detected in the body for several months after administration of the drug (Smith and Taylor, 1974). Cisplatin appears to be nonenzymatically converted to several metabolites which are believed to be inactive (Hayes et al, 1980). These, unlike the parent drug, are highly protein-bound. The renal clearance of parent drug is high, about 45% being excreted in the urine in the first 5 days after dosing. The platinum metabolites, being highly tissue-bound, are cleared more slowly. The reduction in renal function which occurs with ageing is likely to delay cisplatin elimination, and in support of this suggestion some age-related changes in drug toxicity have been noted.

First, cisplatin is a predictable nephrotoxin in patients of all ages. It is known that the occurrence of this reaction can be reduced by hydration and forced diuresis. The use of this drug should be avoided in patients with a glomerular filtration rate of less than 10 ml/min (Bennett et al, 1980). Magnesium wasting has been reported to occur, the incidence of this being approximately 50% in adults but approaching 100% in children. This may be the result of differential renal clearance between different age groups.

Second, ototoxicity is a further complication of cisplatin treatment. It is usually reversible and has an overall incidence of 10–50%, depending on how carefully these patients are screened. Ototoxicity undoubtedly increases with age, possibly as a result of reduced renal clearance of the drug. Pre-existing auditory impairment is a further risk factor (Piel et al, 1974; Helson et al, 1978).

ANTIMETABOLITES

Folate antagonists

Methotrexate (MTX)

MTX is a weak acid which binds to dihydrofolate reductase, thereby blocking the reduction of dihydrofolate to tetrahydrofolic acid. Thymidylic acid and purine synthesis are thereby halted, in turn arresting DNA, RNA and protein synthesis. MTX has a broad spectrum of antineoplastic activity; its use includes the treatment of acute lymphoblastic and myeloblastic leukaemia, and trophoblastic tumours. High-dose MTX with leucovorin rescue is used in the treatment of a variety of tumours, including osteogenic sarcoma and epithelioid carcinomas of the head and neck. The drug is also used in nonmalignant disease, e.g. recalcitrant cases of psoriasis (Weismann, 1976).

MTX can be given orally or systemically. After oral administration it is rapidly absorbed, reaching peak blood levels by 1 h (Henderson et al, 1965). The drug is widely distributed in body tissues, 50–68% of that present in the blood being bound to plasma proteins. Excretion occurs in two phases, the initial phase having a mean $t_{\frac{1}{2}}$ of 2–3 h, is largely determined by the renal excretion of the drug, and takes place in the first 12 h; 50% of an administered dose is excreted unchanged in the urine. The final phase of drug excretion has a mean $t_{\frac{1}{2}}$ of around 10 h.

MTX is believed to be excreted both by glomerular filtration and by tubular secretion (Lankelm and Poppe, 1978). In patients without frank renal impairment, the half-life of the initial phase increases with advancing age, resulting in decreased drug clearance and higher plasma levels. A significant correlation between creatinine clearance and initial $t_{\frac{1}{2}}$ of MTX has also been noted in normal elderly psoriatic patients (Weismann, 1976), and also in patients with renal dysfunction (Kristensen et al, 1975; Chan et al, 1977). These changes in renal excretion of MTX with age are reflected in increased toxicity among elderly patients (Hansen et al, 1971; Kerr et al, 1983). MTX dosage should therefore be reduced in patients with renal impairment and probably in elderly patients (Bennett et al, 1980).

In a further study (Hansen et al, 1971), methotrexate clearance in patients receiving high-dose MTX (1500 mg/m^2) has shown a tendency to decrease with advancing years, although because of large interindividual variation this was not statistically significant. However, all patients under the age of 50 with normal serum creatinine concentrations showed total body clearance of MTX over 60 ml/min/m², while all patients over 70 years had values under 60 ml/min/m².

Studies of differences in the pharmacokinetics of high-dose MTX between children and adults with osteosarcoma have shown lower plasma MTX levels in younger patients up to 24 h after the start of a 6 h infusion, despite similar doses (on a mg/kg basis). Similarly, the half-life of MTX in children was shorter than in adults, with corresponding increased urinary excretion and a greater apparent volume of distribution (Wang et al, 1979).

It would therefore seem that consistent alterations in MTX clearance do occur with ageing, in both normal and high doses. Appropriate dosage adjustments are probably prudent.

Pyrimidine antagonists

Cytarabine

Cytarabine is of particular use in high-growth fraction tumours, usually in combination with other cytotoxic agents. It is a most effective drug in the treatment of acute myeloid leukaemia. After transport into the cell, the drug is deaminated to uracil arabinoside or phosphorylated to arabinosyl cytidine triphosphate, the latter being the active metabolite which competes with deoxyribosylcytidine triphosphate for the binding sites of DNA polymerase, resulting in inhibition of DNA synthesis (Graham and Whitmore, 1970).

Cytarabine must be given parenterally because extensive and rapid deamination occurs within the gut lumen, allowing for only 20% absorption (Finklestein et al, 1970). The plasma disappearance of cytarabine in humans has been determined in several studies, and there are wide discrepancies between the calculated plasma half-lives (Ho and Frei, 1971; Baguley and Falkenhaug, 1975). The former have reported triphasic kinetics with an initial $t_{\frac{1}{2}}$ of around 15 min. A major fraction of the dose is hepatically metabolized by cytidine deaminase, with a secondary elimination $t_{\frac{1}{2}}$ of 2 h. At 24 h, 90% of a given dose has been eliminiated with a clearance of 90 ml/min (Dedrick et al, 1973). The drug crosses the blood–brain barrier, after which it is excreted only slowly, because of a lack of cytidine deaminase activity in the cerebrospinal fluid (Chabner et al, 1977).

Although variable plasma half-lives for both the first and second phases of elimination of cytarabine have been reported, as well as variable clearance rates and volume of distribution, analysis has failed to reveal any correlation between age and pharmacokinetic variables (van Prooijen et al, 1976).

Purine antagonists

6-Mercaptopurine (6-MP)

6-Mercaptopurine is purine-6-thiol hydrate, differing from purine itself by the presence of a sulfhydryl group rather than a hydroxyl group at the 6th position of the purine ring. 6-MP is thought to act as a false metabolite, the nucleotide competing with enzymes responsible for the conversion of iosinic acid to adenine and xanthine ribotide, and the 6-methyl mercaptopurine ribotide inhibiting purine synthesis (Henderson and Patterson, 1973). 6-MP is effective in the induction and maintenance of remission in acute leukaemia in children and adults, and also in chronic granulocytic conditions. Not all patients respond initially, and many responders do eventually become refractory (Freidreich et al, 1963). It is usually given as part of combination chemotherapy and is administered orally.

After oral dosing, the absorption of the drug is variable, with total urinary excretion being no more than 50% of an equivalent intravenous dose (Loo et al, 1968). Maximal plasma levels are attained within 2 h of oral dosing. Approximately 20% of a given dose is bound to plasma protein. Metabolism is largely by hepatic methylation of the sulfhydryl group and oxidation to 6-thiouric acid by xanthine oxidase, although some nonhepatic degradation may occur (Elion, 1967).

The main age-related differences in 6-MP disposition which have been reported occur between children and adults. Plasma clearance is significantly more rapid in children (mean $t_{\frac{1}{2}} = 21$ min) than in adults (mean $t_{\frac{1}{2}} = 47$ min). This may relate to a faster rate of metabolism in children. Specific data relating to the very elderly adult are scanty.

PLANT ALKALOIDS

Etoposide

Etoposide is a semisynthetic epipodophyllotoxin derivative that can be administered both intravenously and orally. It is most active in the treatment of haematological malignancy and small cell carcinoma of the lung. Etoposide causes marked inhibition of cell cycle traverse through metaphase to mitosis (Krishan et al, 1975).

The absolute oral bioavailability of the drug, based on plasma concentrations and urinary excretion, is 48–57%. Approximately 94% of plasma etoposide is protein-bound and the drug exhibits extensive tissue binding (Allen and Creaven, 1975). Plasma elimination is biexponential with a terminal $t_{\frac{1}{2}}$ of around 5.3 h after intravenous dosing, and 6.8 h after oral dosing. Forty-eight hour urinary recovery is 36% of an intravenous dose and 20% of an oral dose. Most of the total urinary excretion occurs within the first 12 h of dosing (Smyth et al, 1985). A substantially lower renal clearance (7.7 ml/min/m²) than total body clearance (21.4 ml/min/m²) is indicative of significant clearance by nonrenal routes such as biliary excretion or presystemic or systemic metabolism. Up to 53% of a dose may be recovered in the stools, predominantly as metabolites.

Although a wide intersubject and intrasubject variation has been noted after both intravenous and oral dosing, the exact cause of this variation is not known. However, it is of particular interest that no significant correlation with ageing or renal impairment has been noted in a very recent study (Smyth et al, 1985).

Vincristine and other vinca alkaloids

The vinca alkaloids, originally derived from the plant *Vinca rosea*, have been used to treat a variety of haematological and non-haematological conditions, including leukaemias, Hodgkin's disease, and non-Hodgkin's lymphoma. The drugs appear to cause mitotic inhibition and to arrest the cell cycle in metaphase.

Vincristine, one of the most commonly used vinca alkaloids, is given by intravenous injection, usually as a bolus dose. Plasma decay is triphasic, with mean $t_{\frac{1}{2}}$ values of around 5 min, $2\frac{1}{2}$ h and 85 h respectively. Vincristine has a large volume of distribution (8.42 l/kg) due to extensive tissue binding. Serum clearance has been estimated to be 0.1 l/kg/h (Nelson et al, 1980). Elimination is mainly biliary, and only 10% of an administered dose is excreted in the urine (Owellen, 1975). Large inter-individual variation in the pharmacokinetics of vinca alkaloids have been demonstrated. Liver disease would appear to be a major factor in determining the elimination of these drugs, and in one study where 39 patients received vincristine, mostly for haematological malignancy, raised serum alkaline phosphatase levels before treatment were associated with a highly significant ($p < 0.001$) increase in plasma area under the concentration/time curve and half-life (Van den Berg et al, 1982).

In the case of vindescine at least, the wide variation in elimination and disposition between the patients does not appear to be related to age (Rahmani et al, 1985).

MISCELLANEOUS AGENTS

Procarbazine

Procarbazine was reported to have activity against Hodgkin's disease in 1963 and is now commonly used in the combination chemotherapy of this disease. The drug and its active metabolites act by interfering with protein, RNA and DNA synthesis. It may be administered orally or parenterally.

Procarbazine is rapidly absorbed from the gastrointestinal tract. It readily crosses the blood–brain barrier (Schwartz et al, 1967). The pathways of metabolism have been extensively studied in rodents. Procarbazine is rapidly spontaneously oxidized in solution to the azo derivative, which is then further oxidized in the liver to azoxy isomers, with subsequent hydroxylation to produce methylating and alkylating agents. It is also possible that free radicals are generated from the azo compound (Weinkam and Shiba, 1978).

Metabolism is swift, and the parent drug has a mean plasma $t_{\frac{1}{2}}$ of less than 10 min. After 24 h, up to 70% of the dose is recovered in the urine, mainly as N-isopropylterephalmic acid, < 5% being excreted unchanged by the kidneys (Oliverio, 1971).

Unfortunately, no data are available on the specific pharmacokinetics of this drug in a geriatric population.

Asparaginase

Asparaginase is an enzyme isolated from the Gram-negative bacterium *E. coli* and from the plant parasite *Erwinia caratovora*. The drug has been used with variable success in a variety of malignant diseases, usually in combination with other cytotoxic agents. Many tumour cells lack the ability to synthesize asparagine, and asparaginase, by hydrolysing asparagine to aspartic acid and ammonia, deprives the tumour cell of this amine which is essential for protein synthesis (Capizzi et al, 1971).

Asparaginase may be given intravenously or intramuscularly, the latter being said to reduce the risk of hypersensitivity reactions (Lobel et al, 1979). After intravenous injection the initial clearance of the enzyme from plasma follows first-order kinetics with a half-life of 14–22 h. Daily administration results in drug accumulation in the blood. Enzyme activity is detectable 13–22 days after single injections (Ohnuma et al, 1970). Volume of distribution approximates plasma volume. Large inter-individual variations in plasma $t_{\frac{1}{2}}$ have been observed. Pharmacokinetic parameters have been shown not to correlate well with sex, body mass, renal function and hepatic function (Ho et al, 1970); furthermore, no specific correlation between pharmacokinetics and ageing has been noted (Ho et al, 1970).

Interestingly, some toxicities may be age-related, such as the appearance of anti-asparaginase antibodies, which occur more frequently in adults than in children (Killander et al, 1976), and central nervous system abnormalities such as depression, personality disorder and organic brain syndrome. These side-effects were shown in one study of 49 patients to be relatively common in adults (31%), but not to occur in children (Haskell et al, 1969). The exact cause of this is obscure.

CONCLUSIONS

Age has been shown to affect the disposition of a variety of all types of drugs. However, studies on drug metabolism in the elderly have consistently shown that concurrent frailty and disease, such as cardiac, hepatic, or renal failure, is always much more important than the ageing process itself. This is particularly relevant to patients with malignant disease, who are often critically ill and debilitated.

Nonetheless, age-related changes in the pharmacokinetics of a variety of anticancer drugs have been reported, particularly drugs which are excreted primarily by the kidney. It is likely that these pharmacokinetic changes are at least partly responsible for the increase in drug toxicity which is seen in elderly patients, although changes in target organ sensitivity may also have an important role.

REFERENCES

Adair CG, Bridges JM & Desai ZR (1986a) Renal function the elimination of oral melphalan in patients with multiple myeloma. *Cancer Chemotherapy and Pharmacology* **17**: 185–188.

Adair CG, Bridges JM & Desai ZR (1986b) Can food affect the bioavailability of chlorambucil in patients with haematological malignancies? *Cancer Chemotherapy and Pharmacology* 17: 99–102.

Alberts DS, Bachur NR & Holtzman JL (1971) The pharmacokinetics of daunomycin in man. *Clinical Pharmacology and Therapeutics* 12: 96–104.

Alberts DS, Chen HSE, Lui R et al (1978) Bleomycin pharmacokinetics in man. Intravenous and administration. *Cancer Chemotherapy and Pharmacology* 1: 177–181.

Alberts DS, Chang SY, George Chen H-S et al (1979) Oral melphelan kinetics. *Clinical Pharmacology and Therapeutics* 26: 737–745.

Allen LM & Creaven PJ (1975) Comparison of the human pharmacokinetic of VM-26 and VP-16, two antineoplastic epipodophyllotoxin glucopyranoside derivatives. *European Journal of Cancer* 11: 697–707.

Andersson B, Beran M, Peterson C et al (1982) Significance of cellular pharmacokinetics for the cytotoxic effects of daunorubicin. *Cancer Research* 42: 178–183.

Bachur NR, Reiter W & Arena E (1975) Cardiac uptake of adriamycin not affected by strophanthine. *Cancer Chemotherapy Reports* 59: 765–766.

Bagley CM, Bosllick FW & DeVita VT (1973) Clinical pharmacology of cyclophosphamide. *New England Journal of Medicine* 295(27) 1522–1533.

Baguley BC & Falkenhaug E-M (1975) Plasma half-life of cytosine arabinoside in patients with leukaemia—the effect of uridine. *European Journal of Cancer* 11: 43–49.

Benjamin RS (1975) Clinical pharmacology of adriamycin (NSC-123127). *Cancer Chemotherapy Reports* 6: 183–185.

Bennett WM, Muther RS, Parker RA et al (1980) Drug therapy in renal failure. Dosing guidelines for adults. Part II. *Annals of Internal Medicine* 93: 286–325.

Blum RH, Carter SK & Agre K (1973) A clinical review of bleomycin—a new antineoplastic agent. *Cancer* 31: 903–914.

Bonadonna G, Monfardini S, Delena M et al (1970) Phase I and preliminary phase II evaluation of Adriamycin (NSC 123127). *Cancer Research* 30: 2527–2582.

Bosanquet AG & Gilby ED (1982) Pharmacokinetics of oral and intravenous melphalan during routine treatment of multiple myeloma. *European Journal of Cancer and Clinical Oncology* 18(4): 355–362.

Bristow MR, Billingham ME & Mason JR (1978) Clinical spectrum of anthracycline antibiotic cardiotoxicity. *Cancer Treatment Reports* 62(6): 873–879.

Bristow MR, Billingham ME & Daniels JR (1979) Histamine and catecholamines mediate Adriamycin cardiotoxicity. *Proceedings of the American Association of Cancer Research* 20: 118(abstract 477).

Bruce DW & Edgcomb JH (1967) Pancytopenia and generalised sepsis following treatment of cancer of the bladder with instillations of triethylene thiophosphoramide. *Journal of Urology* 97: 482–485.

Burnand KG, Boyd PJR, Mayo ME et al (1976) Single dose intravesican thio-TEPA as an adjuvant to cystodiathermy in the treatment of transitional cell bladder carcinoma. *British Journal of Urology* 481: 55–59.

Capizzi RL, Bertino JR, Steel RT et al (1971) L-Asparaginase: clinical, biochemical, pharmacological and immunological studies. *Annals of Internal Medicine* 24: 893–901.

Castleden CM & George C (1979) The effect of ageing on hepatic clearance of propranolol. *British Journal of Clinical Pharmacology* 7: 49–54.

Castelden CM, Volans GN & Raymond K (1977) The effect of ageing on drug absorption from the gut. *Age and Ageing* 6: 138–143.

Chabner BA, Myers CE & Oliverio VT (1977) Clinical pharmacology of anti-cancer drugs. *Seminars in Oncology* 4(2): 165–191.

Chan H, Evans WE & Pratt CB (1977) Recovery from toxicity associated with high-dose methotrexate: prognostic factors. *Cancer Treatment Reports* 61: 797–804.

Cohen BE, Egorin MJ, Kohlhepp EA et al (1986) Human plasma pharmacokinetics and urinary excretion of thioTEPA and its metabolites. *Cancer Treatment Reports* 70(7): 859–864.

Creasey WA, McIntosh LS, Brescia T et al (1976) Clinical effects and pharmacokinetics of different dosage schedules of adriamycin. *Cancer Research* 36: 216–221.

Crooke ST, Comis RL, Einhorn LH et al (1977) Effects of variations in renal function on the clinical pharmacology of bleomycin administered as an intravenous bolus. *Cancer Treatment*

Reports **61:** 1631–1636.

Cusack B, Kelly J, O'Malley K et al (1979) Digoxin in the elderly: pharmacokinetic consequences of old age. *Clinical Pharmacology and Therapeutics* **25:** 772–776.

Dedrick RL, Forrester DD, Cannon JN et al (1973) Pharmacokinetics of 1-β-D-arabinofurano-sylcytosine (Ara-C) deamination in several species. *Biochemical Pharmacology* **22:** 2405–2417.

den Hartigh J, McVie JG, van Oort WJ et al (1983) Pharmacokinetics of mitomycin in humans. *Cancer Research* **43:** 5017–5021.

Di Marco A, Zunino F, Silvestrini R et al (1971) Interaction of some daunomycin derivatives with deoxyribonucleic acid and their biological activity. *Biochemical Pharmacology* **20**(6): 1323–1328.

Edwards G, Calvert RT, Crowther D et al (1980) Repeated investigations of cyclophosphamide disposition in myeloma patients receiving intermittent chemotherapy. *British Journal of Clinical Pharmacology* **10:** 281–285.

Eichelbaum M (1982) Defective oxidation of drugs: pharmacokinetic and therapeutic implications. *Clinical Pharmacokinetics* **7:** 1–22.

Elion GB (1967) Biochemistry and pharmacology of purine analogues. *Federation Proceedings* **26:** 893–904.

Elson LA (1958) Haematological effects of the alkylating agents. *Annals of the New York Academy of Sciences* **68:** 826–833.

Evans WE, Yee GC, Crom WR et al (1981) Clinical pharmacology of bleomycin and cisplatin. *Head and Neck Surgery* **4:** 98–110.

Finklestein JZ, Scher J & Karen M (1970) Pharmacological studies of filtrated cytosine arabinoside (NSC 63878) in children. *Cancer Chemotherapy Reports* **54:** 35–39.

Freidreich EJ, Frei E III & Gehen EA (1963) The effect of 6-mercaptopurine on the duration of steroid-induced remissions in acute leukaemia. *Blood* **21:** 699–716.

Fulton B, James OFW & Rawlins MD (1979) The influence of age on the pharmacokinetics of paracetamol. *British Journal of Clinical Pharmacology* **7**(4): 418.

Galton DAG (1953) Myleran in chronic myeloid leukaemia. *Lancet* **i:** 208–213.

Graham FL & Whitmore GF (1970) Studies in mouse L-cells on inhibition of DNA polymerase by 1-β-D-arabinofuranosylcytosine 5′-triphosphate. *Cancer Research* **30:** 2636–2644.

Hale WE, Stewart RB & Marks RG (1983) Haematological and biochemical laboratory values in an ambulatory elderly population: an analysis of the effects of age, sex and drugs. *Age and Ageing* **12:** 275–284.

Hansen HH, Selawry OS, Holland JF et al (1971) The variability of individual tolerance to methotrexate in cancer patients. *British Journal of Cancer* **25:** 298–305.

Haskell CM, Canellos GP, Leventhal BG et al (1969) L-Asparaginase toxicity. *Cancer Research* **29:** 974–975.

Hayes FA, Green AA, Evans WE et al (1980) Treatment of neuroblastoma with *cis*-platinum and VM-26: response and toxicity. In Nelso VD & Grassi C (eds) *Current Chemotherapy and Infectious Disease*, pp 1642–1643. Washington DC: American Society for Microbiology.

Helson L, Okonkwo E, Anton L et al (1978) *Cis*-platinum ototoxicity. *Clinical Toxicology* **13:** 469–478.

Henderson ES, Adamson RH & Oliverio VT (1965) The metabolic fate of tritiated methotrexate. II. Absorption and excretion in man. *Cancer Research* **25:** 1018–1024.

Henderson JF & Patterson ARP (1973) In *Nucleotide Metabolism: An Introduction*, p 48. New York: Academic Press Inc.

Ho DHW & Frei E III (1971) Clinical pharmacology of 1-β-D-arabinofuranosylcytosine. *Clinical Pharmacology and Therapeutics* **12:** 944–954.

Ho DHW, Therford B, Carter CJK et al (1970) Clinical pharmacological studies of L-asparaginase. *Clinical Pharmacology and Therapeutics* **11:** 408–417.

Huffman DH & Bachur NR (1972) Daunorubicin metabolism in acute myelocytic leukaemia. *Blood* **39**(5): 637–643.

Huffman DH, Benjamin RS & Bachur NR (1972) Daunorubicin metabolism in acute nonlymphocytic leukaemia. *Clinical Pharmacology and Therapeutics* **13**(6): 895–905.

James OFW (1983) Gastrointestinal and liver function in old age. *Clinics in Gastroenterology* **12:** 671–691.

Juma FD (1984) Effect of liver failure on the pharmacokinetics of cyclophosphamide. *European*

Journal of Clinical Pharmacology **26:** 591–593.

Juma FD, Rogers HJ & Trounce JR (1979) Pharmacokinetics of cyclophosphamide and alkylating agents in man after intravenous and oral administration. *British Journal of Clinical Pharmacology* **8:** 209–217.

Juma FD, Rogers HJ & Trounce JR (1980) The pharmacokinetics of cyclophosphamide, phosphoramide mustard and nor-nitrogen mustard studied by gas chromatography in patients receiving cyclophosphamide therapy. *British Journal of Clinical Pharmacology* **10:** 327–335.

Juma FD, Rogers HJ & Trounce JR (1981) Effect of renal insufficiency on the pharmacokinetics of cyclophosphamide and some of its metabolites. *European Journal of Clinical Pharmacology* **19:** 443–451.

Kampmann JP & Molholm-Hansen JE (1979) Renal excretion of drugs. In Crooks J & Stevenson IH (eds) *Drugs in the Elderly*, pp 77–87. London: Macmillan Press.

Kennedy KA, Rockwell S & Sartorelli AC (1980) Preferential activation of mitomycin C to cytotoxic metabolites by hypoxic tumour cells. *Cancer Research* **40:** 2356–2360.

Kerr IG, Jolivet J, Collins JM et al (1983) Test dose for predicting high dose methotrexate infusions. *Clinical Pharmacology and Therapeutics* **33**(1): 44–51.

Killander D, Dohlwitz A, Engstedt L et al (1976) Hypersensitivity reactions and antibody formation during L-asparaginase treatment of children and adults with acute leukaemia. *Cancer* **37:** 220–228.

Krishan A, Paikg K & Frei E III (1975) Cytofluorometric studies on the action of podophyllotoxin and enipodophyllotoxins (VM-26 and VP 16213) on the cell cycle traverse of human lymphoblasts. *Journal of Cell Biology* **66:** 521–530.

Kristensen LO, Weismann K & Hutters L (1975) Renal function and the rate of disappearance of methotrexate from serum. *European Journal of Clinical Pharmacology* **8:** 439–444.

Lankelm AJ & Poppe H (1978) Determination of methotrexate in plasma by on-column concentration and ion-exchange chromatography. *Journal of Chromatography* **149:** 587–598.

Lobel JS, O'Brien RT, McIntosh S et al (1979) Methotrexate and asparaginase combination chemotherapy in refractory acute lymphoblastic leukaemia of childhood. *Cancer* **43:** 1089–1094.

Loo TL, Luce JK, Sullivan MP et al (1968) Clinical pharmacologic observations on 6-mercaptopurine and 6-methylthiopurine ribonucleoside. *Clinical Pharmacology and Therapeutics* **9**(2): 180–194.

McIntyre OR, Leone L & Pajak TF (1978) The use of intravenous melphalan (L-PAM) in the treatment of multiple myeloma. *Blood* **52**(5) (supplement 1): 274.

McLean A, Woods RL, Catovsky D et al (1979) Pharmacokinetics and metabolism of chlorambucil in patients with malignant disease. *Cancer Treatment Reviews* **6**(supplement): 33–42.

Mooney H, Roberts R, Cooksley W et al (1985) Alterations in the liver with ageing. *Clinics in Gastroenterology* **14:** 757–771.

Mouridsen HT, Faber O & Skovsted L (1974) The biotransformation of cyclophosphamide in man: analysis of variation in normal subjects. *Acta Pharmacologica et Toxicologica* **35:** 98–106.

Nelson RL, Dyke RW & Root MA (1980) Comparative pharmacokinetics of vindesine, vincristine and vinblastine in patients with cancer. *Cancer Treatment Reviews* **7**(supplement): 17–24.

Novak LP (1972) Ageing, total body potassium, fat free mass and cell mass in males and females aged 18 and 85 years. *Journal of Gerontology* **27:** 438–443.

Ohnuma T, Holland JF, Freeman A et al (1970) Biochemical and pharmacological studies with asparaginase in man. *Cancer Research* **30:** 2297–2305.

Oken MM, Crooke ST, Elson MK et al (1981) Pharmacokinetics of bleomycin after IM administration in man. *Cancer Treatment Reports* **65:** 485–489.

Oliverio VT, Denham C, De Vita VT et al (1971) Some pharmacologic properties of a new antitumour agent, *N*-isopropyl-δ-(2-methyl-hydrazino-*p*-toluamide) hydrochloride (NSC-77213). *Cancer Chemotherapy Reports* **42:** 1–7.

Owellen RJ (1975) The pharmacokinetics of aromatic ring ³H-vinblastine in humans. *Federation Proceedings* **34:** 808.

Piel IJ, Meyer D, Perlia CP et al (1974) Effects of *cis*-diammine di-chloroplatinum (NSC-119875) on hearing function in man. *Cancer Chemotherapy Reports* **58:** 871–875.

Prestayku AW, Crooke ST & Carter SK (1980) *Cisplatin: Current Status and New Developments.* New York: Academic Press.

Rahmani R, Kleisbauer JP, Cano JP et al (1985) Clinical pharmacokinetics of vindesine infusion. *Cancer Treatment Reports* **69:** 839–844.

Regardh CG, Landahl S, Larsson M et al (1983) Pharmacokinetics of metoprolol and its metabolite OH-metroprolol in healthy non-smoking, elderly individuals. *European Journal of Clinical Pharmacology* **24:** 221–226.

Robert J & Hoerni B (1983) Age dependence of the early phase pharmacokinetics of doxorubicin. *Cancer Research* **43:** 4467–4469.

Robert J, Iliadis A, Hoerni B et al (1982) Pharmacokinetics of adriamycin in patients with breast cancer. Correlation between pharmacokinetic parameters and clinical short term response. *European Journal of Cancer and Clinical Oncology* **18:** 739–745.

Roberts JJ & Warwick GP (1961) Studies of the mode of action of tumour growth inhibiting alkylating agents III. *Biochemical Pharmacology* **6:** 217–227.

Schein PS (1978) Nitrosourea anti-tumour agents. In Umezawa H (ed.) *Advances in Cancer Chemotherapy*, pp 95–106. Baltimore: University Park Press.

Schwartz DE, Bollag W & Obrecht P (1967) Distribution and excretion studies of procarbazine in animals and man. *Arzneimittel Forschnung* **17:** 1389–1393.

Shock NW, Watkin DM, Yiengst MJ et al (1963) Age difference in water content of the body is related to basal oxygen consumption in males. *Journal of Gerontology* **18:** 1–8.

Smith PHS & Taylor DM (1974) Distribution and retention of the anti-tumour agent ^{195m}Pt-*cis*-dichlorodiamminiplatinum (II) in man. *Journal of Nuclear Medicine* **15:** 349–351.

Smithard DJ & Langman MJS (1978) The effect of vitamin supplementation upon antipyrine metabolism in the elderly. *British Journal of Clinical Pharmacology* **5:** 181–185.

Smyth RD, Pfeffer M, Scalzo A et al (1985) Bioavailability and pharmacokinetics of etoposide (VP-16). *Seminars in Oncology* **12**(1) (supplement 2): 48–51.

Theologides A, Yarbro JW & Kennedy BJ (1968) Daunorubicin inhibition of both DNA and RNA synthesis. *Cancer* **21:** 16–21.

Van den Berg HW, Desai ZR, Wilson R et al (1982) The pharmacokinetics of vincristine in man: reduced drug clearance associated with raised serum alkaline phosphatase. *Cancer Chemotherapy and Pharmacology* **8:** 215–219.

van Prooijen R, Vanderkleijn E & Haanen C (1976) Pharmacokinetics of cytosine arabinoside in acute myeloid leukaemia. *Clinical Pharmacology and Therapeutics* **21**(6): 744–750.

Vestal RE, Norris AH, Tobin JD et al (1975) Antipyrine metabolism in man: influence of age, alcohol, caffeine and smoking. *Clinical Pharmacology and Therapeutics* **18:** 425–432.

Vestal RE, McGuire EA, Tobin JD et al (1977) Ageing and ethanol metabolism. *Clinical Pharmacology and Therapeutics* **21:** 343–354.

Von Hoff DD, Layard M & Baja P (1978) Analysis of risk factors for development of adriamycin [A]-induced congestive heart failure. *Proceedings of the American Association of Cancer Research* **19:** 54.

Walker MD & Hilton J (1976) Nitrosourea pharmacodynamics in relation to the central nervous system. *Cancer Treatment Reports* **60:** 725–728.

Wang Y-M, Sutow WW, Romsdahl MM et al (1979) Age-related pharmacokinetics of high-dose methotrexate in patients with osteosarcoma. *Cancer Treatment Reports* **63**(3): 405–410.

Weinkam RJ & Shiba DA (1978) Metabolic activation of procarbazine. *Life Sciences* **22:** 937–946.

Weismann K (1976) Methotrexate therapy for psoriasis in elderly patients with impaired renal function. *Acta Dermato-Venerologica (Stockholm)* **57:** 185–186.

Wilkinson GR (1983) Drug distribution and renal excretion in the elderly. *Chronic Diseases Journal* **36:** 91–102.

Woodhouse KW (1985) Drugs and the ageing gut, liver and pancreas. *Clinics in Gastroenterology* **14**(4): 863–881.

Woodhouse KW & Blain PG (1983) Some organ-specific adverse reactions to cytotoxic drugs. *Adverse Drug Reaction and Acute Poisoning Reviews* **2:** 123–143.

Woodhouse KW, Hamilton P, Lennard A et al (1983) The pharmacokinetics of melphalan in patients with multiple myeloma. *European Journal of Clinical Pharmacology* **24:** 283–285.

Woodhouse KW, Williams FM, Mutch E et al (1984a) The effect of alcoholic cirrhosis on the two kinetic components (high and low affinity) of the microsomal O-deethylation of 7-ethoxycoumarin in human liver. *European Journal of Clinical Pharmacology* **26**: 61–64.

Woodhouse KW, Mutch E, Williams F et al (1984b) The effect of age on pathways of drug metabolism in human liver. *Age and Ageing* **13**: 328–334.

Wynne H, Mutch E, James OFW et al (1987) The effect of age on monooxygenase enzyme kinetics in rat liver microsomes. *Age and Ageing* **16**(3): 153–158.

Zwelling LA & Kohn KW (1979) Mechanism of action of *cis*-dichlorodiammineplatinum (II). *Cancer Treatment Reports* **63**: 1439–1444.

10

Monoclonal gammopathy and multiple myeloma in the elderly

ROBERT A. KYLE

The term 'benign monoclonal gammopathy' indicates the presence of a monoclonal protein in persons without evidence of multiple myeloma, macroglobulinaemia, amyloidosis, lymphoproliferative disease, or other related disorders. The term is misleading because it is not known at diagnosis whether a monoclonal protein will remain stable and benign or will develop into symptomatic multiple myeloma, macroglobulinaemia, other lymphoproliferative disease, or amyloidosis. Consequently, the term 'monoclonal gammopathy of undetermined significance' (MGUS) is preferable.

Analysis of the serum or urine for monoclonal proteins (M-proteins) requires a sensitive, rapid, dependable screening method to detect the presence of an M-protein, and a specific assay to determine its heavy-chain class and light-chain type. Electrophoresis on cellulose acetate membrane is satisfactory for screening but will not detect small monoclonal proteins. High-resolution agarose electrophoresis is more sensitive in detecting small M-proteins. Either immunoelectrophoresis or immunofixation or both should be employed to confirm the presence of an M-protein and to determine its type (Kyle, 1986b).

Monoclonal proteins without evidence of myeloma, macroglobulinaemia, amyloidosis, or related diseases, have been found in approximately 3% of persons more than 70 years of age in Sweden (Hällén, 1963; Axelsson et al, 1966; Hällén, 1966) and in the USA (Kyle et al, 1972). Among 6995 normal Swedish persons more than 25 years old, the overall prevalence of M-proteins was 1%, and among 1200 patients 50 years old or older who were residents of a small Minnesota community, 1.25% had an M-protein. In a survey of 17 968 adults 50 years old or older in Finistère, France, 303 (1.7%) had a monoclonal protein (Saleun et al, 1982). The use of more sensitive techniques will detect a higher incidence of M-proteins. For example, Papadopoulos et al (1982), using agarose electrophoresis, detected homogeneous bands in the sera of 30 (5%) of 600 healthy adults 22–65 years of age.

The incidence of monoclonal gammopathics increases with advancing age. Crawford et al (1987), utilizing agarose gel electrophoresis, detected monoclonal proteins in 11 (10%) of 111 patients older than 80 years of age in a population of ambulatory residents of a retirement home.

Although the incidence of multiple myeloma is greater in American Blacks than in Caucasians, the incidence of monoclonal proteins is essentially the same (Schechter et al, 1986). In a review of 4193 monoclonal gammopathies from three regions in France, Hurez et al (1985) reported a high frequency of IgM (33%), almost twice that reported from other series.

Monoclonal gammopathies are being discovered in clinical practice much more commonly than before. At present, approximately 50 000 serum protein electrophoretic strips are screened each year at the Mayo Clinic. During 1985, 882 new cases of serum M-proteins were recognized. The clinical diagnoses included MGUS (75%), multiple myeloma (11%), primary systemic amyloidosis (8%), lymphoma (4%), macroglobulinaemia (1%), and indeterminate (1%).

Thus, the prevalence of MGUS is considerable, and it is important to both the patient and physician to determine whether the monoclonal gammopathy will remain benign or will progress to multiple myeloma, macroglobulinaemia, lymphoma, or amyloidosis.

MONOCLONAL GAMMOPATHY OF UNKNOWN SIGNIFICANCE

Currently, my colleagues and I are gathering follow-up data on 241 patients who had a monoclonal serum protein recognized at the Mayo Clinic before January 1, 1971. Patients with multiple myeloma, macroglobulinaemia, amyloidosis, lymphoma, or related diseases were excluded. The patients were classified as follows: group 1, patients who had no increase of serum M-protein level during follow-up (benign); group 2, patients who had an increase of more than 50% in M-protein level or who developed urine M-protein but no myeloma or related disease; group 3, patients who died from unrelated causes; and group 4, patients in whom multiple myeloma, macroglobulinaemia, amyloidosis, or related diseases developed (Table 1).

Group 1 (stable)

At the end of 10 or more years (median, 13 years), the number of patients whose monoclonal gammopathy had remained stable and could be classified as 'benign' monoclonal gammopathy had decreased to 88 (37%). Actually, one-fourth of the patients had been followed up for 15–26 years and had not developed multiple myeloma, macroglobulinaemia, amyloidosis, or lymphoproliferative disease. The M-protein disappeared in only one patient.

There was no significant difference in the initial level of haemoglobin, size of the serum M-protein, type of serum heavy and light chains, reduction of uninvolved immunoglobulins, type of IgG heavy chain, and number of plasma cells in the bone marrow between the group with stable or benign monoclonal gammopathy and the total group.

Table 1. Course during first 13 years (median) of follow-up in a series of 241 patients with 'benign' monoclonal gammopathy.

Group	Description	No.	%
		Follow-up (median 13 y)	
1	No significant increase of serum or urine M-protein (benign)	88	37
2	> 50% increase of M-protein from initial value or appearance of urine M-protein	13	5
3	Died from unrelated cause	94	39
4	Developed myeloma, macroglobulinemia, amyloidosis, or related diseases	46	19
Total		241	100

Reproduced with permission of the Mayo Foundation from Kyle RA (1984a).

Group 2 (increase of M-protein only)

In all 13 patients of this group, the serum M-protein level increased by 50% or more (median increase, 1.1 g/dl; range, 0.7–1.5). Multiple myeloma, macroglobulinaemia, or amyloidosis did not develop. The median interval from the recognition of the M-protein to an increase of 50% or more was 126 months (range, 58–178).

Group 3 (died without developing multiple myeloma, macroglobulinaemia, amyloidosis, or related diseases)

The 94 patients in this group died without developing evidence of a plasma cell proliferative process. The median interval from diagnosis of the M-protein to death was 67 months (range, 0–221). Eighteen patients survived more than 10 years after recognition of the serum M-protein. Cardiac disease was the most frequent cause of death (38%), followed in frequency by cerebrovascular disease (14%). Seven patients died of a malignancy not associated with a plasma cell proliferative process.

Group 4 (developed multiple myeloma, macroglobulinaemia, amyloidosis, or related diseases)

Multiple myeloma, macroglobulinaemia, amyloidosis, or a malignant lymphoplasmaproliferative process developed in 46 patients (19%). The actuarial rate at 10 years was 16.2%. Among this group, multiple myeloma accounted for 32 (70%). The interval from recognition of the M-protein to diagnosis of multiple myeloma ranged from 2 to 21 years (median, 8.2). The median survival after the diagnosis of multiple myeloma was 35 months (Kyle, 1984a).

In six patients, macroglobulinaemia of Waldenström developed 4–20 years after recognition of the M-protein. In another six patients, systemic amyloidosis was diagnosed 6–14 years after recognition of an M-protein in the serum. In two other patients a malignant lymphoproliferative process developed—chronic lymphocytic leukaemia in one and an aggressive undifferentiated non-Hodgkin's lymphoma in the other.

Other investigators have had a similar experience. During a 20-year follow-up of 64 Swedish patients with monoclonal gammopathy, Axelsson (1986) found that two had died of multiple myeloma and one had died of lymphoma. Three others had an increase of their M-protein, and another patient had had a high level of IgA and a tentative diagnosis of multiple myeloma. Thus, 10% of their patients had evidence of some progression of their 'benign' monoclonal gammopathy.

DIFFERENTIATION OF MGUS FROM MULTIPLE MYELOMA AND MACROGLOBULINAEMIA

Patients with MGUS have: < 3 g of M-protein per decilitre in the serum and no or small amounts of Bence Jones proteinuria; fewer than 5% plasma cells in the bone marrow aspirate; normal serum albumin level; and no anaemia, hypercalcaemia, renal insufficiency, or osteolytic lesions (unless caused by other diseases). The only basis for deciding that the patient has MGUS is the absence of an increase of the M-protein level or the development of a plasma-cell lyphoproliferative process during long-term follow-up.

In contrast to the patient with MGUS, the patient with smouldering multiple myeloma (SMM) has an M-protein level > 3 g/dl in the serum and > 10% atypical plasma cells in the bone marrow. In addition, the patient with SMM frequently has a small amount of M-protein in the urine and a reduction of uninvolved immunoglobulins in the serum. However, anaemia, renal insufficiency, and skeletal lesions do not develop and the patient's condition remains stable. These patients should not be treated unless laboratory abnormalities progress or symptoms of myeloma develop (Kyle and Greipp, 1980).

Differentiation of the patient with 'benign' monoclonal gammopathy from one in whom myeloma or macroglobulinaemia eventually develops is very difficult at the time that the M-protein is recognized. The size of the serum M-protein level is of some help—higher levels are associated with a greater likelihood of malignancy (Møller-Petersen and Schmidt, 1986). The presence of > 3 g of M-protein per decilitre of serum usually indicates overt multiple myeloma or macroglobulinaemia, but some exceptions, such as SMM, do exist. Levels of immunoglobulin classes not associated with the M-protein (normal polyclonal or background immunoglobulins) may aid in differentiating benign from malignant monoclonal gammopathy. In most patients with multiple myeloma, the levels of polyclonal immunoglobulins are reduced, although a similar reduction in the levels in patients with benign monoclonal gammopathy may also occur. The association of a monoclonal light chain (Bence Jones proteinuria) with a serum M-protein usually indicates a neoplastic process. However, we have seen many patients with a small amount of monoclonal light chain in the urine and an M-protein in the serum whose conditions have remained stable for years. The presence of $> 10\%$ plasma cells in the bone marrow is suggestive of multiple myeloma, but the conditions of some patients with a greater degree of plasmacytosis have remained stable for long periods. Plasma cells in multiple myeloma show morphological atypia, but these features may also be seen in benign monoclonal gammopathy and SMM. The presence of osteolytic lesions is suggestive of multiple myeloma, but metastatic carcinoma may produce lytic lesions and plasmacytosis and may be associated with an unrelated serum M-protein.

β_2-Microglobulin levels are not helpful in differentiating benign monoclonal gammopathy from low-grade multiple myeloma because there is too much overlap between the two entities. The presence of J-chains in malignant plasma cells, or the plasma cell acid phosphatase levels, are not reliable indicators. Reduced numbers of OKT4+ T cells, increased numbers of monoclonal idiotype-bearing peripheral blood lymphocytes, and increased numbers of immunoglobulin-secreting cells in peripheral blood, are characteristic of multiple myeloma, but there is considerable overlap with MGUS.

The plasma cell labelling index using a monoclonal antibody (BU-1) reactive with 5-bromo-2-deoxyuridine (BrdUrd) in an immunofluorescent assay is helpful in differentiating patients with MGUS or SMM from those with multiple myeloma (Greipp et al, 1987). Patients with MGUS or SMM are characterized by having a low plasma cell labelling index. Preliminary studies have revealed that the plasma cell labelling index of peripheral blood is also useful.

In summary, there is no reliable technique for differentiating a patient with a benign monoclonal gammopathy from one who will subsequently develop multiple myeloma or other malignant disease. The most reliable means of differentiating a benign from a malignant course is the serial measurement of the M-protein level and periodic re-evaluation to determine whether features of multiple myeloma, systemic amyloidosis, macroglobulinaemia, or other malignant lymphoproliferative disease develop.

ASSOCIATION OF MONOCLONAL GAMMOPATHY WITH OTHER DISEASES

Although monoclonal gammopathy frequently exists without any other abnormalities, certain diseases do occur in association with it, as would be expected in an older population. The association of two diseases occurring in a person depends on the frequency with which each disease occurs independently. Furthermore, an association may become apparent because of differences in referral practice or the selection of other patient groups. The investigator must utilize valid epidemiological and statistical methods in evaluating these associations reported in the literature. The need for appropriate control populations cannot be overemphasized.

Association of monoclonal gammopathy and hyperparathyroidism has been reported in several series. In an effort to clarify the relationship, we reviewed the records of patients with surgically proven parathyroid adenoma in whom serum protein electrophoresis had been done within the 6 months preceding parathyroidectomy. Among 911 patients who met these criteria and were more than 50 years of age, immunoelectrophoresis revealed an M-protein in nine (1%) (Mundis and Kyle, 1982). This incidence of M-protein is similar to that found in previous studies of normal populations. The association of hyperparathyroidism and benign monoclonal gammopathy seems to be due to chance alone.

An increased incidence of M-protein in association with carcinoma of the colon has been reported. However, in two large studies (Migliore and Alexanian, 1968; Talerman and Haije, 1973), the incidence of M-protein in malignancies was no greater than that expected in a population of similar age.

These studies demonstrate the need for comparison with an adequate control population before an assumption is made that an association exists between monoclonal gammopathy and any disease.

Lymphoproliferative disorders

For 30 years, M-proteins have been recognized in lymphoma and lymphocytic leukaemia. Subsequently, Alexanian (1975) noted an IgM protein in 29 (4.5%) of 640 patients with diffuse lymphoproliferative disease, and in none of 292 patients with a nodular lymphoma. The incidence of an IgM protein was approximately 100 times greater than that found in a normal population. Hobbs et al (1974) noted that 10% of patients with malignant lymphoma proved by biopsy had an IgM protein. Two-thirds of the patients had a diffuse histological pattern, while only 13% had a follicular pattern. Magrath et al (1983) found IgM proteins in the sera of 12 of 21 patients with undifferentiated lymphoma of Burkitt's and non-Burkitt's types.

Although an increase in polyclonal immunoglobulin level is common in angioimmunoblastic lymphadenopathy, six patients with an M-protein have been found (Offit et al, 1986). Sugai et al (1985) reported that five of 10 Japanese patients with Sjögren's syndrome had a monoclonal IgA protein.

Leukaemia

Monoclonal proteins have been found in the sera of some patients with acute leukaemia. Noel and Kyle (1987) have described 100 patients with chronic lymphocytic leukaemia and a monoclonal protein in the serum or urine. The protein was IgG in 51% and IgM in 28%. The median concentration of M-protein was 1.0 g/dl. We found no important differences in patients with chronic lymphocytic leukaemia, whether they had an IgG or an IgM monoclonal protein. Monoclonal gammopathies have been noted in some patients with hairy cell leukaemia (Jansen et al, 1983). Matsuzaki et al (1985) described three patients with monoclonal gammopathy and adult T-cell leukaemia.

Other haematological diseases

Monoclonal proteins have been reported with a wide variety of haematological diseases, including pernicious anaemia, acquired von Willebrand's disease,

Gaucher's disease, pure red-cell aplasia, chronic idiopathic thrombocytopenia, myelodysplastic syndromes, agnogenic myeloid metaplasia, chronic granulocytic leukaemia, and polycythaemia vera (Kyle, 1986a).

Connective tissue diseases

Rheumatoid arthritis, lupus erythematosus, and other connective tissue diseases have been found to be associated with monoclonal gammopathies (Michaux and Heremans, 1969). However, a definite relationship has not been proven. Polymyalgia rheumatica has been noted with monoclonal gammopathy, but because they both occur more commonly in an older population, a relationship is doubtful. Three patients with an IgG κ monoclonal protein have been reported with polymyositis (Kiprov and Miller, 1984).

Neurological disorders

In a series of 279 patients with a sensorimotor peripheral neuropathy of unknown cause, Kelly et al (1981) found 16 with MGUS. Many patients with MGUS have been reported to have an associated clinical peripheral neuropathy. The incidence would be greater if one depended only on electrophysiological evidence of neuropathy.

Latov et al (1980) demonstrated that the small monoclonal IgM λ protein in a patient with peripheral neuropathy was directed against peripheral nerve myelin. This protein was subsequently identified as a specific glycoprotein component of myelin and referred to as myelin-associated glycoprotein (MAG). Dellagi et al (1983) reported 10 patients with an IgM monoclonal protein of < 1 g/dl and peripheral neuropathy with antibody activity against the myelin sheath. Occasionally, the M-protein binds to a peripheral nerve glycolipid and not to MAG (Lieberman et al, 1985).

Dalakas and Engel (1981) reported that four of five patients with peripheral neuropathy and monoclonal gammopathy benefited from prednisone, azathioprine, cyclophosphamide, or chlorambucil treatment. We have seen some patients who had sensorimotor peripheral neuropathy associated with an IgG or an IgM protein who responded to melphalan or chlorambucil respectively.

Motor neurone diseases (including amyotrophic lateral sclerosis and spinal muscular atrophy) associated with monoclonal proteins have been identified (Patten, 1984; Shy et al, 1986). Myasthaenia gravis, ataxia-telangiectasia, or multiple sclerosis has been found with monoclonal gammopathies, but the association may be only fortuitous.

Dermatological diseases

Lichen myxedematosus (papular mucinosis, scleromyxedema) is a rare dermatological condition frequently associated with an IgGλ basic monoclonal protein that has cathodal mobility (James et al, 1967). Scleredema (Buschke's disease) has been associated with a monoclonal protein.

Powell et al (1985) reported that nine (10%) of 86 patients with pyoderma gangrenosum had a monoclonal gammopathy. Seven of the nine had IgA.

Necrobiotic xanthogranuloma is frequently associated with a monoclonal IgG protein (Finan and Winkelmann, 1986).

More than a dozen patients have been reported with monoclonal gammopathy and Sézary syndrome. We have seen several patients with mycosis fungoides and a monoclonal gammopathy. Thus, cutaneous T cell lymphomas have been associated with M-proteins.

Miscellaneous

Gelfand et al (1979) described a patient with angioneurotic oedema and acquired deficiency of C1 esterase inhibitor, and reviewed the records of 14 others reported in the literature, including five with a 7S IgM monoclonal protein. Of nine patients with the periodic systemic capillary leak syndrome (increased capillary permeability), eight had a monoclonal protein in the serum (Löfdahl et al, 1979).

Although polyclonal increases in immunoglobulins are most common in liver disease, M-proteins have been noted. Heer et al (1984) found an M-protein in 11 of 272 patients with chronic active hepatitis. They found M-proteins in the sera of 13 of 50 randomly chosen patients with chronic active hepatitis. M-proteins have also been recognized in patients with primary biliary cirrhosis (Hendrick et al, 1986).

Monoclonal proteins were found in more than half of patients with an acquired immunodeficiency syndrome (AIDS) or with lymphadenopathy syndrome (LAS) (Heriot et al, 1985). M-proteins are seen in 30% of patients with renal transplants who have received immunosuppressive therapy (Radl et al, 1985). We have recognized a number of patients who had transient, persistent, or varying monoclonal gammopathies after liver transplantation.

Monoclonal proteins with antibody activity

In some patients with MGUS, myeloma, or macroglobulinaemia, the monoclonal immunoglobulin has exhibited unusual specificities to dextran, antistreptolysin O, antinuclear activity, von Willebrand factor, various antibiotics, actin, various infections, thyroglobulin, calcium, and copper. This subject has recently been reviewed in detail by Merlini et al (1986).

Biclonal gammopathies

In 1981, we reported that 37 of 57 (65%) patients with biclonal gammopathy had no features of multiple myeloma or lymphoproliferative disease. The findings were similar to those in patients with MGUS. It has also been postulated that in some patients the M-proteins arise from two separate plasma cell clones while in others the proteins behave in a concordant manner that is consistent with incomplete class switching in a single plasma cell clone (Riddell et al, 1986).

MULTIPLE MYELOMA

Multiple myeloma (plasma cell myeloma, myelomatosis, or Kahler's disease) is characterized by a neoplastic proliferation of a single clone of plasma cells engaged in the production of a monoclonal immunoglobulin.

Aetiology

The cause of multiple myeloma is unknown. There is no compelling evidence that environmental or hereditary factors are important in many instances.

Radiation may be a factor in some cases. There was a modest increase in incidence of multiple myeloma in atomic bomb survivors. Cuzick (1981) has reviewed the role of radiation in the aetiology of multiple myeloma. The possibility of a viral cause has been raised, and currently there is much interest in retroviruses and oncogenes, but proof of a viral cause in humans is meagre.

There is little direct evidence that chemicals cause myeloma in humans, even though reports have linked multiple myeloma with benzene or asbestos. Several reports have noted multiple myeloma in farmers, furniture workers, rubber workers, radium dial workers, and cosmetologists, as well as in workers exposed to pesticides and carbon monoxide. A report of two families in which successive spouses who lived in the same house developed multiple myeloma suggests the possibility of environmental causes, but no such agents were identified.

Repeated antigenic stimulation of the reticuloendothelial system could have an effect on the development of myeloma. In one series, more allergies were noted in patients with myeloma than in controls. Chronic disease of the biliary tract has been implicated in the development of plasma cell dyscrasias, but the incidence of cholelithiasis reported in such cases probably does not differ significantly from that in a normal population.

The likelihood of a genetic factor in some cases is supported by well-documented reports of familial clusters of two or more first-degree relatives (siblings or parents and children) with multiple myeloma (Maldonado and Kyle, 1974). A genetic factor is also supported by the report of multiple myeloma occurring in a pair of monozygotic twins (Judson et al, 1985). In a control study of 439 patients with multiple myeloma and 1317 matched controls, only three patients and four controls reported multiple myeloma in their families (Bourguet et al, 1985).

Incidence and epidemiology

Multiple myeloma accounts for about 1% of all types of malignant disease and slightly more than 10% of haematological malignancies. Although two-fold to three-fold increases in the incidence of multiple myeloma in the USA and a five-fold increase in England and Wales have been reported, rates in Malmö, Sweden, have increased only slightly. Data from Olmsted County, Minnesota, revealed an annual rate of three per 100 000 from 1945 to 1954, and a similar rate during the following two decades. The death rate for myeloma probably has not changed significantly; most likely, the apparent increase of rates in recent years is related to increased availability and use of medical facilities and improved diagnostic techniques.

Multiple myeloma occurs in all races and all geographical locations. Its incidence in blacks is twice that in whites. Myeloma is more common in males—60%.

Clinical manifestations

Onset

Multiple myeloma is a disease involving the elderly, having a peak incidence during the seventh decade of life. Only 2% of patients are less than 40 years of age (Kyle, 1975).

Symptoms

Bone pain, typically in the back or chest and less often in the extremities, is present at the time of diagnosis in more than two-thirds of patients. The pain is usually induced by movement and does not occur at night, except with change of position. The bone pain of myeloma should not be attributed to arthritis or 'old age' in the elderly. The patient's height may be reduced by several inches because of vertebral collapse. Weakness and fatigue are common and are often associated with anaemia. Fever from the disease itself is rare. Most patients with myeloma who have fever have an infection. Abnormal bleeding, most often as epistaxis or purpura, may be a prominent feature. The major symptoms may result from acute infection, renal insufficiency, hypercalcaemia, or amyloidosis.

Physical findings

Pallor is the most frequent physical finding. The liver is palpable in about 20% of patients, and the spleen in 5%. Extramedullary plasmacytomas are uncommon but may be present as large, vascular, subcutaneous masses, often having a purplish hue.

Laboratory findings

A normocytic, normochromic anaemia eventually occurs in nearly every patient with multiple myeloma. Increased plasma volume from the osmotic effect of a large amount of M-protein may produce a large decrease of haemoglobin and haematocrit levels. Thus, significant anaemia may be suggested by the haemoglobin or haematocrit level when the red cell mass is only slightly reduced. Typically, erythrocyte sedimentation is increased, but it is normal in 10% of patients. Initially, leukocyte and platelet counts are usually normal, but decreases are common later in the disease. Plasma cells are seen in the peripheral blood in about 15% of patients.

In a group of 457 patients with multiple myeloma seen at the Mayo Clinic from 1981 to 1985, the serum protein electrophoretic pattern on cellulose acetate revealed a peak or localized band in 80% of patients, hypogammaglobulinaemia in 7%, and no apparent abnormality in the remainder. Ninety-four per cent of the 33 patients with hypogammaglobulinaemia had a monoclonal protein in the serum or urine. A monoclonal protein was detected in the serum in 92% of these patients. Fifty-two per cent of the proteins were IgG, 21% were IgA, 16% were light chain only (Bence Jones proteinaemia), and 2% were IgD. Electrophoresis of urine in 446 patients in this group showed a globulin peak or band in 89%, mainly albumin in 8%, and a normal pattern in 3%. Immunoelectrophoresis or immunofixation of the urine reveals a monoclonal protein in 79% of these patients. Almost all (99%) of these 457 patients with multiple myeloma had a monoclonal protein in the serum or urine.

The serum creatinine level is elevated in about half of the patients, and hypercalcaemia is present in 30%. Conventional radiographs reveal abnormalities consisting of punched-out lytic lesions, osteoporosis, or fractures in about 80% of patients. The vertebra, skull, thoracic cage, pelvis, and proximal humeri and femurs are the most frequent sites of involvement. Technetium-99m bone scans are inferior to conventional radiographs for detecting lesions in myeloma. Computed tomography (CT) is helpful in patients with myeloma who have skeletal pain but no abnormality on radiographs (Kyle et al, 1985).

T lymphocyte function declines in the ageing patient. The peripheral blood of patients with myeloma shows a reduction of OKT4+ (helper T lymphocytes) cells and an increase in OKT8+ (suppressor T lymphocytes) cells. The demonstration of the M-protein idiotype and the production of the patient's M-protein by peripheral blood lymphocytes indicate that these cells are part of the malignant clone.

Differential diagnosis

Bone pain, anaemia, and renal insufficiency constitute a triad that is strongly suggestive of multiple myeloma. If the diagnosis is suspected, the physician should obtain, in addition to a complete history and physical examination: determinations of haemoglobin or haematocrit levels; leukocyte, differential, and platelet counts; measurements of serum creatinine, calcium, phosphorus, alkaline phosphatase, and uric acid; radiographic survey of bones, including humeri and femurs; serum protein electrophoresis; measurement of serum immunoglobulins, immunoelectrophoresis, or immunofixation; tests for cryoglobulins and viscosity if the M-spike is large or if symptoms of hyperviscosity are present; bone marrow aspiration and biopsy; routine urinalysis; and electrophoresis, immunoelectrophoresis, and immunofixation of an adequately concentrated aliquot from a 24 h urine specimen.

The diagnosis depends on the demonstration of an increased number of plasma cells in the bone marrow. These plasma cells vary from small and relatively mature to large and anaplastic. The pattern varies greatly among patients, and in some instances the cells may not be recognized as myeloma cells because they may have a very lymphoid appearance suggestive of lymphoma or macroglobulinaemia. A monoclonal immunoglobulin can be identified in plasma cells by the immunoperoxidase method, and this technique is very helpful in differentiating monoclonal plasma cell proliferation in multiple myeloma or MGUS from reactive plasmacytosis due to carcinoma, connective tissue disease, liver disease, hypersensitivity states, and viral and bacterial infections. The immunoperoxidase technique is also helpful in recognizing neoplastic plasma cells that have the appearance of signet-ring cells simulating metastatic adenocarcinoma, large foamy histiocyte-like cells resembling lipid storage cells, mononuclear cells with abundant clear cytoplasm suggestive of hairy cells, and large anaplastic cells resembling proerythroblasts, large-cell lymphoma, or undifferentiated carcinomas. Bone marrow involvement is often focal rather than diffuse; consequently, specimens may vary greatly. In some instances, a bone marrow aspirate must be obtained from another site.

Although the finding of large homogeneous nodules or infiltrates of plasma cells in bone marrow sections is the most reliable morphological criterion for the diagnosis of multiple myeloma, Buss et al (1986) noted that 2% of patients with reactive plasmacytosis had this feature while 26% of patients with well-documented multiple myeloma did not. Therefore, large homogeneous nodules or infiltrates of plasma cells in bone marrow sections are the most specific finding in making the diagnosis of multiple myeloma, but they are not always diagnostic of the disease nor are they always present.

Minimal criteria for the diagnosis of multiple myeloma include the presence of at least 10% abnormal, immature plasma cells in the bone marrow, or histological proof of an extramedullary plasmacytoma, the usual clinical features of multiple myeloma, and at least one of the following abnormalities—an M-protein in the serum (usually > 3 g/dl), M-protein in the urine, or osteolytic lesions. Connective tissue diseases, chronic infections, metastatic carcinoma, lymphoma, and leukaemia may simulate some of the characteristics of myeloma and should be excluded in the differential diagnosis, unless other features make the diagnosis of multiple myeloma definite.

Patients with multiple myeloma must be differentiated from those with MGUS. Patients with MGUS should be observed indefinitely and not be given therapy. Not all patients who fulfil the criteria for the diagnosis of multiple myeloma should be treated. Patients with SMM also should not be given therapy.

A plasma cell labelling index (LI) using [^{3}H]thymidine or a monoclonal antibody to 5-bromo-2-deoxyuridine is helpful in differentiating a patient with MGUS or SMM from one with multiple myeloma. Patients whose plasma cells have a low LI ($< 0.8\%$) most likely have a stable condition but should be followed-up closely.

Organ involvement

Renal

Renal insufficiency is common in myeloma and is seen in about half of patients. It is most commonly due to hypercalcaemia or 'myeloma kidney', in which the distal and occasionally the proximal convoluted tubules and collecting tubules become obstructed by large laminated casts. These casts are composed of precipitated Bence Jones protein as well as albumin, IgG, Tamm–Horsfall mucoprotein, and polyclonal light chains of both types. Giant cells are often seen, and dilatation and atrophy of the renal tubules develop. Some Bence Jones proteins have a nephrotoxic effect but others do not. The mechanism of nephrotoxicity by Bence Jones proteins is unknown. There is no direct relationship between the isoelectric point of the Bence Jones protein and renal damage. Cooper et al (1984) reported that almost every patient with monoclonal free light-chain excretion had impaired proximal renal tubular function. They did not find that λ light chains were more nephrotoxic than κ light chains. Hyperuricaemia, pyelonephritis, infiltration of the kidney by plasma cells, deposition of amyloid, and increased blood viscosity may all contribute to renal insufficiency.

Multiple myeloma may be associated with the Fanconi syndrome (Maldonado et al, 1975). In these patients, Bence Jones proteinuria is almost always of the κ type. Crystalline cytoplasmic inclusions are commonly seen in the plasma cells of the bone marrow and in the renal tubular cells. Plasmacytosis or frank myeloma is present in the bone marrow.

Monoclonal light chains may be deposited in the renal glomerulus and are manifested by a nephrotic syndrome or renal insufficiency. This condition has been designated as light-chain deposition disease. The most typical lesion is nodular glomerulosclerosis. Electron microscopy shows finely granular, electron-dense deposits on the outer aspects of the tubular basement membranes. The deposits consist mainly of κ light chains (Tubbs et al, 1981).

Rapidly progressive proliferative (crescentic) glomerulonephritis has been reported to be associated with monoclonal IgA or IgG proteins (Kebler et al, 1985). The kidney in myeloma has recently been reviewed by Hamblin (1986).

Neurological

Radiculopathy is the single most frequent neurological complication and is usually lumbosacral. Root pain results from compression of the nerve by the vertebral lesion or by the collapsed bone itself. Compression of the spinal cord or cauda equina occurs in about 5% of patients with myeloma.

Sensorimotor peripheral neuropathy may occur in multiple myeloma. Most frequently it is associated with amyloidosis.

Intracranial plasmacytomas usually represent extensions of the myelomatous lesions of the skull. Infrequently, plasmacytomas may involve the hypothalamus, temporal cortex, corpus callosum, posterior fossa, or dura mater. Destruction of the sella, with involvement of the third, fourth, and sixth cranial nerves, may be seen. Meningeal involvement has been reported in a number of instances (Gomez and Krishnamsetty, 1986).

Gastrointestinal

Multiple myeloma may involve the stomach and be seen as prominence of the rugal folds. Involvement of the liver, biliary ducts, and head of the pancreas may occur. Ascites has been reported (Greer et al, 1985).

Respiratory

The most frequent abnormality on thoracic radiographs is the presence of lytic lesions. Plasmacytomas occur in more than 10% of patients. Pleural effusion is uncommon and is usually due to congestive heart failure from cardiac amyloidosis. Myeloma rarely involves the pleura but has been well-documented.

Skeletal

Radiographic evidence of abnormalities of the skeleton is seen initially in about 80% of patients with multiple myeloma. Generalized osteoporosis may be the only skeletal manifestation in myeloma. It is difficult to differentiate between postmenopausal osteoporosis and osteoporosis associated with multiple myeloma. The vertebrae, skull, thoracic cage, pelvis, and proximal humeri and femurs are the most common sites of involvement.

The mechanism of bone resorption in myeloma is mainly osteoclastic. Osteoclast-activating factor (OAF) represents a family of bone-resorbing factors produced by lymphocytes and monocytes (Mundy and Bertolini, 1986). Durie et al (1981) demonstrated a close relationship between the production of OAF by bone marrow cells and the extent of skeletal destruction.

Technetium-99m bone scans are generally inferior to conventional radiographs for detecting lesions in myeloma. Computed tomography (CT) is particularly helpful in myeloma when skeletal pain is atypical but radiographs are normal. In this situation, CT often reveals lytic lesions. CT also has been helpful in differentiating overt multiple myeloma that involves the skeleton from smouldering multiple myeloma or MGUS in which a large monoclonal serum protein is associated with postmenopausal osteoporosis and compression fractures (Kyle et al, 1985). Magnetic resonance imaging (MRI) is apparently more sensitive, and revealed abnormalities in all 30 patients with multiple myeloma. Radionuclide bone scans were positive in only six, while 20 showed abnormality on the radiographs. Eleven of 15 patients had abnormal findings on CT studies (Daffner et al, 1986).

Durie et al (1986a) reported deletion or translocation involving all or part of the 6q chromosome in patients who had myeloma with bone disease, whereas patients without this chromosomal abnormality had no bone lesions.

Muscle hypertrophy due to enlarged muscle fibres was reported in a man with κ light-chain myeloma. The monoclonal κ protein had a specific enhancing effect on human muscle cell differentiation (Delaporte et al, 1986).

Infections

The incidence of infection is increased in multiple myeloma. Diplococci and *Staphylococcus aureus* were the most frequent pathogens, but, more recently, Gram-negative organisms have been reported to account for more than half of all infections (Shaikh et al, 1982). The greatest risk of infection in multiple myeloma is during the first 2 months after initiation of chemotherapy.

Elevated serum creatinine levels and decreased polyclonal serum immunoglobulins were associated with a higher incidence of infection (Perri et al, 1981).

The impairment of antibody response, deficiency of normal immunoglobulins, reduction of delayed hypersensitivity, and, in some instances, depression of reticuloendothelial function and impaired activity of the neutrophils, all may contribute to the increase of infections among patients with myeloma. The propensity to infection is further increased by chemotherapeutic depression of the immune response and production of neutropenia. Herpes zoster is not uncommon in patients with myeloma.

Coagulation abnormalities

Bleeding may be a prominent feature. The qualitative platelet abnormalities may result from coating of platelets by myeloma protein. Inhibitors of coagulation factors and thrombocytopenia from marrow involvement or chemotherapy may contribute. Intravascular coagulation, amyloid deposition, and hepatic or renal insufficiency may produce bleeding.

Course and prognosis

Multiple myeloma runs a progressive course, with a median survival of 2–3 years. The major causes of death are infection and renal insufficiency.

A clinical staging system based on a combination of findings that correlate with the myeloma cell mass has been frequently utilized. Patients with high cell mass (stage III) have at least one of the following: haemoglobin < 85 g/l, serum calcium > 2.99 mmol/l (> 12 mg/dl), IgG > 70 g/l, IgA > 50 g/l, urinary Bence Jones protein > 12 g/24 h, or advanced lytic bone lesions. Patients with low cell mass (stage I) had all of the following characteristics: haemoglobin > 100 g/l, normal serum calcium, serum IgG < 50 g/l or IgA < 30 g/l, Bence Jones protein < 4 g/24 h, and no generalized lytic lesions. Patients whose cell mass was between the limits specified were designated as having stage II disease. Patients were subclassified according to their serum creatinine values as stage IA (< 177 μmol/l or < 2 mg/dl) or IIB (> 177 μmol/l or > 2 mg/dl). Median survival was 61.2 months for patients with stage IA disease and 14.7 months for patients with stage IIIB disease (Durie and Salmon, 1975).

The serum β_2-microglobulin level is an important prognostic factor in multiple myeloma. Cuzick et al (1985) reported that β_2-microglobulin levels, uncorrected for serum creatinine level, were the single most powerful prognostic test in 476 patients with multiple myeloma. Multivariate analysis showed that only the addition of the haemoglobin level provided additional prognostic data. In a series of 147 untreated patients with multiple myeloma, Bataille et al (1986) also reported that the β_2-microglobulin level was the most powerful indicator of prognosis at the time of diagnosis and found that the serum albumin level was the only other variable of value in prognosis.

In a recent review, Durie (1986) summarized the available data on staging and kinetics in multiple myeloma. He emphasized the role of staging systems as well as the plasma cell labelling index.

Low tumour cell RNA content is associated with resistance to chemotherapy. In fact, a stepwise increase in response rate with increasing levels of RNA has been demonstrated. Patients with myeloma who have hypodiploidy have a poor response to chemotherapy (Barlogie et al, 1985).

The serum creatinine and calcium levels are also variables that affect the survival of patients with multiple myeloma. However, the most important factor in prognosis is response to treatment. Prognosis is poorer in patients who respond rapidly to chemotherapy (Durie et al, 1980).

Treatment

Chemotherapy is the preferred initial treatment for overt, symptomatic multiple myeloma. In most patients, analgesics, together with chemotherapy, can control pain. This approach is preferred to the use of local irradiation, because pain frequently recurs at another site and radiation may further reduce the bone marrow reserve. Therefore, the use of palliative irradiation should be limited to patients who have disabling pain from a well-defined focal process that has not responded to chemotherapy.

The major controversy, still not resolved, is whether melphalan and prednisone or a combination of alkylating agents should be used. Although combinations of chemotherapy produce more objective responses, a significant difference in survival has not yet been proved. Furthermore, a combination of chemotherapeutic agents is less convenient and more costly, produces more side-effects, and reduces the therapeutic options for future treatment.

The oral administration of melphalan (Alkeran) (0.15 mg/kg daily for 7 days) and prednisone (20 mg three times daily for the same 7 days) every 6 weeks is a reasonable, easily administered, well-tolerated regime and produces objective response in 50–60% of patients. Leukocyte and platelet counts must be determined at 3 week intervals, and the dose of melphalan altered in order to achieve modest cytopenia at midcycle. Melphalan should be given while the patient is fasting, because absorption is delayed and reduced to about half after food is taken. Some patients do not absorb melphalan adequately. The dose of melphalan should be calculated on the basis of the patient's ideal body weight. At least three courses of melphalan and prednisone should be given before this therapy is discontinued, unless there are serious side-effects or the disease progresses rapidly despite adequate doses of melphalan. Objective evidence of response may not be achieved for several months, and change to another therapeutic regimen should not be made unless there is evidence of progressive disease or intolerable side-effects from melphalan and prednisone. Resistance to melphalan and multiple myeloma has recently been reviewed, and possible approaches to overcome this problem have been suggested (Hall et al, 1986).

Many combinations of chemotherapeutic agents have been used because of the obvious shortcomings of melphalan and prednisone. The best known combination, the M-2 Protocol, includes melphalan, cyclophosphamide, carmustine (BCNU), vincristine, and prednisone. In an uncontrolled study, this regimen produced objective response in 78% of 81 previously untreated myeloma patients and a median survival of 38 months (Lee et al, 1982). In a randomized trial comparing this regimen with melphalan and prednisone therapy, objective response was noted in 74% of patients receiving the M-2 combination of chemotherapeutic agents and in 53% of those receiving melphalan and prednisone. However, the median survivals of 33 and 29 months, respectively, were not significantly different (Oken et al, 1984). Furthermore, the frequency of severe, life-threatening, or lethal toxicity was greater in patients receiving the combination of chemotherapeutic agents.

In a prospective study, courses of a combination of vincristine, melphalan, cyclophosphamide, and prednisone were alternated with either the combination of vincristine, cyclophosphamide, doxorubicin and prednisone, or the combination of vincristine, carmustine, doxorubicin and prednisone. These alternating combinations produced a 75% reduction of tumour mass in 53% of patients and a median survival of 40 months, whereas therapy with only melphalan and prednisone produced a 32% response and a median survival time of 24 months (Salmon et al, 1983). These findings were confirmed in a subsequent analysis of the data, which revealed a median survival of 48 months for patients who received alternating combinations of chemotherapy, and 23 months for patients who received melphalan and prednisone (Durie et al, 1986b). Another report (Alexanian and Dreicer, 1984), using the same combinations of alternating chemotherapeutic agents with only a minimal difference in dosage, had response rates that were virtually the same as for melphalan and prednisone (53–60%). The slightly longer survival of patients treated with melphalan and prednisone (38 months versus 28 months) was attributed to the higher frequency of favourable prognostic features and the use of vincristine and doxorubicin combinations when the myeloma became resistant.

In an evaluation of registered and published trials, Simes (1986) suggested a significant survival advantage for combination chemotherapy. However, the magnitude of this survival advantage was less when based on registered rather than published trials. He noted that the pooled analyses would not have resulted in a significant survival advantage for combination chemotherapy if the Southwestern Oncology Group (SWOG) report was excluded (Salmon et al, 1983). Sporn and McIntyre (1986) have presented an analysis of therapy in patients with multiple myeloma who were previously untreated.

The controversy of single versus a combination of alkylating agents has not been resolved. The use of melphalan–prednisone is a reasonable choice. It is important to realize that there is no satisfactory chemotherapy for myeloma.

The ideal duration of chemotherapy is unknown. Cessation of chemotherapy usually results in relapse, but continued treatment may lead to a myelodysplastic syndrome or overt acute leukaemia (Kyle, 1984b). Chemotherapy probably should be continued for 2 years and then discontinued, provided that the M-protein level in the serum and urine has been stable for at least 6 months and the patient has no other evidence of active disease. The patient must then be followed up carefully, and chemotherapy reinstituted when relapse occurs.

Therapy for refractory myeloma

All patients with multiple myeloma who have a response to chemotherapy will eventually have a relapse if they do not die of another disease. In addition, approximately one-third of patients treated initially with chemotherapy will not obtain an objective response.

The highest response rates reported for patients with multiple myeloma resistant to alkylating agents have been with VAD—i.e. the combination of vincristine, doxorubicin (Adriamycin), and dexamethasone. Vincristine and Adriamycin in a 4-day continuous infusion with dexamethasone (40 mg daily) produced a response in 14 (70%) of 20 patients with resistant multiple myeloma. Infection represented the most frequent complication, but cytopenias were moderate (Barlogie et al, 1984). In a subsequent report, Alexanian et al (1986) found that approximately one-fourth of patients who were unresponsive to chemotherapy obtained an objective response with VAD or high-dose dexamethasone alone. They reported that VAD induced remission in two-thirds of patients who had relapses, whereas dexamethasone produced remission in only 21%. VBAP—a combination of vincristine (2 mg), carmustine (BCNU) (30 mg/m^2), doxorubicin (Adriamycin, 30 mg/m^2), and prednisone (60 mg)—daily for 5 days has produced some benefit in approximately 40% of patients. Interferon has had considerable notice in both the lay and medical presses, but the overall response has been disappointing. Combination of interferon with chemotherapy may be of benefit and this is being initiated (Cooper and Welander, 1986). Results from combinations of chemotherapeutic drugs as well as newer single agents, along with radiation therapy for previously treated myeloma patients, have recently been summarized (Kyle et al, 1986). New chemotherapeutic agents with greater specificity for the plasma cell but without increased toxicity must be found before major progress can be made with chemotherapy.

Newer therapeutic approaches

Currently available agents used in different dosages, combinations, schedules, or routes of administration may provide some benefit. McElwain's group reported that seven of 30 patients with previously untreated myeloma who were less than 60 years of age achieved a complete remission after a single intravenous dose of melphalan (140 mg/m^2) (Selby et al, 1985). Only one of the seven patients had a relapse during follow-up. The results using a high dose of melphalan for patients with previously treated myeloma have been disappointing.

Small doses of cyclophosphamide or melphalan have been beneficial in the treatment of murine plasmacytomas. This approach could be utilized in human myeloma. A soft agar colony assay for stem cells in human myeloma represents an opportunity for the in vitro determination of sensitivity to chemotherapeutic agents. This technique shows promise, but the assay system must be improved before it can be of practical value.

Bone marrow transplantation from an identical twin (syngeneic) (Fefer et al, 1986) or from a matched donor (allogeneic) (Gahrton et al, 1986) has been performed. Some patients have received benefit, but the morbidity is high and generally the myeloma cannot be eradicated.

Autologous bone marrow transplantation is potentially applicable to treat far more patients than is allogeneic transplantation, because the problems of graft versus host disease or graft rejection are circumvented. Two major problems exist for patients with myeloma. First, multiple myeloma is difficult to eradicate from the bone marrow, even with large doses of chemotherapy and radiation. The second major problem is that of removing myeloma cells and their precursors from the autologous bone marrow before reinfusion. A panel of monoclonal antibodies directed against myeloma cells and their precursors or chemotherapy (or both) may be used. The therapeutic use of monoclonal antibodies to plasma cell antigens may be possible in the future, but many hurdles must be overcome. Much more needs to be learned about the biological basis of multiple myeloma before real progress can be made in therapy.

Management of complications

Hypercalcaemia, which occurs in one-third of patients with multiple myeloma, should be suspected if the patient has anorexia, nausea, vomiting, polyuria, increased constipation, weakness, confusion, stupor, or coma. Treatment is urgent because renal insufficiency commonly develops. Hydration, preferably with isotonic saline, is essential. Caution must be exercised to avoid fluid overload in the elderly patient. In addition prednisone in an initial dose of 25 mg four times daily should be given, but the dose must be reduced and discontinued as soon as possible. Calcitonin has been used with some success. If these measures fail, mithramycin should be given intravenously in a dose of 25 μg/kg. Its effect is produced within 24–48 h, but hypercalcaemia often recurs after 2 or 3 days. Furosemide (Lasix), 40 mg every 4 h, may be used, but adequate hydration must be maintained. If hypercalcaemia recurs after an initial response, inorganic phosphate (Neutra-Phos) may be used on an outpatient basis, but it must not be given if renal insufficiency or hyperphosphataemia is present. Because prolonged bed rest often contributes to hypercalcaemia, patients with myeloma should be encouraged to be as active as possible.

Allopurinol is necessary if hyperuricaemia is present. If the patient is allergic to allopurinol, sodium bicarbonate and acetazolamide taken at bedtime can make the urine alkaline. Polycitra (an oral alkalizer) may also be used.

Patients with acute renal failure must be treated promptly with alkalinization and maintenance of fluid and electrolyte balance. Haemodialysis may be necessary. Acute renal failure may be benefited by total plasma exchange, but this has not been proved in a randomized study. In the presence of chronic renal failure, long-term dialysis can prolong life if the multiple myeloma can be controlled. Survival has been increased in some patients by renal transplantation for myeloma kidney.

Prompt and appropriate treatment of bacterial infections is important. Significant fever is an indication for appropriate cultures and radiography and for consideration of antibiotic therapy. There is considerable doubt as to the efficacy of injections of γ-globulin for the prevention of infection. Intravenously administered γ-globulin can be considered, but it is very expensive. In patients with multiple, recurrent, serious Gram-positive infections, penicillin given prophylactically has achieved good results. Although antibody response is impaired, pneumococcal vaccine and influenza immunization should be given to all patients.

Bone lesions manifested by pain and fracture constitute a major problem. Frequently, a brace or supporting garment is helpful initially; but avoidance of trauma is more important because even mild stress may result in multiple fractures. The patient should be encouraged to be as active as possible because confinement to bed increases demineralization of the skeleton. Analgesic agents should be given to control the pain and to allow the patient to be ambulatory. Fixation of fractures of long bones with an intramedullary rod and methyl methacrylate has given very satisfactory results. The use of fluoride, which stimulates osteoblastic activity, and calcium, which aids calcification of the osteoid tissue, may be of benefit. Oral diphosphonates, which reduce osteoblastic activity, may be helpful. The symptoms of hyperviscosity include oronasal bleeding, blurred vision, neurological symptoms, and congestive heart failure. Most patients have symptoms when the relative serum viscosity reaches 6 or 7 centipoises (normal, < 1.8), but the relationship between serum viscosity and clinical manifestations is not precise. Vigorous plasmapheresis with a cell separator will relieve the symptoms of hyperviscosity, but chemotherapy is necessary for long-term benefit. Plasmapheresis should not be done unless the patient is symptomatic.

For patients with multiple myeloma who state that their legs are weak or that they have difficulty in voiding or defecating, the possibility that an extradural myeloma is compressing the spinal cord must be considered. The sudden onset of severe thoracic pain or the presence of a paraspinal mass also raises the possibility of compression of the spinal cord. If any of these symptoms or signs occur, magnetic resonance imaging (MRI), computed tomography (CT), or myelography is essential. Radiation therapy in a dose of approximately 3000 rad (30 Gy) is helpful. Dexamethasone should be administered daily during radiation therapy to reduce the oedema. If the neurological deficit worsens during irradiation, surgical compression must be done and radiotherapy resumed.

Any patient with a serious disease such as multiple myeloma has psychological problems that need substantial, continuing emotional support. The approach must be positive. Physicians must have confidence in their ability to cope with a patient's problems and the patient should be able to sense this confidence. Potential benefits of therapy should be emphasized. It is reassuring to the patient to know that some patients survive for 10 years or more while receiving treatment. It is vital that the physicians caring for patients with multiple myeloma have an interest and the capacity to deal with incurable disease over a span of months to years with assurance, sympathy, and resourcefulness.

SUMMARY

The term 'benign monoclonal gammopathy' indicates the presence of a monoclonal protein in persons without evidence of multiple myeloma, macroglobulinaemia, amyloidosis, lymphoproliferative disease, or other related disorders. The term 'monoclonal gammopathy of undetermined significance' (MGUS) is preferable because it is not known at diagnosis whether an M-protein will remain stable and benign or develop into symptomatic multiple myeloma or related disorders. Immunoelectrophoresis and immunofixation of the serum and urine are necessary to determine the presence and type of M-protein. At the Mayo Clinic, follow-up data have been gathered for more than 13 years on 241 patients with an initial benign monoclonal gammopathy. Nineteen per cent of these patients developed multiple myeloma, macroglobulinaemia, amyloidosis, or related diseases during the follow-up period. There is no reliable technique for differentiating a patient with a benign monoclonal gammopathy from one who will subsequently develop a serious disease. It is necessary to follow these patients indefinitely. Important in the complete understanding of the elderly patient with monoclonal gammopathy are the following: clinical manifestations, laboratory findings, and differential diagnosis of multiple myeloma; the course and prognosis and the induction therapy and treatment of multiple myeloma; newer therapeutic approaches; and the management of complications such as hypercalcaemia, hyperuricaemia, renal failure, bacterial infections, skeletal disease, and neurological problems.

Acknowledgements

The author was supported in part by Research Grant CA-16835 and CA-15083 from the National Institutes of Health, Public Health Service, and the Toor Fund.

REFERENCES

Alexanian R (1975) Monoclonal gammopathy in lymphoma. *Archives of Internal Medicine* **135:** 62–66.
Alexanian R & Dreicer R (1984) Chemotherapy for multiple myeloma. *Cancer* **53:** 583–588.
Alexanian R, Barlogie B & Dixon D (1986) High-dose glucocorticoid treatment of resistant myeloma. *Annals of Internal Medicine* **105:** 8–11.
Axelsson U (1986) A 20-year follow-up study of 64 subjects with M-components. *Acta Medica Scandinavica* **219:** 519–522.
Axelsson U, Bachmann R & Hällén J (1966) Frequency of pathological proteins (M-components) in 6995 sera from an adult population. *Acta Medica Scandinavica* **179:** 235–247.
Barlogie B, Smith L & Alexanian R (1984) Effective treatment of advanced multiple myeloma refractory to alkylating agents. *New England Journal of Medicine* **310:** 1353–1356.
Barlogie B, Alexanian R, Dixon D et al (1985) Prognostic implications of tumor cell DNA and RNA content in multiple myeloma. *Blood* **66:** 338–341.
Bataille R, Durie BGM, Grenier J & Sany J (1986) Prognostic factors and staging in multiple myeloma: a reappraisal. *Journal of Clinical Oncology* **4:** 80–87.

Bourguet CC, Grufferman S, Delzell E, DeLong ER & Cohen HJ (1985) Multiple myeloma and family history of cancer: a case-control study. *Cancer* **56:** 2133–2139.

Buss DH, Prichard RW, Hartz JW, Cooper MR & Feigin GA (1986) Initial bone marrow findings in multiple myeloma: significance of plasma cell nodules. *Archives of Pathology and Laboratory Medicine* **110:** 30–33.

Cooper EH, Forbes MA, Crockson RA & MacLennan ICM (1984) Proximal renal tubular function in myelomatosis: observations in the fourth Medical Research Council trial. *Journal of Clinical Pathology* **37:** 852–858.

Cooper MR & Welander CE (1986) Interferons in the treatment of multiple myeloma. *Seminars in Oncology* **13:** 334–340.

Crawford J, Eye MK & Cohen HJ (1987) Evaluation of monoclonal gammopathies in the 'well' elderly. *American Journal of Medicine* **82:** 39–45.

Cuzick J (1981) Radiation-induced myelomatosis. *New England Journal of Medicine* **304:** 204–210.

Cuzick J, Cooper EH & MacLennan ICM (1985) The prognostic value of serum β_2 microglobulin compared with other presentation features in myelomatosis. (A report to the Medical Research Council's Working Party on Leukaemia in Adults.) *British Journal of Cancer* **52:** 1–6.

Daffner RH, Lupetin AR, Dash N et al (1986) MRI in the detection of malignant infiltration of bone marrow. *American Journal of Roentgenology* **146:** 353–358.

Dalakas MC & Engel WK (1981) Polyneuropathy with monoclonal gammopathy: studies of 11 patients. *Annals of Neurology* **10:** 45–52.

Delaporte C, Varet B, Fardeau M, Nochy D & Ract A (1986) In vitro myotrophic effect of serum kappa chain immunoglobulins from a patient with kappa light chain myeloma and muscular hypertrophy. *Journal of Clinical Investigation* **78:** 922–927.

Dellagi K, Dupouey P, Brouet JC et al (1983) Waldenström's macroglobulinemia and peripheral neuropathy: a clinical and immunologic study of 25 patients. *Blood* **62:** 280–285.

Durie BGM (1986) Staging and kinetics of multiple myeloma. *Seminars in Oncology* **13:** 300–309.

Durie BGM & Salmon SE (1975) A clinical staging system for multiple myeloma: correlation of measured myeloma cell mass with presenting clinical features, response to treatment, and survival. *Cancer* **36:** 842–854.

Durie BGM, Salmon SE & Moon TE (1980) Pretreatment tumor mass, cell kinetics, and prognosis in multiple myeloma. *Blood* **55:** 364–372.

Durie BGM, Salmon SE & Mundy GR (1981) Relation of osteoclast activating factor production to extent of bone disease in multiple myeloma. *British Journal of Haematology* **47:** 21–30.

Durie BGM, Baum VE, Vela EE & Mundy GR (1986a) Abnormalities of chromosome 6q and osteoclast activating factor (OAF; TNF β) production in multiple myeloma. *Blood* **68**(supplement 1): 208a(abstract).

Durie BGM, Dixon DO, Carter S et al (1986b) Improved survival duration with combination chemotherapy induction for multiple myeloma: a Southwest Oncology Group study. *Journal of Clinical Oncology* **4:** 1227–1237.

Fefer A, Cheever MA & Greenberg PD (1986) Identical-twin (syngeneic) marrow transplantation for hematologic cancers. *Journal of the National Cancer Institute* **76:** 1269–1273.

Finan MC & Winkelmann RK (1986) Necrobiotic xanthogranuloma with paraproteinemia: a review of 22 cases. *Medicine (Baltimore)* **65:** 376–388.

Gahrton G, Ringdén O, Lönnqvist B, Lindquist R & Ljungman P (1986) Bone marrow transplantation in three patients with multiple myeloma. *Acta Medica Scandinavica* **219:** 523–527.

Gelfand JA, Boss GR, Conley CL, Reinhart R & Frank MM (1979) Acquired C1 esterase inhibitor deficiency and angioedema: a review. *Medicine (Baltimore)* **58:** 321–328.

Gomez GA & Krishnamsetty RM (1986) Successful treatment of meningeal myeloma with combination of radiation therapy, chemotherapy, and intrathecal therapy. *Archives of Internal Medicine* **146:** 194–196.

Greer JP, Pinson RD, Russell WG et al (1985) Malignant plasmacytic ascites: a report of two cases and a review of the literature. *Cancer* **56:** 2001–2004.

Greipp PR, Witzig TE, Gonchoroff NJ et al (1987) Immunofluorescence labeling indices (LI) in myeloma and related monoclonal gammopathies. *Mayo Clinic Proceedings* (in press).

Hall A, Proctor SJ & Harris AL (1986) Melphalan resistance in myeloma. *British Journal of*

Haematology **63:** 1–6.

Hällén J (1963) Frequency of 'abnormal' serum globulins (M-components) in the aged. *Acta Medica Scandinavica* **173:** 737–744.

Hällén J (1966) Discrete gammaglobulin (M-)components in serum: clinical study of 150 subjects without myelomatosis. *Acta Medica Scandinavica* **462**(supplement): 1–127.

Hamblin TJ (1986) The kidney in myeloma. *British Medical Journal (Clinical Research)* **292:** 2–3.

Heer M, Joller-Jemelka H, Fontana A et al (1984) Monoclonal gammopathy in chronic active hepatitis. *Liver* **4:** 255–263.

Hendrick AM, Mitchison HC, Bird AG & James OFW (1986) Paraproteins in primary biliary cirrhosis. *Quarterly Journal of Medicine* (July) **60:** 681–684.

Heriot K, Hallquist AE & Tomar RH (1985) Paraproteinemia in patients with acquired immunodeficiency syndrome (AIDS) or lymphadenopathy syndrome (LAS). *Clinical Chemistry* **31:** 1224–1226.

Hobbs JR, Carter PM, Cooke KB, Foster M & Oon C-J (1974) IgM paraproteins. *Journal of Clinical Pathology* **28**(supplement): 54–64.

Hurez D, Youinou P, Gombert J & Preud'Homme JL (1985) Survey of monoclonal gammopathy in western France: incidence and unexpected high frequency of IgM. *Immunology* **56:** 557–560.

James K, Fudenberg H, Epstein WL & Shuster J (1967) Studies on a unique diagnostic serum globulin in papular mucinosis (lichen myxedematosus). *Clinical and Experimental Immunology* **2:** 153–166.

Jansen J, Bolhuis RLH, van Nieuwkoop JA, Schuit HRE & Stenfert Kroese WF (1983) Paraproteinaemia plus osteolytic lesions in typical hairy-cell leukaemia. *British Journal of Haematology* **54:** 531–541.

Judson IR, Wiltshaw E & Newland AC (1985) Multiple myeloma in a pair of monozygotic twins: the first reported case. *British Journal of Haematology* **60:** 551–554.

Kebler R, Kithier K, McDonald FD & Cadnapaphornchai P (1985) Rapidly progressive glomerulonephritis and monoclonal gammopathy. *American Journal of Medicine* **78:** 133–138.

Kelly JJ Jr, Kyle RA, O'Brien PC & Dyck PJ (1981) Prevalence of monoclonal protein in peripheral neuropathy. *Neurology (New York)* **31:** 1480–1483.

Kiprov DD & Miller RG (1984) Polymyositis associated with monoclonal gammopathy. *Lancet* **ii:** 1183–1186.

Kyle RA (1975) Multiple myeloma: review of 869 cases. *Mayo Clinic Proceedings* **50:** 29–40.

Kyle RA (1984a) 'Benign' monoclonal gammopathy: a misnomer? *Journal of the American Medical Association* **251:** 1849–1854.

Kyle RA (1984b) Second malignancies associated with chemotherapy. In Perry MC & Yarbro JW (eds) *Toxicity of Chemotherapy*, pp 479–506. New York: Grune & Stratton.

Kyle RA (1986a) Benign paraproteinaemia. In Delamore IW (ed.) *Multiple Myeloma and Other Paraproteinaemias*, pp 171–192. Edinburgh: Churchill Livingstone.

Kyle RA (1986b) Classification and diagnosis of monoclonal gammopathies. In Rose NR, Friedman H & Fahey JL (eds) *Manual of Clinical Laboratory Immunology*, 3rd edn, pp 152–167. Washington, DC: American Society for Microbiology.

Kyle RA & Greipp PR (1980) Smoldering multiple myeloma. *New England Journal of Medicine* **302:** 1347–1349.

Kyle RA, Finkelstein S, Elveback LR & Kurland LT (1972) Incidence of monoclonal proteins in a Minnesota community with a cluster of multiple myeloma. *Blood* **40:** 719–724.

Kyle RA, Robinson RA & Katzmann JA (1981) The clinical aspects of biclonal gammopathies: review of 57 cases. *American Journal of Medicine* **71:** 999–1008.

Kyle RA, Schreiman JS, McLeod RA & Beabout JW (1985) Computed tomography in diagnosis and management of multiple myeloma and its variants. *Archives of Internal Medicine* **145:** 1451–1452.

Kyle RA, Greipp PR & Gertz MA (1986) Treatment of refractory multiple myeloma and considerations for future therapy. *Seminars in Oncology* **13:** 326–333.

Latov N, Sherman WH, Nemni R et al (1980) Plasma-cell dyscrasia and peripheral neuropathy with a monoclonal antibody to peripheral-nerve myelin. *New England Journal of Medicine* **303:** 618–621.

Lee BJ, Lake-Lewin D & Myers JE (1982) Intensive treatment of multiple myeloma. In Wiernik

PH (ed.) *Controversies in Oncology*, pp 61–79. New York: John Wiley & Sons.

Lieberman F, Marton LS & Stefansson K (1985) Pattern of reactivity of IgM from the sera of eight patients with IgM monoclonal gammopathy and neuropathy with components of neural tissues: evidence for interaction with more than one epitope. *Acta Neuropathologica (Berlin)* **68:** 196–200.

Löfdahl C-G, Sölvell L, Laurell A-B & Johansson BR (1979) Systemic capillary leak syndrome with monoclonal IgG and complement alterations: a case report on an episodic syndrome. *Acta Medica Scandinavica* **206:** 405–412.

Magrath I, Benjamin D & Papadopoulos N (1983) Serum monoclonal immunoglobulin bands in undifferentiated lymphomas of Burkitt and non-Burkitt types. *Blood* **61:** 726–731.

Maldonado JE & Kyle RA (1974) Familial myeloma: report of eight families and a study of serum proteins in their relatives. *American Journal of Medicine* **57:** 875–884.

Maldonado JE, Velosa JA, Kyle RA et al (1975) Fanconi syndrome in adults: a manifestation of a latent form of myeloma. *American Journal of Medicine* **58:** 354–364.

Matsuzaki H, Yamaguchi K, Kagimoto T et al (1985) Monoclonal gammopathies in adult T-cell leukemia. *Cancer* **56:** 1380–1383.

Merlini G, Farhangi M & Osserman EF (1986) Monoclonal immunoglobulins with antibody activity in myeloma, macroglobulinemia and related plasma cell dyscrasias. *Seminars in Oncology* **13:** 350–365.

Michaux J-L & Heremans JF (1969) Thirty cases of monoclonal immunoglobulin disorders other than myeloma or macroglobulinemia: a classification of diseases associated with the production of monoclonal-type immunoglobulins. *American Journal of Medicine* **46:** 562–579.

Migliore PJ & Alexanian R (1968) Monoclonal gammopathy in human neoplasia. *Cancer* **21:** 1127–1131.

Møller-Petersen J & Schmidt EB (1986) Diagnostic value of the concentration of M-component in initial classification of monoclonal gammopathy. *Scandinavian Journal of Haematology* **36:** 295–301.

Mundis RJ & Kyle RA (1982) Primary hyperparathyroidism and monoclonal gammopathy of undetermined significance. *American Journal of Clinical Pathology* **77:** 619–621.

Mundy GR & Bertolini DR (1986) Bone destruction and hypercalcemia in plasma cell myeloma. *Seminars in Oncology* **13:** 291–299.

Noel P & Kyle RA (1987) Monoclonal proteins in chronic lymphocytic leukemia. *American Journal of Clinical Pathology* **87:** 385–388.

Offit K, Macris NT & Finkbeiner JA (1986) Monoclonal hypergammaglobulinemia without malignant transformation in angioimmunoblastic lymphadenopathy with dysproteinemia. *American Journal of Medicine* **80:** 292–294.

Oken MM, Tsiatis A, Abramson N & Glick J (1984) Comparison of standard (MP) with intensive (VBMCP) therapy for the treatment of multiple myeloma (MM). *Proceedings of the Annual Meeting of the American Society of Clinical Oncology* **3:** 270(abstract).

Papadopoulos NM, Elin RJ & Wilson DM (1982) Incidence of γ-globulin banding in a healthy population by high-resolution electrophoresis. *Clinical Chemistry* **28:** 707–708.

Patten BM (1984) Neuropathy and motor neuron syndromes associated with plasma cell disease. *Acta Neurologica Scandinavica* **70:** 47–61.

Perri RT, Hebbel RP & Oken MM (1981) Influence of treatment and response status on infection risk in multiple myeloma. *American Journal of Medicine* **71:** 935–940.

Powell FC, Schroeter AL, Su WPD & Perry HO (1985) Pyoderma gangrenosum: a review of 86 patients. *Quarterly Journal of Medicine* **55:** 173–186.

Radl J, Valentijn RM, Haaijman JJ & Paul LC (1985) Monoclonal gammopathies in patients undergoing immunosuppressive treatment after renal transplantation. *Clinical Immunology and Immunopathology* **37:** 98–102.

Riddell S, Traczyk Z, Paraskevas F & Israels LG (1986) The double gammopathies: clinical and immunological studies. *Medicine (Baltimore)* **65:** 135–142.

Saleun JP, Vicariot M, Deroff P & Morin JF (1982) Monoclonal gammopathies in the adult population of Finistère, France. *Journal of Clinical Pathology* **35:** 63–68.

Salmon SE, Haut A, Bonnet JD et al (1983) Alternating combination chemotherapy and levamisole improves survival in multiple myeloma: a Southwest Oncology Group study. *Journal of Clinical Oncology* **1:** 453–461.

Schechter GP, Shoff N, Chan C & Hawley HP (1986) The frequency of asymptomatic mono- and biclonal gammopathy in hospitalized black and Caucasian veterans. *Blood* **68**(supplement 1): 214a(abstract).

Selby P, Ayliffe M, Behrens J & Mcelwain TJ (1985) High-dose treatment with melphalan and methylprednisolone for multiple-myeloma. *Abstracts of the Proceedings of the Symposium on Monoclonal Gammopathies: Clinical Significance and Basic Mechanisms*, 19–20 September, Brussels, Belgium.

Shaikh BS, Lombard RM, Appelbaum PC & Bentz MS (1982) Changing patterns of infections in patients with multiple myeloma. *Oncology* **39**: 78–82.

Shy ME, Rowland LP, Smith T et al (1986) Motor neuron disease and plasma cell dyscrasia. *Neurology* **36**: 1429–1436.

Simes RJ (1986) Publication bias: the case for an international registry of clinical trials. *Journal of Clinical Oncology* **4**: 1529–1541.

Sporn JR & McIntyre OR (1986) Chemotherapy of previously untreated multiple myeloma patients: an analysis of recent treatment results. *Seminars in Oncology* **13**: 318–325.

Sugai S, Shimizu S, Hirose Y et al (1985) Monoclonal gammopathies in Japanese patients with Sjögren's syndrome. *Journal of Clinical Immunology* **5**: 90–101.

Talerman A & Haije WG (1973) The frequency of M-components in sera of patients with solid malignant neoplasms. *British Journal of Cancer* **27**: 276–282.

Tubbs RR, Gephardt GN, McMahon JT et al (1981) Light chain nephropathy. *American Journal of Medicine* **71**: 263–269.

11

Bleeding and coagulation disorders in
the elderly

J. ADRIAN COPPLESTONE

Haemorrhage accounts directly for approximately 4% of all the deaths in the over 60 age group in England and Wales (OPCS, 1985). The major sites of fatal bleeding are intracranial, subarachnoid, rupture of aortic aneurysms and gastrointestinal (predominantly from peptic ulceration). The first three are all consequences of degenerative conditions of the blood vessel walls. Fatal bleeding due to defects in blood coagulation and platelets is rarer (1–2% of haemorrhagic deaths) but a haemorrhagic diathesis occurs in a wide variety of conditions and poses considerable clinical problems. It is this group of disorders which are discussed in this chapter.

The serious consequences of bleeding in the elderly have prompted studies to determine whether in old people there are major changes in the coagulation, fibrinolytic systems or platelets which would make bleeding or thrombosis more likely. In one study of 61 subjects aged 66–96 years, factors XI, XII and antithrombin III tended to increase in women and decrease in men, while factors X, VII, V and fibrinogen increased in both sexes. No changes were found in factor VIII levels, or fibrinolysis (as measured by euglobulin clot lysis time) (Hamilton et al, 1974a, b). The trends were small and variations in factor assays were considerable. Another study (Todd et al, 1973) found normal values in prothrombin times and fibrinogen in 87 subjects aged 50–80. Platelets are present in similar numbers as in young people (Hamilton et al, 1974b) and have a normal or slightly shortened lifespan (Sie et al, 1981). Minor changes with in vitro testing have been reviewed by Hyams (1985) but are clinically insignificant. Thus there are no major changes which occur with ageing; rather, particular bleeding problems arise in some diseases that are commoner in the older population.

The commonest form of bleeding is localized blood loss from the gastrointestinal, respiratory and urogenital tracts. This is often the presenting feature of underlying pathology, particularly carcinoma. The bulk of these patients will not have a haemostatic disorder, but some have unusual features or more generalized bleeding. This chapter outlines the clinical approach to the assessment of a possible bleeding diathesis. The disorders which can cause problems are divided into platelet, vascular, and coagulation abnormalities, reflecting the main physiological pathways of haemostasis. However, these are artificial divisions and many diseases cut across their boundaries.

CLINICAL APPROACH

History

The clinical history has major importance in determining the cause of bleeding and in assessment of the likelihood of bleeding occurring, giving vital clues to the aetiology of bleeding and also allowing interpretation of laboratory tests.

Bleeding due to reduced or defective platelets tends to be from mucosal membranes. Bleeding is immediate and prolonged. It results from oozing of blood from small vessels. Tiny pinpoint haemorrhages in the skin (petechiae) or larger purpuric spots appear, often on the ankles first in ambulant patients. In vascular diseases, petechiae and purpura appear but profuse bleeding is rare. Following injury, patients with defective coagulation may stop bleeding initially, but as the fibrin clot fails to form, bleeding recurs and may be prolonged. Bleeds into joints, muscles and deep tissues are characteristically seen when the defect is severe.

The age of onset of bleeding and the haemostatic response to previous trauma, operations and childbirth may give an indication of whether there has been a lifelong congenital defect or recently acquired diathesis. Whether the bleeding is spontaneous or related to trauma should also be noted.

The elderly may have multiple pathology, and as well as asking the patient about any other medical problems, it is usually helpful to question their other medical attendants and peruse their medical notes. Problems may arise not only from medical conditions such as liver disease or carcinoma, but also from the treatments, e.g. chemotherapy or radiotherapy. It is essential to determine the medication the patient is taking, including nonprescribed drugs or tablets borrowed from friends and relatives. In particular, aspirin and nonsteroidal anti-inflammatory drugs may compound bleeding problems through their platelet-inhibiting action.

A family history of a bleeding or clotting problem must be sought. Descendants are likely to be more helpful than antecedents, and negative response does not exclude a mild congenital deficiency.

Examination

Examination of the patient permits evaluation of skin bleeding—petechiae, purpura and bruising, subcutaneous haematomas, haemarthrosis or localized bleeding. Recurrent haemarthrosis will produce joint deformities and reduced mobility. The site of purpura is important—on the legs in thrombocytopenia, on the forearms in senile purpura, on the face in amyloid and on the extensor surfaces of legs, arms and buttocks in Henoch–Schönlein allergic purpura.

Purpura, bleeding gums and corkscrew hairs suggest scurvy. Telangiectasia of the mouth and fingers is seen in Osler's disease. Abnormal skin elasticity or joint hypermobility suggests a connective tissue disorder such as Erhler–Danlos syndrome.

Clinical signs may reveal underlying diseases which are associated with an acquired defect of haemostasis. Signs of chronic liver disease, abdominal masses due to carcinoma, splenomegaly and lymphadenopathy involved with lymphoma or leukaemia, skeletal tenderness and deformity arising from metastatic carcinoma or myeloma, and joint swelling of connective tissue disorders, may all suggest the cause of bleeding.

Investigation

The clinical diagnosis can be confirmed by further investigation which includes a full blood count including platelets, basic clotting tests, liver function and renal function tests; and, where indicated, immunoglobulin levels and electrophoresis, autoantibody screening, radiography and tissue biopsy are performed.

LABORATORY TESTS

Initially a series of simple tests are performed. The platelet count is commonly measured on automated blood counters and low values need to be checked on the blood film (Payne and Pierre, 1984), which will also reveal abnormalities in platelet morphology. The best overall test of platelet function is the skin bleeding time, which is increased by abnormal platelet function (often drug-induced) or connective tissue disorders (Lind, 1984; Hamblin, 1985). In the UK, the most commonly performed method uses a commercial template, the Simplate device (Poller et al, 1984).

The prothrombin time, now usually reported as the international normalized ratio (INR), tests the extrinsic coagulation pathway and is prolonged by reduced levels of factors VII, X, V, II and fibrinogen. The activated partial thromboplastin time (APTT) reflects changes in factors VIII, IX, X, XI, XII and defects of the contact phase. To a lesser extent it is prolonged by deficiencies in factors II, V and fibrinogen (Thomson and Poller, 1985). The thrombin time is prolonged by abnormalities in fibrinogen, raised fibrin degradation products (FDP), and the presence of heparin.

If prolonged clotting times are found, but can be corrected by the addition of normal plasma, a deficiency in coagulation factor(s) is present. If there is no correction, the presence of an inhibitor is inferred, as the immunoglobulin inactivates the clotting factor added.

The coagulation screening tests are best interpreted in the light of information from the history and examination of the patient. Where multiple defects are present, e.g. in liver disease, the abnormalities may be explained. A raised FDP level is helpful when diagnosing disseminated intravascular coagulation (DIC). Further specific factor assays may be necessary and can be measured by their clotting effect, antigen level, or other effects, e.g. by factor

Table 1. Platelet disorders causing bleeding in the elderly.

Thrombocytopenia
Decreased marrow production
 vitamin B_{12} or folate deficiency
 marrow infiltration by carcinoma or lymphoma
 leukaemia and myelodysplasia
 radiation and chemotherapy
 drugs, e.g. thiazides, chloramphenicol
 aplastic anaemia

Increased platelet destruction
 Immune mechanism
  autoimmune (ITP)
  disease-associated: collagen disorders, lymphoproliferative diseases
  drugs, e.g. *quinidine*
  infections
  acquired immunodeficiency syndrome (AIDS)
  post-transfusion purpura (PTP)
  heparin-associated thrombocytopenia (HIT)
 Nonimmune mechanism
  disseminated intravascular coagulation (DIC)
  massive transfusion and cardiopulmonary bypass

Increased platelet pooling
 splenomegaly and hypersplenism
 hypothermia

Abnormal Platelet Function
Drugs—nonsteroidal anti-inflammatory, dipyridamole, heparin, alcohol
Myeloproliferative disorders
Myelodysplastic syndromes
Dysproteinaemia
Renal failure
Liver disease
Cardiopulmonary bypass

VIII ristocetin cofactor assay. If thrombocytopenia is a problem, a marrow aspirate and trephine can provide information on platelet production. Platelet-associated immunoglobulins may also be helpful if immune destruction is possible. Platelet function can be assessed in vitro (Greaves and Preston, 1985).

PLATELET DISORDERS

Bleeding due to thrombocytopenia is unlikely to occur until the platelet count falls below $50 \times 10^9/l$ but is frequently not seen until after the count has fallen below $20 \times 10^9/l$. It may occur at higher counts if there is abnormal platelet function, a local lesion, or if there are other coagulation deficiencies. A classification of platelet disorders causing bleeding is shown in Table 1. There may be inadequate marrow production, excessive breakdown or increased pooling of platelets. Platelets may be present in normal numbers but fail to function correctly.

Decreased marrow production

This is one of the commonest causes of thrombocytopenia and is often associated with marrow infiltration by metastatic carcinoma or lymphoma. The marrow may be affected by myelodysplasia or acute or chronic leukaemias, which have a higher incidence in the elderly. Dietary deficiency of vitamin B_{12} or folate, or pernicious anaemia, causes megaloblastic haemopoiesis and results in pancytopenia. These conditions are associated with characteristic features in the blood count and film. Drugs may cause thrombocytopenia by a toxic effect on the megakaryocytes or by causing aplastic anaemia. The commonest agents causing thrombocytopenia are cytotoxic drugs and radiation treatment.

A bone marrow aspirate and trephine is helpful, revealing abnormal haemopoiesis or an infiltrate. In disorders of decreased production, megakaryocytes are decreased in number. If they are increased, this suggests excessive breakdown or increased peripheral pooling of platelets. When assessing hypocellularity, the trephine should be at least 15 mm, as pelvic marrow cellularity falls in old age and small areas of low cellularity are normal.

Treatment of thrombocytopenia is by platelet transfusion if the patient is bleeding. If the cause of severe thrombocytopenia cannot be treated the prognosis is poor, as patients will eventually become refractory to platelet transfusions, due to alloimmunization. Low-dose prednisolone (10 mg/day) and antifibrinolytic drugs such as tranexamic acid can be useful and reduce bleeding episodes in very thrombocytopenic patients.

Drug-related thrombocytopenia

Drugs can cause problems through a wide variety of mechanisms—by direct marrow toxic effect, by immunological effects or by affecting platelet function. The list of drugs implicated is enormous (Packham and Mustard, 1977; Aster, 1983; Rao and Walsh, 1983). Thrombocytopenia may be predictable following the use of chemotherapy or radiotherapy, or idiosyncratic.

The drugs which have been most frequently reported in the UK to the Committee of Safety of Medicines (CSM) as being associated with thrombocytopenia are shown in Table 2 (CSM, personal communication). The commonest reports are following the use of co-trimoxazole, phenylbutazone, a wide range of nonsteroidal anti-inflammatory drugs, cimetidine, sodium valproate, frusemide and thiazide diuretics. Acute alcohol intoxication has a direct effect on megakaryocytes, as well as through its chronic effects on the liver. In some cases, the drug effect is immune-mediated (quinine and quinidine) and in these situations the marrow will show normal or increased numbers of megakaryocytes. In all cases the suspected drug should be stopped. Thrombocytopenia will usually correct itself within 3 weeks.

Table 2. Drugs reported to the Committee on Safety of Medicines as associated with thrombocytopenia (1964–1986).

	No. of reports*			No. of reports*
Antibiotics			*Anticonvulsants*	
Co-trimoxazole	132		Sodium valproate	60
Rifampicin	27		Carbamazepine	24
Ampicillin	15			
Nalidixic acid	9		*Antacids*	
			Cimetidine	60
Nonsteroidal anti-inflammatory drugs			Ranitidine	21
Phenylbutazone	73			
Indomethacin	62		*Diuretics*	
Ibuprofen	56		Frusemide	41
Benoxaprofen	37		Cyclopenthiazide	20
Naproxen	34		Hydrochlorthiazide	17
Piroxicam	29		Bendrofluazide	11
Diclofenac	21			
Mefenamic acid	19		*Miscellaneous*	
Ketoprofen	19		Methyl dopa	21
Fenprofen	15		Oxprenolol	19
Flurbiprofen	10		Chlorpropamide	11
Fenpyrazone	10		Quinine	10
Fenbrufen	9		Quinidine	10
			Carbimazole	10
Other Antirheumatic drugs			Thioridazine	10
Gold compounds	31		Nitrazepam	10
D-Penicillamine	43			

* The number of reports refers to the frequency of reports where thrombocytopenia was the most important reaction and does not take account of the usage of each drug prescribed.

Increased platelet destruction

Immune thrombocytopenic purpura (ITP)

Immune thrombocytopenia is characterized by reduced platelet survival due to premature destruction by the reticuloendothelial system of autologous platelets coated with antiplatelet antibody. It is associated with a wide variety of autoimmune diseases—most often systemic lupus erythematosus (SLE) and rheumatoid arthritis—and lymphoproliferative diseases—chronic lymphocytic leukaemia and lymphoma. The application of many new assays which demonstrate increased levels of platelet-associated immunoglobulin (PAIg) and the introduction of high-dose intravenous immunoglobulin treatment have led to continuing interest in ITP (Kelton and Gibbons, 1982; McMillan, 1983a; Von dem Borne, 1984; Karpatkin, 1985). Although classically a disease of young women, ITP can affect both sexes and all ages. In one series of 62 adult patients, one-third were aged over 60 years (Difino et al, 1980).

Patients usually present with bruising and purpura but milder forms may be detected circumstantially. A careful drug history is essential and any drugs that are suspected of causing thrombocytopenia (see Table 2) stopped. Suspicion of underlying lymphoproliferative disorder or collagen disease arises if splenomegaly is present. Marrow examination typically shows normal or increased numbers of megakaryocytes. Increased levels of PAIg can be shown using one of a large number of tests which measure the immunoglobulin on whole or lysed washed platelets. Most use antihuman immunoglobulin antisera labelled with ^{125}I (LoBuglio et al, 1983), fluorescein (Von dem Borne, 1986) or enzymes such as immunoperoxidase (Hegde et al, 1985). PAIgG is elevated in 68–90%, and PAIgM in 49–79%. Platelet-associated complement is also found (Hegde et al, 1985; Kurata et al, 1985). The wider use of these assays has shown that raised PAIg does not necessarily mean that specific antiplatelet antibody is involved. Raised levels are found in conditions with circulating immune complexes: autoimmune diseases, AIDS, viral infections and drug-induced thrombocytopenia. Other nonimmune disorders include myeloma, acute leukaemia, myeloproliferative disease, myelodysplasia, carcinoma, liver disease, hypersplenism and septicaemia (Von dem Borne, 1984). While these tests provide a useful adjunct to diagnosis, the results need to be interpreted with caution.

Treatment

ITP can occur in an acute form following viral infection but this form is rare in the elderly. It is more usual for the disease to follow a chronic course with remissions and relapses. The initial management should be with prednisolone (1 mg/kg) (McVerry, 1985), which produces a response in approximately 70–75% of cases (Difino et al, 1980; Pizzuto and Ambriz, 1984; Jacobs et al, 1986). If after 3 weeks there has been no response, the steroids should be stopped, but responders should have the dosage gradually reduced over several months. Some patients require very small amounts of prednisolone (2–3 mg/day) to maintain a normal count. If the patient requires long-term steroid, it is important to use the lowest dose possible which will keep the platelet count above $50 \times 10^9/l$ and achieve haemostasis, rather than higher doses in an attempt to normalize the platelet count. Alternate day dosage will minimize long-term side effects.

Patients who do not respond to steroids or who require an unacceptably high maintenance dosage may respond to splenectomy. This produces remissions in 65–73% (Difino et al, 1980; Pizzuto and Ambriz, 1984) but older patients are less likely to respond (Difino et al, 1980). In this latter study, five of 11 nonresponders were found to have an accessory spleen. When present, its removal may be helpful.

More recently the use of high-dose intravenous monomeric IgG (IVIgG) has enabled some patients to remit without splenectomy (Newland et al, 1983). IVIgG can also be used to prepare for splenectomy those who have a short-lived response. In elderly patients with severe atherosclerotic disease, fatal thrombotic events have been associated with the use of IVIgG (Woodruff et al, 1986). This complication, and the cost of the infusion, suggest that its use will remain secondary to that of steroids.

Refractory ITP patients, who do not respond to treatment, can be difficult to manage and the main aim is to achieve adequate haemostasis (McVerry, 1985). Vinca alkaloids (Marmont and Damasio, 1971; Ahn et al, 1974) produce an increase in platelet count after 7–24 days but responses are transient and limited by neurotoxicity. Immunosuppressive drugs—cyclophosphamide or azathioprine—can be used in a steroid sparing role.

Danazol is an anabolic steroid which has been reported to produce some benefit (Ahn et al, 1983) and has an effect on macrophages (Schreiber et al, 1987). No measures are entirely satisfactory, and it is this group of patients that are at risk of dying from cerebral haemorrhage.

Heparin-induced thrombocytopenia (HIT)

Thrombocytopenia develops following heparin administration in approximately 5% of patients (review by Kelton, 1986). The frequency has fallen from the 30% initially reported (Bell et al, 1976), partly due to better study design, but also due to the increasing use of porcine intestinal heparin, which has a lower risk of causing thrombocytopenia. While the majority have only mild thrombocytopenia, the importance of the syndrome is that a few patients with HIT develop severe acute arterial or venous thrombotic complications, usually 8–11 days after starting treatment. In this group, platelets were found to have increased PAIgG and C3 (Cines et al, 1980), and an IgG was found which induced heparin-dependent thromboxane B2 synthesis, [^{14}C]serotonin release and platelet aggregation (Chong et al, 1982). Western blotting has shown that the IgG binds to platelet antigens in the presence of heparin (Lynch and Howe, 1985). The IgG also reacts to heparin bound to endothelial cells (Cines et al, 1987). The thrombosis and thrombocytopenia are due to massive intravascular platelet aggregation.

The diagnosis is partly by exclusion—repeating the platelet count, reviewing previous counts and considering other drugs and DIC. A heparin-dependent platelet-aggregating factor may be found in the patient's serum using platelet-rich plasma (Fratantoni et al, 1975) but can be difficult to demonstrate. Recently, a specific test using [^{14}C]serotonin release has been reported (Sheridan et al, 1986).

The treatment of HIT depends on the degree. The majority of cases have mild to moderate HIT and are less at risk of thrombotic complications. Heparin can be continued until oral anticoagulants are effective, and the platelet count should be carefully monitored. In severe cases heparin must be discontinued and oral anticoagulants started. Defibrinating agents may be needed for 2–3 days until coumarins become effective. Aspirin has a role as a platelet-aggregation inhibitor. Low molecular weight heparin has been used but it too can cause HIT (Roussi et al, 1984).

Post-transfusion purpura (PTP)

This is a syndrome characterized by the onset of severe thrombocytopenia 5–10 days after transfusion of blood or platelets. Although rare, PTP is increasingly being recognized and 150 cases have been reported up to 1986 (Mueller-Eckhardt, 1986). The majority of cases were female and many were aged 60–80 years. All have a history of exposure to platelet antigens through pregnancy or blood transfusion. Virtually all patients have PLA1/ZW^a-negative platelets and have an alloantibody anti-PLA1/ZW^a in their serum, often accompanied by HLA antibodies. The mechanism of destruction of autologous platelets remains obscure.

High-dose IVIg is the treatment of choice and produces a rapid response. Prior to IVIg, patients were treated with exchange transfusions or platelets which were often accompanied by severe adverse reactions (Mueller-Eckhardt, 1986).

Increased pooling of platelets

In splenomegaly there is increased splenic sequestration of platelets, and the peripheral blood count is $45–90 \times 10^9/l$ (Karpatkin, 1983). Bleeding is not usually a problem, as platelets can be mobilized during haemostatic stress.

During hypothermic episodes, platelets remain in the peripheral capillary bed, but the count returns to normal on rewarming.

Abnormal platelet function

Myeloproliferative disorders

Proliferative polycythaemia, essential thrombocythaemia, myelofibrosis and chronic myeloid leukaemia are associated with both bleeding and thrombotic events, despite an increase in platelets. A wide variety of platelet abnormalities have been reported and they do not correlate well with the risk of bleeding (Waddell et al, 1981; Rao and Walsh, 1983; Schafer, 1984). Abnormal platelet function may be helpful in distinguishing myeloproliferative from secondary reactivity thrombocytosis. The bleeding time does not help to distinguish those who are likely to haemorrhage. In a study of 38 patients, no correlation was found between bleeding and the extent of thrombocytosis (Kessler et al, 1982). Bleeding was twice as frequent in those aged over 59 years and occurred with anti-inflammatory drugs in 32% of episodes. In polycythaemia patients, treatment with aspirin and dipyridamole is associated with an increased risk of major gastrointestinal haemorrhage (Tartaglia et al, 1986).

Myelosuppressive treatment may improve the bleeding tendency (Schafer, 1984) and hydroxyurea, melphalan or busulphan can be used (de Pauw et al, 1985; Van de Pette et al, 1986). In an old, noncompliant patient, ^{32}P may be useful, despite the increased risk of acute leukaemia (Landlaw, 1986).

Myelodysplastic syndrome (MDS)

Thrombocytopenia is common in MDS, but in addition many patients have abnormal platelet function (Rasi and Lintula, 1986). The most common finding is impaired or absent aggregation by adrenaline or collagen. Bleeding can be troublesome in these patients, requiring platelet transfusions, to which they eventually become refractory.

Drugs

Platelet function can be modified by a wide variety of drugs (Packham and Mustard, 1977). The commonest inhibitory drugs are aspirin and nonsteroidal anti-inflammatory drugs such as indomethacin, phenylbutazone and sulfinpyrazone. Other drugs that adversely affect platelet function are: clofibrate, propranolol, cyproheptadine, high doses of penicillin and cephalosporins especially in the renal failure, frusemide, membrane-active drugs such as amitryptyline and anaesthetics, and some prostaglandins of which the best example is prostacyclin.

Drug-related abnormal platelet function rarely causes bleeding but may commonly exacerbate localized bleeding or other haemostatic defects.

Uraemia

Bleeding complicates uraemia and the bleeding time is often prolonged. Abnormalities of platelet aggregation have been reported (Carvalho, 1983; Weiss, 1983). The prolonged bleeding time may be shortened by cryoprecipitate (Janson et al, 1980) or DDAVP (Mannucci et al, 1983). Haemostasis may also be improved by dialysis (Di Minno et al, 1985).

Cardiopulmonary bypass

Cardiopulmonary bypass has enabled many patients to have heart surgery, but bleeding is a problem requiring approximately 3% of patients to have re-exploration of the chest (Salzman et al, 1986). In Salzman's series, 60% of the patients were aged over 60 years. Bleeding is usually due to defective platelet function and thrombocytopenia. Other less important factors are reduction in coagulation factors, heparin and protamine dosage, abnormal factor polymerization and increased FDPs and fibrinolysis (Bick, 1985; Mammen et al, 1985; Harker, 1986). Patients who have abnormal bleeding after bypass can be treated with platelet transfusions (Bick, 1985) or DDAVP (Salzman et al, 1986).

VASCULAR DISORDERS

In this group of disorders the initial screening tests are normal. They have been reviewed by Forbes and Prentice (1981).

Senile purpura

Purpura appears on the exterior surfaces of forearms and hands, and gradually fades over 1–3 weeks, often leaving a brown stain. It arises due to alterations in collagen which allow small vessels to rupture with minor trauma. No correlation with ascorbic acid deficiency has been noted (Banerjee and Etherington, 1973; Hyams, 1985) but a reduction in serum zinc has been reported (Haboubi et al, 1985). Similar purpura is seen in patients taking long-term corticosteroids.

Scurvy

Vitamin C deficiency is associated with purpura and more widespread bleeding, including mucosal surfaces and periosteum. It is due to abnormal collagen synthesis and there is also abnormal platelet function (Hyams, 1985). It is an uncommon disease in the western world and is associated with malnutrition, food faddism and alcoholism.

Hereditary haemorrhagic telangiectasia

Originally described by Osler, this autosomal dominant-inherited disease causes telangiectatic lesions in skin and mucous membranes. They are multiple and tend to bleed, leading to chronic iron deficiency. The number of lesions increases with age. Treatment of bleeding is by local pressure, and cautery, especially in the nose, but gastrointestinal bleeding can be troublesome. Patients may require lifelong iron therapy and even transfusion support. Tranexamic acid may sometimes help.

Amyloidosis

Amyloidosis may complicate paraproteinaemia or may follow chronic infections or collagen disorders. Amyloid deposits in the skin lead to an increase in vascular fragility. Purpura is common and occurs after minor trauma. Periorbital purpura may follow coughing or straining. In rare cases, adsorption of factor X by the amyloid causes factor X deficiency (Greipp et al, 1981).

COAGULATION DISORDERS

Congenital deficiencies

Haemophilia

Congenital coagulation deficiencies are usually associated with the younger age groups, and because afflicted patients die prematurely of haemorrhage these deficiencies have not usually been thought to be a problem in old age. In fact, one-tenth of the UK's 5931 registered haemophiliacs (factor VIII and IX) are aged over 60 years (570 cases). Treatment with factor concentrates has increased life expectancy to near normal (Larsson, 1985; Rizza and Spooner, 1985). Whether this progress will be maintained with the emergence of AIDS in haemophiliacs (Jones et al, 1985) remains to be seen.

The elderly haemophiliac, although suffering less frequent haemarthroses, usually has severe arthritic damage which requires analgesics, and may need artificial joint replacement. He is also prone to the ordinary diseases of

Table 3. Case illustrative of the problems arising in an elderly haemophiliac.

FD Male born 2.10.05
Haemophilia diagnosed as child (Factor VIII: 4 iu/dl)
        Bleeding   4 weeks post dental extraction
                       13 weeks post tonsillectomy
        Infrequent haemarthroses
1975 *Diabetes mellitus* (DM)—controlled by diet, later oral hypoglycaemics.
1975 *Recurrent iron-deficiency anaemia* due to gastrointestinal (GI) bleeding from unknown site.
1978 *Transurethral resection of prostate*. Bled for 3 weeks despite factor VIII cover.
1980 Recurrent GI bleeding requiring red cell transfusion. Colonoscopy reveals *angiodysplasia*
        of colon and polyps.
1984 DM required insulin.
        GI bleeding required regular transfusion.
        Hepatitis B surface and *e antigen* positive and *human immunodeficiency virus antibody*
        positive due to infection from factor VIII concentrates.
        Ba enema reveals *constricting carcinoma of sigmoid colon*.
        Resection complicated by secondary haemorrhage and breakdown of anastamosis. Factor
        VIII support needed for 4 weeks.
1985 Further transfusions for GI bleeding.
        Pulmonary metastases developed.
        Died aged 79 years.

---

advancing years. An illustrative case showing some of the problems encountered is shown in Table 3. The mainstay of treatment for the severe haemophiliac remains heat-treated factor VIII or IX. Desamino-8-D-arginyl-vasopressin (DDAVP) can be used with antifibrinolytics for minor operations in milder VIII-deficient patients (Editorial, 1983), who may occasionally be diagnosed late in life following an abnormal preoperative clotting test.

Von Willebrand's disease

The incidence of Von Willebrand's disease (VWD) is not well-established and may amount to half that of haemophilia (Tuddenham, 1984). By postal questionnaire, the incidence of severe VWD was estimated as 1.38 (USA)–1.51 (Europe) per million population (Weiss et al, 1982), of which 48/1077 were aged over 65 years. The clinical features are abnormal bruising and mucous membrane bleeding from nose, mouth and gastrointestinal tract. The bleeding time is prolonged and factor VIIIC, Von Willebrand's factor (VWF) Ag and VIII Ristocetin cofactor assays are reduced. The VWD can be classified into subtypes based on molecular size, distribution and function of the plasma VWF (Tuddenham, 1984; Holmberg and Wilsson, 1985). Some patients have been found to have abnormal platelets that avidly absorb VWF. This defect has been termed pseudo Von Willebrands disease (Weiss et al, 1982).

Cryoprecipitate has mainly been used to replace VWF. More recently, DDAVP has been introduced (Mannucci et al, 1977; Editorial, 1983) and found to produce a 2–4 fold rise in factor VIII and shortening of the bleeding time (Kobrinsky et al, 1984). Its use is contraindicated in type IIB VWD and pseudo VWD, as DDAVP causes platelet aggregation and thrombocytopenia (Holmberg et al, 1983). With limited cardiovascular reserve in the elderly, the lower dose of 0.3 μg/kg is recommended, with patients being carefully monitored for the hypertensive and fluid-retaining side effects of DDAVP. Repeated doses may have less effect. Antifibrinolytic drugs such as tranexamic acid should also be given concurrently with the DDAVP.

Acquired coagulation disorders

Anticoagulants

Heparin. This is used widely for treatment of thromboembolism and in lower doses for prevention. Bleeding is an important complication (Loeliger et al, 1984; Levine and Hirsh, 1986). It is more likely to occur with intermittent intravenous injection (9–33%) than following continuous infusion (0–5%). Haemorrhage is more likely in patients who have had recent surgery, and the risk may be increased in elderly women. In general, monitoring the effect of heparin has not predicted haemorrhage, but those who bleed do have more abnormal assays (Holm et al, 1985). Nevertheless, routine monitoring using the APTT (ratio 1.5–2.5) is recommended. When serious bleeding occurs, heparin can be neutralized by protamine sulphate. Low-dose subcutaneous heparin (in doses 5000–9000 units 12 hourly) has a very small haemorrhagic risk.

Oral anticoagulants. Much has been done to improve the laboratory control of oral anticoagulant therapy (Shinton, 1983; Poller, 1985) and there has been greater interest in therapeutic quality control (Loeliger, 1985). The risk of bleeding increases with the increasing intensity of anticoagulation (Loeliger et al, 1984). The elderly are likely to be on other medication, increasing the risk of drug interactions with warfarin. A large number of drugs are known to interact with coumarin anticoagulants (Standing Advisory Committee, 1982).

The commonest causes of bleeding are the addition of antibiotics (often co-trimoxazole), increased consumption of alcohol, or the use of aspirin and nonsteroidal anti-inflammatory drugs. The aged are more prone to be confused by frequent changes or complex drug schedules. The regime needs to be simple and written down. Should bleeding occur, the INR should be checked, and if it is over 4.0 fresh frozen plasma (FFP) will immediately correct the defects. Further FFP may need to be given the next day. Vitamin K may be given but takes at least 6 h to be effective. Where anticoagulation is to be continued, small doses of vitamin K (1–5 mg) should be used. Bleeding may arise from an underlying pathology, even if the INR is in the therapeutic range.

Liver disease

The liver is the site of synthesis of the majority of the coagulation proteins: fibrinogen, factors II, V, VII, IX, X, XI, XII, XIII, plasminogen, antithrombin III and $\alpha 2$ antiplasmin. It is also responsible for clearing activated coagulation factors and plasminogen activator (Prentice, 1985). Vitamin K-dependent γ-carboxylation of certain glutamic acid residues in factors II, VII,

IX, X and protein C completes the synthesis of these factors, which remain inactive without carboxylation. Vitamin K is a fat-soluble vitamin and its absorption is reduced in obstructive liver disease. The short half-life of the clotting factors means that failure to synthesize them in acute liver disease may result in a prolonged prothrombin time while other biochemical tests of liver function are still normal (Chisholm, 1985). In severe disease the fibrinogen level falls and the thrombin time will be abnormal. Abnormal fibrinogen with increased sialic acid content and abnormal fibrin polymerization has been reported (Francis and Armstrong, 1982) and may be associated with hepatocellular regeneration. Raised levels of FDPs also affect fibrin polymerization. Low-grade DIC may be present due to activated clotting factors triggering DIC, or slow clearance of fibrinolytic enzymes resulting in excessive fibrinolysis, but is rarely of clinical significance. Thrombocytopenia is commonly present due to splenomegaly or DIC. Although very low levels are not usually present, they may have abnormal function and aggravate bleeding from oesophageal varices and peptic ulceration.

In asymptomatic patients, no treatment may be necessary, but vitamin K parenterally will help if there is an element of biliary obstruction. For patients needing surgery or biopsy, correction with fresh frozen plasma, or, if fluid overload is a problem, with prothrombin complex concentrates (PCC) will be needed. Because of reports of thrombotic complications and transmission of hepatitis and other viruses, PCC are rarely used (Chisholm, 1985). It is possible that heat treatment may make them safer. The bleeding time can be helpful in assessing the significance of thrombocytopenia. Significant prolongation requires cancellation of the procedure or transfusion with prophylactic platelet concentrates.

Bleeding in patients with liver disease is usually from the gastrointestinal tract—oesophageal varices, duodenal ulcer or gastric erosions. Energetic correction of coagulation defects with FFP (and possibly PCC) and platelets is needed. The haemostatic problems may be compounded by the additional burden of massive blood transfusion and DIC.

Disseminated intravascular coagulation

Disseminated intravascular coagulation (DIC) is a syndrome characterized by pathological intravascular activation of the clotting factors and platelets, excessive fibrinolysis and eventual depletion of fibrinogen and platelets. It may be acute, overwhelming, and result in total defibrination with extensive bleeding and shock; or more commonly, it is mild with a slow depletion of coagulation factors. Microthrombosis in small vessels causes organ dysfunction in the kidneys, brain, heart and adrenals. It also causes red cell fragmentation and intravascular haemolysis.

The causes of DIC are numerous and are shown in Table 4. In newly presenting patients the commonest cause is metastatic carcinoma. DIC may complicate septicaemia, particularly meningococcal meningitis. It is commonly present during dissection or rupture of aortic aneurysms. Any cause of shock can produce DIC, especially following major trauma. Diagnosis can usually be made rapidly with initial tests showing thrombocytopenia,

Table 4. Main causes of DIC in the elderly.

Infections	Septicaemia—Gram-negative bacilli, meningococcus
	Infections—protozoa, viruses, rickettsiae
Malignancy	Acute leukaemia—AML M3, M4, M5
	Carcinoma—breast, prostate, lung, pancreas, stomach
	Lymphoma
Surgery	Major trauma
	Cardiopulmonary bypass
	Aortic aneurysm
Liver disease	(Often difficult to distinguish whether DIC present)
Miscellaneous	Chronic renal failure
	Diabetic ketoacidosis
	Collagen vascular diseases
	Heat stroke
	Burns
	Incompatible blood transfusion
	Snakebite (vipers, rattlesnakes and adders)

fragmented red cells on the blood film, prolonged INR, APTT and thrombin time, reduced fibrinogen and raised FDPs (Donati, 1980). In one study of 346 patients with DIC, the most useful tests were the FDP, fibrin monomer and antithrombin III (ATIII) levels (Spero et al, 1980). There was an overall mortality of 68%.

Treatment involves: supporting the patient with fluid replacement; maintaining oxygenation and renal output; identifying and dealing with underlying cause of the DIC; and replacing depleted clotting factors and platelets. FFP will replace all coagulation factors, but if severe hypofibrinogenaemia is present, cryoprecipitate is a useful adjunct. The use of heparin is controversial (Prentice, 1985) and perhaps its role is when replacement alone has failed. Heparin will be ineffective in the presence of low ATIII levels and it is possible that in the future patients will be given infusions of ATIII–heparin complex and antiplatelet agents.

Systemic fibrinolysis

On rare occasions, defibrination can be due to excessive fibrinolysis caused by increased release of plasminogen activator (PA). Bleeding is present at sites of trauma, wounds and venepuncture, and later progresses to become widespread. The prostate gland contains large quantities of PA and hyperplasminaemia may follow prostatic or pelvic surgery. Some tumours, especially carcinoma of the prostate, may release PA. Therapeutic fibrinolysis with streptokinase, urokinase and recombinant tissue plasminogen activator may cause bleeding in 45% and fatal bleeding in 1–3% (Verstraete and Collen, 1986) and at present is usually restricted to younger patients.

The distinction from DIC is difficult but important. In both, fibrinogen is low and FDPs raised. In excessive fibrinolysis, the platelet count is normal and euglobulin clot lysis time is shortened. Treatment with an inhibitor of fibrinolysis, such as tranexamic acid, is indicated, whereas in DIC, fibrinolytic inhibitors can exacerbate organ dysfunction by causing microvascular thrombi.

Circulating anticoagulants

Circulating anticoagulants are autoantibodies that are directed against specific coagulation factors. There have been several recent reviews of these rare syndromes (Shapiro, 1979; Furie, 1983; Hougie, 1985; Prentice, 1985).

Factor VIII inhibitors. Acquired factor VIII inhibitors in patients not previously transfused are associated with autoimmune disease (SLE, rheumatoid arthritis, pemphigus, ulcerative colitis), penicillin sensitivity and paraproteinaemias. However, half the patients have no associated disease and these patients are usually elderly females (Editorial, 1981; Green and Lechner, 1981). Severe cases usually present with spontaneous bleeding, especially into joints and muscles. The APTT is prolonged and does not connect with normal plasma. The factor VIII clotting activity is very low and the specific factor VIII inhibitor can be titred.

Most inhibitors are IgG. The clinical course is variable and treatment should aim to prevent haemorrhage. Acute bleeding episodes can be treated with high doses of factor VIII concentrates, porcine factor VIII, and activated factor IX products (FEIBA and Autoplex). It may be possible to reduce the inhibitor titre by plasma exchange or immunosuppression (azathiaprine/cyclophosphamide and steroids). Suppression of the inhibitor after high-dose IVIg has been reported in two patients (Sultan et al, 1984).

Other inhibitors. Other patients have had inhibitors reported to von Willebrand factor, factor V, factor IX and factor XIII. These cases are rare and are discussed in more detail by Furie (1983) and Hougie (1985).

The lupus anticoagulant (LA). This was first described in a patient with SLE (Conley and Hartmann, 1952), and is an IgG or IgM antibody thought to be directed against phospholipid in the prothrombin activation complex (Exner et al, 1975). The LA may well have more than one site of action (Hougie, 1985). As well as showing inhibition effects in the APTT, the LA shows increased activity as the concentration of thromboplastin is reduced (Schleider et al, 1976). Another more sensitive test is the kaolin clotting time (Exner, 1985).

The LA is commonly found when a preoperative clotting screening shows a long APTT (Hougie, 1985). It is not associated with excessive bleeding, even with major surgery, unless it is accompanied by thrombocytopenia or a second inhibitor. Its presence is more often associated with thrombotic complications (Mueh et al, 1980; Elias and Eldor, 1984).

Paraproteinaemias

Paraproteins can affect haemostasis by several mechanisms which are shown in Table 5 and have been reviewed by Brozovic (1981). In one series (Perkins et

Table 5. Bleeding disorders in paraproteinaemia.

Platelet defects	Thrombocytopenia
	Abnormal function due to coating of platelet by paraprotein
Coagulation factor defects	Abnormal fibrin monomer polymerization
	Specific coagulation inhibitors: VIII, VWF, XI, XII
	Low factors due to adsorption to paraprotein: VIII (IgA), VII (IgG), II, V and X
	Heparin-like activity
Amyloidosis	Vascular purpura
	Factor X (and IX) deficiency

al, 1970) bleeding occurred in 15% of patients with IgG myeloma, in 38% of patients with IgA myeloma, and in 60% with Waldenstrom macroglobulinaemia. Where the paraprotein is having a blocking effect, plasma exchange can be expected to help. When a heparin-like proteoglycan is present (Khorry et al, 1980; Palmer et al, 1984), protamine sulphate may help. Bleeding may be difficult to control in amyloidosis where amyloid factors bind factor X and to a lesser extent factors IX and II (Furie et al, 1981; Greipp et al, 1981). Splenectomy may be helpful (Rosentein et al, 1983). Plasma exchange is unsuccessful (Copplestone et al, 1984).

SUMMARY

Ageing does not bring with it any major changes in the coagulation or fibrinolytic proteins or platelets. It does bring a greater burden of disease, with less reserves, and so when haemorrhage occurs in the elderly it has more serious consequences.

The cause of a bleeding diathesis can usually be determined after a careful history, and examination of the patient followed by simple tests—the platelet count, blood film, bleeding time, prothrombin time, partial thromboplastin time, thrombin time, fibrin degradation products and the euglobulin clot lysis time. Other confirmatory tests, assays and inhibitor titres, will seal the diagnosis.

Treatment is mainly directed at removing the underlying cause, if possible, and remedying the defect, with platelet transfusion, fresh frozen plasma or factor concentrates. These treatments will not be effective where there is an inhibitor or antibody present; steroids, splenectomy (for ITP), plasma exchange or immunosuppression are needed. Two major advances have occurred in the early 1980s. One has been the introduction of high-dose intravenous immunoglobulin in the management of ITP, although worries remain about thrombotic events in elderly patients. The other is the spreading use of DDAVP, originally introduced for von Willebrand's disease and mild haemophilia, and now finding a role in uraemia and with cardiopulmonary bypass.

Drugs are a significant and potentially preventable cause of bleeding in the elderly. The most frequent problems arise with anticoagulants. The risk of interactions increase with the number of other medications which are prescribed.

Acknowledgements

I would like to thank Dr G. Burton and the Committee on Safety of Medicines for providing the information for Table 2, Drs M. Chisholm and R. Hyde for helpful comment, and Miss J. Nesbitt for typing the manuscript.

REFERENCES

Ahn YS, Harrington WJ, Seelman RC & Eytel CS (1974) Vincristine therapy of idiopathic and secondary thrombocytopenias. *New England Journal of Medicine* 291: 376–380.

Anh YS, Harrington WJ, Simon SR et al (1983) Danazol for the treatment of idiopathic thrombocytopenic purpura. *New England Journal of Medicine* 308: 1396–1399.

Aster RH (1983) Thrombocytopenia due to enhanced platelet destruction. In Williams WJ, Beutler E, Erslev AJ & Lichtman MA, (eds) *Hematology*, 3rd edn, pp 1313–1314. New York: McGraw Hill.

Banerjee AK & Etherington M (1973) Senile purpura and platelets. *Gerontologica Clinica* 15: 213–220.

Bell WR, Tomasulo PA, Alving BM & Duffy TP (1976) Thrombocytopenia occurring during the administration of heparin. A prospective study in 52 patients. *Annals of Internal Medicine* 85: 155–160.

Bick RL (1985) Hemostasis defects associated with cardiac surgery, prosthetic devices and other extracorporeal circuits. *Seminars in Thrombosis and Hemostasis* 11: 249–280.

Boey MI, Colaco CB, Gharavi AE et al (1983) Thrombosis in system lupus erythematosus: striking association with the presence of circulating lupus anticoagulant. *British Medical Journal* 287: 1021–1023.

Brozovic M (1981) Acquired disorders of blood coagulation. In Bloom AL & Thomas DP (eds) *Haemostasis and Thrombosis*, pp 411–438. Edinburgh: Churchill Livingstone.

Carvalho ACA (1983) Bleeding in uraemia—a clinical challenge. *New England Journal of Medicine* 308: 38–39.

Chisholm M (1985) Haematological disorders in liver disease. In Wright R, Millward-Sadler GH, Albert KGMM & Karran S (eds) *Liver and Biliary Disease*, 2nd edn, pp 203–214. London: Baillière Tindall.

Chong BH, Pitney WR & Castaldi PA (1982) Heparin-induced thrombocytopenia: association of thrombotic complications with heparin-dependent IgG antibody that induces thromboxane synthesis and platelet aggregation. *Lancet* ii: 1246–1248.

Cines DB, Kaywin P, Bina M et al (1980) Heparin associated thrombocytopenia. *New England Journal of Medicine* 303: 788–795.

Cines DB, Tomaski A & Tannenbaum S (1987) Immune endothelial-cell injury in heparin-associated thrombocytopenia. *New England Journal of Medicine* 316: 581–589.

Conley L & Hartmann R (1952) A haemorrhagic disorder caused by circulating anticoagulant in patients with disseminated lupus erythematosus. *Journal of Clinical Investigation* 31: 621–622.

Copplestone JA, van der Star RJ, Chilsholm DM & Hamblin TJ (1984) Factor X deficiency in primary amyloidosis: treatment by plasmapheresis. *Apheresis Bulletin* 2: 60–63.

de Pauw BE, van Bergen ANL, Haanen C & Steenbergen J (1985) Intermittent melphalan in the treatment of essential thrombocytosis with haemorrhage or thrombosis. *Scandinavian Journal of Haematology* 35: 448–450.

Difino SM, Lachant NA, Kirshner JJ & Gottlieb AJ (1980) Adult idiopathic thrombocytopenic purpura. Clinical findings and response to therapy. *American Journal of Medicine* **69**: 430–442.

Di Minno G, Martinez J, McKean ML et al (1985) Platelet dysfunction in leukaemia. Multifaceted defect partially corrected by dialysis. *American Journal of Medicine* **79**: 552–559.

Donati MD (1980) Acquired defects of haemostasis. In Thompson JM (ed.) *Blood Coagulation and Haemostasis*, 2nd edn, pp 159–199. Edinburgh: Churchill Livingstone.

Editorial (1981) Acquired haemophilia. *Lancet* **i**: 255.

Editorial (1983) DDAVP in haemophilia and von Willebrand's disease. *Lancet* **ii**: 774–775.

Editorial (1984) Lupus anticoagulant. *Lancet* **i**: 1157–1158.

Elias M & Eldor A (1984) Thromboembolism in patients with the 'lupus'-type circulating anticoagulant. *Archives of Internal Medicine* **144**: 510–515.

Exner T (1985) Comparison of two simple tests of the lupus anticoagulant. *American Journal of Clinical Pathology* **83**: 215–218.

Exner T, Rickard A & Kronenberg H (1975) Studies on phospholipids in the action of a lupus coagulation inhibitor. *Pathology* **7**: 319–323.

Forbes CD & Prentice CRM (1981) Vascular and thrombocytopenic purpuras. In Bloom AL & Thomas PP (eds) *Haemostasis and Thrombosis*, pp 268–278. Edinburgh: Churchill Livingstone.

Francis JL & Armstrong DJ (1982) Acquired dysfibrinogenaemia in liver disease. *Journal of Clinical Pathology* **35**: 667–672.

Frantantoni JC, Pollet R & Gralnick HR (1975) Heparin-induced thrombocytopenia: confirmation of diagnosis with in vitro methods. *Blood* **45**: 395.

Furie B (1983) Acquired anticoagulants. In Williams WJ, Beutler E, Erslev AJ & Lichtman MA (eds) *Hematology*, 3rd edn, pp 1424–1432. New York: McGraw Hill.

Furie B, Voo L, McAdam KP et al (1981) Mechanism of factor X deficiency in systemic amyloidosis. *New England Journal of Medicine* **304**: 827–830.

Greaves M & Preston FE (1985) The laboratory investigation of acquired and congenital platelet disorders. In Thomson JM (ed.) *Blood Coagulation and Haemostasis. A Practical Guide*, 3rd edn. Edinburgh: Churchill Livingstone.

Green D & Lechner K (1981) A survey of 215 non-hemophilic patients with inhibitors to factor VIII. *Thrombosis and Haemostasis* **45**: 200–203.

Greipp PR, Kyle RA & Bowie EJW (1981) Factor X deficiency in amyloidosis. A critical review. *American Journal of Haematology* **11**: 443–450.

Haboubi NY, Haboubi NAA, Gyde O, Small NA & Barford AV (1985) Zinc deficiency in senile purpura. *Journal of Clinical Pathology* **38**: 1189–1191.

Hamblin TJ (1985) What about the bleeding time? *British Medical Journal* **291**: 91.

Hamilton PJ, Dawson AA, Ogston D & Douglas AS (1974a) The effect of age on the fibrinolytic enzyme system. *Journal of Clinical Pathology* **27**: 326–329.

Hamilton PJ, Allardyce M, Ogston D, Dawson AA & Douglas AS (1974b) The effect of age upon the coagulation system. *Journal of Clinical Pathology* **27**: 980–982.

Harker LA (1986) Bleeding after cardiopulmonary bypass. *New England Journal of Medicine* **314**: 1446–1448.

Hegde UM, Bowes A & Roter BLT (1985) Platelet associated complement components (PAC$_{3c}$ and PAC$_{3d}$) in patients with autoimmune thrombocytopenia. *British Journal of Haematology* **60**: 49–55.

Holm HA, Abilgaard U & Kalvenes S (1985) Heparin assays and bleeding complications in treatment of deep venous thrombosis with particular reference to retroperitoneal bleeding. *Thrombosis and Haemostasis* **53**: 278–281.

Holmberg L & Wilsson IM (1985) Von Willebrand disease. *Clinics in Haematology* **14**: 461–488.

Holmberg L, Nilsson IM, Borge L, Gunnason M & Sjorin E (1983) Platelet aggregation induced by 1-desamino-8-D-arginine vasopressin (DDAVP) in type 11B von Willebrand's disease. *New England Journal of Medicine* **309**: 816–821.

Hougie C (1985) Circulating anticoagulants. In Poller L (ed.) *Recent Advances in Blood Coagulation*, vol. 4. Edinburgh: Churchill Livingstone.

Hyams DE (1985) The blood. In Brocklehurst JC (ed.) *Textbook of Geriatric Medicine and Gerontology*, pp 879–898. Edinburgh: Churchill Livingstone.

Jacobs P, Wood L & Dent DM (1986) Results of treatment in immune thrombocytopenia. *Quarterly Journal of Medicine* **58:** 153–165.

Janson PA, Jubelirer SJ, Weinstein MJ & Deykin D (1980) Treatment of the bleeding tendency in uraemia with cryoprecipitate. *New England Journal of Medicine* **303:** 1318–1322.

Jones P, Hamilton PJ, Bird G et al (1985) AIDS and haemophilia: morbidity and mortality in a well defined population. *British Medical Journal* **291:** 695–699.

Karpatkin S (1983) The spleen and thrombocytopenia. *Clinics in Haematology* **12:** 591–604.

Karpatkin S (1985) Autoimmune thrombocytopenic purpura. *Seminars in Haematology* **22:** 260–288.

Kelton JG & Gibbons S (1982) Autoimmune platelet destruction: Idiopathic thrombocytopenic purpura. *Seminars in Thrombosis and Haemostasis* **8:** 83–103.

Kelton JG (1986) Heparin-induced thrombocytopenia. *Haemostasis* **16:** 173–186.

Kessler CM, Klein HG & Havlik RJ (1982) Uncontrolled thrombocytosis in chronic myeloproliferative disorders. *British Journal of Haematology* **50:** 157–167.

Khorry MS, Nesheim ME, Bowie EJW & Mann MG (1980) Circulating heparin sulphate proteoglycan anticoagulant from a patient with plasma cell disorder. *Journal of Clinical Investigation* **65:** 666–674.

Kobrinsky NL, Israels ED, Gerrard JM et al (1984) Shortening of bleeding time by 1-deamino-8-D-arginine vasopressin in various bleeding disorders. *Lancet* **1:** 1145–1148.

Kurata Y, Curd JG, Tamerius JD & McMillan R (1985) Platelet-associated complement in chronic ITP. *British Journal of Haematology* **60:** 723–733.

Landlaw SA (1986) Acute leukaemia in polycythaemia vera. *Seminars in Haematology* **23:** 156–165.

Larsson SA (1985) Life expectancy of Swedish haemophiliacs, 1831–1980. *British Journal of Haematology* **59:** 593–602.

Levine MN & Hirsh J (1986) Haemorrhagic complications of anticoagulant therapy. *Seminars in Thrombosis and Hemostasis* **12:** 39–57.

Lind SE (1984) Prolonged bleeding time. *American Journal of Medicine* **77:** 305–312.

LoBuglio AF, Court WS, Vinocur L, Maglott G & Shaw GM (1983) Immune thrombocytopenic purpura. Use of a ^{125}I-labelled antihuman IgG monoclonal antibody to quantify platelet-bound IgG. *New England Journal of Medicine* **309:** 459–463.

Loeliger EA (1985) Laboratory control, optimal therapeutic ranges and therapeutic quality control in oral anticoagulation. *Acta Haematologica* **74:** 125–131.

Loeliger EA, van Dijk-Wierda CA, van den Besselaar AMHP, Broekmans AW & Roos J (1984) Anticoagulant control and risk of bleeding. In Meade TW (ed.) *Anticoagulants and Myocardial Infarction: A Reappraisal*, pp 135–177. Chichester: John Wiley and Sons.

Lynch DM & Howe SE (1985) Heparin associated thrombocytopenia: antibody binding specificity to platelet antigens. *Blood* **66:** 1176–1181.

Mammen EF, Koets MH, Washington BC et al (1985) Hemostasis changes during cardiopulmonary bypass surgery. *Seminars in Thrombosis and Hemostasis* **11:** 281–292.

Mannuci PM, Ruggeri ZM, Pareti FI & Capitanio A (1977) 1-Deamino-8-D-arginine vasopressin: a new pharmacological approach to the management of haemophilia and von Willebrand's disease. *Lancet* **1:** 867–872.

Mannucci PM, Remuzzi G, Pusineri et al (1983) Deamino-8D-arginine vasopressin shortens the bleeding time in uraemia. *New England Journal of Medicine* **308:** 8–12.

Marmont AM & Damasio EE (1971) Clinical experiences with cytotoxic immunosuppressive treatment of idiopathic thrombocytopenic purpura. *Acta Haematologica* **46:** 74–91.

McMillan R (1983a) Immune thrombocytopenia. *Clinics in Haematology* **12:** 69–88.

McMillan R (1983b) *Immune Cytopenias—Methods in Haematology Series*. New York: Churchill Livingstone.

McVerry BA (1985) Management of idiopathic thrombocytopenic purpura in adults. *British Journal of Haematology* **59:** 203–208.

Mueh JR, Herbst KD & Rapaport SI (1980) Thrombosis in patients with the lupus anticoagulant. *Annals of Internal Medicine* **92:** 156–159.

Mueller-Eckhardt C (1986) Post-transfusion purpura. *British Journal of Haematology* **64:** 419–424.

Newland AC, Treleaven JG, Minchinton RM & Waters AH (1983) High dose intravenous IgG in adults with autoimmune thrombocytopenia. *Lancet* **1:** 84–87.

OPCS (1985) *Mortality Statistics: Cause*. Review of the Registrar General on deaths by cause, sex and age in England and Wales, 1984 Series DH2, No. 11. London: HMSO.

Packham MA & Mustard JF (1977) Clinical pharmacology of platelets. *Blood* **50:** 555–573.

Palmer RN, Rick ME, Rick PD, Zeller JA & Gralnick HR (1984) Circulating heparin sulfate anticoagulant in a patient with a fatal bleeding disorder. *New England Journal of Medicine* **310:** 1696–1699.

Payne BA & Pierre RV (1984) Pseudothrombocytopenia: a laboratory artifact with potentially serious consequences. *Mayo Clinic Proceedings* **59:** 123–125.

Perkins HA, MacKenzie MR & Fudenberg HH (1970) Hemostatic defects in dysproteinaemias. *Blood* **35:** 695–707.

Pizzuto J & Ambriz R (1984) Therapeutic experience on 934 adults with idiopathic thrombocytopenic purpura: multicentric trial of the cooperative Latin American group on Haemostasis and Thrombosis. *Blood* **64:** 1179–1183.

Poller L (1985) Advances in oral anticoagulant treatment. In Poller L (ed.) *Recent Advances in Blood Coagulation*, vol. 4, Edinburgh: Churchill Livingstone.

Poller L, Thomson JM & Tomenson JA (1984) The bleeding time: current practice in the UK. *Clinical and Laboratory Haematology* **6:** 369–373.

Prentice CRM (1985) Acquired coagulation disorders. *Clinics in Haematology* **14:** 413–442.

Rao AK & Walsh PN (1983) Acquired qualitative platelet disorders. *Clinics in Haematology* **12:** 201–238.

Rasi V & Lintula R (1986) Platelet function in the myelodysplastic syndromes. *Scandinavian Journal of Haematology* **36**(supplement 45): 71–73.

Rizza CR & Spooner RJD (1985) Treatment of haemophilia and related disorders in Britain and Northern Ireland during 1976–80: report on behalf of the directors of haemophilia centres in the United Kingdom. *British Medical Journal* **286:** 929–933.

Rosenstein ED, Itzkowitz SH, Pensiner AS, Cohen JI & Mornaghi RA (1983) Resolution of factor X deficiency in primary amyloidosis following splenectomy. *Archives of Internal Medicine* **143:** 597–599.

Roussi JH, Houbouyan LL & Goynel AF (1984) Use of low-molecular weight heparin in heparin-induced thrombocytopenia with thrombotic complications. *Lancet* **1:** 1183.

Salzman EW, Weinstein MJ, Weintraus RM et al (1986) Treatment with desmopressin acetate to reduce loss after cardiac surgery. *New England Journal of Medicine* **314:** 1402–1406.

Schafer AI (1984) Bleeding and thrombosis in the myeloproliferative disorders. *Blood* **64:** 1–12.

Schlieder MA, Nachmann RL, Jaffe EA & Coleman M (1976) A clinical study of the lupus anticoagulant. *Blood* **48:** 499–510.

Schreiber AJ, Chein P, Tomaski A & Cines CB (1987) Effect of Danazol in immune thrombocytopenia purpura. *New England Journal of Medicine* **316:** 503–508.

Shapiro SS (1979) Antibodies to blood coagulation factors. *Clinics in Haematology* **8:** 207–214.

Sheridan D, Carter C & Kelton JG (1986) A diagnostic test for heparin-induced thrombocytopenia. *Blood* **67:** 27–30.

Shinton WK (1983) Standardisation of oral anticoagulant treatment. *British Medical Journal* **287:** 1000–1001.

Sie P, Montague J, Blanc M et al (1981) Evaluation of some platelet parameters in a group of elderly people. *Thrombosis and Haemostasis* **45:** 197–199.

Spero JA, Lewis JH & Hasiba U (1980) Disseminated intravascular coagulation. Findings in 346 patients. *Thrombosis and Haemostasis* **43:** 28–33.

Standing Advisory Committee for Haematology of the Royal College of Pathologists (1982) Drug interaction with coumarin derivative anticoagulants. *British Medical Journal* **285:** 274–275.

Sultan Y, Kazatchkine MD, Maisonneuve P & Nydegger UE (1984) Anti-idiotypic suppression of autoantibodies to factor VIII (antihaemophilic factor) by high dose intravenous gamma globulin. *Lancet* **2:** 765–768.

Tartaglia AP, Goldberg JD, Berk PD & Wasserman LR (1986) Adverse effects of antiaggregating platelet therapy in the treatment of polycythaemia vera. *Seminars in Haematology* **23:** 172–176.

Thomson JM & Poller L (1985) The activated partial thromboplastin time. In Thomson JM (ed.) *Blood Coagulation and Haemostasis. A Practical Guide*, 3rd edn, pp 301–339. Edinburgh: Churchill Livingstone.

Todd M, McDevitt E & McDowell F (1973) Stroke and blood coagulation. *Stroke* **4:** 400–405.
Tuddenham EGD (1984) The varieties of von Willebrand's disease. *Clinical and Laboratory Haematology* **6:** 307–323.
Van de Pette JEW, Prochazka AV, Pearson T et al (1986) Primary thrombocythaemia treated with busulphan. *British Journal of Haematology* **62:** 229–237.
Verstraete M & Collen D (1986) Thrombolytic therapy in the eighties. *Blood* **67:** 1529–1541.
von dem Borne AEG, Vos JJE, van der Lelie J, Bossers B & van Dalen CM (1986) Clinical significance of positive platelet immunofluorescence test in thrombocytopenia. *British Journal of Haematology* **64:** 767–776.
Waddell CC, Brown JA & Repinecy YA (1981) Abnormal platelet function in myeloproliferative disorders. *Archives of Pathology and Laboratory Medicine* **105:** 432–443.
Weiss HJ, Meyer D, Rabinowitz R et al (1982a) Pseudo-von Willebrand's disease. An intrinsic platelet defect with aggregation by unmodified human factor VIII/von Willebrand factor and enhanced adsorption of its high-molecular-weight multimers. *New England Journal of Medicine* **306:** 326–333.
Weiss HJ (1983) Acquired qualitative platelet disorders. In Williams WJ, Beutler E, Erslev AJ Lichtman MA (eds) *Hematology* 3rd (edn). pp 1355–1362. New York: McGraw Hill.
Weiss HJ, Ball AP & Mannucci PM (1982b) Incidence of severe von Willebrand's disease. *New England Journal of Medicine* **307:** 127.
Woodruff RK, Grigg AP, Firkin FC & Smith IL (1986) Fatal thrombotic events during treatment of autoimmune thrombocytopenia with intravenous immunoglobulin in elderly patients. *Lancet* **2:** 217–218.

12

Terminal care in haematology

FIONA RANDALL

The care of any patient in the terminal phase of an illness makes special demands on the professionals involved. It is normally accepted that a doctor's duty is 'to serve his patient's interests in being cured', but when we know that death cannot be averted our goals change, and our duty is to serve his interests in attaining a peaceful death, both physically and emotionally. To achieve this, basic skills in both therapeutics and counselling are needed, plus the inner resources to cope with distressing encounters with the dying.

The skills involved in terminal care are the same whatever the illness, and a certain level of competence is essential if we are to do the best for our patients. One thing is certain – eventually 100% of patients die, so it is clearly our duty as professionals to learn these skills.

The needs of the dying person, both emotional and physical, are described below with suggestions as to how we might provide the most effective care. Particular emphasis is given to the problems most commonly encountered in those with haematological diseases.

It is helpful at the outset to consider our goals in the simplest terms. Firstly, we would all wish our patients to enjoy physical comfort so far as we can achieve it. Secondly, we would wish to minimize emotional distress, and to work towards peaceful acceptance of death. It is obvious that physical and emotional well-being are interdependent, but for ease of discussion I will consider them separately.

PHYSICAL CARE

Nursing care is rarely the province of doctors, but an awareness of the patient's needs in this regard is essential if the doctor is to work most effectively as part of the caring team.

The person who is not 'curable' is just as deserving of time and effort as the one who will leave hospital well. It is difficult to give adequate time on busy medical wards, but at least terminally ill patients should not receive less than their fair share. Unfortunately, as working with the dying is particularly stressful, it is easy for us, quite unconsciously, to make the excuse we are too busy, or to avoid real contact by keeping conversation superficial. Because of this a deliberate effort is frequently needed to ensure that the patient is not suffering from subtle forms of isolation.

Competent, practical nursing care is essential. However, we should be aware that the way care is delivered is an indication to the patient of his worth. Compassion and gentleness are the most eloquent expression to the patient of his unique value. Fortunately, the haematology patient has often had a long course of treatment from one team before the terminal phase of the illness, and during that time a relationship of mutual respect, trust, and hopefully honesty should have been established.

Since doctors actually spend a very limited amount of time with the patient it is essential that good communication between nursing and medical staff exists, so that pain and other symptoms not obvious when the doctor visited are reported. The attitude of doctors towards nursing staff is important in this respect – we must be prepared to trust the observations of the nurses on duty, and to act upon their information without viewing their comments as an adverse judgement on our care. Fortunately experienced nurses become quite skilled at approaching their doctor in the way most likely to achieve the desired result, but we have no excuse for making their task more difficult.

Another area of uncertainty is that of independence. How hard should we push the terminally ill person to maintain mobility and self care when at any moment their condition may deteriorate? What is the point? Isn't it easier to allow them to do as much or as little as they please? In fact there are several good reasons for encouraging the reluctant patient to maintain mobility and independence. First, the development of painful pressure sores is reduced or avoided. Secondly, a greater degree of dignity and self-respect may be preserved. Thirdly, the encouragement of independence affirms to the patient that although dying he is still an adult, is respected as such, and has responsibilities to those around him to facilitate his care. Finally, improvement in strength or a change in home circumstances may come about at any time, and the more independent the patient the more likely it is he can be managed at home, where most people prefer to remain.

The help of an enthusiastic physiotherapist is invaluable, and the use of facilities such as a hydrotherapy pool or gymnasium is often beneficial.

Diversional therapy helps to distract patients from their physical and mental problems, and so serves to give them a period of emotional rest. Moreover, most enjoy the experience of creativity, often forgotten since childhood.

Whilst practical care is the province of our nursing colleagues, the responsibility of symptom control rests mainly with the doctor.

The discipline of symptom management is exactly the same in the situation of terminal illness as in a first consultation with the doctor. The routine of careful history, examination and appropriate investigation should be followed with as much attention as when a primary diagnosis has not been made. One is most likely to achieve relief of discomfort when its cause is known and treatment follows a logical course.

Thus a meticulous history remains important. Where a pain is described, its site, character, radiation, severity, etc. will frequently suggest the pathology responsible. Physical examination is essential, and may yield some surprise.

Investigation is appropriate where its results may influence management – not simply to satisfy academic curiosity.

It is also helpful to try to understand the significance of the symptom to the patient – unfortunately it is not uncommon to discover that a person harbours horrible images of the illness. When the cause of the symptom and its treatment is explained, fears can usually be allayed. Finally, if the cause of the symptom cannot be resolved, the discomfort needs to be relieved by analgesics, antiemetics, etc.

The range of symptoms encountered in haematological malignancies is obviously smaller than in oncology as a whole. However, some particularly distressing situations can arise, which merit discussion so that we are better equipped to deal with them.

PAIN CONTROL

Bone pain occurs frequently in multiple myeloma. It can be very severe, and diagnosis, suggested strongly by history, is confirmed by X-ray or more rarely, bone scan. It is essential that radiotherapy is considered early since it is very often effective in reducing pain. Benefits are usually not felt till after treatment is finished. Where vertebrae are involved, radiotherapy helps to prevent collapse with its attendant complications. Even if radiotherapy has already been given to the painful site, one should always enquire whether the total dose has been reached. Patients often need reassurance about the effects of radiotherapy – some think that treatment inevitably causes alopecia and nausea. Where palliative radiotherapy is used in terminal care courses of treatment are as short as possible and frequently only one fraction may be necessary.

The more complex issue of continuing chemotherapy to retard bone disease is resolved by balancing possible benefits and side-effects. Bone pain is also responsive to non-steroidal anti-inflammatory drugs, since their anti-prostaglandin activity reduces pain mediated by prostaglandins released by the tumour. Regular analgesics, as discussed later, will be used in conjunction with these specific measures.

Nerve compression pain is particularly difficult to relieve. It occurs most often in myeloma where vertebral collapse can cause pressure on nerve roots, usually in the lumbar region. Masses of lymph nodes in the cervical region can also press on the brachial plexus. Nerve compression pain typically radiates, may be described as stinging, shooting or burning and may be associated with parasthesiae. Once again, one should endeavour to relieve the cause of the nerve compression. This may entail radiotherapy, or perhaps chemotherapy.

High dose steroids, e.g. dexamethasone 4–16 mg daily, may reduce peri-tumour oedema, and may be tried if not contra-indicated. Where shooting pains and parasthesiae occur an anticonvulsant may help. Carbamazepine and clonazepam have been used and are sometimes dramatically effective. However, side-effects can be a problem with both drugs. If anticonvulsants fail, tricyclic antidepressants, usually amitriptyline 25–50 mg at night, may be effective. Their mechanism of action is uncertain, and their effect is not contingent upon depression being present.

In some cases, transcutaneous nerve stimulation may help, but it is essential to experiment with the position of the electrodes. Many patients appreciate the ability to manipulate their own analgesia by adjusting the stimulator, and most physiotherapists are experienced in the use of the stimulator and can teach them.

Finally, a nerve block may be considered. Since this procedure requires considerable technical expertise, only anaesthetists generally practise this treatment. It is frequently worth asking their advice, as potential risks of loss of function must be clearly understood. Temporary blocks with local anaesthetic are usually tried first. Whilst these manoeuvres are tried analgesics are used. However the opiates seem relatively ineffective against nerve compression pain, even when high doses are used.

Fortunately most fatal haematological diseases do not cause very severe pain, but regular analgesia is needed in many patients, and a brief review of the general principles of analgesic use is helpful.

Most pains are constant. Therefore regular analgesia is, by definition, the only way to achieve complete pain relief. The analgesic effect of consecutive doses overlaps, keeping blood levels in the therapeutic range. The dose interval is obviously dependent on the duration of action of the drug used. For instance, 4 hourly paracetamol, 4–6 hourly for co-proxamol (Distalgesic), 4 hourly for diamorphine and morphine in solution, 2–3 hourly for dextromoramide and 12 hourly for morphine sulphate slow release MST (Napp).

The oral route of administration is preferred. Not only is it most convenient, but absorption is gradual causing a slow rise in blood level, which is then less likely to reach toxic levels. The intravenous route is impractical, and bolus injections are likely to cause overdose. If the oral route is impractical, parenteral administration is usually by intramuscular injection, but diamorphine can be given either intermittently or continuously subcutaneously – in the latter case a small battery-operated pump is used and the daily dose of diamorphine is placed in a 10 ml syringe which fits into the pump. When using opiates it is important to remember that oral absorption is poor. Therefore when changing from oral to parenteral administration one halves the oral dose.

It is obviously imperative that an adequately potent analgesic is used. Regular doses of paracetamol may be tried first, but if not sufficient regular co-proxamol (up to eight tablets daily) or co-codamol (paracetamol + codeine) or co-dydramol (paracetamol + dihydrocodeine tartrate) may be used. If pain still breaks through a regular opiate is needed. Traditionally morphine or diamorphine in water or chloroform water are used, but a 10 mg tablet of diamorphine is also available. One begins with a small dose – 2.5 mg diamorphine 4 hourly – and increases gradually, titrating the dose against the pain. Most patients will be pain-controlled on 30 mg diamorphine 4 hourly or less.

Opiate side-effects can cause problems. Nausea and drowsiness may occur, but both tend to resolve in a few days. However constipation tends to occur in all patients, because opiates reduce gut peristalsis and intestinal transit time is greatly prolonged. This results in the passage of an infrequent and very hard stool. A stimulant laxative e.g. bisacodyl (Dulcolax) is usually needed as well as a faecal softener e.g. lactulose or dioctyl sodium sulphosuccinate.

Many patients fear the addiction they have heard about in cases of opiate abuse. They need to be reassured that when the opiate dose balances the pain, euphoria is not experienced, so they do not become addicted to a euphoric effect. Explanation is also needed about the necessity for regular analgesia.

When pain control has been achieved on a 4 hourly opiate in solution and the patient is in a stable condition, a change may be made to the slow-release morphine preparation MST. This drug, although considerably more expensive, is very convenient as it is designed to be used in a 12 hourly regime. If given more frequently, e.g. 4–6 hourly, excessive nausea, drowsiness or confusion may occur. It is available in 10 mg, 30 mg, 60 mg and 100 mg tablets.

Some difficulties can occur with drug combinations. Buprenorphine (Temgesic) is a partial agonist, and to some extent will act antagonistically if prescribed with other opiates. Therefore it should *never* be given in a regime with other opiates. Moreover it frequently proves ineffective in malignant diseases, and may also cause nausea and confusion. For these reasons I feel buprenorphine is best avoided in the terminally ill.

If pain control proves difficult, even with increasing doses of opiate – more than 90 mg diamorphine 4 hourly is unusual – a review of the patient and the pain is helpful. The degree of pain perceived by a person is influenced by his emotional state. Fear, anxiety, guilt, and particularly depression need to be alleviated to render a patient pain-free. The organic cause of the pain should also be reviewed. Sometimes alternative treatments such as previously described have been omitted.

Finally, since so little is still understood about opiate action and metabolism, the appropriate dose can be established only by titration against the pain as reported by the patient.

SYMPTOM CONTROL

Other symptoms besides pain can cause severe distress, and unless they are alleviated little energy remains to resolve vital emotional issues. Once again a meticulous history and examination, with appropriate atraumatic investigation, are essential to establish the cause of the symptom, so that where possible the cause itself may be treated.

Anorexia can be a very distressing symptom to both the patient and relatives. Food is one of the great pleasures in life and loss of appetite is particularly noticed by patients whose other pleasures have been curtailed by illness. Unfortunately failure to eat has a very sinister significance for patient and family. Food is associated with life and failure to eat ultimately equates with death. Some patients and families can accept a poor food intake only when they are able to accept death as the probable final outcome.

It is worth attempting to improve appetite artificially by using steroids. I have not found any other drug which really helps. A high dose is used for about one week e.g. prednisolone 30 mg or dexamethasone 4 mg daily. If ineffective it should be reduced and stopped. If effective it can be reduced to a maintenance dose of 10–15 mg prednisolone or 1–2 mg of dexamethasone daily. Of course this treatment can be used only if steroids are not contra-indicated e.g. by diabetes, peptic ulcer, etc. The main problems associated with steroids in the terminal situation are a cushingoid appearance and increased incidence of stomach bleeding. Long-term side-effects are not a worry.

A sore mouth is a frequent cause of failure to eat. By far the most common pathology in the immunosuppressed and debilitated patient is oral thrush. Typical white plaques may not be visible, and if in doubt a mouth swab should be sent whilst oral nystatin is commenced. In very resistant cases a course of ketoconazole (Nizoral) may be used. If the infection extends down the oesophagus severe pain on swallowing and even dysphagia can result. In these cases treatment with nizoral gives faster results. Alternatively patients may take 2–3 ml of nystatin suspension at each dose and swallow it.

Nausea and vomiting are less frequent complications of terminal haemato-logical diseases. They may be iatrogenic, or due to metabolic disorders such as uraemia or hypercalcaemia, particularly in myeloma. If the cause cannot be removed regular anti-emetics should be given. Unfortunately, selection is largely a matter of trial and error, plus a consideration of sedative properties. In severe cases the phenothiazine methotrimeprazine is often effective, but it produces unacceptable sedation in some patients.

Constipation is another problem which causes enormous patient distress, and can ultimately lead to nausea and vomiting and a deterioration in physical condition. A regular laxative should always be prescribed with an opiate, but even patients not on analgesics may need an aperient because of poor diet, immobility, change of routine, etc.

Dyspnoea can produce great physical discomfort and is often aggravated by fear. Sometimes it is appropriate to treat the cause, e.g. chest infection, pleural effusion, anaemia, but sometimes in the terminal situation to do so merely prolongs the end. The discomfort of dyspnoea is usually eased by small regular doses of diamorphine, e.g. 2.5–10 mg 4 hourly. Diazepam is also useful.

Anaemia, causing lethargy and dyspnoea, can become a difficult chronic management problem, and one wonders whether repeated transfusions are appropriate. Obviously if the patient is ambulant and not actively bleeding, with a reasonable quality of life, regular transfusions are continued. However, is it reasonable to transfuse very frequently if the patient is suffering blood loss as well as marrow failure, or if quality of life seems poor? The alternative is likely to be death from cardiac failure, secondary to anaemia. If a patient indicates that he has 'had enough' then it is reasonable to cease transfusions and treat the symptoms of anaemia, principally dyspnoea, as described above. Diuretics may help. However some patients wish to live as long as possible whatever is entailed, and one may have to continue transfusions until some catastrophic event supervenes. Others do not cling so tenaciously to life, but rather fear death. It is helpful to the patient to discuss specific fears and give reassurance where possible. In the absence of openness for discussion, the patient may assume the future is so terrifying that the staff are unwilling to talk about it.

Depression is easily overlooked, since we expect patients to be sad, but a completely flat effect, with lack of pleasure in anything, and sleep disturbance with early morning waking are abnormal and indicate a depressive state which usually improves with treatment. Tricyclic antidepressants in small doses very often give relief. Since they take about two weeks to act, treatment should not be delayed, and shorter acting drugs e.g. dothiepin (Prothiaden) may be preferred. Mianserin and flupenthixol are alternatives, having a different range of side-effects. If two anti-depressants have failed, and the patient is clearly depressed, with flat effect and no enjoyment of life at all, the help of a psychiatrist should be sought.

Unfortunately, some of the terminal events which can occur in haematological diseases, particularly acute leukaemias, are extremely distressing. It is important that nursing staff (or relatives if the patient is at home) should be warned of the risks, whilst causing as little alarm as possible. A plan of action should be prepared in advance so that hopefully those in the caring team will not panic, for if they do the patient surely will. Not one of us would want to see or remember our loved one dying in terror and physical distress.

A massive haemorrhage is always a possibility when a patient's platelet count is very low. In the terminally ill person, heroic resuscitation is obviously inappropriate. The scene is particularly frightening if a large amount of blood is visible – the simple expedient of using a red blanket reduces the horror of the situation. Sedation is the kindest course of action. An injection of an opiate at least equal to their regular 4 hourly dose will help relieve dyspnoea. Hyoscine is an excellent sedative, and 0.4–0.6 mg can be given with the opiate. Chlorpromazine or methotrimepazine given as well will ensure the patient is not aware. Obviously this 'disaster regime' is useful only if prescribed in advance so that it can be given intramuscularly without delay. If a doctor is on hand intravenous diazepam and/or diamorphine can be administered. It is possible that the patient will die soon after the injection, as a result of the effects of blood loss. If an excessive dose of opiate has been given, e.g. 4–6 times the person's usual dose, the nurse giving the injection will feel responsible for the patient's death, and I feel it is wrong to place the staff in this situation. I also feel it is ethically wrong, even in these circumstances, to give a deliberate overdose.

Infections, particularly pneumonia and septicaemia, are frequent terminal events. The use of antibiotics is often inappropriate. Opiates may be used to relieve dyspnoea, and in the unconscious patient with 'bubbling' respirations due to secretions in the throat, intramuscular hyoscine given with the 4 hourly opiate may dry up secretions. It should not be given alone as unpleasant side-effects occur.

When the person with overwhelming disease slips into unconsciousness, analgesics and sometimes sedatives need to be administered parenterally. Explanation to the family as to the nature of the injections is necessary or they may think euthanasia is being practised. Conversely, intravenous hydration of the dying person serves no useful purpose. Nursing staff need to be particularly watchful for signs of discomfort, most often obvious on turning.

Grimacing, rigidity or restlessness may all indicate pain, and if there is doubt analgesia should be increased. If the patient is generally stiff diazepam may help, and since 10 mg is a 2 ml injection intramuscularly and is poorly absorbed the rectal route is often preferable.

The unconscious patient should look peaceful and relaxed. In a hospice situation they are not moved to a single room because of the sinister significance this move then acquires, and because other patients usually cope well with the sight of a friend peacefully asleep and well cared for. Always assume that until the moment of death is past the patient can still hear.

EMOTIONAL CARE

Obviously in order to meet our patient's emotional needs, we must be willing to talk with him about problems relating to his illness and death. However, talking with terminally ill patients is so emotionally demanding that we may endeavour to avoid any real communication. Why do we do this? First, we may regard the death of our patient as our failure to cure so that we feel inadequate or guilty. Secondly, talking with our dying patients reminds us of our own mortality, and brings our own fears about death to the surface. Thirdly, when faced with a very distressed person, the cause of whose suffering we cannot remove, we may feel inadequate, and inadequacy is painful. Finally, the patient and family may blame us for our failure to cure – if this happens, it may be best to ask another counsellor to help.

Thus it is not surprising if faced with a dying person we feel 'this hurts too much – I can't deal with it', and avoid discussing emotive issues at all. However this attitude is no help to our patient. It may be necessary for us to face our own fears about death before we can bear to come close to the dying.

Our first 'communication crisis' is likely to surround the disclosure of the diagnosis and prognosis. I believe patients should be told as much of the truth as they want to know. However, until the patient appreciates the seriousness of the illness he does not know how much information he wants. So gentle negotiation is used. One offers the truth a little at a time, ascertaining at each stage if the patient would like more details. This allows the patient to control the flow of information at the interview, and to ask questions. If a person obviously does not want to know, there seems little justification for telling him. Lying is also unhelpful – it destroys the basis for trust in the future. However there are obvious problems with this general philosophy.

The young fit patient may have no reason to guess the serious nature of the illness, and may seem not to want to know the truth. However practical preparation is often very important, and frequently it is necessary to divulge the diagnosis in order to avoid unnecessary trauma and so that essential arrangements are made.

Similarly, where unpleasant treatment such as chemotherapy is indicated, the serious nature of the illness must usually be explained so that the patient can make a decision about treatment. However, some patients prefer to cast the doctor in the parental role, and simply say 'whatever you think best'.

In this country there seems to be an established practice for telling relatives the truth but not necessarily the patient. Difficulties arise when following this policy if having told the family they then ask or insist that the patient should not know. We must remind ourselves and sometimes the family that our first duty is to the patient who is entitled to the truth *if* he indicates he wants it. It is usually best to explore with the family the reasons why they wish the patient to remain in ignorance. They may believe the truth will so depress their loved one that they will 'give in' and so die sooner. Or the family may feel unable to face the mutual distress when the diagnosis is disclosed. I think we should try to persuade the family to allow the patient as much information as he wants, because we know that without shared knowledge communication barriers are likely to occur, which may cause distressing isolation to all parties.

Finally, one of the hardest aspects of illness to bear is uncertainty, and patients whose prognosis cannot be predicted need much support to live with a precarious future.

Many patients with haematological diseases require prolonged active treatment, and wish to understand the nature of their illness and its progress. Frequently they need to feel in control of their own lives. Discussions about the treatment and its effects will arise, and the patients do have the right to participate in decisions about their care.

Whether treatment should be continued depends on the patient's informed decision, but one must explore what motives lie behind that decision. For instance the depressed patient may opt to discontinue treatment as a way of committing suicide 'by default'. The judgement of the depressed person is obviously impaired.

If a patient wishes to continue a treatment which does not seem likely to bring about a remission, and which increases the suffering of the illness, one should ask 'Is he really fighting to live?' In which case any hope of extension of life should be pursued or 'Is he simply afraid to die?' In which case his fears need to be explored, rather than continuing forlorn attempts to delay death.

Obviously this policy of discussing treatment with the patient is not always appropriate. Some people wish to hand over the responsibility of decision-making to the doctor, and make this clear. We have then to do our best on their behalf. Patients may also find it difficult to discuss treatment with their own doctor, because it may then seem that they are questioning his judgement. This is a good argument for asking another professional, perhaps a Social Worker, to clarify their thoughts with them and communicate these thoughts to the doctor.

Patients may feel a need to discuss their fears about death. This is particularly difficult to handle, as we are unable to provide reassurance about many of their worries, but at least we should be willing to listen, share their thoughts, and by that sharing try to alleviate their inevitable loneliness in dying. Fears of physical pain, of loss of control over external events and bodily function, of disfigurement and rejection and of leaving all other human contact are very common. If as a doctor we are the chosen confident we should pay tribute to that trust with our time, giving reassurance where possible.

Generally, it seems that the last weeks or months of life are most comfortable for the patient, family and caring staff where the patient reaches acceptance of death. However, this is not possible for everyone, and the path towards acceptance is often tortuous.

Initially, denial of the diagnosis is so common, particularly in the young, to be regarded as normal. It does not indicate that we made a mistake in divulging the diagnosis, and we should not react by denying the truth ourselves. Denial is a protective mechanism and generally one should not bludgeon the patient with the truth. However, if outward denial is being maintained whilst inner panic causes an anxiety state, or physical symptoms of fear, one should attempt to re-explore the truth, giving reassurance where possible. Anger and grief are also normally experienced, and should be allowed expression. Depression (as opposed to sadness) should be treated actively.

Spiritual anxieties are common in all persons approaching death. Those not certain about the existence or nature of an after-life or God may want simply to share their thoughts, or they may request spiritual guidance. In the former case we should be willing to listen if the subject is raised, but if spiritual guidance is requested the pastor of the patient's choice should be sought. Surprisingly, the person with a deep commitment to a faith is by no means exempt from spiritual suffering. Feelings of desertion by God and inability to pray do occur. Some people think that their illness is a punishment for previous wrongs. Others, particularly when depressed, may feel worthless and that they are past being forgiven. Doubts may arise in a person who has felt quite secure in his faith all his life. Usually these problems can be resolved with the help of an appropriate minister once the patient has summoned up the courage to disclose them. Disclosures may first be to those providing physical care, whom the patient has learned to trust, and if they feel 'out of their depth', professional help should be sought.

Fortunately many people, particularly the elderly, manage to reach a state of acceptance of death. This is not simply resignation to the inevitable, but implies an accurate appraisal of their changing situation, with positive adjustments as their physical condition and role in the family alters.

The great strength and courage of those who battle towards acceptance of death is always impressive. Those of us privileged to share in that struggle owe them our best.

SUMMARY

As doctors, it is clearly our duty to continue to care for our patients if their illness is not curable. Basic skills in symptom control and counselling are needed, and if we have taken the trouble to acquire some knowledge in these respects we will be much better equipped to help the dying patient.

Pain control is not complicated if approached logically. The exact cause of the pain should be treated if possible, and regular, adequately potent analgesics used to balance the pain so that analgesia is achieved throughout the 24 hours. There is nothing to be gained by withholding opiates when moderate analgesics are ineffective. The approach to the control of other symptoms is similar.

Emotional care is generally more difficult and taxing to the doctor than physical care. Initially it may be difficult to decide what to tell the patient about his illness. Mistakes are less likely if the patient is allowed to indicate how much information he wants, and a vital relationship of trust can be maintained only if we tell the truth. Once this relationship of trust is established we should continue to give the opportunity for discussion of fears and worries, or sometimes simply show that we are willing to share our patient's distress. Those who depend upon us for their care deserve our commitment to them until the moment of death.

Acknowledgements

The various writings of Dr Avril Stedeford on the subject of emotional care of the terminally ill have been very helpful.

Index

Note: Page numbers of article titles are in **bold** type.